Trials of Irish History

In *Trials of Irish History*, Evi Gkotzaridis brings her original insights into theory and philosophy to bear upon the controversial question of the revision of Irish history. In an incisive restaging of the passionate joust that took place between revisionists and traditionalists in the shadow of the "Troubles", the author prises open conflicting intellectual notions about the function of history in a divided society. She compares this Irish *Kulturkampf* with similar discussions in Germany and France in order to identify and magnify the strengths, weaknesses and temptations hidden in the arguments propounded by each side.

Here for the first time, the historical and the theoretical fuse in an attempt to enter the minds of those trailblazer historians who in 1938, against considerable odds including the painful memory of the Irish Civil War, the cultural contraction of the first decades of independence, the estrangement between two regimes and the devastation of the Second World War, spearheaded an unpoliticized history. Drawing on hitherto unused archives, the book shows how the venture to disenthral Irish and European history from the fiend of official propagandas proved challenging and perilous. *Trials of Irish History* unveils a crucial chapter in the history of Irish revisionism when the "new historians" clashed with the Bureau of Military History over the handling of oral records related to the War of Independence – refuting later accusations of collaboration with the Political Establishment laid at the door of the revisionist school.

This book represents a spirited defence of the first revisionists. While it recognizes that revisionism is a path littered with booby traps which needs to be trod carefully, it nonetheless commends the courage and ingenuity of those historians, by showing how the postmodern interpretative turn at the end of the twentieth century has by and large vindicated it. At once playful and responsible, it shows that if facts cannot be trusted because, to use the phrase of Hubert Butler, they are just seasonings to theoretic puddings, scholastic theories can also be mis-used to invigorate sentimental and foregone political conclusions.

Evi Gkotzaridis is Jean Monnet Fellow at the European University Institute of Florence.

Routledge studies in modern European history

Trials of Irish History

Genesis and evolution of a reappraisal
1938–2000

Evi Gkotzaridis

Routledge
Taylor & Francis Group

LONDON AND NEW YORK

First published 2006
by Routledge
2 Park Square, Milton Park, Abingdon, Oxon OX14 4RN

Simultaneously published in the USA and Canada
by Routledge
270 Madison Ave, New York, NY 10016

Routledge is an imprint of the Taylor & Francis Group, an informa business

© 2006 Evi Gkotzaridis

Typeset in Garamond by Wearset Ltd, Boldon, Tyne and Wear
Printed and bound in Great Britain by MPG Books Ltd, Bodmin

British Library Cataloguing in Publication Data
A catalogue record for this book is available from the British Library

Library of Congress Cataloging in Publication Data
A catalog record for this book has been requested

ISBN10: 0–415–32918–3 (hbk)
ISBN10: 0–203–34069–8 (ebk)

ISBN13: 978–0–415–32918–7 (hbk)
ISBN13: 978–0–203–34069–1 (ebk)

Contents

Acknowledgements

This book began as a PhD thesis. It all started when the late Paul Brennan, my supervisor, at once amused and mystified by some of my naïve statements in my first dissertation tried in his typical wry repartee, which used to throw me every time, to correct my vision. To this day I remain in doubt if he meant his displeasure, his touchiness or if he wanted to tell me not to breathe too casually what the French call "l'air du temps". I suppose there must have been a bit of both. He did shake me out of my youthful satisfaction though and for this, the inspiration to embark on a beautiful journey and all his boundless solicitude for the rebellious one I was, I will always be grateful. He is sorely missed.

I am deeply obliged to the librarians and archivists of Cambridge University Library, the National Archives of Ireland, the National Library of Ireland, University College Dublin Archives, the Manuscript department of Trinity College Library and the Irish Military Archives for all their help, patience and kindness. A special thanks to Commandant Victor Laing of the Military Archives for sharing with me his knowledge of a crucial episode.

The life-blood of this book has been two fellowships. In 2001, I was lucky to be awarded the prestigious Government of Ireland postdoctoral fellowship in the Humanities and Social Sciences which gave me the opportunity to start research on this project in the most auspicious and congenial conditions. It was held in the department of history at the National University of Ireland, Maynooth. I would like to thank especially my mentor Prof. Vincent Comerford who on a hazy, anguished day welcomed me in his office, listened to my ideas, advised me to apply for the fellowship and in his gentle, unassuming way gave me two things I needed most; trust and support. His friendship has meant a lot to me and he has my unconditional affection.

I would like to thank also my colleagues and friends at the department, Fergus Campbell, Fearghal McGarry, Terence Dooley and Querciolo Mazzonis with whom I had interesting and enjoyable times speaking about Irish and Italian revisionism and Mike Cronin for reading part of the work and for always being his happy, smiley and loyal self with me.

Three other people have been important in the preparation of this project:

my external examiner Tom Dunne and Roy Foster for expressing curiosity and enthusiasm for a more conscious theoretical approach to Irish historiography and for lavishing on me their precious help and steady encouragement, and Michael Laffan for pushing me more in the direction of the archives and reading, commenting on and criticizing parts of the manuscript.

I am also thankful to the European University Institute for awarding me with the Jean Monnet fellowship in 2004 and to Prof. Anthony Molho and Niki Koniordou for making life and work in Florence a very pleasant, stimulating and cheering experience.

This book has also benefited from an exchange grant from the European Science Foundation (Scientific Programme in the Humanities) within the framework of an activity entitled "Representations of the Past: The Writing of National Histories in Europe".

This book is dedicated to my father, Triandafillos Gkotzaridis and to the dear memory of my mother, Vassilia Tzoura.

Preface

The purpose of this book is to trace the genesis of modern historical scholarship in Ireland and explain what obstacles it has encountered in its search for truth and social progress. In the 1980s, this work of decontamination from propaganda came under violent attack from a group of theorists sympathetic to Irish nationalism and concerned to prove its relevance in the future of a more just and peaceful Northern Ireland. Determined to bring into disrepute the new approach which was at times too iconoclastic to be deferential and generally too desirous to contemplate paradoxes and disturb complacency, these opponents painted a nasty and unfair picture of Irish revisionism. They contended that the new history was, despite its scientific pretences, no more objective and a lot less decent than the nationalist history that had preceded it. They also implied that it was dangerous because it amounted to a form of denial, presenting similar seamy undertones as the outrageous revisionism espoused by the Fascist Right and the Stalinist Left on the Continent.

According to these opponents, the "new historians" had conspired to wipe out of the pages of Irish history the reality of English colonialist terror and oppression. The "new history" was denounced as being Fascist in its general inclination because it was too soft on the machinations of mighty England and too harsh on the blunders of weak Ireland. Theory was deliberately used as a weapon in a battle to outwit the revisionists. Yet, I could not help being struck and puzzled by the intuition that their infatuation with postmodern theory was a rather skin-deep, artificial and disingenuous affair. Equally, I could not dispel the ever-imposing thought that Irish revisionism and postmodern theory presented an astonishing twin-ship in sensibility, spirit and method. Even so, I had as yet no inkling of where this strange revelation would lead me to. I mused it was like having a cryptic intelligence message in front of my eyes and feeling frustrated at not having found the means to break the code yet. I knew i had in my possession a precious piece of information. Unfortunately, it failed to speak to me intelligibly. I do not remember precisely when the secret code began to unravel, but it did. It gradually dawned on me that this knowledge was vital because it contained *in nuce* the means not only to define with more precision the philosophical and methodological pedigree of Irish revisionism but also more boldly to point at the contradictions, incoherences and overall lack of rigour of the discourse of literary criticism in Ireland; a discipline which had claimed a monopoly on theoretical exegesis. I set out therefore first to explore this connection and then to turn the theoretical weapon against Irish theorists so as to attack them on their ground with the use of their own concepts.

A major incentive behind this work was to familiarize others and myself with the ethical, political and theoretical problems that occur when an attempt is made to reform a tradition, as it happened in Ireland when Moody and Edwards embarked on their corrective mission. I have taken into account in all seriousness the objections raised against revisionism while at the same time not departing from my original commitment, which was to defend it. I have always been drawn to history and philosophy; two disciplines that have traditionally been rivals and functioned on the basis of opposed premises. Through the study of the Irish historiographic controversy, I was able to rekindle my curiosity for them and understand better the epistemological barrier that separates them.

Finally, my instinct was telling me it was time to introduce a comparative dimension to the Irish debate. I deemed that the debate on the pros and cons of revisionism had been conducted wrongly in a too parochial manner. Time was ripe, as I saw it, for a more cogent analysis of this phenomenon; one which was to distance me from the cynical opinion which regarded it as a distillation of the embers of the Great Treaty Split or as a clever device calculated to shore up Northern Ireland by manufacturing intellectual justification for partition. Archival research has an exceptional heuristic quality and is pregnant with meaning in a way that theoretical demonstration can never be. Deprived of a revivifying plunge into the reality of the past, however fragmented and warped, theoretical analysis can quickly turn into navel-gazing; the illusion of making a point when one is in fact only thinking round in circles. Instead when it is performed with integrity and open-mindedness, empirical investigation can break the monologue by digging up information that qualifies and sometimes drastically quashes a priori hypotheses. The freshness of historical study resides precisely in the demonstration of what Herbert Butterfield used to call "the fallacy of our arm-chair logic" – the proof of the superficiality of all our disembodied speculations and presumptions when compared with the surprise of what actually took place. Good history is one that neither slips in manic obsession with useless facts nor in their impetuous deletion. It is, as Richard Evans put it, "the product of a tension between commitment and objectivity, between the desire to argue a case and the wisdom to recognise the constraints placed on the fulfilment of this desire by the intractability of the evidence".[1] Identifying those same limits, R.D. Edwards wrote: "When, therefore, a scholar, in the course of his research, meets with a situation, where insufficient evidence prevents him drawing definite conclusions, he does not hesitate to declare his doubts, leaving it for the controversialist, whose primary interest is in his case rather than in the truth, to explain away any awkward facts and make the most of his conjectures".[2]

When I first set out to write this book, I had this tenacious taste of the impossible in my mouth. The lack of primary sources that could have made it richer and more penetrating was all too conspicuous and demoralizing and prevented me from realizing what I had imagined. Since then some of those papers (the papers of D.B. Quinn and J.C. Beckett) have been organized and released, unfortunately too late for this book. Therefore this is just a first instalment in the effort to enter the minds of the historians who pioneered a new Irish history. A more thorough picture will have to wait until the release of all the papers of the first and the second generations. With this modest contribution my ambition is to oppose the perception still prevalent in Ireland today that history is made solely by political actors and that historians are not that much involved in the transformation of mentalities and sensibilities. This view is anything but constructive as it tends to lead, as a result, to a complete concentration on traditional narrative, at the expense of a more conceptual, analytical and intellectual kind of history. If historians were approached not only as specialists, but also as thinkers and makers of Ireland's modern destiny, that is as intellectuals compelled to revisit their assumptions, interrogate their traditions after registering the shock of momentous events and grapple with stubborn problems it would, I think, make it less easy for certain literary critics to dismiss historical reflection as a mere appendage to politics. It is with this rationale in mind and to extend an invitation to look at Irish historiography for what it did accomplish rather than what it did not, that this book has been written.

Part I

History and theory in the Irish debate

Foes or allies?

1 The intellectual mood in the 1990s

In a tribute to T.W. Moody, F.S.L. Lyons declared: "Of late years the phrase 'the historiographical revolution' has been used so often that it is in danger of becoming a cliché to which everyone subscribes, but which nobody pauses to analyse".[1] For a long time, especially outside academia, when one dared to speak favourably of revisionism the vision of sitting on an automatic seat waiting for one's imminent rejection from an entire community came frightfully into view. One may be forgiven therefore for having trepidations at the thought of pondering in earnest the implications of such a vexatious topic.

For two decades, it was impossible to raise the question of its origins and objective meaning without being embroiled in the sterile debate over England's wrongdoing in Ireland. Those righteous patriots who wanted no truck with the tendentious hermeneutics of revisionism imposed on all what ought to be defined as the acceptable terms of the discussion. Everyone was summoned to display at once his colours, to take sides in the ancient quarrel between England, the ruthless oppressor and Ireland, this small nation that showed remarkable resilience and resourcefulness in its struggle for survival and freedom. The positions were presented in a deceptively simple manner and whoever dithered or straddled this intellectual fence was deemed to be at best cowardly or at worst a mind harbouring renegade tendencies. Revisionists were the henchmen of imperialist Britain and the revisionist school of history was merely an appendage to the reactionary ideologies of colonialism and unionism. Soon, revisionism became a word of defamation against those who spoke with casualness and disrespect of the national heroes. All those sceptical voices who perversely relished acting the devil's advocate became the victims of a witch-hunt instigated by those whose Irishness felt offended by their declarations. Others dismissed it as an irrelevant relic, a pathetic time bomb, a belated reaction from the descendants of a deposed elite against the men who were propelled to the reins of power only two years after the 1916 Rising.[2]

Carried on in this moralizing way, not only the controversy poisoned the atmosphere by creating hostility and rigidifying disciplinary boundaries, but more tragically perhaps it aborted discussion on the sort of critical and methodological practice that this school stood for. All dignified efforts to ascertain what were its strengths and weaknesses were relentlessly swallowed up by the obsessive question of its ideology. Because the other side foregrounded only the political repercussions of this new outlook and rushed to revile it on grounds of ethical slackness, many historians withdrew into a defensive corner and simply refused to be more openly reflective and dialogic. Compelled to respond to attacks that couched the issues in a dualistic manner and bordered sometimes on the personal, they had no time to think about their method, the theoretical intimations or even the ethical concerns that had guided them in their reform. Instead as Boyce and O'Day suggested it, the polemic had the effect of "inviting them to take refuge in their own primordial loyalties – perhaps even threatening them if they did not take refuge".[3]

However, this politicization of the debate concealed the fact that Irish revisionism was not a phenomenon unique to the culture of Ireland but just one local expression of a larger reappraisal. Indeed there is little distinctively Irish about revision. French revisionists following the path-breaking work of the American Robert Paxton have destroyed the Gaullist myth of France's universal resistance to Germany and disclosed the extent of collaboration with the enemy.[4] Similarly the 1980s saw in Germany the explosion of a tempestuous quarrel opposing historians to philosophers over how to contextualize, analyse and make sense of the Holocaust. In Greece, the notion of a pure race going back in a straight line to the Golden Age of Classical and Hellenic Byzantium and presenting all Greeks as direct descendants of Alexander the Great has been shown for what it was; a myth invented by a State anxious to establish its authority over a multi-ethnic people. Perhaps the most sensitive revision happening nowadays in Greek history is that on the Civil War. Stathis Kalyvas and Nikos Marantzidis have questioned the most axiomatic and hegemonic assumption of the Left; mainly that the latter was the main, if not the only, victim of violence.[5] An assumption which could gain credence because the Left had lost in the Civil War and suffered heavy persecution in the aftermath but also because references to Left-wing terror were often dismissed as an appalling lie cooked up by the Greek Right. In Italy Luisa Passerini and Patricia Dogliani have challenged the alleged Marxist dominance over Italian culture in the post-war years and revealed how the artificially repackaged memory of the Italian Resistance failed sometimes to disguise that the Italian nation was too convulsed by a Civil War.[6] In Spain, Stanley G. Payne, by looking dispassionately at the spectacle of the irresponsibility of revolutionary obsession, has revived, in a most problematic fashion, the Right's accusation that the Civil War began not with the rising of the Nationalist Generals in July 1936, but with the armed revolt of the Left in October 1934.[7] The case of Israel where Avi Shlaim[8] and Benny Morris[9] have shown how selective, varnished and self-serving was the Zionist version of the birth of the State of Israel in 1948 may yet offer the most compelling comparison with Ireland as the "new historians" in both countries had to wrestle with the not negligible problem that the actual political conflicts raging in their midst – the Northern Irish Troubles and the Israeli–Palestinian conflict – could only prejudice their "objectivity" and bolster accusations that their project was ideologically purposive.

Furthermore, it is the firm belief of this author that in order to uncover the real impetus behind this revisitation, it is indispensable to locate it in the context of the paradigmatic shift, which occurred inside European political imagination. For the question of what are the origins of Irish revisionism cannot be answered wisely unless one is also prepared to examine its method against the backdrop of Enlightenment philosophy and its refutation with postmodern theories. Although there is little evidence to show that Irish revisionists were acquainted with continental thinkers such as Foucault, Barthes, Lyotard or Derrida, the morphological relationship of their conjectures to concurrent developments in European thought is hard to ignore. Their anxieties about finding an epistemology that could decontaminate and unlock a "superior" or more lasting "truth" about the past was more than just a coincidence.

Theirs was also a local manifestation of the anxieties of the postmodern age, a result of a complex set of circumstances that had affected other countries in parallel ways. This interlocking between postmodern theory and Irish revisionism does not however arise out of a rush for uniformity with the Continent, but rather by the premonition of a spontaneous harmony between the sort of issues treated by late twentieth century theory and those raised by the sequels of a local conflict-ridden past. Undoubtedly those who are most likely to dismiss the connection between postmodernism and revisionism are also those who are not comfortable with the proposition that history can benefit from philosophy. But the chances are this idea will also meet the resistance of those who in a sermonizing tone rush to declare history's method terminally backward and condemned to repeat the partiality embedded in the documents it sieves. Hayden White wrote: "Historians have systematically built into the notion of their discipline hostility or at least a blindness to theory and the kind of issues that philosophers have raised about the kind of knowledge they have produced".[10] If this is so it may be because the majority in the English-speaking world, and especially those in Ireland, were and very much still are self-proclaimed empirical experts who view theorizing as a diversion from their real work, which consists of interrogating primary sources. To conclude however that the new school of Irish history was conceitedly indifferent to philosophy would be inaccurate as Michael Oakeshott, Herbert Butterfield and William Henry Walsh were all invited to expound their philosophy of history at the meetings of the Irish Historical Society.

Two major intellectual currents may have inspired historical reform in Ireland, but when one looks closely at these, one realizes that they are themselves closely interrelated. It is usually assumed that history in England, rooted as it was in a strong empirical tradition, managed for this reason to shelter itself from continental philosophical scepticism and to become only superficially affected by the apprehension of a crisis in historicism. But this is not exactly borne out by a close look at the evolution of historical reflection there. Indeed what was the attack of the Cambridge scholar Sir Herbert Butterfield on the Whig interpretation of history if not the symptom of a profound disagreement with the Whig historians mirroring at a local level the European loss of faith in Hegelian historicism? Ronald Hutton drew attention to the affinity between Marxist revisionism and Butterfield's contention with the Whigs when he said that both were examples of a reaction against a historiography too much organized around teleological assumptions.[11]

The argument of this book does not rest on some rigid hierarchy wherein theory is regarded as superior and history as inferior. Besides, in the context of Ireland it would be absurd to suggest the primacy of theory, since the first wave of historical revision predates the theoretical revolution that really began in the late 1960s on the continent. If anything, the opposite would seem to be nearer to the truth. As we hope to show in this study, theory underwent a profound conversion to a historical cast of mind in the second half of the twentieth century. Postmodernism's retreat from totalizing theories could be attractive to historians because it confirms that they had been right all along, that their dominant practice of emphasizing the peculiarities, the ambiguity and untidiness of the past and displaying a measure of modesty about the possibility of any durable prognosis or judgement on the whole had been qualities too hastily denigrated by theoreticians. The polysemous and Siamese quality of political concepts enshrined in the theory is no revelation for the historian whose empirical observations often give him a heightened sense of the exceptionally dynamic and interactive aspects of human thought and action across time and space.

Rather local historical factors, for instance the existence of a strong tradition of political violence that had more than once jeopardized the infant state, the frustrating persistence of partition, the failure to revive the Irish language or the disappointing record of the isolationist economic policies of Fianna Fáil up to the 1950s, were reasons strong enough to cause an "Irish" introspection. What occurred, therefore, was no crude borrowing, but rather a natural congruence in intuition and in the common decision to stop genuflecting or, as François Furet put it, "commemorating the past".

The adoption of an interdisciplinary approach is vital to our demonstration. With this method we hope to replace an impressionistic opinion of revisionism with a more cogent one. Revisionism has found itself at the crossroads between positivism and relativism. This straddling of two epochs is very important to remember because it has given Irish revisionism its unique profile. In truth this epistemological entanglement has been a mixed blessing. On the one hand, it deterred this school from venturing into a cul-de-sac by espousing the last principle of post-structuralism. For even though it enjoyed its own special brand of heuristic radicalism, it managed to avoid the nihilistic trap in which the extreme version of post-structuralism foundered. On the other hand, it invited charges of philosophical innocence or even, and this proved more harming, of bad faith and collaboration with hostile ideologies.

Comparing Irish revisionism with postmodern theory is just one possible approach. One which in historical terms makes of course little sense since Moody and Edwards embarked on their project of demythologization in the late 1930s long before the French gurus of the postmodern school thought of submitting Western philosophy to the same critical dissection. So our interest in entertaining this hypothesis is less historical than analytical. It is founded on the argument that Irish historiography, because of a primeval rift in the entrails of Irish society, had been stupendously precocious in divining the serious obstacle created by the intrusion of power in knowledge. Conditions unique to the trajectory of this nation, as the treacherous closeness between history and politics and the profound dissensions among Irish people, precipitated a crisis. The loss of faith in historicism, in the capacity of history to elucidate and explain human truths, let alone providing solutions to the problems of the community of which it reflected the destiny, the hope and the predicament, was experienced prematurely in Ireland. There is no doubt that revisionism in its journalistic form sprang from feelings of outrage and disgust at the terrible actions of the IRA. It was a visceral reaction against them and what the IRA presumably stood for. This journalism, concerned with the urgency of hammering into the heads of the Irish public the dangers in condoning this violence, has not always displayed the much-needed qualities of good judgement and moderation. In its condemnation of Irish republicanism it has wrongly collapsed into an anti-totalitarian and reductionist turn of mind, the main failing of which was that it hastily emptied Irish nationalism of any legitimacy.

There is also no doubt that this journalism has drawn some inspiration from a scholarly revisionism, which overall was more nuanced, sober and restrained and more meaningfully perhaps preceded the outbreak of the conflict. Indeed, there is no causal link between the conflict and the historiographic revolution. The work of rectification had been a reality of the Irish historical profession for nearly thirty years before the political commotion began. That this revision too ended up being coloured by the events is almost certain, but the fact remains that the forensic re-examination of the Easter Rebellion for instance, started well before the reappearance of violence in the streets of Derry and Belfast. Often upheaval becomes a distorting prism and one forgets that other factors internal to the evolution of the Republic facilitated historical re-evaluation. In 1965, Ireland signed an agreement of free trade with Great Britain. In 1973, it played a leading role in the organization of the United Nations by refusing to bow to the authority of the American administration and abide by its dictates. It also became a member of the European Community. By obtaining an international platform, the nation gained a self-confidence which no cult of a heroic past, no matter how consoling, could inspire. These developments were indubitable signs that national sovereignty had been proved and historians felt that it no longer needed its traditional apologists.[12]

The country was showing its abilities and its unique identity was asserting itself day after day inside a powerful structure. With its membership of the European Union, the appeal of absolute sovereignty diminished and naturally presaged the future obsolescence of a large part of the nationalist rhetoric.[13] At the seventy-fifth Annual Dinner of the Scots-Irish society at Pittsburgh on Friday 27 April 1962, R.D. Edwards explained that independence had been tantamount to creating the conditions for the birth in Ireland of a real scientific history. The tasting of this independence was a prerequisite for the blossoming of intellectual freedom.[14] In the concept of Europe, Ireland found also the prototype model for the resolution of a nationalist conflict and its adherence became not purely economical but intellectual and, it needs to be said, also ideological. Its parochial outlook softened and an increasingly pragmatic style of politics blossomed. By then, the country had also espoused the European challenge at its own level. Like its European neighbours, it sought to strike a balance between the local and the global, or between regionalism and European cosmopolitanism.

Finally the opening of new archives accelerated the pace of historical revision. But above all, this reform reflected the situation of a discipline undergoing a process of professionalism by aligning its method on the European model. Michael Laffan said as much. By looking at the past with a critical eye, by putting emphasis on complexity and ambivalence, Irish historians had simply applied the same techniques, which were deemed self-evident by their European counterparts.[15] But if the revision of Irish history proceeded for a long period unobtrusively and remained the affair of professional historians, the situation in the 1970s and 1980s was to change dramatically as the crisis in Northern Ireland escalated and political revisionism embodied itself officially for the first time with the sustained series of discussions that took place under the umbrella of the Forum for a New Ireland. It is then when serious calls were made for the need to reappraise unionism and nationalism with at once the same level of respect and realism that the word revisionism acquired, in the words of Ciaran Brady, a new political valence in popular usage.[16]

2 The Revisionist

A new type of intellectual

Ireland, like other European countries, had eventually to wake up to its postmodern condition. The singularity of the Irish historical case has challenged more than one Utopian narrative. The hopes of unionism of creating an Ireland fully integrated with England and playing a vanguard political and economic role in the strengthening of the British Empire were dashed by the disruptive initiatives of an ever more assertive separatist force. The republican vision of a united, free and Gaelic Irish nation was gainsaid by the existence of an obdurate unionist element, whose fierce and unrequited love for Britain brought Ireland to the verge of a civil war and to actual partition. The socialist illusion of overthrow of the capitalist structure and of future unity of the Irish working class, through the virtues of Marxist education, remained just that, an illusion, enticing, rational, scientifically convincing and yet forever elusive. James Connolly rightly foresaw at least one thing: partition was to give a new lease of life to the hysteria of the national question and further divide and emasculate the labour movement.

Everything happened as if the ideologies originated on the Continent could not graft themselves conclusively on the Irish soil. In the second part of the twentieth century, the impression of a deep cultural crisis in Ireland as a result of the failures of these ideologies to gain hegemony over the hearts and minds of all the people of Ireland and the memory of the violence they left in their wake when they clashed, led to a retreat from the conventional championship of a partisan and teleological history. The mood was one of introspection and history reflected this new temper by assuming a new experimental form. Thus, Irish revisionism pulsates with the same scepticism that has traversed the soul of Europe since the end of the Cold War. This cerebral commotion as it was described by the French historian, Jacques Julliard, arose out of a mounting disappointment in the great "isms" that had stamped the world. But far from being the ill-fated omen of a new nihilism, the introversive mood of the intellectuals, which translates in withdrawal from the political scene, testifies to a new willingness to understand history and its inchoative aspects better.[1] Vaclav Havel, Boris Souvarine, Alexsander Solzhenitsyn, personalities trapped inside Soviet Russia or its old satellite countries and bearing witness to the appalling abuses of human rights there, endured a chilling awakening as they realized that the doctrine in which they had put all their energies had deteriorated into something utterly inhuman. They were the first bearers of a stupefying wisdom, the premonition that there may be no global solution to the ills of this world. Communism should be distrusted because it incubates lethal viruses that are not easily detectable as they are hidden behind a benevolent façade. They learnt that a non-theological definition of the nation is not sufficient to guarantee freedom and security for its citizens.

Concurrently, Sean O'Faolain, Owen Sheehy Skeffington and Hubert Butler, men often steeped in the faith and fatherland mentality, had the scales fall from their eyes when they realized that the marriage between nationalism and Catholicism sabotaged the union of hearts; the construction of a pluralist nation capable of drawing the lessons from a legacy of internal division and manipulation at the hands of a common oppressor. Like their continental counterparts, they learnt the paradoxical truth that an emancipating creed could too harbour oppressive if not downright aggressive tendencies. They were soon joined by a new generation of historians, R.D. Edwards, T.W. Moody, J.C. Beckett and D.B. Quinn, who pioneered a revolutionary way of approaching history. By proclaiming and integrating as a key epistemological rule the idea that historiography ought to find the methods to distance itself from the totems and myths of the nationalist and unionist tribes, that indeed it should not connive with any tribe, their profile strikingly resembled that of François Furet who was to devote most of his mature years to the task of decoupling European history and Marxism from one another. In 1938, the same year that the fathers of Irish modern history were launching their academic journal, *Irish Historical Studies*, Raymond Aron, wrote *Introduction á la philosophie de l'histoire*, his doctoral dissertation on the nature and limits of historical knowledge.[2] Aron was building a case against the historical positivism then dominant in the French university but now long defunct. Nowadays his claim forms the core of what passes for relativism in post-structuralist thought. Others in France at the time were also breaking from the straitjacket of French positivism; March Bloch and Lucien Febvre, the founders of the Annales School or Marcel Mauss and Claude Lévi-Strauss who were beginning to shape the school of cultural anthropology. But Aron was different, precisely because he was not abandoning old schools of thought but engaging and dismantling them on their own ground. It seems that the new historians in Ireland were doing something very similar with nationalist and unionist history. They chose not to leave it but to dismantle its methodological and metaphysical assumptions from within by spotting contradictions, illogicalities, ambiguities and what Roy Foster has called "awkward elisions".

Hence, when he addressed an American audience in the 1960s Edwards showed he was aware of the sensitivities his new history was bound to provoke among the emigrated Catholic Irish who had survived exile drawing emotional nourishment from the faith and fatherland staple. Audaciously he explained: "Now, I don't want in any way to be regarded as a debunker. I am proud to see a creative artist whose first concern is to build up a mighty edifice. There is no room here for debunking; but in the process of construction, it is necessary to get away from, and if necessary to tear down, the obstacles that have prevented such a construction in the past".[3] All these men sought to "leaven the sodden lump"[4] of the Irish mind by bravely challenging clerical and political authoritarianism and unremittingly denouncing the shallow and destructive solutions posited by Party, Church or State, solutions which typically only attended to the shell and not to the core of the difficult problems facing Irish society. This harried minority, authentic champions of freedom in a society where political correctness was paid at a high price gave shape to an authentic Irish self-critique and set the conditions that were to empower later generations to think for themselves. They argued self-sufficiency as defined by historic Sinn Féin had turned into a mockery, demonization of the Other had stifled creative energies, shrivelled conscience and stunted sympathy. They urged Ireland to repossess its place inside the great European family, find the trails to the best incarnations of liberal humanism and confront the reality of Irish discord instead of indulging in harmful wishful thinking.

The new historians in Ireland denounced with mounting anguish the irresponsibility of those who still advocated the global solution of good old-fashioned nationalism and they buckled down to the unrewarding task of breaking the "great enchantment". What came to be known as revisionism in the 1960s in fact started much earlier in the 1930s and 1940s by this minority who set out to dissolve imaginary borders and "clarify the founding myths of the nation". If we keep in mind that this travail of exposure of nationalism's fallacies and exaggerations was happening in the midst of inquisitional watchdogs who watched warily for internal and external enemies of the revolution, "the intellectual courage that was required for such dissolving reflection was truly admirable".[5] In 1991, Fintan O'Toole observed that the citizens of the Irish Republic were "the children of a failed revolution" who like all European citizens had learnt the bitter truth that "revolutions fail, that changing the flag does not necessarily solve the problems that made you want to revolt in the first place". Revolution could never be the alpha and omega of history nor deliver humanity from "emigration, poverty, intolerance, or violence". For neither of them ceased "when we won our 'freedom' just as they will not cease in Romania or Czechoslovakia". He contrasted the baffling complexity of the Southerners with the righteous attitude of the Northerners who still lived under the illusion of a final solution, "where the notion that if only this or that were to happen everything would be all right, survived".[6] With the end of the Cold War as symbolized by the demolition of the Berlin Wall and the collapse of Communism in Eastern Europe, some intellectuals dared to air the anathematic idea that perhaps the traditional cleavage between Right and Left had, far from facilitating reflection on the means to improve the human condition, impoverished thought and created a false problem.

The finer minds were quick to intuit that this compartmentalization was inherently reductive and could not any more, if ever it did, adequately explain the awesome complexity of late twentieth century society. Like other countries on the continent, Ireland was in a period of serious spiritual, emotional and intellectual transition and revisionism registered this moment of interregnum. From then on, many held that the challenge for postmodern states was to create equilibrium and harmony between Right and Left and that true social wisdom consisted in learning to utilize ingeniously the positive insights of each tradition. The contradiction perhaps entailed in espousing such a position was henceforth regarded as only superficial and one claimed it was possible to be socialist and favourable to a market economy, a patriot and an exponent of a united Europe, an environmentalist and a defender of technological progress. In the same vein, the former Taoiseach, Garret FitzGerald thought that there was no incoherence in being in favour of the reunification of the island and concerned with the legitimate fears of the Unionists and above all respectful of their veto against territorial unity.[7] In November 1969 when the West still seethed of the emotions unleashed by the Students' revolt against imperialism and capitalism Conor Cruise O'Brien obliquely pressed for the opening of a dialogue between Right and Left. He argued that the Left failed in its socialist project not because it was thwarted by the forces of the Right but because it had not concerned itself enough with what man was actually like. If it had, it would have made less "wildly optimistic assumptions about transforming man through education or revolution", indulge less "its taste for dialectical polemics and high abstractions" and instead turned its attention more on psychology and "in that depth of human understanding which exists in the work of the great imaginative writers [such as] Edmund Burke's".[8]

The embrace of complexity, the wager on its enriching qualities, is one of the most outstanding features of the revisionist method. Roy Foster explained it signalled an end once and for all to "the compelling Manichean logic of the old 'Story of Ireland', with a beginning, a middle and what appeared (up to about 1968) to be a triumphant end".[9] It had jettisoned the illusions of Manichaeism and wanted to explore Irish history in all its complexity and opacity. Again in 1969, Conor Cruise O'Brien articulated the principle that the exercise of power and free intellectual activity were incompatible, anticipating by at least a decade the French Marxist "recession" from political commitment. For him, "the intellectual who surrendered to [the] pressures of power [was] not so much apostatizing as abdicating his function; he ha[d] already turned into something else".[10] In December 1995 Denis Donoghue and Edna Longley advised their colleagues to elevate the debate on revisionism by removing it from the political domain.[11] This refusal of political hijacking of new intellectual discoveries is reminiscent of the decision of the French intellectuals to quit the political platform. Régis Debray who once went to fight in the Bolivian *maquis* beside Ernesto Che Guevara now explained: "For a long time we have lived on Ludwig Feuerbach's principle that the intellectual was not here to interpret the world but to change it. Let us say that today it is the reverse: we have reached a point where absolute priority is given to interpretation". For Jean-Claude Guillebaud who appraised the state of thinking in 1993, it represented "The beginning of a freedom. That of questioning, of pioneering exploration, of obstinate deciphering, and not always spectacular, of a radically new modernity which still awaits, for a large part, to be thought out".[12]

Part II

The genesis of modern historical scholarship in Ireland

3 Internal critique

Vicissitudes and potentials

The most resounding and damning charge brought against revisionism in the last two decades has been that of a tacit collaboration between the historians and the government. This accusation is too serious to be left unanswered. It must be proved or else rejected. Traditionalists denounced it as a dubious device designed to prop up the border and demolish the work of the revolution. Desmond Fennell declared categorically: "both in its ultimate thrust, and as a matter of objective fact, [it] is the historiography of the counter-revolution".[1] Seamus Deane defined it as "a provincial phenomenon" and dismissed its practitioners as "neo-unionists".[2]

This pigeonholing tactic was a cunning way of imposing once more a Manichean turn to the debate, instantly calling into question the democratic credentials of these historians and their authority in their own field of expertise. By dubbing them mere mouthpieces of unionism, they were accused of being reactionary and this guaranteed the discussion never strayed from the beaten tracks, giving to the non-specialist the illusion this was a repetition of the never-ending polemic on the national question, rehashed and served on a more flamboyant plate. This stubborn will to politicize the debate said a great deal about the fear this new outlook might turn into an orthodoxy and forever dissipate whatever remained of the old naïve infatuation with Irish nationalism. If this emotional severance occurred, the old republican dream of completing the revolution in the North would have receded a little further from the horizon of political probabilities. Would traditionalists have been so anxious to cast these new findings into the old moulds, if they had not guessed the real destabilizing potential behind them? This very apprehension conceded a value of some sort to the new cogitations. We cannot of course peremptorily declare that such complicity never was. This requires demonstration. In 1991 Michael Laffan opined: "Historians anticipated as well as responded to the problems posed by violence in Northern Ireland. Some politicians may now share their reservations and mixed feelings about the role of force in Irish history, but it was the historians and not the politicians who led the way."[3] Later during a conversation, Laffan repeated to me he was still convinced of the truth behind this thesis. But he hastened to add a caveat by saying that if the historians did effectively play an avant-garde role in this respect, it did not necessarily ensue the politicians followed the historians' example. He conceded some took the same path but insisted it often happened morally and politically for different reasons.

When we abide by the rules of chronology we find ample evidence supporting the view that the new historians announced precociously the need for a change of attitude to the Northern problem and the Civil War trauma. In the Ireland of the 1980s the real nature of Irish nationalism continued to be a vexing enigma and the subject of an acerbic polemic between traditionalists and revisionists. The latter held that Irish nationalism had too from time to time displayed in a dormant manner sectarian, racialist and totalitarian features, thus implying that its righteousness was unjustified. The former dismissed such notions and wisecracked with the sledgehammer argument of a conspiracy to discredit the achievements of the Irish Revolution, the real intention of which was to rehabilitate and revamp the blemished reputation of Ulster Unionism. In *Modern Ireland*, Roy Foster declared:

> The Irish nationalism that had developed by this date (The start of the Home Rule crisis of 1912) was Anglo-phobic and anti-Protestant, subscribing to a theory of the "Celtic Race" that denied the "true" Irishness of Irish Protestants and Ulster Unionists, but was prepared to incorporate them into a vision of "Independent Ireland" whether they wanted it or not.[4]

Later Brian Murphy riposted: "By branding the native Irish as racialist, revolutionaries and sectarian, Foster has made separation and partition more reasonable and respectable. He has conferred an unmerited legitimacy on the two nations' theory".[5] Murphy's opinion on revisionism as surreptitiously advancing a political agenda is exaggerated. If a politicization of the historical debate occurred in the 1980s it is not so much because the Establishment and Irish revisionists were conspiring behind the scene in moulding public opinion in favour of the Unionists but more likely because historians were writing under great strain. The violence of the Provisionals became a distorting prism that constantly beckoned at the emotional chord of historians and sometimes lured them into the pitfall of oversimplification and exaggeration. But perceptions are as tenacious as reality.

So Murphy's evaluation of the situation should not be written off lightly for it shows that politicization of history is inevitable when issues that were not resolved in the past continue to fester and jeopardize society. The fact that politicization could be as well in the eye of the beholder is of little comfort for in those circumstances it only takes one party to voice its conspiratorial doubts for the other party to find itself instantly embroiled in a rhetorical repartee battle of accusation and counter-accusation, which eventually causes politicization to happen anyway. If on the surface the reform commenced in 1938 seems a positivist exercise, the concerns which begot it were truly theoretical. The generation of Moody, Edwards, Quinn and Beckett knew that the past had been unsparingly plundered unsparingly for propagandist uses and so they came from a lineage that had deeply internalized the problem of history's ideological utility. Ciaran Brady insists that in their public and semi-public utterances, recurring allusions revealed that what had principally motivated the efforts of these men had been something more profound than a mere rudimentary empiricism.[6] The abiding situation of two tribes locked in a never-ending cycle of hate and suspicion stood as a frustrating reminder of the chronic inadequacy of academic history when faced with the power of irrational emotions. Ideology looked triumphant and made a mockery of the pursuit of the truth. In a country where it always appeared to have had the upper hand, the obstacles facing the new historians were not only of a professional nature but also, more fretfully perhaps, of a personal kind. They had to trust their gut feeling and fasten their minds onto the value of their work of correction whatever political effects were to accrue from it. Hence, in December 1962 when Moody launched his project of a New History of Ireland, he recalled "the counsels of despair that endeavoured to save the founders of IHS from themselves in 1937–8" and "he was cheered to see that on this occasion the pessimists were far fewer than they were then" especially when they realized that "much of the head-shaking and hand-wringing was due to mere apprehension or to misapprehension".[7]

Still one can easily see how the charge of a *trahison des clercs* would awaken old doubts and carry quite an important amount of weight in the Irish situation. In the past, prior to the setting-up of the Free State, historians found it virtually impossible to extirpate themselves from political issues, be it the 1641 massacres, the United Irishmen Rebellion of 1798, the defence of Repeal of the Union, Home Rule, the Rebellion of 1916, or the split over the Anglo-Irish Treaty of December 1921. And often, they became wittingly or unwittingly "the kept men" of one faction or another. This phenomenon of collusion was no less conspicuous for happening under the cover of professionalism and due respect for Rankean empiricism. The historians who followed in the footsteps of Moody and Edwards knew all too well about this daunting paradox as the remarks of Brady testify: "Yet it was also clear that this apparently sound academic history was shot through with the concerns of contemporary ideological debates in which the pretence to objectivity and impartiality was a powerful rhetorical weapon".[8] Thus, in a country that had witnessed more than once historians fighting about the correct interpretation of Irish history with "all the paraphernalia of scholarship" but with a clear ideological intent in mind, the loss of faith in objectivity and truth was bound to become rampant and chronic. This perhaps gives us a better appreciation of the enormity of the task that awaited the new historians, in that they had to find ways to spark off a new enthusiasm for these idealistic values that had been manhandled.

The phrase "historiographic revolution" that has been applied to the arrival of Irish revisionism is not just some ostentatious metaphor; the new historians did truly subject Irish historiography to a complete philosophical and epistemological transformation. The steps they devised to obviate the intrusion of politics is at the heart of this demonstration. Despite overtones of radicalism, the accusation of complicity with power laid at the door of the *Irish Historical Studies* school is more a hangover, a projection from the past, and all too often a convenient stick with which to beat into silence any historian who professes to have found embarrassing truths; at any rate something which the evolution of historical scholarship since the late 1930s does not in the least substantiate. Of course there is also the fact that in the late 1970s collusion theories would have been fashionable because Michel Foucault had propounded a theory that claimed that knowledge and power could not be divorced. In every age, he argued, there was a dominant "discourse" which, in the language it used, framed and restricted the possibilities of thought and its expression in such a way as virtually to remove the possibility of disagreement. If one version of the past was endorsed more than others, it was not because it matched more closely with the evidence, but because its exponents wielded more power within the historical profession than their critics and above all because governments deemed their interpretations more auspicious for the policies and strategies of political establishments.[9]

However, a truth overlooked amidst the intensity of exchanges was that Irish history was undergoing the same paradigmatic shift as European historiography and philosophy.[10] Far from being a mere ideologically driven exercise in the narrow sense of the word, seeking merely to manufacture theoretical underpinnings for partition, Irish revisionism was simply testing methods and concepts that had also been intensely debated and criticized on similar grounds on the continent. In France, François Furet challenged the traditional Marxist reading of the French Revolution and explored whether the Terror was not a product of the rationalistic or wilful culture of the Enlightenment. Rejecting the notion that the Terror was a mere accidental skidding off with extenuating circumstances, Furet held it was of the same substance as the Revolution itself.[11] In Greece, Anastasia Karakasidou carried out an ethnographic study in a village of the Macedonian region and discovered that the habitual division between native and refugee was deceptive and hid in reality a phenomenon of ethnic amalgamation a lot more complex. She excavated a rich history containing not only the interaction and commingling between Greeks originating from various regions, but the more intriguing process by which the natives came to regard themselves as Greeks and identify with the fortunes of the Greek State.[12] However true this is it does not mean that Irish traditionalists did not voice some legitimate concerns. Since the French Revolution, Europe had been the site of bold theoretical experiments, the quixotic attempt to impose systematic projections on the irrational and erratic flux of human affairs. Ventures to emulate the French model and to do, it was supposed, better, launched equally from positions which were conventionally the far

Left and the far Right, only proved one thing; it was always possible to do much worse.

Since the 1950s and 1960s, some men of the Left who had devoted them-selves wholeheartedly to the Marxist dream finally took into account the abysmal gap between theory and reality and it compelled them to confront those facts contradicting their system of beliefs, as well as to question their dogmas, rationalizations and hopes. This self-critique and the re-adjustment entailed in it created, however, a problem, at once philosophical and polit-ical. Can a tradition be reformed without risking complete negation and destruction? Will this dismantling not go too far, thereby undermining its foundations and playing right into the hands of the rival one? In the entrenched climate of the Cold War, the instinct of the Left was to reject all theoretical revision as a hypocritical fiddling with the doctrine amounting in fact to a disguised concession to the values and methods of the Right. And who suggested concession to the Right, implied also loss of influence for the values and methods of the Left. Revision was a slippery slope whose termi-nus was the capitulation of the Left to the Right. As described by Boris Ponomaryov, revisionism is "a trend in the working class movement that, to the benefit of the bourgeoisie, seeks to debase, to emasculate, and to destroy Marxism by means of revision, that is by way of re-examination, distortion and negation of its basic tenets".[13] This definition captures well its perceived danger and most significantly the way in which an internal critique has embedded in itself a potential of erosion of dogmatic certitudes infinitely mightier than that of an external critique. The aversion to internal critique out of fear of turning into a political gangplank for the enemy or being labelled a turncoat has had a long and onerous legacy in Ireland. It has led to fanatic entrenchment and withdrawal behind the illusive shelter of a rigid political blueprint. The history of Irish conflict North and South shows recurrently that this reluctance to accept and learn from stalemates or engage with the opposite viewpoint is ultimately counter-productive. But with the exception of some artificial and hollow gestures, the lesson remains to this day unheard. Compromise, especially when it comes after hundreds of deaths sacrificed in the name of an unimpeachable truth, tastes intolerably bitter.

Emotional investment in this truth is so unconditional, so consuming that all of us, consciously or not, feel in a confused and nagging way that our truth, the full version in all its black and white glory, ought to have tri-umphed. The 1921 Anglo-Irish settlement could not satisfy the absolutist tendencies raging and wrestling in the minds of the combatants. They had to find a new outlet and so the Civil War broke out between the diehards and the compromisers. Patrick Pearse, the leader of the 1916 Rising, announced most chillingly the fate of ostracism that was to be meted out on the traitors: "The man who in the name of Ireland, accepts as final settle-ment something less than separation between Ireland and England, even if it is only by a fraction of a iota, is guilty of such an immense disloyalty, such an immense crime against the Irish nation, that it would be better for this man if he had never been born".[14] In 1912 the Unionists thrust violence onto the Irish chessboard again when they vowed to resist the much reviled yet modest Home Rule and the British, by turning a blind eye to subversion coming from one quarter, sanctioned both the Unionist and the Nationalist use of violence.[15] The revisionist historian, F.S.L. Lyons, maligned for being pro-unionist, always refused to rehabilitate the anti-Home Rule cause precisely because Home Rule was an "innocuous measure", whose import if correctly weighed by English and Ulster Unionists could have revealed that "far from being disruptive of the Empire, it was (under the advocacy of John Redmond and John Dillon) a bulwark against other and far more destructive forces".[16]

The question of how reformable is a tradition without suffering irreparable damage is crucial all the more so since it is at the heart of the polemic that has opposed revisionists to traditionalists in Ireland during the historiographic disputation in the 1980s and 1990s. Even if the problem is not always thus couched, the most frequent criticism raised against revision is arguably its tendency to go too far. The feeling is that its demythologizing zeal is to drastic because it presents Irish nationalism as an unmitigated mistake, thereby depriving it of all ethical justification. The difficulty with revision is compounded by the fact that Irish Nationalism and Ulster Unionism do not present just a scholastic interest. In Northern Ireland, in a not too remote past, people still fought sometimes with violent means to get recognition of the legitimacy of Nationalism and Unionism. Each tradition felt somehow besieged and deprived of its fundamental right to exist and express itself freely. So any tinkering that might shake or weaken the foundations of a narrative by hinting at artificiality, contradiction, elision or even complexity was felt understandably as an insuperable menace and a symbolic concession of territory. In any case it was viewed as a dangerous exercise that could reverse the gains wrested out of an already strenuous struggle for political survival.

The habit to pour scorn on the whole revisionist adventure was a favourite pastime of some Irish intellectuals in the 1980s who had a vested interest in jettisoning it as an "impoverishing", "irrelevant" and "encumbering" influence. From the perches of posterity's condescension, glib accusations of archaism in method and intention were vituperatively thrown at the faces of those trailblazer historians who had dared to imagine the empowerment of the Irish intellect inside two regimes, which had instead thrived on its emasculation. Soon it became a reflex for all to grieve contritely over the missed opportunity of Irish historiography. Students learnt to despise the principles for which this school stood before learning anything about the profundity and sagacity of the minds which had grappled with them and the difficulties they raised. Would they be turning in their graves if they could see the insolence and affectation with which their writings were later ransacked in search of "incriminating" evidence of theoretical ignorance?

Would they be distressed by the allegation that their scholastic effort is a mere exercise in collaboration on behalf of the imperial culture, or the powers that be? Most likely. Yet another fair guess is that those with a more mischievous or philosophical disposition would also be smiling secretly at this last twist of irony, which turned their preferred weapon, suspicion, against them. After all suspicion towards all orthodoxy is what they strove to implant in the Irish minds and if now some excelled in this game or gorged on this staple, it could also be a sign that they, the masters of suspicion, had done their job only too well.

This chapter is an invitation to leave aside for a moment our arrogant assumptions and to experience, hopefully in a more mind-walloping fashion, the freshness of those voices as they were brimming with hope, daredevilry and enthusiasm for their craft. Our intention is to delve into the origins of Irish revisionism and flesh out expressly with the use of historical evidence its move away from the trammels of power and its gradual assertion of independence. Historians are here approached not only as specialists but also as thinkers and makers of Ireland's modern destiny. It is suggested that those intellectuals have contributed in no small way to the transformation of mentality and sensibility by showing that moral responsibility and critical surgery cut both ways. Indeed if Britain had ultimately a lot to answer for in the troubles of Ireland, Irishmen could no longer afford to think of her as personifying the miraculous solution around which everything else hinged, that to do so was to concede to her the powers of a God and so their best chance to regain control of their own fate was to better themselves and put the onus for change squarely on themselves. Although there had been inspiring forerunners before 1938, such as Professor James Eadie Todd (1885–1949) from Queen's, who had taught Theodore William Moody (1907–1984), or Eoin MacNeill (1867–1945) and Mary Hayden (1862–1942) who had taught Robert Dudley Edwards (1909–1988) at UCD, and other eminent predecessors such as Aubrey Gwynn (1892–1983) and Edmund Curtis (1881–1943), the revision of Irish history undertaken from 1938 was the most persistent effort to accomplish a separation between sophistry and knowledge.

This new generation decided to free Irish historiography from the clutches of propaganda and the bridles of a "Cold War" frame of mind. Those historians were passionate advocates of European unity convinced as they were that the only way to free their country from paranoid Anglophobia and internal debilitating strife was to convey to Irish citizens a sense that a drama similar to their own was acted out on a much bigger scale and with more horrible humanitarian consequences. Individual states had sown the seeds of hatred to satisfy their lust for power and world domination. Europe was going to be the Great Healer: a warning and an example for Ireland. Recently Willy Maley declared that the comparative approach was never a priority for revisionism.[17]

However, in "History, Politics and Partition", written on 12 March

1955, Edwards underlined how comparison made one approach the history of mankind with deeper sympathy and penetration and helped to bring down the "Iron Curtain of prejudice" erected by propaganda. The problem resided in the fact that "the text-books of Irish history concentrated on the English aggression and left [one] with no clear impression of any other community tradition" to emulate and be proud of. It was high time that Ireland followed the example of these European states which were "seeking to break down old prejudices by weeding their educational book lists of works emphasizing mutual hatred". He supported the position of the Council of Europe for which there could be no European identity until "each state ceased to be obsessed with the rights denied it by its neighbour". The contact with Europe was "particularly valuable to the people of a small country in the shadow of a greater one" for "it enabled them to realise that there were some foreign ideas which were not the sole monopoly of their dominant neighbour".

The awareness of partaking in a common condition could "reveal [to the Irish nation] that [its] own peculiarities [were], after all, more in the mainstream of European development than their neighbour's propaganda might suggest", thereby setting the psychological conditions for a lessening of its paranoia and a recovery of its self-esteem. The Irish needed to realize that "good propaganda can be bad history", and he trusted that with such collective awakening, the Irish would "have established a claim to be classified as self-critical". His hope was that Irish historians "would accustom [themselves] to studying conflicting propaganda, and might [eventually] produce real history".[18] Hence comparison with the fate of other European nations could foster a healthier sense of Irishness and moderate crippling feelings of victimization or inferiority. Propaganda was an affront to the intelligence of all Irish citizens inculcating as it did "a vague notion that, in 1916, the Irish drove the English out, but, by some sort of absent-mindedness, forgot to finish the job around Belfast [and] that King Billy was an Orangeman who saved [the Protestants] from the massacring Papists by the victory of the Boyne".[19] To dampen down the Irish Cold-War mentality, Edwards emphasized – not without wit – the common intellectual reflexes in the old enemies. Hence, despite an apparent unbridgeable gulf:

> [Both] think more in terms of politics than of culture. They both seem to think that the nation and the state are identical. They both forget that the nation is a cultural concept and the state a convenient political mechanism, that if another world war takes place, there will be far fewer states after it than there are today. They both fail to realise that the states of Western Germany and Eastern Germany may yet be embodied in greater states, called Western Europe and Eastern Europe, while the German national culture may remain an element common to both.[20]

Edmund Curtis (1881–1943), who belonged to an earlier generation, thought comparison indispensable for good history. Already in 1925, Curtis deplored that no effort was made to compare the Penal Laws with similar laws in other European countries, as if Ireland was the only country to have suffered religious discrimination. He held that the role of teachers and text-books should be to tell children that Protestants were also persecuted out of existence in France, Spain and Italy, that Bohemia in the Thirty Years War had been converted from Calvinism back to Catholicism by armed force and finally that none of the great Churches believed in religious toleration until a hundred years ago. He explained: "No one will grudge our Catholic fellow-countrymen the glory and honour of having stood so true to their faith and endured so much for it, yet that glory will not be diminished by being set beside a parallel picture of what other nations and minorities have suffered for their creed in other countries".[21] And he added: "This compara-tive picture we must have if we are to have history, in the true sense, for the essence of an understanding of history is to put things and men in their time and place and judge them by such circumstances".[22] Anticipating charges of partiality, Curtis insisted that: "The heroes who are worshipped in the North, and such subjects as the rise and progress of the Orange Order, are every bit as distorted and out of proportion as much of our National History here in the South, and probably with less saving grace of humour and tolera-tion".[23] He thought that the nationalism which had conditioned the Irish to think their virtues were all their own and their defects put into them by their conquerors had now "curdled on the national stomach".

Did Curtis and Edwards know that in their championship of comparison they were refreshing the intuitions of the Belgian historian, Henri Pirenne (1862–1935) and the French historian, Marc Bloch (1886–1944) who together with Lucien Febvre radically changed the face of history as it had hitherto been practised? In 1924 during the International Congress of historians, Pirenne argued that the First World War with its nationalist hysterical outpourings to which historians had been accomplices had torn apart the original unity of European culture. He saw comparison as a whole-some and curative tool to fight the lies of propaganda and restore the belief in the oneness of European consciousness. Only comparison could lessen the power of prejudice. The reason why so many historians lacked objectivity was their ignorance of the ancient ties and contacts that linked countries together. He who engrosses himself too much in the contemplation of his people will inevitably puff up their originality and honour them with dis-coveries which in reality were only borrowed. The narrowness of his know-ledge exposes him to the deceit of "the idols of sentiment". Comparison put history in its true perspective. What formerly looked like a mountain turns out to be just a little mound and the national genius so glorified suddenly becomes a mere manifestation of the spirit of imitation.[24]

Four years later, in his speech at the International Congress of Historians at Oslo, Bloch was reluctant to linger on the political import of comparison and more concerned to demonstrate that it was a "technical instrument", practical, scientific, productive and thus stood apart from the more tautological and teleological practices of philosophy of history and sociology. Yet despite his professed cautiousness, he could not help stressing that comparison thanks to its excavation of rituals that had survived time often released "the fundamental unity of the human mind". Refusing to endow this method with grandiose goals he deemed that it would have fulfilled its promise if only it succeeded in "reconciling terminologies, reducing the dialogue of the deaf" and prompted historians to engage with the germane questions.[25] Whether Curtis and Edwards were aware or not of Pirenne and Bloch is perhaps less important than the fact that faced with the emotional and intellectual challenge posed by national discord, even though they wrote in relatively peaceful times, they, like the latter, searched for a common scientific language; one with which they hoped to peel back the layers of time until the recovery of an irreducible and unassailable core of Irish human condition. Since they praised this method, a second and third generation of revisionists, personalities like Tom Garvin,[26] Brian Walker,[27] Sean J. Connolly,[28] Liam Kennedy[29] and Alvin Jackson[30] have analysed their objects of research by comparing them to parallel objects, processes and phenomena in Europe. Yet this approach, no doubt because of its intellectual demands, was slow to take off. It was only when in the 1980s Irish theorists began to toy with comparisons that the historians considered far-fetched and politically laden that they began themselves to examine in earnest the potentials of this method.

The fate of Irish history changed irrevocably when two young graduates met in the summer of 1931 on the steps of the National Library of Ireland. Their paths met again in 1932 at the famous Institute of Historical Research in London, co-founded in 1921 by A.F. Pollard. Alfred Frederick Pollard was director of the Institute between 1920 and 1939, founding editor of *History*, the journal on which *Irish Historical Studies* was modelled, and in the words of David Cannadine, "the most outstanding Tudor historian of his day". His age fervently believed in the value and attainability of objectivity and emphasized unflagging industry, precision and bibliographical thoroughness.[31] The Institute was conceived as "a world centre" for the dissemination of scholarly knowledge about history. V.H. Galbraith, the successor of Pollard, once explained that what was remarkable about the Institute was that it promoted "the study of the past as a vital international enterprise, which offered a great hope for the future". The liberal profile of this training ground no doubt offered a unique window of opportunity to realize how much bigger, more complex and multifarious was the world beyond the British Isles. This realization, to two historians whose destinies were to lie in Ireland, no doubt worked as a deterrent against provincial isolation and was felicitous to the historiographic revolution they were to initiate.

Born in 1909, Robert Dudley Edwards came from Dublin and was the progeny of a mixed marriage. His mother, Bridget MacInerney, from Co. Clare was a redoubtable woman, a convinced suffragette, an unapologetic republican, who never forgave de Valera for reconciling himself to the abominable idea of the democratic game and who tried with dogged determination but without success to instil the same faith to her two sons. Describing her grandmother, Ruth wrote: "She was a revolutionary and a virago. She hid guns in 1914, cheered on the 1916 Rebellion, sent her young sons into the Fianna and when they were, respectively, thirteen and eleven, instructed them to fight in the Civil War on the republican side".[32] Robert refused and the recruiting sergeant sent his younger brother, Ralph, home. She was also an enthusiastic supporter of Mussolini and Hitler and when her granddaughter asked her how she justified concentration camps she dismissed the allegation as an invention of British propaganda. Such an opinionated woman could not fail to have a profound impact on Robert as a reflective piece on his mother written in 1956 reveals most tenderly:

> The very strength of her convictions created a subconscious antagonism among those who feared the dominant. Her passionate denunciation of injustice created an automatic feeling in favour of those denounced. She trusted too much to a mind, which could penetrate unerringly to the weak spot in an argument or of a character and failed lamentably to take account of the frailty of human nature, which must move more timidly by the light of reason. The man in her may have detected the time-server in her brother or the feminity of my father; the woman in her was too passionate to spare their failure to line up to her ideals. It is a warning as to the hopelessness of trying to be impartial when one's viewpoint is an internal one.[33]

Walter Edwards, Robert's father, came from Gloucestershire from a mining family, but acquired sufficient education to have a white-collar job. He was a Methodist turned Quaker, unassuming, well read, of liberal inclinations and who – it seems – suffered patiently his wife's dramatic effusions. Growing under the influence of such contrasting temperaments probably led the young Robin to identify subconsciously with both, be torn between both and aspire silently to hammer these tendencies into some harmony in his heart and mind. Certainly the wish to steer an independent path for oneself freed from the oppressive shadow of one's mother must have been an important personal drive. This coupled with a desire to express his loyalty to a father dwarfed by the fanaticism of his wife may have played a key role in his maturation, his awareness of the necessity to strive for autonomy of judgement and balance at the same time and in his decision to attain these qualities through a single-minded pursuit of historical truth. That said, it was no surprise to realize that Edwards inherited every inch of his mother's impatience, impetuosity and truculence. Garret FitzGerald, the former Foreign Minister and Taoiseach remembered affectionately his old teacher, "as a character with a slightly malicious sense of humour, which he was never inhibited from employing to take people down a peg or two". Looking back with amusement he added: "An ability to cope with this phenomenon was for students over many decades a prerequisite for survival".[34] F.X. Martin, also a student of his, once complimented him on being the "one man sufficiently big, capable, and interested enough to lift Irish history from its present pedestrian condition" but advised him to abstain from making "witty, true, but cutting remarks" that wounded "thin-skinned people", gave licence to "small-minded yappers" and prevented people from savouring his more likable and genial self.[35]

Theodore William Moody was born in 1907 in Belfast. His father worked in the Harland and Woolf shipyard at a time when Belfast had reason to be proud of the output and international renown of its prosperous industry. His parents, William John Moody and Ann Isabella Dippie, were committed Christians, belonging to the Plymouth Brethren. This background taught him a strong work ethic and a heightened moral sensibility. Quakerism is convinced of the ameliorative power of education and of the potential for good in all men. At the heart of its philosophy is the notion of "Inner Prompting", a quickening of the heart secretly coercing us all, in spite of the dominion of our selfish wills, to care for our neighbour. The imponderables of conscience and compassion worked their mysterious ways through men's choices and decisions. In 1963 in a letter to Prof. Oppenheimer, Butterfield introduced Moody as the historian who in partnership with Edwards "really put modern Irish historical study on the map and brought it into connection with European Scholarship". He added: "He is a man everybody really loves because he has the Irish charm without the Irish wilfulness – in a sense quite a businesslike person but also awfully tactful, which explains why so many calls have been made on him".[36] At the impressionable age of five, Moody received his first shock when standing at a back window of his home he saw against the skyline the flames of houses of Catholic workers being burned in the riots of 1913. This event "seared itself in his memory" writes F.X. Martin and explains why "his manifest dedication to scholarship" was not "self-explanatory" and could not exhaust a rich personality whose heart was filled with a deep and sincere altruism. He saw in him an "affirmative" optimism, "which gave direction, dynamism, and deliberation to his thinking and activities".[37] Certainly this quality of optimism Moody had in abundant measure when he resolved to curb sectarianism in Belfast by waging a "mental war of liberation from servitude to myth" and projected a blueprint, both imaginative and practicable, to reverse the stagnation of Irish history in schools.

The word "stagnation" is no overstatement as the remarks of Aubrey Gwynn, Acting Professor of Modern History at UCD, on 1 March 1930, bleakly reveal. Responding to a suggestion by Eoin MacNeill to start a Historical Society, Gwynn wrote: "Something tangible ought to be done to encourage students to practical research work in History. There is far too much spoon-feeding at present, and the ordinary student does little or no independent reading of his own". He too urged the creation of such a society but on the condition that it would be "limited to those only who are keen on historical study for its own sake". He also counselled that it should not confine itself solely to Irish history but it should cover European history as well. For he felt that although "Irish History has plainly first claim, it would be a bad thing for Irish scholarship to become limited to Irish problems".[38] Desmond Gleeson's letter to Edmund Curtis on 6 February 1936 struck a final note of pessimism when he sarcastically commented:

> There is little interest in any sort of scholarship nowadays except on a cash basis. I don't think it has ever been at a greater discount in Ireland. In the N.U.I., the number of theses in Irish history for the past twenty years could be counted on one's fingers – there is no money in it or job at the end of it. People like myself who spend their spare time in picking up a crumb or two from the past are regarded as harmless lunatics and gently encouraged to "make a fourth" or study syncopation.[39]

Moody arrived at the Institute a year before Edwards and there, during the seminars, both men learnt how to process and analyse historical evidence in a more scientific way. By the time they returned to Ireland, both men were ready to instigate profound changes in the teaching of history inside the university and in the public at large. The broad lines of this wonderful journey are known and the author will not repeat here what can be found elsewhere; suffice to say that a measure of their success is that most of their far-seeing schemes, their BBC Ulster lectures, the Thomas Davis lectures, the New History of Ireland, the UCD archives, the Irish History Students' Association, all survived their progenitors and became true landmarks and precious assets in the refashioning of Irish history in a spirit of real and open-minded curiosity. Among their most lasting achievements was the creation of the Irish Committee of Historical Sciences, the umbrella organization for historians in the Republic and Northern Ireland who obstinately continued their liberal dialogue even during the most uncongenial of times of the hunger-strikes and the spiralling of sectarian violence in Northern Ireland. Their cooperative effort was the reflection of a faith, some would call it naïve, in the didactic energies underpinning it. In 1969, Moody evinced his fine egalitarian sensibility by declaring: "History, the study of human thought and action in the stream of time, in so far as they can be reconstructed in the mind from the surviving evidence, achieves its highest fulfilment only when it is intelligible to men as such and not only merely to historians".[40] On 19 July 1960, Edwards fretted over the performance of his students in a Matriculation exam:

It is deplorable to see how many have no notions beyond what they get in notes dictated by teachers. The approach is largely unreal because of the failure to realise that history is not concerned with faith and fatherland. This style of propaganda indubitably affects adversely all who do not get driven into the church or into the IRA. What is needed is a history of Ireland in its relations with civilisation in which the unity of Europe gets more emphasis and can be balanced against English aggression and Protestant bigotry. And it ought to be made a high priority.[41]

Like Jacques Derrida, they believed that what has been thought, written and learnt can be thought, written and learnt anew.[42] Technical history, the task of establishing the facts as precisely as possible, was not an end in itself but literally a foundation, a stepping stone to conveying a more clear-headed, magnanimous and responsible understanding of a troublesome past. In 1792 Condorcet reminded Frenchmen of a crucial truth: "As long as there are men who do not obey their reason alone, who receive their opinions from a foreign opinion, all chains are broken in vain".[43] This is a sentiment to which the first revisionists would also have shared. Hence Aidan Clarke remembers with thankfulness that Edwards had introduced into History at UCD "a famed 'marathon' in which, for days on end, students first criticised one another's work and then criticised one another's criticisms".[44] Tom Dunne recollects how history at UCD, presided over by the same "volatile and stimulating" character, had a "special air of excitement and innovation", an impression reinforced by his deliberate shunning from hierarchical haughtiness especially with students he considered talented.[45] The decision to step down from the editorship of *Irish Historical Studies* and to pass on the torch to the following generation was inspired by similar egalitarian feelings. In a statement he made at a meeting of the Irish Historical Society on 20 May 1957, Edwards suggested that the old faces had to make room for new ones because even though "they had laboured in the heat of the sun", "they were not entitled to take up a possessive attitude towards the journal". With a rare display of modesty which his students and colleagues may be forgiven for having missed sometimes when they were the dazed victim of his biting tongue, Edwards explained:

> While we may pride ourselves upon being in large part its creators, we cannot regard it as our creature. To deny that younger scholars are fit to take our places today is to refuse to a younger generation what Edmund Curtis did not refuse to us when we were younger than is any member of this committee at the present time: the chance of trial and error.[46]

Hearsay has it though that there was more to it. Maybe a thing that the fathers of modern Irish history forgot in the first spur of grit is that before being first-quality intellects they were also men with foibles, doubts and prejudices. Those faults had their origin in two personalities who could not have been more unlike. But they were also the residual imprint of two estranged societies. And so whilst they were engaged on the gigantic mission of changing how their compatriots saw their past, themselves and one another, in the hope of achieving a reapprochement, they eventually tumbled to the fact that their personal collaboration was not going to be a smooth one either. And truly it wasn't. They notoriously enraged each other so much that the story of their chaotic friendship became an unmissable part of the legend they created. The mischievous and conspiratorial Dudley with his younger crony Desmond would play malicious tricks on Theo whom they liked to cast as a "pompous paragon of rectitude, sobriety and good sense". Needless to say the high-principled, responsible and industrious Theo did not find the devil-may-care and obstructive attitude of his eccentric rivals amusing.[47] Apparently on this occasion Dudley was trying to embarrass Theo into resigning from the editorship of the journal. Something that Theo for his own good reasons was not ready to do. Owen Dudley Edwards the son of Robert explained the rationale behind the creation of the new historical school:

> They sought a discipline whose findings would be made and disclosed as impartially as human frailty permitted. They were guided by the pursuit of objectivity laid down (if not always successfully practised) by Acton and Ranke – and before them by William Robertson. They were animated by their knowledge that history took lives in the worlds they came from, Edwards' Dublin and Moody's Belfast, notably in 1919–1923 when they were boys between the ages of 10 and 14. They wanted to shape schools of history, the products of which future generations could read with intellectual but not political profit, and above all without being driven to bloodshed by it.[48]

From its origins, Irish revisionism was actuated by ethical concerns, which by essence could capsize the new state's artificial self-image. This moral imperative was paramount in the thinking of this first generation and there was something truly subversive about it because it flew in the face of topical electoral majorities. The peace and stability of the 1940s and 1950s, later intensified by the economic optimism of the 1960s, made for a mentality prone to complacency similar to what Herbert Butterfield called the Whig interpretation of history: a tendency "to praise revolutions provided they have been successful, to emphasize certain principles of progress in the past and to produce a story which is the ratification if not the glorification of the present".[49] However the woolly balloon enveloping the South was soon to be punctured by the scalpel of the revisionism of the 1960s with increasing pungency if not provocation in the voices of such different writers as Conor Cruise O'Brien,[50] F.X. Martin[51] and Francis Shaw,[52] compelling Irishmen and women to think again of emotions and beliefs too passively held.[53]

The decades after independence were a time when national introspection, freedom of expression and right of dissent were discouraged. Even though Ireland was a democracy, the circumstances in which this had been secured were not conducive to the growth of a real open society. Partition with the actual opting out of one million Ulster Protestants meant tragically the loss of a fine opportunity to lay the foundations of a real dialogue across political and confessional divides. With them out of the equation, it became more acceptable to impose the precepts of Catholicism and Gaelicism on a uniform and acquiescent majority. Social homogeneity bred intellectual smugness, a general loathsomeness to envision the possibility of other types of Irishness let alone to empathize with them and their dilemma.[54] In a rural society shaped by the ethos and interests of farmers and where the priest had gained an untrammelled moral superiority over its parish, socialism was presented either as an irrelevance or a dangerous toxin causing depravity. Alarmed by the advance of socialism on the continent, an egalitarian credo whose professed mission was to rescue men from the limbos of superstition and inculcate them with a new faith in their mental faculties, the Church sought to devise a means to protect its spiritual monopoly in Ireland. And so it did by entering into an alliance with the Pro-Treaty camp. Since socialism with its secular and anti-clerical overtones was sometimes expressed by Republicans, the Church was wary of them and in due time turned against them by threatening the Irregulars with excommunication and branding them as murderers.[55]

For a long time after the Civil War a question mark hung over the legitimacy of the Free State. Born surrounded by intimate enemies who accused it of cowardly forgoing the Republic and degenerating into a puppet regime, the Free State felt painfully vulnerable and was thankful for a chance to draw on the "superabundant reserves" of authority enjoyed then by the Catholic Church.[56] With the fear of *coup d'état* prying over the minds of the Free Staters, the compulsion to drive their own revolutionary past out of the window and to adorn themselves with all the trappings of legality became an obsession. Thus the imperatives of popular acceptance and survival of the regime came to rest on the invention of a state mythology by which to convince Irish citizens that the Free State was the embodiment of the goal that all nationalists had with such self-abnegation and bravery fought for. This ontological insecurity at the heart of the new political dispensation operated more and more like a straitjacket. It forced the government to exhibit with ever more rhetorical extravagance its patriotic probity, especially when in 1925 an intractable reality, in the unforeseen failure of the Boundary Commission to yield significantly more territory for the Southern jurisdiction, disclosed to the eyes of the Northern Nationalists and the Republicans their embarrassing powerlessness in the face of partition. This fiasco gave the opposition the ideal weapon with which to attack Cumman na nGaedheal for inefficiency, bungling and betrayal.[57] Thus, as Clare O'Halloran showed in her analysis on the evasions of Southern nationalism, the Treaty's most frustrating legacy was the way the formulation of an innovative policy was hampered by mutual paranoia and an obligation to outshine in calculated jingoism. Thus the narrow competitiveness of the Southern parties froze all deliberation on what might prove auspicious to a future thawing in the mind of Ulster.[58]

Moreover, the principle of the priority of the national over the social, which kept the Labour Party abnormally attached to Sinn Féin, led the former to commit two serious mistakes, in the decision not to contest the elections of 1918 and 1921, thereby putting the cause of organized labour at a disadvantage in the early years of independence. Labour's success in 1922 gave the impression that its prospects were not irreversibly damaged by its deference to Sinn Féin but the truth was not as promising. Far from indicating that Ireland was awakening to a radical mood, it merely betrayed weariness about the angry feuding that had paralysed Sinn Féin during the six months since the Treaty.[59] The Civil War which followed automatically provoked, as Michael Laffan put it, the electoral retrogression of Irish Labour in the 1923 general elections because: "The bitterness of guerrilla warfare polarized loyalties and hatreds in a way in which the skirmishing during the first half of 1922 had failed to do. The civil war enhanced the primacy of the national question. The civil war restored Irish normality, European abnormality, to Independent Ireland".[60] Irish social radicalism was also inhibited by another factor. To remain united at an institutional level with its sister organization in the North and to avoid alienating Protestant workers, Irish Labour was compelled to pursue a strictly economic or Labourite policy. Labour's concern with doing nothing which might further divide Northern and Southern workers often forced the Northern leadership to seek integration into and recognition from the Unionist State and imperceptibly to collaborate with its sectarian and repressive character.[61]

The theocratic direction taken by the Southern state, with the banning of divorce, the outlawing of birth control, together with its totalitarian proclivities with the setting up of the Censorship Board in 1929, and the Church's imposition of the "Ne Temere" decree which obliged children of mixed marriages to be raised as Catholics, all these features signalled a sort of overreaction to a cultural malaise which Irish society was at pains to conceal. The cause of this malaise was the protracted decline of the Irish language and the Gaelic culture of the past, which from the vantage point of post-independence made the Cultural Revival look increasingly like a half-baked chimera. Beset with the problem of this lack of cultural distinctiveness, devotional and strident Catholicism assumed the role of psychological "ersatz" so that the searing memory of a terrible paradox could be tolerated. The same function was fulfilled by militant nationalism at the beginning of the twentieth century. Declan Kiberd diagnosed the cause of this uneasiness:

The Irish speakers in Connemara were never great nationalists. They didn't have to prove they were Irish, unlike the more anglicised Irish people in Dublin ... Nationalism began to thrive in Ireland at the end of the 19th century partly in the vacuum left by the virtual collapse of the Irish language. People became assertive because they were unsure as to whether they had anything left to assert.[62]

In the minds of many patriots, independence was conceived as a thing of the spirit. Up until the late 1930s, it was very much the fashion to emphasize Ireland's superiority over England. De Valera's political project sought to rationalize economic disadvantage by presenting it as the deliberate choice made by a spiritually fulfilled and morally serene people. The *Catholic Bulletin*, which in the words of Margaret O'Callaghan exemplified "the most extreme manifestation of reactive cultural confusion", had spread the myth that in ancient Gaelic society, the poorest rural families relieved themselves of the burden of their grinding toils by sitting around the fire to discuss scholastic philosophy.[63] Whether uttered with racialist venom or in more debonair fashion, the anxiety was that foreign invasions would quench the Gaelic cultural fire. Given how few people had a good command of Irish, the Gaelic League soon became a dyke to protect Irish culture from engulfment or disintegration. Cosmopolitanism was disparaged because it produced a shallow and arid literature, lacking in "moisture" and "depth", as Seosamh O'Neill replied to George Russell's incitation to let down the dykes.[64] For O'Neill, the promises of the cogito are deceitful. The mind cannot escape from the control of tribal values without becoming shrivelled up, devitalized, like a tree emptied of its sap. Only national culture, nourishing mother "par excellence", can feed the intellect with treasures of wisdom that stem from centuries of Irish tradition and infallible majoritarian precepts. The equation between wisdom and tradition is however problematic. It begs entirely the question of the possibility that a tradition could conceal repressive tendencies whose purpose is to thrust a too mechanical conception of truth on a guileless people. Truth and tradition are not synonymous. If to immerse oneself in the prejudices of previous generations can help to understand the instinctual in us, and even provide comfort and rejuvenation, it can, to a same degree, tragically spell the surrender of critical resistance, which is so vital to the improvement of both individual and society.

The core message of the Enlightenment urged men to find the courage to use their own judgement without the succour of a director of conscience or the crutch of received opinions. When O'Neill implies that imagination and meditation are destined to dry up unless they are rooted deep into the organic soil of a nation, he repeats the reasoning of the German romantic Herder or the French counter-revolutionary de Maistre. Like them, he dismisses the notion that these faculties can ripen and flourish without the humus of a national culture or from some critical distance of it. Not surprisingly the reluctance to open up to the example of other nations became even more acute when that nation was England. It became a problem for the new historians who sought the advice and expertise of English historians in their efforts to professionalize and publicize Irish history. As Roy Foster astutely put it, "to suggest that Irish historical scholarship could benefit by follow-ing English example automatically raised hackles";[65] not least among Irish historians themselves who although they agreed on the need to rescue and reveal a real Irish past, could not always brush aside their quickly aroused nationalism. For instance on 20 January 1954 James Hogan complained about the over-representation of English historians in the role of external examiners to the detriment of "graduates from the National University or Trinity College" who had specialized in Irish history.[66] The first decades of independence also marked the inexorable decline of the Southern Unionists. Although the founders of the Irish Free State, Arthur Griffith and Kevin O'Higgins, were anxious to allay their fear of becoming the victims of intimidation and discrimination for their selfish part in the defence of the English interest in Ireland, by making an effort to integrate them in the Senate, defeatism and passivity had overwhelmingly set in, pushing many to emigrate.[67] The sociological portrait outlined above shows conspicuously that all the conventional avenues of political opposition, including the Republican element which stayed aloof from the democratic process until 1927, had of their own strange volition sidelined and muzzled themselves.

Nor is there any doubt that this self-imposed silence contrasted vividly with the invigorating clash of point of views of the years before political independence when radicalism assumed more than just a militarist form and was sometimes actively competing against it. Equally certain is that this retreat of the other political forces, apart from giving free reign to the authoritarian propensities both of the Church and the Government, could have totally blunted the critical capabilities of a people already shattered and cowered by the realization of the human cost of the Revolution if it had not been for the intervention of a few revisionists who courageously embarked as early as the 1930s on the gruelling journey of rediscovering the true goals of Irish nationalism; goals which had dwindled to mere ornamental symbols or hair-splitting trivia and suffered from a harmful loss of perspective in the heat and passion of civil war. It is against this mentality of evasion and con-formism and a most frigid political landscape that the revisionist endeavour must be appreciated. A theoretical speculation of the sort propounded by Michel Foucault who spoke of a regime of truth imposed by power to which academic activity is abidingly at best compliant or at worst complicit, often used in the Irish debate to belittle the work of those Irish dissentients, over-looks a far from negligible fact. That fact is that the serious questions these men posed were too unsettling and too fundamental, and above all too reflective of a European condition, to really serve the needs of any single faction which held power during that time. One must also bear in mind an important reflex in Cumman na nGaedheal and Fianna Fáil alike in that both tended to stake their electoral stamina on the suppression of those very same questions.

Symptoms of a retreat from the blithe certainties of historicism can be glimpsed already in the 1930s and 1940s. The stigma of Irish disunity, in all its manifestations, affects deeply the classical scholar Michael Tierney (1894–1975) and forces him to curb his antipathies. Writing in February 1935 at a time when he is an outspoken advocate for the powerful right-wing section of the opposition to de Valera, Tierney is no longer content with criticizing just one side. Mysticism and the sterile compartmentalization of the Civil War had paralysed Irish nationalism. If its vigour was "running to seed" it was for want of positive inner unity of purpose. Since the Treaty, the nation had been kept "milling round in circles like a blind bull in a ring" because neither the "little free staters" nor the "little republicans" had the courage to implement the principles they professed. Nationalism was confronted with a clear choice between two alternatives; declaring a Republic or fully associating with the British Commonwealth. "Postponement of choice between these real alternatives in the hope that something would turn up to render it unnecessary" was "the worst disservice to Ireland" because "it merely succeeded in getting for our country the disadvantages of both alternatives without any of their advantages, and in lengthening an ordeal which true statesmanship should be above all concerned to cut short". "Sham" republicanism which "keeps the so-called ideal dangling out of reach and thereby fosters and perpetuates the pathology of unrest" but desists from explaining the means by which it proposes to achieve it, is dangerous. So is "sham" dominionism which because it is still eager to justify itself and has incapacitating qualms about the Treaty, feels the need to mimic the Republicans by "knocking away, one by one, all the very light and easily-borne chains that now bind us to that system" while secretly hoping to continue benefiting from the advantages derived from that same system.[68] Thus the observation that the Hegelian narrative has suffered one too many qualifying clauses in the form of the Ulster Loyalist Rebellion of 1912, the Treaty, Partition and the Civil War, that it is a palimpsest bespeaking much uncertainty, cross purposes and commotion, makes him doubt the feasibility of some happy closure. Of course he has not yet jettisoned from his mental apparel the historicist dream, but he is intent on hammering home that it is doomed to extinction unless Nationalists abandon their petty bickering and adopt a cohesive and coherent policy.

Interestingly enough, his father-in-law, the famous historian Eoin Mac-Neill was also an opponent of Hegelianism. The qualities that singled him out as one of the first Irish Rankean historians were his philological technique which involved the decipherment, edition and interpretation of texts and gave him in the words of Daniel Binchy an "uncanny sense of communion with a long-dead past",[69] his total immersion in the manuscript sources of Gaelic Ireland and above all his critical appraisal of them. His unstinting patriotism however sometimes coloured his original research and prevented him from making the emotional leap towards a more detached view of the recent past. He saw no contradiction between scholarship, espousal of a golden past of Gaelic civilization, and belief in an Irish Manifest Destiny. "Island of saints and scholars", faith and knowledge, as is evident by the phrase, naturally cohered and were not perceived as antinomic. His rejection of the hypothesis commonly upheld by both Nationalists and Unionists that Gaelic Ireland was a *tribal* society did not emanate solely from scientific deliberations. If his unique merit is to have shown that the word was used too loosely in a way that seemed to absolve the historian from further serious investigation of the people so described, his edginess with this analogy was also due to the fact that it implied a complete negation of "national unity". The strange contradiction in MacNeill is that although he could rightly claim to be free from the illusions of political Hegelianism, he never quite freed himself from its more elusive emotional appeal, as his search for an embryonic manifestation of an organic unity with legal and political basic components as early as the third century, unveils. These hidden trammels become more noticeable when one looks at journalistic interventions in which again he reads history entirely backwards and sees in Ulster radicalism an anticipation of some latent unity. In "The Exclusion of Ulster", he writes: "The Volunteer rally in Dungannon church, the triumphal reception of the Catholic delegates in Protestant Belfast, ... these and not the temporary aberrations of hatred fostered to enslave, are the inextinguishable realities of Ulster's blended past; and these heroic memories will triumph, are daily winning, against the foul infection".[70] Hence this paradox in that his method which in some aspects was impeccably empirical and could have provided an escape from Hegelianism, was also subordinated to the purpose of establishing the ancient credentials of the twentieth century Irish state. His conviction was that:

> Notwithstanding an extensive intercourse with neighbouring and distant peoples, and notwithstanding an extremely decentralised native polity, the Irish people stand singular and eminent in those times, from the 5th century forward, as the possessors of an intense national consciousness. Instead of apologising for [our] past, we should not be ashamed of it, and we should recognize that Ireland stands in history the leading example of the development and fulfilment of the idea of nationality and also − "the hidden Ireland" − the leading example of tenacious fidelity to that idea under the most adverse conditions.[71]

It is on the strength of this principle of continuity that MacNeill can defend with confidence the notion of English manipulation of the Irish mind. It is neither religious sentiment nor actual difference in race but an "illusion of race" that makes Ulster Unionists pro-British and anti-Irish. Sectarian antagonism did not "arise from an ingrained common hatred for centuries" but "operated from above" to prevent "good feeling" between the two sections of the nation. Part of the reason why it was, according to him, so hard to dislodge this "solid and irrefragable fact of history" – the fomenting of animosity – derived from people's reluctance "to admit, even to themselves, that their prejudices are the product of deliberate manipulation by others".

When it ushered in the impetuous decade of the 1960s Irish society was almost choking on the agonizing questions that eventually began to tumble out of their mouths. A disconcerting feeling that the social, cultural and political reality of contemporary Ireland scarcely reflected the aspirations of the revolutionary martyrs of 1916, provoked the surge of articles of a speculative and counterfactual kind concerned with the question of how Ireland would have fared without 1916, and whether, considering everything, the rising came out as a positive good.[72] The outbreak of the conflict in Northern Ireland in 1969 suddenly crystallized in the collective consciousness what many had tried to erase from their minds but never quite succeeded; the tenacity of the sectarian sentiment. Thus, the confrontation with this violence struck at the intellectual and moral foundations of Irish nationalism. The presentiment that the struggle for independence had, in its revolutionary haste, dodged vital issues, cropped up and the discipline stopped at once its praise of separatism and began reassessing the latter's methods and ends with unprecedented critical and at times severe caution. However it is important to bear in mind that this critical mood was not solely the result of the onset of the Troubles in Northern Ireland nor only the sign of a modernizing society impatient to forgo an outdated mythological equipment that had outlived its usefulness. It predated the reappearance of sectarian violence and was more like a premonition that problems that had not been addressed and worked through in Irish society were bound to backfire sooner or later. Hence, from the start a unique feature of revisionism's interpretative style was that it gave priority to the testimonies of these personalities whose complex stance was severely slated by nationalist history; those who already in the first decade of the twentieth century, represented revisionist voices, wayward and troubled minds, such as Eoin MacNeill, the leader of the Irish Volunteers who boycotted the Rising by countermanding his order of general mobilization, Francis Sheehy-Skeffington the pacifist who expressed doubts about the militarist path to which the Separatists were committing themselves with unadulterated enthusiasm, or even John Redmond, the head of the IPP who thought that violent separatism was self-defeating because it hardened the opposition of Ulster Unionism.

It is patent that the recourse to these buried testimonies helped to denaturalize if not invalidate Republican discourse by showing that as early as 1915 there were men who held diverging opinions on such crucial issues as the degree and shape of independence, the precise conditions in which violence should be brought to bear and the strategic attitude to adopt vis-à-vis Britain. A hermeneutic angle which for the first time gave a respectful attention to these marginalized voices undeniably targeted the legitimacy of the action, method, logic and discourse embodied by the Easter Rebellion since it infiltrated a crippling doubt at the very heart of the revolution commenced in 1916. What made these heterodox statements a disturbing piece of information was above all that they came from men who by and large belonged to the same political family. The sceptical interrogation they prompted was for this very reason more corrosive and harder to eliminate from memory precisely because they disclosed that uncertainty had always been the hidden coin of the nationalist discourse.

In March 1961, F.X. Martin published the memoranda of Eoin MacNeill in *Irish Historical Studies* and suddenly another face of the revolution, one either despised or forgotten, gained coherence, respect and rehabilitation again.[73] It was less dogmatic, less fanatic and more humane since it flinched from enslaving man to the strictures of some platonic idea and the imperatives of romantic idealism. With this disclosure, Republicans could no longer claim that MacNeill was trying to justify the countermanding orders issued on Holy Saturday since these notes (memorandum I), were composed in mid-February 1916, over two months before the Rising. Apparently these notes were intended for Pearse, MacDonagh, Connolly, Ceannt, MacDermott, Plunkett and Clarke. MacNeill was warning them against a blind obedience to the archaic maxim, "England's difficulty is Ireland's opportunity" and enjoined them to pay more attention to the material situation.

MacNeill, a reputed historian of Medieval Ireland was a moderate, a supporter of Home Rule. If he rallied to the militarist solution it was only to ensure that Ireland would effectively obtain the local autonomy voted in Westminster, but whose implementation was postponed until the end of the Great War. Bulmer Hobson and Eoin MacNeill agreed that the Irish Volunteers should take up arms only if the country found itself under impending imposition of conscription or if the authorities were to ban the army. MacNeill planned to train, organize and arm a body of volunteers so that at the end of the European war, the country could launch a serious attack against the British government if it reneged on its promise to implement Home Rule. He also hoped that the Volunteers would be joined by hundreds of disillusioned ex-soldiers who after all had also fought on the European front on behalf of the rights of small nations. Once the war was finished, the instant adoption of Home Rule would be demanded and if ignored, then guerrilla tactics would begin.[74] The level-headedness of MacNeill ran counter to the prophetic shock-elitism of Pearse. He was opposed to the blood-sacrifice theory. He opposed it because he suspected that this repugnant theory concealed a personal tragedy, a feeling of crushing and bitter failure and because the "actualities" did not call for such an extreme action. MacNeill had an intimate knowledge of the psychological profile of the Easter leaders; and so he entreated them not to succumb to the treacherousness of emotion:

> To my mind, those who feel impelled towards military action on any of the grounds that I have stated are really impelled by a sense of feebleness or despondency or fatalism or by an instinct of satisfying their own emotions or escaping from a difficult, complex and trying situation. It is our duty, if necessary, to trample on our personal feelings and to face every sort of difficulty and complexity, and to think only of our country's good.[75]

Behind Pearse's heroic façade and his urge for self-immolation, he senses a fear of existential complexity. In Connolly's impatience, he discerns rage and frustration; Connolly wants to retaliate against those who erected obstacles across his path during all these years of socialist struggle.[76] But MacNeill, unfaltering in his fierce democratic patriotism, will not be mellowed and disarmed by excuses of this kind. His belief is that "no man has a right to seek ways of discharging his feelings at the expense of his country".[77] To launch an insurrection without a reasonable chance of military success boils down to murder and no militaristic speech, no matter how virile or mystical, should disguise this disgraceful logic. It is a murder to lead one's men to an inevitable slaughter, it is a crime to venture out in the streets and start shooting at the police or the soldiers, and he concludes: "The only possible basis for successful revolutionary action is deep and widespread popular discontent. We have only to look around us in the streets to realize that no such condition exists in Ireland".[78] MacNeill's chief concern was that the aim and the name of the revolution remained unsullied by egotistical considerations. The revolution, if it was to win a large mandate, had to be blameless and unimpeachable. It had to meet the maximum conditions of legitimacy and the possibility of a political and moral advantage gained after the failure of the operation was, according to him, an unacceptable argument. The estimation of chances for success must depend on facts, "the actualities known to us". It must not depend on impressions, instincts, premonitions or any a priori maxims. A man's feelings, "his unreasoned propensities" are dangerous because they are not amenable to reason. "They may seem to him to be simple interior voices" when in fact they are the outcome of his circumstances, experiences and unconfessed ambitions. Thus, it is a mistake to place one's trust in them and choose them as unfailing guides in a matter involving the fate of a whole country.[79]

Intractable in his moral standards, he writes: "To put forward these or any other dogmas of the kind without associating them with the actualities, or so as to overrule the actualities, would be a proof of mental incapacity. To act on them would be madness, to act on them without otherwise justifying the action would be criminal".[80] The Irish people had a right to be consulted and patiently won over to the idea of revolution. No one was entitled to act righteously in matters pertaining to national interest or foist carelessly on the people his elitist prejudices. The revolution had to be a collective undertaking, not a secretive and isolated one. Finally MacNeill hinted that if the

Irish Volunteers were unquestionably a military force, they were not militaristic for all that and thus they did not rule out the possibility of a peaceful solution. Fundamental distinction, though a fine one, unfortunately, and Francis Sheehy-Skeffington did not fail to predict an inexorable swerve. In May 1915, the *Irish Citizen*, published an *Open Letter* addressed to Thomas MacDonagh in which the pacifist astutely asked, "Will not those who rejoice in warfare inevitably take the prominent place in the direction of the organization?"[81] He believed the army was steering a dangerous course. Convinced that it was on a slippery slope, he brought home the glaring contradictions that commitment to martial means had already begotten in the separatist movement and above all in the very mind and heart of MacDonagh. Vigilant, he characterizes the speech delivered by his friend at the Women's Protest Meeting, "a vivid example of the kind of tangle we have all got ourselves into under the existent militarist and de-humanizing system". Indeed, the sharp-eyed integrity of Sheehy-Skeffington cannot help noticing the half-confessed incoherences behind MacDonagh's speech:

> You spoke in advocacy of peace. You traced war with accuracy to its roots in exploitation. You applauded every effort made by the women to combat militarism and establish a permanent peace. You hoped it would never be necessary to use the arms of the Volunteers, and that we should never see war in this country. You yourself said your position was somewhat anomalous at a peace meeting.[82]

Yet he is baffled by the discovery that all this wisdom does not elicit from his friend more scepticism for a warmongering that has always, throughout the history of mankind, disguised its vampiric intentions behind a devotion to lofty ideals. A military solution is de-humanizing, debasing and misleading. Its greatest paradox is that it proceeds to defend peace with military methods. He suspects that the monster of violence will crush the desire for justice and equality. He compares the Irish embryo with its frantic and necrophilic unleashing in Europe:

> European militarism had drenched Europe in blood. Irish militarism may only crimson the fields of Ireland. For us that would be disaster enough. You fervently hope never to employ armed force against a fellow Irishman. But a few weeks ago, I heard a friend, speaking from the same platform with me, win plaudits by saying that the hills of Ireland would be crimsoned with blood rather than that the partition of Ireland should be allowed. That is the spirit that I dread. I am opposed to partition; but partition could be defeated at too dear a price.[83]

If he foresees a hijacking of the Volunteer Army by extremist elements it is because he knows all too well the uncanny power that violence yields over the minds of early twentieth century men. Violence can release very potent unconscious drives; hence the mysterious fascination it exerts. The laborious effort to think about peace, equality, better economic opportunities and social justice is too monotonous or pedestrian to satisfy these passions. The Irish Volunteers are in truth infected by the same virus which rages all over Continental Europe. It is the outrageous idea that to win immortality for a cause, man must be valiant and expose himself to the ultimate peril and sacrifice. They are impelled by the belief that martial feat is glorious, that it is virile and brave to take life or give one's life and cowardly to want to achieve one's objectives without bloodshed. Furthermore, he suspects that the Volunteers are by essence reactionary because they comprise no women. Their conspicuous absence from the ranks of the army is not mere neglect but deliberate exclusion: itself just a symptom of its retrograde nature. He is convinced that the fanatics will eventually squeeze the potential for radicalism out of the organization. From that moment on, the contradictions hidden in it will become blatant and the minority which was always reticent to organized violence will find itself, sooner or later, faced with the necessity of either abandoning its principles or withdrawing from a system which by definition could only cancel out or parody those ideals.[84] Besides, the human cost of the Great War became a sombre warning to all future generations who still harboured any illusion about Draconian militaristic solutions. When death changes in degree and nature, it becomes harder to ensure the survival of the name in the renown; all that remains to do is to ratify the disappearance of the name in the number.[85]

The murderous logic of ends and means, a fortiori when those means are supported by an ever higher-performance technology and when the relief of the dead soldier is already waiting in the reserve, transforms men into mere pawns. Henceforth individuals count for nothing and it is the humanity of every friend, foe or innocent victim, which, by losing its unique character, suffers an unprecedented devaluation. Because Sheehy-Skeffington did not flinch from studying the gruesome implications of this logic, he knew that violence was not the answer. On the contrary, it represented a backward step. Far more could, in fact, be achieved by intelligent, organized, positive resistance to injustice wherever it was detected. That's why he fervently pleaded for a new education of men, one that would lay bare the scandalous and appalling lie at the bottom of militarism, and show people the real meaning of patriotism and self-sacrifice. The logic being reversed with the digging up of this disquieting evidence is a totalitarian one. Totalitarianism hates and recoils from ambivalence. When it tries to articulate vaguely its objections to it, it declares arbitrarily that it is synonymous with confusion and chaos. This is why, historically, it has constantly tried to eradicate any trace of dissent by giving the fake impression that this erasure of complexity imposes itself by the incontrovertible imperative of having to choose between confusion and order. It is the rationale of "either" this option "or" the other frenetically invoked in the political domain often to justify the adoption of repressive measures by a strong state. Totalitarian thought senses the danger hidden in internal dissent. It knows it can undermine its absolute power.[86] One can weigh better now the unsettling effect of a historiography which does not hesitate to exhume all these levels of discord that were once buried and dispelled under a façade of purity, the deceptive appearance of a noble and unanimous vision and an unshakeable logic. The retrieval of this information has the effect of refuting the very notion of an absolute truth and intimates instead the competition between relative truths. The elements that were suppressed by tradition are henceforth tracked down, re-evaluated and their creative potential tested. The historical retrospective of revisionism obviously entails more than a process of destabilization. It re-opens historical vistas in an attempt to initiate an expedition of discovery and renewal.

It is no coincidence if the new historians snatched on this forgotten and bizarre evidence. The resort to it betrayed the hope that in its critical evaluation, these historians would find answers to these seditious and nerve-racking questions that no one in and out of power dared to raise. Was it reasonable to advocate a separatist solution in a country where one million Protestants were opposed even to the notion of a form of political autonomy? Had the sinking into revolutionary dogmatism increased the differences between North and South and further damaged the possibility of a rapprochement between these hegemonic blocs? Did the Home Rule constitutionalist policy of Redmond and Dillon of the 1890s offer a better chance of healing the emotional breach between Ulster and the South? Did the men who died in 1916 and especially after 1923 in the name of the separatist ideal go to their death for nothing since this dream could never adequately materialize itself in the Irish context? Had the violence, destruction and bitterness of the years between 1916 and 1923 done little more than hasten developments, which, at least in their broad outlines, would have happened in any case? Did the military campaign of Michael Collins in the 1920s influence in a negative way the consecutive shape and practices of the Stormont regime in Ulster? These questions were devastating in their implications and the fact they did not always arise from a scrupulous reading of the historical sequence did nothing to dispel their traumatic potential. As Michael Laffan put it, in the nature of things, such hypotheses could not result in firm answers, let alone in any agreement; yet for the majority of the new historians, these became legitimate forms of inquiry.[87]

4 The loss of history and the new historians' fight against propaganda on the Irish and continental "front"

Like its European counterparts, Irish historiography has felt the tremors of the demolition of historicism. Irish revisionism is both symptom and cure. It represents one brave effort to rehabilitate history and reaffirm its originality. This chapter situates the revisionist project against a larger historical backdrop in order to give a more thorough impression of the European climate of post-historicist reappraisal and define with more detail its methodological profile. Since the end of the Second World War, history has suffered a major theoretical challenge. This crisis, as it will be underscored, had a long gestation. However, it gathered pace and reached a climax in the 1960s and 1970s when the insights of postmodernism became hostile weapons in the hands of rival disciplines, such as philosophy and anthropology. Because historicism is at once a worldview and a method of scientific inquiry, some examination of how the shattering events of the twentieth century affected both aspects of the sensibility is essential. It is Ciaran Brady who suggested the need to reposition the explosion of Irish mythology in the context of Europe's post-historicist climate.[1] He defined Irish revisionism as an effort to respond to the disintegration of the methodological principles that had informed the practice of history. Our intention here is to flesh out this phenomenon of parallel retreat from historicism. In the aftermath of the Second World War, a few revisionist historians sought to refashion a discipline mired in complicities with the omnipotent governments by changing the canons of selection and interpretation of facts and imposing higher scientific standards. Unfortunately what they failed to anticipate was that this revision brought with it its own dangers, temptations and quandaries.

Although Moody and Edwards shared in the general optimism of the society and the age in which they lived, their own optimism was offset by a sharp consciousness of the serious challenges that still loomed ahead and demanded courage and vision. Optimism was there but guarded, intuiting that some metamorphosis of the heart and the mind had to take place if the Irish nation was to blossom into a genuinely self-respecting, confident and cosmopolitan culture and the two rival states that had been jealously watching one another's every move were ever to develop a friendly *entente*. Thus

Edwards did not mince his words when he denounced the total lack of vision of the Government. He was concerned that political life in the Republic had become a sham because it was hindered by the pusillanimous mood bred by the Civil War and because Fianna Fáil shirked from confronting the implications of the gap between their policies and the obduracy of Ulster or the cultural leanings of Irish youth. As early as 29 January 1955, in "The Future of Fianna Fáil", Edwards protested that the revision of Fianna Fáil's agenda proposed by Sean Lemass was futile in view of the failure to achieve any of the party's popular goals, and that the leadership had to reflect seriously on whether there was a valid reason for keeping the party in existence:

> Three times in the last ten days, Mr. De Valera has spoken publicly on the revival of Irish. "If the language was to be saved it must be saved now". Yet with far greater facilities than there were forty years ago, it would appear that the children were not anxious to speak it. He complained that the history of the last thirty years was not well known, and he attributed this to the difficulties which would arise for a teacher who might have in his class the descendants of people who took opposite sides after the Treaty. Elsewhere he referred to the unification of this small island and he stated he did not see at the moment a direct way to achieve unity. I suggest the continued existence of Fianna Fáil as at present constituted is one of the several obstacles to the revival of Irish, the teaching of recent Irish history and the re-unification of the thirty-two counties. As long as our recent history is presented as a one-sided justification of the roles played by our leaders in 1922, so long will it be impossible to make it palatable to the children. When will all the survivors of the civil war – on both sides – be big enough to admit their failure of judgment? As long as they keep silent their followers are committed to justifying Fianna Fáil and Fine Gael in terms of mutual hate. The coming generation is looking to the future – to an ideal that will bring about the unification of Ireland. And they are not so sure that it can be brought about on the old issues which split the country in 1920 and caused a civil war in 1922 ... Until it is clear to the meanest intelligence that one can be a good Irishman and disagree with Fianna Fáil or Fine Gael or even with the Rising of 1916, Irish unity will continue to be a vain hope.[2]

Undoubtedly, this passage reveals intransigence, but one which is not ideological or partisan. Rather it seems to arise out of a moral and intellectual disquiet. It would be no hyperbole to say that these lines bespeak a stubborn refusal to play the ideological game and an unflinching determination to expose all manners of political cowardice and double standards. What Edwards finds dangerous is Fianna Fáil's persistence in the illusion that the Irish historicist dream is still attainable if only the party stands faithfully by its antediluvian methods. This refusal to interrogate tradition in the light of a disappointing experience and record is what pushes him to the conclusion that the current leadership is not properly equipped in intelligence and courage to make the laborious readjustments needed if Irish society is not to ruin irretrievably its last chances for the realization of its laudable dream of unity. Edwards does not intend to leave his tradition for it is not so much the ends he disputes but rather their narrow definition and especially the measly and inane means employed to achieve them. Nor is he deterred by how fraught is this exercise in critique as this passage attests:

> The debates over the Treaty, the struggle to save the Republic, the years of civil war and political exile, the existence of a Belfast government, provoked in many minds a serious doubt whether Irish nationalism had not, perhaps, been expressed too extravagantly. And if pro-Treaty administrations since 1922 have had second thoughts, the tendency of Fianna Fáil has been rather in the reverse. Claiming more effectively than any other party to be the apostolic successors of the pre-1922 movements – republican, Gaelic and democratic – the Fianna Fáil party has never attempted to qualify constitutionally the revolutionary teaching which a more secure position might have dictated ... How can de Valera now attempt to qualify that theoretical nationalism unless, perhaps, by introducing compulsory courses in contemporary history?[3]

Those bent on attaching a pro-Treaty label to the "new history" could lunge at this passage as good proof of their suspicions. However, other passages from the same article refrain from pandering to the pro-Treaty accusation of de Valera as the man who craftily orchestrated the Civil War and bore an enormous responsibility for it. As early as 1957, prefiguring by at least thirty years the more outspoken revisionism which swept along academia, the press and the political circles, Edwards spoke of the futility of blaming one side or the other given that partition was already a *fait accompli*, thus not easily removable either in December 1921 or in 1925 at the time of the Boundary Commission meetings. Too much "concentration on the instrument negotiated on the 6 December, 1921", tended "to blind [one] to the weakness of the negotiators in dealing with the North and the extent to which English tradition was rooted in the reverence for monarchy". Moreover de Valera being a product of "the Pearse School" could not conceive that "his apparently historical approach to the question was beyond the comprehension of a Craig" and "wholly justifiable only by those accepting fully his own assumptions". Provocative in his "longue durée" approach, he put forward the argument that the Civil War was a diversion which prolonged the Republican fiction and postponed the traumatic realization that a more portentous war between North and South had all along hovered in the background:

If Mr. De Valera may be held responsible for incitement to civil war in 1922 or even for failing to prevent it, it is important to recollect that those who say so cannot escape the logic of attributing the same to Pearse in 1916; nor can they ignore the fact that in 1922 it may have been the only alternative to a war between North and South ... It is hard to see how the South would have escaped from such an ordeal without such substantial losses as could not have been repaired for several generations and indeed the possibility cannot be excluded that no separate Irish State could have survived ... Little as he can have welcomed the civil war, much as he may have desired to terminate it, the determination of the militant republican element to resist was something on which he was to have little influence ... If the civil war between former colleagues was a tragedy it was infinitely preferable to the destruction of the republican idea as de Valera saw it or to a civil war between North and South as none of them [de Valera and Collins] saw it at the time.[4]

Writing before the eruption of violence in Northern Ireland in 1968, Edwards could still afford some optimism and think that Ireland had survived its worst phase of sectarianism and was riding safely away from a destructive wave:

For strife between former colleagues might ultimately be smoothed over, and the history of the last thirty-five years has shown how successfully that was accomplished. But the recollection of warfare between unionist Ulster and the nationalist South might have created a mutual antipathy, which could not be eradicated in centuries. However wide the division today between North and South it has not been rendered unbridgeable by any renewal of that warfare of hate which had infected the opposing sides after 1641 and maintained in our own time a legend of Protestant Ulster's particularism.[5]

What is remarkable is that Edwards' reading of the actual balance of power at Westminster, besides being noticeably composed and perceptive, was confirmed by the work of his talented research assistant, Maureen Wall.[6] Better known for her pioneering findings on the penal era, which threw light on how eighteenth-century Catholics coped under the weight of civil disabilities, she also produced the first scholarly analysis of the origins of partition. Until then, the understanding of what caused the Split hinged on the governing belief spread by anti-Treaty survivors that partition had been the crux, the key reason. But in a close examination of the Treaty debates, Wall discovered how relatively little complaint there was about partition compared with complaint about the oath.[7] A repeated charge in the propagandist parlance of Fianna Fáil and the press was that the Treaty "created" partition or "gave away" Northern Ireland. It was the merit of Wall to show that most Republican assumptions rested on slim and illogical grounds. The postulation that Sinn Féin could have secured better terms if only de Valera had gone to London or if only the plenipotentiaries had referred back to him and called Lloyd George's bluff when he imposed a deadline and threatened them with resumption of war, failed to appreciate that by December 1921, Northern Ireland had already embarked on a separate legal destiny with the sympathetic blessing of the British and most crucially the August 1921 implicit pledge of de Valera who had stated that Sinn Féin did not intend to use force to settle the Ulster question.[8] If partition did figure in the negotiations it was entirely, in the words of Joe Lee, "shadow-boxing" as all the Irish knew since they chose not to quarrel over it in vain but to trust a very vague promise of a readjustment of the border in ways favouring the territory of the Free State. Even if Dail Eireann had remained united in 1922, in rejecting or accepting the Treaty, Wall thought, there was no evidence to support that this would in any way have diminished the resolve of Northern Unionism to remain apart.[9] Indeed she firmly believed that the Boundary Commission and the Council of Ireland were stratagems used to "obscure the harsh realities of partition", and agreed with R.D. Edwards to say that the Civil War deflected attention from the rapidly erupting North and "prevented an even more serious conflict between Nationalists and Unionists, with all the frightful implications of a sectarian war, and the extension of the Belfast pogroms to the whole Northern Ireland area".[10] During a lecture on "The Origins of the Civil War", at UCD in the 1950s, Desmond Williams declared: "The struggle over jurisdiction and authority did not arise out of any bad faith or personal wickedness; it found its roots in the whole revolutionary tradition between 1916–21." He continued:

> It is difficult only to view the theme chosen strictly as a historical problem. And this is so for two reasons: the first of which is the passion evoked still by discussion on the Civil War among many people and the second of which relates to the paucity of original documents written at the time by the participants in that struggle. The clauses in the Sinn Féin constitution, in the constitution of Dail Eireann, and of the Oath of Allegiance, were at the basis of [the] controversy. The oath was a symbol that could be interpreted in different ways: it was in fact interpreted in different ways ... It is not our business to examine whether or not Collins and Griffith had exceeded their powers. All I am concerned with here is to indicate that men in good faith, or men carried away by passion and distrust, also in equal good faith, could hold contrary views. In the same way in which the position of the oath had never been clarified, so also did the authority of the plenipotentiaries rest in obscurity.[11]

In this passage, we see Williams rejecting the Manichean logic, the black and white, good and evil mindset. It is as if he is saying there are other ways, more reasonable and compassionate, of looking at the history of Irish disunity; ways which could make room for the welcoming and serene contemplation of other truths, no less legitimate and no less worthy of sympathy and respect. On 14 June 1958, Michael Harrison shared with Florence O'Donoghue his enthusiastic impressions of the event:

> On Thursday week last Professor Williams of UCD gave a lecture on the "Causes of the Civil War". He spoke for two hours and three quarters to a large and most attentive audience pulling no punches but drawing deductions and making conclusions purely as a historian. Your book *No Other Law* was the basis of his entire theme. I had re-read it in anticipation and indeed had a copy on my lap. He kept so close to your script that I felt like protesting but he redeemed himself by attributing his sources to you as the talk developed. The main thing now is that the period has emerged from the emotional context and is beginning to be appreciated as history. Williams would not impute an unworthy motive to either side and I hope that is how our children will be made to see the period. It is generally accepted that there is a scarcity of material particularly on the Executive side which militates against a true exposition of the facts.[12]

On hearing that Williams had thrown himself into a serious rethinking of this sensitive issue, O'Donoghue urged Harrison to pass on the information that the Civil War was, contrary to the prevailing belief, far better documented than the War of Independence. Whether and when these documents would be released, he could not tell, but he was given between two and three thousand documents, under the condition he would return them when he was writing *No Other Law*,[13] and could therefore testify to a "mine" of original information.[14] The announcement of the new epistemological benchmarks was done, not at all surprisingly, by methodically critiquing the old nationalist history. Hence, in a review of P.S. O'Hegarty's *A History of Ireland under the Union*, Edwards clarified why the author fell short of the qualities that a true historian should possess. His "outlook" was too "intolerant of opposition and oblivious of others' interests". His method was inadequate and led to inconsistency, as when O'Hegarty asserted his inability "to accept the economic or the class conscious interpretation of history" and yet, as Edwards pointed out he "infiltrates the non-political aspects of history whenever he is convinced they illustrate his viewpoint".

The work was overly influenced by "the literature of the conflict" and chained to the "principles of revolution", and ideological burden, preventing him from appreciating the need to "give the benefit of the doubt" to the "opponents of his heroes". His failure to apply "the exact principles of historical criticism in the analysis of the evidence" reduced him to a mere "commentator on commentaries rather than the historical critic of the contemporary documents which are the real quarry of research work". Thus, O'Hegarty's claim to be a true historian was overblown because his criticism was demonological when it should be scientific, and above all because he showed no understanding of the "multiplicity of forces which are needed to destroy a movement or cause a civil war". In Edwards' definition of the historian's craft, method and generosity of spirit are inseparable to such an extent that a defective range of historical techniques breeds navel-gazing, obtuseness and a most disheartening lack of empathy. Last but not the least cause for concern was that "in his determination to blame the opponents of his old comrades for the anti-climax of 1921, he shows recklessness and unawareness that an historian ought to reconcile feelings and avoid at all costs exacerbating them".[15]

In 1988, Father Brendan Bradshaw denounced the *Irish Historical Studies'* school as being anti-national. Its value-free principle hid a "tacit bias", encouraged "tacit evasion", and led to the normalization of the exploitative and violent fact of colonization.[16] However, on 31 July 1959 Edwards condemned attempts at mitigating the conduct of the *Black and Tans* in occupied Ireland. To the reviewer who on 10 July 1959 wrote: "Mr. Bennett's presuppositions do not allow him to present fairly the difficulties of a Government straining to restore public order", Edwards replied: "It appears [to me] that it is your reviewer who has presuppositions which preclude him from presenting fairly the difficulties of an author in dealing with a controversial subject". To the reviewer who could not wait to dispel "the myth of Black and Tan villainy and licentiousness, of wanton and widespread brutality", just because "the world opinion has had the opportunity to reflect upon the more effective methods of Hitler", he retorted that British methods of repression in Ireland were no less cruel and shameful for having since been replaced by Hitler's exterminating ones. He warned the reader against lapses into dubious forms of amnesia, which may be induced by comparing English atrocities with German atrocities. The appalling record of British rule in Ireland should not be diminished or rationalized out of existence with impunity because the Jews met an even more horrible and arbitrary fate in the hands of the German State. He then took issue with the word "murder" when applied to the actions of Kevin Barry, because the top priority of an astute reviewer should be to refrain from "reproducing the controversial terms of 1920" when referring to "the consequence of a clash between British forces and Irish guerrillas". His special attention to terminology reveals a mind acutely sensitized to the clandestine character of ideology, the manner in which it frames language or narrows perceptions, and trying at all cost to escape its snares. In his opinion, this review "read like the hysterical effusions of committed parties with bad consciences or with blind obsessions" preventing them from grasping the real purpose of Bennett's book.[17] Offering his own estimation of Bennett's qualities as a historian, he too voiced reservations about his gift in "divining the official lie or in discriminating between fact and propaganda" but he conceded at least one merit in Bennett he did not notice in his reviewer; "he had the sense to see that brutality breeds brutality; at least he had the imagination to realize that the methods of Gandhi were morally superior to those of the Irish who resorted to armed resistance". Inflexible in his detection of bias he countered: "May [I] suggest that the reviewer may have failed to note the purpose of this book because of his tortuous obsessions with the justification of one side against another in a conflict of forty years ago".

On 2 March 1957, Edwards wrote: "The history of partition could well be included in the school courses for the history of Ireland. The absence of any word on the northern movement except as an incidental aspect of the British conspiracy condemns the *Indivisible Island* of Frank Gallagher".[18] In 1954, Edwards wrote an article for the *Irish Press* under the heading "Padraic MacPiarais – The Leader" in which he couched the Northern problem in conciliatory terms. In honouring the gospel of Pearse, the Irishman of 1954 had to convince his compatriots that "there is in the Irish tradition a thousand priceless heirlooms". "Education" could become a window of discovery of this cultural richness, "if it is based upon belief in youth and can be conveyed in words of love". In stressing the importance of educating the new generations with words of love, Edwards not only reminded his audience that education in the past was geared to intensify discord and hatred, but also made the point that Christian magnanimity does not require approval of and identification with the political choices of others. Man can and ought to find in himself the spiritual resources to tolerate difference especially when it comes to motives he does not understand. He then raised courageous questions:

> Can Cuchulain help to remind us that the men of Ulster may still be Irish in defying the men of Ireland who would coerce them as Connacht or Leinster would wish? The Cuchulain of Patrick Pearse wears the trappings of the hopeful Christian. He depicts the freedom and individualism of the historic defender of Ulster's liberties. Who can deny the right of the men of Ulster to resist the coercive violence of the men of Ireland? They are all Irishmen, and the men of Ulster may yet believe it when all temptations to political advancement are resisted. Would Patrick Pearse have preached a civil war? Will they remember that even if they succeeded in overwhelming Orange Ulster by force, the recollection of that deed would keep in Ulster Orangemen an indignation and a resistance to spiritual unification which could, like a canker, eat into the soul of Ireland?[19]

Edwards was making a political statement here. It is clear that his historical perspective tempted him to espouse a distinct political sensibility steeped in the philosophy of liberal humanism. His definition of Irishness was optimistic and generous since it sought to reconcile apparently antagonistic principles. A man could defend partition and still be an Irishman. His being exceeded the limits of politics. If it were not for the temptation of power, Ulstermen would feel comfortable with acknowledging their Irishness. In his worldview, the battle for power was what truly poisoned human relations. Cultural or religious differences were not such an obstacle to harmony. The role of religion in exacerbating the political division was fudged. On 18 April 1966, when the commemoration of the 50th anniversary of the 1916 Rising was in full swing, he declared soberly: "The great failure of the republican tradition in Ireland has been its inability to see the viewpoint of those who were not republicans and of those who wanted to maintain close association with Britain".[20] This sentence strengthens the impression that he and other "new historians' were about to denounce the bogus success story which claimed that everything had gone well in the struggle for liberation. The tone is so subdued that it can almost lull our judgement to the radicality of what is being said. Edwards was fighting to shake off a Southern bourgeois complacency that thought of Ulster as just a little and manageable "loose end", a small obstacle that could not alter the fundamental destiny of the nation.

For there was at the heart of Irish revisionism an unshakeable determination to reintroduce the Other in the pages of history: the Protestants of Ulster. Here he departed from the republican assumption that Ulster Unionists were mere pawns, stooges of British imperialism. They were a force to be reckoned with and needed to be treated as separate with valid motives of their own for resisting the break up of the Union. The most intelligent way of reversing partition was still to avoid falling into the trap of a partitionist history. Unless the South confronted the inadequacy of its thinking on the North, real change would remain forever a will-o'-the-wisp. Thus revisionism was obsessed with the failure of Irish nationalism to appeal to all Irishmen and instead of sweeping this unpalatable fact under the carpet, it looked hard at the evidence with a view to establish what exactly went wrong during nation-building. R.D. Edwards' daughter, Ruth, explained that because he was half Protestant, Robert entertained no romantic illusions about this tribe. However this level-headedness which shied away equally from idealization and demonization was also the reason why he "wanted Irish Protestants to have their proper place in Irish history – not to be represented as interlopers and foreigners who should accept the Catholic nationalist ethos or go home to wherever they had come from three, five or eight hundred years before".[21] The notion that mutual understanding between rivals involves a work of patient parturition and that history's real vocation is to be its midwife, is here implicit, and is redolent of Herbert Butterfield's own conception of history. In 1945, before the Conference of Irish historians, he identified partisanship as a pernicious reflex which needed to be overcome if European diplomacy and peace were to flourish:

> Nothing is more needed today than the surmounting of this particular hurdle, this national barrier to understanding, and nothing is more futile than merely to blame the foreigner and to rail at his wickedness, when somewhere or other there is involved also an intellectual incapacity of our own – a neglect to measure our own selfishness as nations and a failure adequately to put ourselves in another's place. The overcoming

of this particular hurdle between nations is the real service that historical study might do in our own time if it maintains its autonomy and
integrity as an academic study, seeking only to make human understanding more profound.[22]

Butterfield approved of Ranke's observation that all generations are
equidistant from eternity and that it is often an act of ignorant and impru-
dent arrogance to impose our own criteria in our analysis of their actions,
values and goals. And if the dead generations deserved some respect so did
even more the living generations. He wanted to restore the Christian values
of moderation and sympathy at the centre of diplomacy and thus correct the
wrong-headed course it had followed since the Versailles settlement had
regrettably repudiated the wisdom of the balance of power. On 14 January
1956, in a review of Butterfield's book *Man on his Past*, Edwards underscored
the superior insights to be gained into the dangerous ways the past was distorted by propaganda thanks to the use of a theoretical history:

> One of the few small services for mankind which the study of history
> can offer is to break down prejudices which have survived from the past.
> Between neighbouring communities the perpetuation of disagreements
> is only too often due to misreading the past or perhaps to continuing to
> believe in war propaganda. While there had formerly been students of
> universal history, it was not until the Gottingen school of historians
> began to study the history of history that the subject can be said to have
> been put on a scientific basis. It was from these 18th century scholars
> that Ranke, and later Acton, developed their ideas on the scientific
> methods which are essential if we would see mankind as a whole.[23]

Remarkably enough, Edwards rightly situates the origins of a critical,
self-reflexive impulse in the practice of history inside German empiricism
itself. This may sound like a truism until one remembers that the philosophers of the second half of the twentieth century invented an unhelpful
antithesis between Rankean empiricism and philosophy and unfairly dismissed the former as a crudely factual, uncritical and old-fashioned method
when in reality a familiarization with its nascent insights and enduring
quandaries as pondered by Herder, Ranke and later Droysen and Dilthey
unmistakably shows that postmodernism has inflated the novel character of
some of its discoveries. German empiricism, far from being agnostic or
hostile to theory, steadily increased its engagement with it. Early historicism as represented by Ranke registered a healthy balance between a quest
for overarching universals and the commitment to the description of an infinitely diffracted reality. Idealism was no mere palliative against relativism
but was a coeval and equivalent element.[24] It was while he was engaged in
an important debate with his colleague Georg Hegel at the University of
Berlin that Ranke made in 1824 the famous statement which asserted the

separateness of history and its right to be treated as an autonomous discipline with a status at least equal if not superior to philosophy: "To history has
been assigned the office of judging the past, of instructing the present for
the benefit of future ages. To such high offices this work does not aspire: it
wants only to show what actually happened".[25] Running contrary to Hegel's
teleological vision of history which disposed of events, people and facts if
they were deemed irrelevant to or did not conform to an "ultimate design",
Ranke set out to prove that it was not metaphysical speculations on the
ulterior meaning of history but empirical research, the meticulous study of
facts, which furthered knowledge.

A more theoretical Ranke can be gleaned from this phrase: "from the
particular, one can carefully and boldly move up to the general; from general
theories, there is no way of looking at the particular". Here Hegel's theory is
turned upside down. The deciphering of traces or "hieroglyphs" to use the
Rankean term, will naturally unveil the idea. But the theory cannot uncover
the myriad of incarnations of the idea in this life. It seems that Ranke advocated a historical interpretation no longer subordinated to a metonymic reasoning, where each component was seen as a reflection of the whole, but one
shaped or inferred analytically and dialogically on the basis of the evidence
found; an evidence which was not always acquiescent to the demands of the
initial hypothesis. However, from Dilthey onwards, this fragile balance
between idealism and relativism is tilted in favour of a radical notion of
change which denied absolute standards of judgement outside the object of
research, paved the way for an "anarchy of convictions" and irreversibly
dented the ideal of attainment of an Archimedean point in the knowledge of
the past.[26]

That said, what these statements of Butterfield and Edwards have in
common is what postmodern thinkers would call a naïve notion of the workings of ideology. In Edwards and Butterfield's worldview, propaganda is
undeniably a major obstacle to harmonious co-existence, but it is posited as
extraneous, vaguely superimposed on the mind and thus removable. Its
noxious effects can be effaced with a proper dissemination of historical
knowledge. Both men were convinced that historical thinking could play a
part in removing the blinkers that hampered amicability between opposite
tribes. It is no exaggeration to say that Butterfield's entire intellectual activity had focused on rousing consciences to how hindsight, prejudice and fore-
knowledge hemmed in true understanding. He helped historical minds to
reach higher critical maturity and distance from their society and the unreliable evidence found in the archives. Despite occasional doubts about the
feasibility of averting the encroachment of ideology with any degree of finality, doubts which, granted, increased over time in Edwards' mind and led
him as Aidan Clarke put it, "to erect depersonalisation into a private principle" and perhaps by way of rebuffing them to invest a growing amount of
his attention on the organization of archives, these men remained
positivists.[27]

No matter how percipient were their intuitions, they were still imbued with a certain philosophical climate. They thought it was possible to hone the methods of logical verification, improve the philological techniques and add substantially to the critical armoury of the historian. They were also rationalists who believed that the imparting of a purer form of history purged of crude contaminations would loosen in the minds the deadening grip of ideology. The fact that against all the odds, in a time of rival jurisdictions, cultural isolation, fanatical entrenchment and European war, the founding fathers of the new history, T.W. Moody and R.D. Edwards, created an inclusive fraternity by gaining the trust of both Nationalist and Unionist historians is itself a monument to that extraordinary faith. Such demonstration of bold ingenuity and organizational perseverance is not compatible with minds totally overcome by epistemological torment. This beautiful faith infuses a letter sent to Moody from H.S. Richardson on 5 March 1942: "I find historical work a distraction at times from painful and unprofitable reflection. And I like to believe that we are helping to keep alight a torch for which future generations may bless us, though we are nameless. If learning is mutilated, the enemy will have triumphed".[28] Thus however misguided and conceited this faith appears to a twenty-first century phlegmatic theorist who thinks he knows better, it served nevertheless as an absolute prerequisite for the blossoming of a real historical debate in Ireland.

There is little doubt that the revisionist initiative was eminently political although not in the sense commonly alleged by latter-day detractors. Good history is subversive because through its recovery of forgotten or defeated sensibilities and its appreciation of the structural complexity of past society, it removes the illusion of fatality that enshrouds present constitutional arrangements. The new historians were dangerous to the orthodoxy enshrined in de Valera's 1937 Constitution precisely because they knew and did not flinch from showing – as Conor McCarthy half admitted it – "that the nation and the state were neither singular nor wholly coincident, nor were they beyond dispute".[29] In this sense their project was not that different from Michel Foucault's who once explained that historical enquiry made sense only as a method used to throw light on the revocability of the codes, signs and myths of a society. The function of historical erudition was to discover the "immense and proliferating questionable nature (criticabilité) of things"[30] and to note with relief and delight not our dependence towards an origin which transcended us but on the contrary, "the general fragility in the very bedrock of existence" once imagined to be solid and familiar. The analysis of the limits imposed on us reveals how penetrable and crossable these limits were. Hence, the thrust of Foucault's new history and that of Irish revisionism was to erode the foundations of the dogmatism which eventually contaminated all traditions. This anti-foundational approach, to use a word borrowed from Derrida, which sets out to challenge the foundations of all authoritative discourse and to test their claims to moral and political infallibility, is indeed a core theme of the revisionist mode of critique. The definition of the 1916 Easter Rebellion as a military coup, the questioning of the actual depth and continuity of the separatist sentiment, and the search for the missed opportunities of the past when Irish fortunes may have taken a more positive turn are all local indications of the deconstructive moves carried by postmodernism.

When he opened the 21st Annual Congress of the Irish University Students Association on 3 February 1971, Edwards stated: "The Congress gave rise to opportunities for discussion and cooperation amongst erstwhile rivals". And he added: "The one thing that they all had in common was an interest in history and a desire to become familiar with her peculiarities". However, this immersion into the intricacies of the past was not activated by simple antiquarian predilections. There was an urgency behind it as the editorial of the Third Annual Congress of the IUSA bulletin revealed: "The papers are indeed on subjects upon which people will be anxious to express their views; a fact which augurs well for the Congress, especially as the issues involved do not lie in the mists of academic past, but are vital to all who seek in history an answer to the problems, not only of living in Ireland in peace, but of living at all".[31]

When our two ingenious idealists took the steps to gain representation for Ireland on the *Comité International des Sciences Historiques* as a single cultural unity and discount the constitutional split on the ground, they knew they had possibly hit an obstacle that demanded to be negotiated with caution and legerdemain. On 27 January 1938, Edwards drew the attention of Harold Temperley, the then President of the CISH to the fact that "the question of political boundaries" arose "for the first time" and the danger was that "the political administrators of Northern Ireland might come to regard the scheme as one which would favour Mr de Valera's 'all Ireland' policy and would bring 'the border' into ridicule". If the Northern Government's suspicions were thus aroused "no effort would be spared to compel the Ulster Society of Irish Historical Studies to have nothing to do with the matter". Queen's University which had associated itself with Trinity College and the National University of Ireland in subsidizing Irish historical studies could be threatened with budgetary cutbacks and the Northern historians foresaw even becoming "the objects of a persecution campaign with the aim of bringing their resignations from the University". On 29 January 1938, Moody had indeed sounded the alarm bells when in his gentlemanly manner he sought assurance that "such cooperation could be arranged without exposing our society to criticism" and that nothing would be done to "endanger that very happy and successful form of cooperation between the two societies which had produced Irish Historical Studies".[32] Given the risk of a backfire at the hint of a project designed to call attention to a unity more resilient than the transient severance Moody chose sensibly not to broadcast this aspect.

But those who welcomed the journal of *Irish Historical Studies* in the press did not fail to detect its higher political import which in their eyes represented also its most irresistible and attractive feature. Terence O'Hanlon wrote in the *Irish Times* how inspired he felt by this timely harbinger of hope to a sundered nation.[33] The *Irish Press* enthused at the splendid start it had made in the vital need "to sweep away the vast heap of rubbish emanating from the patriotic school. It afforded striking proof that in Irish culture there is no boundary and that men of learning are united by the common bonds of love of truth and love of country".[34] For the famous historian A.J.P. Taylor writing in the *Manchester Guardian* with an awareness of the deep imminent shadows threatening Europe with unsurpassed regression, the journal was the last sanctuary of sanity, the guarantee that "if in the near future Ireland might once again, as in the Dark Ages, be called upon to preserve the last remnants of civilisation it could discharge this mission with success".[35] In his valedictory recollection of his teacher and friend T.W. Moody, F.S.L. Lyons articulated with some poignancy the dilemma facing the second generation of the new historians. He captured with arresting precision the emotionally exacting transition from the modern era to the postmodern condition and the existential chasm which grew ever more dismaying between Moody and his successors:

> The point rather is that a historian who grew to maturity between the wars necessarily has a different view of life, and therefore of history, from one who has grown to maturity after 1945 ... In Moody, there remains a good deal of the liberal historian of the old school who still cherishes a lingering belief, if not in the perfectibility of man, at least in his improvability, and who has not entirely discarded the idea of progress from his mental equipment. His students, on the other hand, inhabit a world where such liberalism begins to seem increasingly an intellectual luxury, which they can scarcely afford. Too much has happened to our society, too many axes have been laid to the roots of the tree of knowledge, for us easily to ascribe any longer purity of aim and disinterestedness of motive to men and women who, we sense, were as muddled and vulnerable in their day as we are in ours.[36]

The belief that cognition and society can be bettered is what declines inexorably as the implications of the atrocious crimes committed during the World Wars and the unashamed way in which history as a discipline was compromised, sink in. The credibility of the scientific method was seriously undermined in the 1920s and 1930s, when German historians collaborated with their government to provide arguments for the revision of the Treaty of Versailles and the recovery of the territories lost at the end of the Great War. This attempt to escape the material implication of the war-guilt clause in the Treaty compelled by force of example British and French historians to follow suit and contribute too their share of distortion.[37] The fact that this *trahison des clercs* assumed its most bare-faced form in Germany, the country which had embarked on a crusade to extol objectivity and spread the Rankean method, only intensified the sense of a profound crisis. The need to protect the interests of states had damaged the interests of truth and humanity so much so that it took twenty years of historiography on the origins of the First World War, for the most brilliant historians, men like Sidney Bradshaw Fay (1876–1967)[38] and Luigi Albertini (1871–1941)[39] to arrive at the opinion voiced earlier by the shrewd Lloyd George that Europe had slipped into the abyss rather than marched into war. They had realized that "Prejudice, passion, absence of magnanimity in the true sense of the word, and most of all, fear, were responsible for the failures and weaknesses of the diplomats of 1914". Thus observing the same phenomenon happening all over again with the same mournful regularity after the Second World War, Desmond T. Williams wrote:

> Documents were never wholly reliable. Today they are less so than ever. In more senses than one, contemporary history has been responsible for assisting the forces of darkness. The power of real history to pierce deep to the marrow of things has been reduced. History becomes an instrument in a cause; it becomes a servant and not a master. The influence of moral passion, to be distinguished from moral judgment is more misleading than helpful for the historian. Making all allowances, passion enters less into the study of remoter periods than into that of our own times, and the distortions caused by ideological prejudice are open to greater check … I do feel that the damage done to history by an unwise concentration on modern history is disastrous. In our small country, this is not so obvious, but on larger fields the evil effects are cumulative.[40]

This statement may throw light on Edwards' disinclination, after he took up the joint editorship of *Irish Historical Studies* with T.W. Moody in 1957, to change the rule dictating the exclusion of articles on contemporary history from the pages of the journal. The cause of this "conformist" approach was something more profound than a mere fear of controversy and bias. A kind of scientific disquiet with ethical ramifications not unlike the undertones of postmodern sensibility is apparent here. More precisely he had grounds both epistemic and philosophical for doubting the attainment of a first class science of contemporary history. He had noticed that this genre was afflicted by a greater obsession to go back to the origin, or the crossroads in the hope of locating the exact moment when the situation reached a point of no return. This obsession was also governed by the fear of having perhaps missed out on what might have happened if other options had been tried. Hence the hypothesis that the Second World War would not have occurred if certain people's opinions had been adopted was strictly speaking, insisted Williams, non-historical, because it had a strong normative flavour about it and was not amenable to the rules of logical and empirical verification or what he called "the rules of thumb". What is said here is that in a "might-have-been" argument one could adduce as much evidence as one could find without fearing at all being categorically refuted. For this reason it was a circular reasoning of a more frustrating degree because the chances of breaking it were next to nil. He also called attention to the fact that in the case of the problems raised by contemporary history, "abstraction" and "practice" did not contradict each other. Hence, "those who reason out from first principles" and "those who work on the basis of technical data" will assuredly find themselves in agreement. Granted there is a possibility that one may hit upon different reasons from the other, still the conclusions are the same. Thus he refused to side with the cold-shouldering attitude of a more austere English empiricism represented by L.B Namier (1888–1960) or Geoffrey Elton (1921–1994), historians who would have no truck with theory and recognized that "abstraction surveys from the heights of general reason; practice peeps up from the lowlands of empirical experience. But they meet eventually, and will not disagree".

Desmond T. Williams (1921–1987) is the other great name of the revisionist school. He studied at UCD and after graduation he showed his outward looking, broad-minded orientation by specializing on the origins of National Socialism in Germany. In 1944 he went to Cambridge, more precisely Peterhouse that boasted an excellent tradition of diplomatic history and counted among its fellows the iconoclastic and much revered Herbert Butterfield (1900–1979). While he was external examiner for the National University of Ireland, a role that both Harold Temperley and Michael Oakeshott took on before him, Butterfield met Williams and confident that he had discovered a rare gem he, with the encouragement of Edwards, facilitated Williams' acceptance at Peterhouse to work on "pan-Germanism in Austria, 1898–1902". Williams impressed him as "the most able and promising young historian I have ever had anything to do with" and "an extraordinarily stimulating person to have about the place".[41] There were bountiful elements of eccentricity, theatricality and brilliance in his personality, which endeared him to his seniors and juniors alike and of course to Butterfield for whom he became a *protégé* and an intellectual intimate. Oliver MacDonagh, his junior by three years, who had also gone to Cambridge in 1947 to prepare his MA under the supervision of Denis W. Brogan, wrote to Edwards that "Williams is quite a legend in Peterhouse and lives up to the part very vigorously".[42] No doubt the pinnacle of his training as a historian came when he was elected by the Foreign Office along with British, French and American historians to go to Berlin to edit the papers of the German foreign ministry for the period 1919–1945. This position gave him the unique opportunity to examine primary material of the utmost importance and of startling immediacy. In a letter of reference written on 4 May 1949 Butterfield commended Williams as immensely qualified to take up the history of the World Wars, especially the origins of the War of 1914, because "no other contemporary historian was so aware of the traps and dangers in contemporary history" and possessed at the same time such "a strong background of European history over many centuries".[43]

That Williams presented these original qualities to an astounding degree may be accounted for by his experience as an "Official" historian and perhaps by an intriguing event, which occurred while he was engaged in this diffi-cult task. In March 1949, Williams informed Butterfield, who was respons-ible for introducing his name to the Foreign Office, that the latter had apparently broken a previous undertaking – on the basis of which Williams had accepted the job – of not withholding any document from the scrutiny of the historians. Later during a famous speech called "Some Aspects of Contemporary History" given at UCD, he made an oblique allusion to this incident by declaring, "Historians on occasion lend themselves and edit 'offi-cial' history subject to the censorship of a departmental chief. The severity of the censorship varied widely of course in different countries but the prin-ciple is one which formerly would have been rejected out of hand by all historians".[44] On reading this disconcerting news, Butterfield reasoned that this was no "mere internal matter" since it had an immediate bearing on the crucial questions of "keeping faith with the public" and "maintaining" the "honour" of academic historians. Butterfield advised his former student "to resign in a signal manner, making the reason as public as possible, and doing this as soon after he had clarified the situation as he could reasonably manage". Butterfield felt so strongly about this unforgivable instance of interference of power into knowledge that he told Williams that no external pressure or consequence to himself "would deter him from airing a matter so important to the public and to historical science".[45]

The advocacy of the revocability of perceptions is an immensely problem-atic exercise. Williams and Butterfield were a brave minority who set out to do precisely this, to heighten in people's minds the flimsiness of seemingly ineradicable prejudices on the most sensitive European issue of the time, the Second World War. The Irish contribution to this revisionism as spear-headed by T.D. Williams and later pursued by Kevin B. Nowlan was acknowledged in 1961 by A.J.P. Taylor who in a book that aroused furious debate, wrote rather enticingly without further comment, "a few neutrals raised a peep of doubt, particularly from Ireland".[46] These historians were rightly or wrongly suspicious of the demonization of Germany, the depic-tion of an irredeemably evil and warmongering people, the unqualified dese-cration and condemnation of an entire culture because of the abominable sins Nazism had committed. In fact the "otherness" or "abnormality" of German character was frequently stated in a fashion that re-affirmed the early twentieth century racist stereotyping of which German anti-Semitism was only the most obscene form. Both men were pitiless in their detection of the vulgar propaganda of the Allies and the Axis forces alike and were espe-cially impatient with the version of the causes of the War propounded by the British Foreign Office. English Historians whose conclusions were too close to the official line, such as L.B. Namier, John Wheeler-Bennett, Eliza-beth Wiskemann, Hugh Trevor-Roper and Alan Bullock, did not convince them; hence their principled and at times dogmatic rejection of official history. The foundations on which the old humanist education was based were now gone and Williams felt it did not bode well when history supplanted the Classics in education. Given that youth had lost all contact with the Classics and the Bible, "the twin foundation stones of our culture", only history could spread prescience, acuteness and sympathy, if only it was taught properly. But recent developments belied this because history was compressed into a general theory and had become fatally fused with "political life" as in the example of "Marxism [which] provided the most monstrous and colossal attempt to build a *Weltauschaung* on history" or that of the rise of national states with "Pan-Germanism" and "Pan-Slavism", which preceded and outlasted the former. This unhealthy fusion was also visible in Western democracies where the public was calling for the inclusion of contemporary history in university courses.

Williams did not agree with those historians who out of academic snobbery scorned contemporary history on account of the inadequacy of material, lack of available evidence or difficulties in connection with "objectivity". The air of superiority they affected was unbefitting because he had noticed that they too could not resist drawing practical lessons or unscientific conclusions in their treatment of remoter periods. Still he admitted that contemporary history "exposed in more dramatic and self-evident fashion" "the [indelible] pressure of emotional prejudice", which was "greater among historians in relation to what concerned the living than what concerned the dead". This tendency was "magnified by the ideological conflicts which characterised struggles for world power". Hence, the passion invested lately in national wars had equalled that of the religious wars in the remote past and this new phenomenon of international relations was aggravated if not caused by the entry of the masses into political action. Finally "the savagery and self-righteousness of modern war had invaded the cloister of the historian as well as the platform or the Press".[47] These observations led him to the dour conclusion that scholars could no longer claim immunity from this odium and the charge of *trahison des clercs* was not wholly unjustified. The palpable sign that historical scholarship had regressed was that "what was once obvious to working historians had now to be established; and what was once known by instinct required ratiocination".[48] The prime lesson history taught was "the simple Christian truth of original sin and the simple Christian admonition 'not to cast the first stone'". But the world refuses to heed it with the result that since the end of the Second World War, the same ruinous habit of corruption of history has started all over again out of this bizarre and creepy combination of "demand for justice, passion for revenge, itch of curiosity" and a rush for self-justification on the part of omnipotent governments.[49]

This digression into the Second World War and German historiography is everything but fortuitous. If its immediate purpose is to contextualize and fathom out the nuances of the revisionist sensibility of Butterfield and Williams, its other purpose is to winkle out the opposing impulses or the undercurrents of meaning which provide a clue to those higher stakes involved in revisionism in general. In those years, Butterfield and Williams worked in close alliance in their efforts to expose the ideological charge, the errors and the myths that clustered Hitler's rise to power and his territorial aggressions. Their methods were complementary as Butterfield criticized the "outer framework of reference" of those works while Williams, thanks to his impressive knowledge of war documents, was able to pinpoint the problems in interpretation that did arise out of excessive reliance on or too literal reading of one set of records. They were very much aware of being a beleaguered minority and Butterfield spurred his younger ally to reach ever higher levels of rigorousness and stringency in his microscopic critique of evidential material as used by official historians. Above all he advised him to refrain from answering one dogmatic statement by another and always to justify scientifically his objections. He concluded: "Since we who question the great gang of contemporary historians are in such a minority, we do have to make out our case, and it is not we who can convince the world by dogmatic statement or by a laconic authoritative verdict."[50]

"The minds of men", pronounced oracularly Butterfield in 1948 in a contribution to *Studies*, were "prone to deadly inelasticities" which narrowed their affective and mental universe and coerced them into repeating perpetually the kind of error made in 1814–1815. Then France was singled out as the "perpetual aggressor", the one and only formidable "menace to Europe". Now it is Germany who has become the epitome of evil. Then the British government saw fit to place a "strong Prussia in the Rhineland", and by doing so it "prepared for a new age of history by actually strengthening Germany against France". Now the British government had put all its zeal in the fight and the complete emasculation of Germany by punitive sanctions, but by doing so, he warned, "it may actually prevent us from adjusting our minds to the situation and to the possible conflicts of this new era that has now arisen" with the increasing signs of tension emanating from Russia.

Butterfield drew attention to an incredible irony; up to the early 1900s, English historians in "the voices of Acton and Maitland", "admired" and even "worshipped" German historical scholarship for its impeccable scientific criteria, now it was vilified in no uncertain terms and the founding fathers of historicism, Hegel and Ranke were chastised for not anticipating the consequences of their spiritualization and sanctification of the State. Up to that time, all English freedom was imputed to "the Teutonic element in our history" while Germany itself was remembered for its emphasis on regionalism and local autonomy. It was the Latin peoples who were condemned for being unrepentant authoritarians – "the French with their Bonaparte, the Spaniards with their Inquisition and the Italians with their Pope". Now the "prejudices" had turned, "with equal exaggeration to the opposite side of the compass" and Butterfield cleverly remarked "it is difficult to see how any person with a sense of humour can help being struck by the fact that the great change in the English attitude to German historiography coincided so closely with the change of British foreign policy towards

Germany".[51] Equally Butterfield and Williams opposed the theory prevalent at the time, which claimed total continuity between Bismarck and Hitler and thus hastily rejected what had been hitherto, before the trauma of dictatorial repression, a vibrant culture. They feared the passions the war had unleashed had also distorted history, with treacherous hindsight unerringly mutilating the past realities of the German–English relationship and forcing an unhealthy sort of amnesia.

In Butterfield and Williams' definition of revisionism, historical truth seems to be an absolute in the sense that it cannot in any circumstance be subordinated to any other values or temporal ideologies. This means that so long as truth and an ideal of social and political justice coincide, the marriage runs smoothly. But if by misfortune, revisionism hits upon information which shows that this ideal of justice has compromised itself by violence or mendacity and defiled the very principles of human rights it purports to defend, then the marriage breaks up because the historian will refuse to silence those embarrassing facts to protect the interests of this ideal. By the same token, if evidence is discovered which directly or indirectly bolsters the cause of a national foe, the historian will still feel obliged to release it in the public domain regardless of its immediate moral and political implications and irrespective of its consequences. For instance, A.J.P. Taylor wrote:

> There is only one profound responsibility on the historian, which is to do his best for historical truth. If he discovered things which were catastrophic for his political beliefs he would still put it in his books. He has no responsibility whatsoever to fiddle the past in order to benefit some cause that he happens to believe in.[52]

Professional ethics are here observed almost in a deontological or Kantian fashion, as it were, because historical truth is deemed a categorical imperative. Hence the first revisionists of the 1920s and 1930s to whom Desmond Williams refers with approval, Americans like Sidney Bradshaw Fay[53] or Harry Elmer Barnes (1889–1968)[54] were a nuisance, real troublemakers chiefly because their analyses, by challenging the claim of sole German responsibility for the outbreak of the Great War, were undermining the credibility of Versailles and strengthening the case for revision of the entire settlement. Put in crude terms, their work was helping the Germans. Of course revisionists did not see it that way. They claimed that a territorial revision of Versailles if undertaken soon enough could forestall the rise of Hitler and spare humanity another wasteful war. In April 1961, a reviewer diagnosed precisely the most disturbing aspect about Taylor's thesis in *The Origins of the Second World War*: "it did to Nuremberg what inter-war German propaganda tried to do to Versailles".[55] Put differently, Taylor, who even in the wildest flights of imagination could not be branded a Germanophile, found himself in a state of inadvertent collusion with the

German Right because some of his conclusions could be lifted to argue that the trials at Nuremberg lacked moral validity.

At the bottom of revisionism there are also strong anti-Establishment feelings. Its research hinges on the crucial notion that there is not a single government in Europe which wants the public to know all the truth, for if there is one all it needs to do is to "open its archives to the free play of scholarship, to friends, enemies, neutrals, devil's advocates and independent observers, so that everything may be put into the crucible and we may know the worst that the eagle eye of a hostile critic may pounce upon, the clash of controversy ultimately producing a more highly-tested form of truth".[56] The fact that none had hitherto done so confirmed Butterfield in his suspicions. It is therefore a history which prides itself in the distance it takes from motives of *raison d'état* and is attentively on the look out for the key to the one drawer which the government does not want it to peer in.

There were of course grounds for concern about certain tendencies in post-war German historiography and English historians were not just the prisoners of official propaganda. In 1948, Gerhard Ritter (1888–1967) published *Europa und die deutsche Frage*. In it he argued that National Socialism was an aberration, an *Irrweg*, a deviation from a pure origin, and even more unforgivably, an infection which reached Germany from the West. Ritter thought it was outlandish to consider Hitler the heir of Frederick II and of Bismarck, for neither preached global war. In 1946, Friedrich Meinecke (1862–1954) published *German Catastrophe*. In it he contended that Nazi Germany was not uniquely evil in as much as the "amoral element" at its core infected the whole of Western civilization and was in fact the upshot of a more general fermentation occasioned by a monstrous process of change. "This truth", he nonetheless cautioned, "ought not to be a justification for us Germans. Ethical and historical considerations demand that we Germans should mind our own business, and seek to understand Germany's special part in it".[57] However, in spite of or perhaps because of this warning, Meinecke's mitigating tactics became even more attractive and were easily smuggled in undetected.

He equated Nazism with a simple Machiavellian type of ideology and most disconcertingly perhaps he did not mention the Holocaust, which undeniably was symptomatic of an unparalleled degree of premeditation, one that went way beyond the dishonest machinations of a few individuals. This omission in the midst of the de-Nazification attempts of the Allied occupation, and the Nuremberg war crimes tribunals, seemed itself disingenuous, and it was hard not to read into it passive denial or worse, denigration of the event. Meinecke's use of language was also eloquent. His choice of metaphor, when he described the Third Reich as an overpowering wave that "burst upon Germany" reduced Nazism to a devastating natural cataclysm upon which Germans had no control and where they too became victims. He was most anxious to expel Hitler from the collective memory of the Germans, through some semantic magical trick. Thus he was at pains to convince that: "This fellow does not belong to our race at all. There is something wholly foreign about him". By dissociating Germans from Nazis as thoroughly as possible, he hoped to absolve the former by transferring the guilt for their crimes onto a third category, the Nazis. This attractive estrangement overlooked however that Nazism could not have invaded the country and its hegemony lasted for so long without the tacit condoning or active collaboration of its citizens. In fact, Meinecke and Ritter were the first post-war German historians to toy with the concepts of totalitarianism or fascism as a means to remove the singularity of Nazi ideology and transfer responsibility for its crimes onto outside influences. Under their pen, the forerunners of Hitler were Robespierre and Napoleon III, and not Frederick the Great and Bismarck. The intellectual roots of National Socialism lay, startlingly, in the French Revolution and its by-product, plebeian democracy. In a letter to Butterfield on 8 November 1955, Williams described Meinecke as a historian "who for all his industry and aptitude, was too much under the influence of an ideology and of Germanic pre-suppositions",[58] thereby implying that he did not agree with his type of historical revision.

However, neither did Williams agree with the sensational continuity theory best exemplified by the zealous Lewis Namier who believed that the Third Reich had not been "a gruesome accident or a monstrous aberration, but the correct consummation of the German era in history". If Germany was dangerous it was not primarily because of fascism, which on balance was merely a doctrine likely to rise and fade, but because this country was the psychotic of Europe. "States, like planets, moved in predestined courses" and Namier warned the West that Germany, trapped in her own inherent evil, was bound to set it loose chronically.[59] Later Williams took issue with Namier's retrospective, determinist and teleological interpretation of German and Austro-Hungarian developments in the period between 1812 and 1918 in a review of *Side Lines of History*. A positivist method that wanted to uncover "iron-laws" or "the logic of situation and the rhythm of events", to quote from the book, made one skim over important details such as the fact that German Nationalism in Austria was not a homogeneous block of opinion but comprised a wide variety of attitudes and beliefs. Namier's approach was tautological because, "he had found the answer before, he had put all the relevant questions, and he had read the present back into the past".[60] This determinist hypothesis was initially also defended by A.J.P. Taylor (1906–1990) who spoke of an unbroken continuity "from Luther to Hitler" in the form of an aggressive, expansionist militarism in the German–Prussian State, of which National Socialism was only the most radical manifestation.[61] Taylor blamed Martin Luther for fomenting disunity amongst the various German States, for etching in the collective psyche "the German nationalist sense of being different" and for instilling mindless obedience to the orders of their rulers. Where Herbert Butterfield wrote more than ever in a spirit of "appeasement", to mollify "the jangled state of people's nerves",[62] Taylor was not afraid to voice his anti-German animus by delivering such pronouncements as, "it was no more a mistake for the German People to end up with Hitler than it is an accident when a river flows into the sea".[63]

Even his openly revisionist book on the origins of the war, which challenged the idea of Hitler as the "system-maker" who planned the destruction of Western civilization and described him as a traditional statesman whose only separateness lay in a "terrifying literalism", only did so with the robust intention of shouldering the German people with as great if not the greatest responsibility. In a perverse fashion, he said what others, perhaps official historians, knew but dared not contemplate so unflinchingly or say so brusquely; the reality of German complicity. Hence, he writes: "It seems to be believed nowadays that Hitler did everything himself, even driving the trains and filling the gas chambers unaided. This was not so. Hitler was a sounding board for the German nation. Thousands, many hundred thousand, Germans carried out his evil orders without qualm or question".[64] After having taken cognisance of this literature, we must ask ourselves what did Desmond Williams, Ireland's first diplomatic historian and a pioneer of the revisionist method later espoused by the sulphurous Taylor, think of those two poles? From a close reading of his work one can presume that he found them both crude, deficient and suspect chiefly because they were a mirror image of each other and because not only the historical analysis of war diplomacy was encrusted with "practical, sociological and political presuppositions" but even the choice of archival material that was released bore the mark of similar fetters.

In his junior capacity as editor of the captured German archives, he had experienced at first hand the censoring proclivities of the victors who were anxious, "to anticipate the results of any attempt by historians in vanquished countries to challenge the accepted version of responsibility for the war, which had been laid down at the Nuremberg trials". The Allies tightly vetted all documents brought into the public sphere as "they were determined to get their 'historical' blow in first" and prevent a repetition of the Versailles scenario when the defeated countries reversed the moral judgements imposed by unilateral act in the peace treaties, and later reaped important political advantages out of the conversion world opinion underwent in regard to the moral issues.[65]

If by postmodern standards of historical criticism, Irish revisionism may sound naïve in some of its methodological postulations, it ceases to do so when we compare it to the state of contemporary continental scholarship. Williams deplored the fact that as late as the 1950s, continental historians still felt obliged to defend the part played by their government during the Second World War. Theirs were mere official histories, the research for which relied heavily on the release of State sources. Therefore, the historical profession there was still split on strict partisan lines. In his review of Williams' paper in 1958, Edwards joined him in his attack against Namier, who in his study on the Second World War, "assumed the forces of 'light' to be on one side, and of darkness to be on the other". When provoked by a critic who charged sneeringly that it was all very well for Irish historians to take up a neutral attitude, Edwards riposted that it was "a sad reflection upon the courage of some English historians if ten years and more after the end of the war, they still felt committed to the propaganda of the past". Furthermore, there is a sense in which Edwards and Williams welcomed Irish neutrality as beneficial in as much as it placed Ireland at an emotional remove from the horrors, falsifications and collusions of the War, and gave Irish historians the golden opportunity to reflect upon these with increased sharpness. They believed that cool meditation on how during the war history on the continent was manhandled with the complicity of historians could become a major incentive for the handling of Irish history with new valiance and audacity and influence for the better the way Irish disputes were perceived:

> Perhaps it is some consolation that historical neutrality can be reckoned a merit to the Irish who have so frequently been accused of being unable to see their own history impartially because of the seven-century struggle with England. But it should also be an incentive to us, now that it has been shown that a conference of Irish historians can present their studies within these austere limits, to continue to show other countries how history should be written. There is plenty of room in the study of Irish history for such work ... If we can show we have the detachment here, as well as the scholarship, it will ensure that that work is done well.[66]

In his seminal essay on the historiography of the Second World War, remarkable for its level of maturity, considering it was written just a decade after the end of the War by a scholar still in his early thirties and who, what is more, was not daunted by the task of critiquing the still contentious issue of Appeasement, it is again Namier who is the target; the historian who embodies the kind of contemporary history Williams cannot respect. Williams objected to the Namierite type of history because it credulously provided justification for the judicial and political verdicts passed at Nuremberg in September 1946. His conclusions were – strictly speaking – not scientific because they were too much moored to two presuppositions which, granted, if accepted, rendered them intelligible and convincing. Hence, he was aghast at the spectacle of a historian of Namier's standing, a man who alone personified the empirical and objective benchmarks laid down by Leopold von Ranke, "sally forth" in "the murky waters" of a Manichean, po-faced and sanctimonious official history where "one side was (conveniently) wrong and bad, and most persons directly or indirectly connected with that side (were) as wrong and as bad as the causes for which they stood" and where one held the "valid" but unverifiable notion that if the Resisters had outweighed the Appeasers the war would not have occurred. However, the main weakness of this history was that it could only declaim pedestrian truths such as, "Hitler wanted war". But "Nobody would, on the whole now contest this fact" retorted Williams, and "it is easy to draw the conclusion that the British Foreign Office was right in supporting the general decision to resist him". This history was however neither probing nor heuristic enough to raise new questions, and thus to teach us something about the play of the contingent in diplomacy or allow us to learn from past mistakes. Its effect was to curtail the effort of historical understanding. Its almost sycophantic attitude to the Allies' version of events stymied any exploration along unconventional routes such as:

> When did Hitler really want to go to war, or over what issues he would have preferred to take that decision …? Namier does not consider if between March 16th and April 3rd, mistakes of judgment were not committed by Foreign Office advisers, or if the facts upon which they based their advices did not subsequently prove to be false. Nor does he ask if some of Hitler's own actions were not themselves partly the product of either real or presumed British, French or American policy.[67]

Williams' own interpretation of the War placed a great deal of stress on the blundering factor: the power of prejudice and fear to misconstrue intentions and actual realities on the ground, to be exceedingly excited by confusing evidence and to ruin chances of devising more profitable and wiser policies. During his close reading of diplomatic documents, he discovered that Neville Chamberlain's decision to overthrow Appeasement took place not so much as a result of the pressure of domestic opinion caused by Hitler's occupation of Prague on 15 March 1939, but more so on the basis of misleading information he received from the Romanian Tilea who told the Foreign Office that the Germans had delivered an ultimatum to Romania and from a journalist who informed the government of an "imminent German attack on Poland". Both reports proved to be unfounded and Chamberlain, thought Williams, was to blame for not double-checking them.

Assuming the Poles were in danger, he offered them a unilateral guarantee against a German threat to their independence; and the Poles were accorded the right to decide what constituted such a threat. This move was, in Williams' estimation, a mistake first because British policy was thus made dependent on the views of Poland, freeing the Poles from any obligation to compromise on Danzig or to cooperate more closely with Soviet Russia, and second because it put flesh on Hitler's fear that Poland had entered into a general encircling front against Germany. Chamberlain did not have in his possession all the pieces of the jigsaw. He did not know the Poles had rejected German advances to solve the Danzig problem and had partially mobilized. The Poles did not wish to be associated with Chamberlain's Four Power Consultation, but by their unwillingness to compromise over Danzig and their partial mobilization, they convinced Hitler that they were, as Hitler reasoned that Joseph Beck would not have put up such a show of resistance if he had not already joined the peace-front.[68] Williams thought that Poland had made a suicidal miscalculation when it chose not to concede Danzig since the Polish Corridor no longer guaranteed the security and independence of the Polish state once the Germans secured rearmament in 1939.

The real protection for Poland lay in the preservation of the balance of power and, to this end, Williams declared emphatically, "the gaining of one's year respite would have been worth a thousand Danzigs". Against her own best interest, Poland by calling Hitler's bluff, precipitated Britain and France into a war for which neither of them was militarily ready. Beck was equally wrong in his judgement that the Fuehrer would be deterred by the Anglo-Polish barrier that was supposed to thwart his plan to occupy Danzig as "Hitler was induced to act sooner than he had intended, and to hit Poland hard before either she or Britain were prepared to face the prospect of general war".[69] Williams concluded: "Everyone, I think, misunderstood the exact position of the other; and this was as true of Hitler's conception of Polish, as it was of Chamberlain's or Beck's view of German, policy".

In a letter to Butterfield, Williams confided his fear that his questioning of the judiciousness and foresight of British statesmanship during this crucial period might give the impression that he also contested the more general threat posed by German Nazism. His position was subtler. He insisted that the assumptions about what were German realities proved to be false, as far as Hitler's immediate intentions were concerned, though Williams made a distinction between Hitler's long-term and short-term policies, between his ultimate goal and the means he might have chosen as the best way to attain it. But he did not doubt that the War was likely to have happened anyway owing to Hitler's determination to have sovereignty in Danzig and the strength of feeling against Poland among the German masses. And yet he remained convinced that it was not inevitable and came at the wrong time for everyone concerned. He writes:

> I would be disappointed if the manner in which I handle the whole problem is one which indicates any particular view about the moral issues concerned. I am sure that one can accept the Foreign Office view of the danger of Hitler and Germany, and yet condemn the details of the execution of that policy. This may seem to be avoiding issues, but it is not one in which I feel it is necessary to be involved.[70]

In reserving for himself the right to abstain from answering whether the Allies were right or wrong to perceive Hitler as a danger for humanity and thus to try and stop him, in questioning only the pertinence of the timing and the conditions in which the decision to go to war was taken, Williams echoed Butterfield's opinion that it was best for historical explanation not even to touch the realm in which words like right or wrong carried meaning. All the same, Williams did sense a problem here even though he seemed to have flinched from looking into it. The problem is that grabbed by less scrupulous hands, Williams' findings could be to suggest that Hitler's aggressiveness was wildly overstated, that he was just reacting, that he was the first to be dismayed by the war because he did not imagine that the democracies would actually go to war over Poland since Danzig and the Polish Corridor were the regions where the German case for revision of the Versailles Treaty were stronger and because the Allies had already appeased Berlin over more-contestable territorial issues. Put another way, his findings could be contrived to suggest as Taylor did, that the war was a terrible accident that nobody had wanted. However, even if one is prepared to swallow Taylor's more ambitious conclusion which considerably weakens the perception of Hitler as a blood-thirsty and imperialist warmongerer, one may riposte that it still leaves unaccountable and inexcusable the policy of the concentration and death camps. Raring to go into uncharted land and to contemplate with glee ironical facts, Williams noticed that "historians of the defeated countries" profited from the fact that in "defeat", "recrimination" triggered uncomfortable questions and this usually prompted a speedy release of documents from those in power who were anxious to respond to accusations. The Nuremberg trial had, in his opinion, harmed its reputation of moral rectitude when the prosecuting governments had not authorized inspection of their archives.[71] This was a remark Taylor echoed in 1961 when with terse provocation he wrote:

> The documents at Nuremberg were chosen not only to demonstrate the war-guilt of the men on trial, but to conceal that of the prosecuting Powers. If any of the four Powers who set up the tribunal had been running the affair alone, it would have thrown the mud more widely ... Of course the documents are genuine. But they are "loaded"; and anyone who relies on them finds it almost impossible to escape from the load with which they are charged.[72]

Williams' reading was structuralist but not crudely determinist. He thought that Versailles, instead of making the world safer for freedom and democracy, exacerbated insecurities, moral doubts and especially fears; that of the "extinction of German tradition and German power", that of "unemployment and starvation that followed from it". Hitlerism fed itself on those fears and its own methods "created" in turn, "other fears" among other people, that of "European dictatorship" and that of "extinction of 'inferior' nationalities and races". He thought those fears affected judgement, action and behaviour to the point of "bringing nearer to reality objectives which might otherwise have remained as among the more absurd and irrelevant preoccupations of the statesman".[73] Those sets of fears were alone a powerful and terrible crucible which ultimately got the better of everyone's nerves and undoubtedly made the war seem, when it came like a self-fulfilling prophecy. What deserves attention here is that Williams was already in the mid-1950s expounding the hypothesis that Taylor formulated apparently in a more blanket fashion in 1961. Like Taylor he did not subscribe to the teleology that attributed to Hitler a methodically worked-out plan for the conquest of Europe and the triumph of the German Empire. Instead he thought that neither his policy nor his character had been absolutes but he managed to adapt them craftily according to environment, external reactions and circumstances. Hence for instance, the Hitler of *Mein Kampf* with his "countrified style" did not impress the cultured middle class of the Weimar Republic steeped as it was in cosmopolitanism. But he reversed this indifference when at a later date, "he learned the advisability of being, on many issues, all things to all men". Determined to win the support of the middle class and secure at least the neutrality of the army, between 1930 and 1933, he "softened the acerbity of some of his views, and toned down their implications where it became politically advisable to do so".[74] Hitler before 1923 was a pure revolutionary, who was determined to overthrow government by force. After 1923, while maintaining his original contempt for parliamentary democracy, he decided to capture power by means of the democratic process. This was forced upon him, not by any change in objective, but by tactical necessities.

What's more, Williams' more nuanced reading of German history presented similarities with the *discontinuiste* method of Geoffrey Barraclough (1908–1984). In June 1961, Barraclough gave an interesting paper to the Conference of Irish historians in Galway in which he questioned the teleological bend of nineteenth-century German historiography. He rejected the consensus which defined Bismarck's Reich of 1871 as only a stepping-stone towards the full accomplishment of German unity. The logic behind Bismarck's creation and the logic behind Hitler's ambitions were not the same. Bismarck, Barraclough insisted, was a pragmatist and a realist, who knew that the other European powers would never accept the existence of a new and powerful state in the heart of Europe. After 1871 the thrust of his diplomacy consisted in securing a period of peace during which the new Reich would be stabilized and accepted. His choice to appeal to the nationalist feelings of his people was tactical for he needed to secure the allegiance of all Germans under Prussia.

But his own nationalism did not entail the return home of the Germans of Austria or the happiness of the Germans of Holstein and he had no intention of becoming the servant of a febrile, uncontrollable and dangerous pan-Germanism of the kind advocated by the Liberals who unreasonably dreamt of making state and folk coincide. Barraclough campaigned for a writing of nineteenth-century German history in which the movement for unification would no longer be interpreted as the be-all and end-all of the German peoples between 1813 and 1871, for he believed that such a revisitation unyoked from "the political overtones which have so often sounded a false note" could give rise to a better appreciation of the more lasting

achievements of the German peoples and of the essential values they
have brought to European civilization, sometimes in spite of and sometimes
because of political disunity.[75] Reviewing the volume in which the
essay appeared, J.C. Beckett, another important name of Irish revisionism,
wrote:

> Professor Barraclough's discussion of the attitudes of various German
> historians indicates clearly enough, what we in Ireland know only too
> well, that historical interpretation can have a very direct connection
> with politics. Perhaps in the long run one of the strongest justifications
> for the serious study of history is the need for protecting the public from
> policies based on a false interpretation of the past.[76]

For "Bismarck" read "Daniel O'Connell", for "febrile pan-Germanism" read
"Irish Fenianism", for "German disunity" read "Irish disunity" and one starts
to get an inkling into the paradigmatic skeleton that the new historians, especially those of the second generation, were to adopt in their own original
reconsideration of Irish modern history. However, one should not deduce here
that Irish historiography was being pushed, merely responding to external
methodological stimuli. The rejection of linear, *continuiste* and teleological
accounts of the Irish past was already detectable in the work of the critic Sean
O'Faolain[77] and the classical scholar Michael Tierney;[78] even though those
early revisionist analyses had sometimes a polemical edge which disqualified
them from the title of "objective history". In 1949, Michael Tierney complained about a writing of Irish history so monopolized by the doctrine of
nationality that it categorically dismissed all other explanations as aberrant.
The result was "the setting aside or the condemnation as somehow irrelevant
of [Daniel O'Connell], the greatest Irish political figure because he could not
be fitted into it".

As for O'Faolain's decision to restore O'Connell to the pedestal from
which more radical nationalists from Mitchel to Griffith had toppled him
it was itself too enmeshed in the writer's own disillusionment with
the physical force tradition he had himself once believed in, to break free
completely from the principle of identity. The aspects of O'Connell he chose
to highlight and sometimes to exaggerate, such as his moderation, his
non-sectarian definition of Irish democracy and his liberal, anti-theocratic
conception of the state were also the remedies that O'Faolain was pre-
scribing at the time to an Ireland still recovering from the traumas and
sequels of its jaunt into political extremism. It is still the tentacles of the
principle of identity which one sees creeping up again although it is being
inflected on a different level; here it is a case of the writer himself identifying with his object of enquiry because he thinks that object validates his
personal choices.

The *continuiste* and *discontinuiste* readings both share the same fundamental
assumption, but inverted. It is the idea of the German *Sonderweg*. It means

special or separate path but with a clear implication of divergence from the West. Originally coined by German academics in the nineteenth century in order to explain Germany's exceptional vitality and its promising evolution removed from the shallow values of "Latin imperialism"; later the meaning of the word changed from "divergence" to "deviance" or "skidding off" to provide a seemingly scientific explanation for Germany's descent into dictatorship and genocide. Here the message is that something went wrong on the journey to accomplish Germany's Manifest Destiny. Germany lagged behind Western Europe. Although it had known modernity with the advancement of technology and industrialization, it had failed to internalize the values of democracy, thereby creating a dangerous imbalance. Butterfield did not agree with the outlandish views of Gerhard Ritter who saw Nazism as an alien or extraneous phenomenon bearing no relation to the history of the German society or the German mind. However, one thing which stands out compellingly from the evidence is that he was particularly anxious to maintain good feeling and amicability between German and English historians, even going so far as to take on the role of ambassador who always tried to make amends for the slights and curtness of others and spoke the reassuring, sensible, respectful word. Equally obvious is that he took his self-appointment in earnest, with a deep personal conviction and that this desire to repair the broken trust and rekindle mutual esteem across national divides may have led him to silence or play down certain intellectual or moral doubts he had. Others were not as reticent to voice their doubts.

Hence, in April 1950 Geoffrey Barraclough, speaking for himself and on behalf of other English and German historians, accused the *Historische Zeitschrift*, "of taking refuge in dreary banalities", and "deliberately shirking", indeed, "cold-shouldering the great moral and political issues facing German historians today". He also admitted to being disturbed by its "subtly reactionary and nationalist trends". Barraclough was outraged at the suggestion in one article of the journal that the "German Catastrophe" was primarily due to the failure of England, France and the United States in 1931 "to show friendship and understanding" to the Heinrich Brüning Government. It was, as the published British documents would undoubtedly have proven, a lie and he was riled as much by the lie as by the negligence which allowed it to spread so effortlessly. He then attacked Gerhard Ritter for spreading the idea that the tradition of human rights and liberal parliamentary democracy derived from England and France were "the historical source of totalitarianism", and that the only way to check "this western disease" was "a strong remedial dose of German 'Rechtsstaat', i.e., of constitutionalism (in the German sense) à la William I and Bismarck". Barraclough noticed that this "sophisticated flank-attack" against the West had already formed the core of Ritter's *Europa und die Deutsche Frage*; a work which without hesitation he described as "the coolest piece of propaganda yet to come from Germany". With unconcealed pessimism and dread, he concluded:

The situation in the German universities is grave – far graver than is commonly realized. Every word and gesture on our part is watched intently for signs of weakening in the face of the growing nationalist propaganda, particularly when (as I am sure is the case with your reviewer) we weaken unknowingly and in good faith. The approving reception you have given to the "new" *Historische Zeitschrift*, if it is accepted as a final judgment from this side of the Channel, cannot but be a source of encouragement to all those in Germany who are still fighting, not of course for Hitler, but for the ideas and ideals of those who, from Hindenburg downwards, backed Hitler. Equally it will be a source of bewilderment and discouragement to those few in the German Universities today, who still are genuinely concerned to bring to life in Germany (what does not yet exist) a sense of democracy in the sense in which that word has been historically understood in England and France.[79]

Soon Ritter felt provoked to respond to those accusations. These remarks, he declared, were "a total misapprehension of his views", for he had often criticized both the constitutional monarchy and the absolute monarchy as conceived by William I and "forcibly and unambiguously rejected Treitschke's nationalism and militarism". He was "painfully disappointed" to discover that his work "had remained outside of Professor Barraclough's ken" and "alarmed" that a historian of his great "integrity" could "perceive nothing except nationalistic presumption and obduracy" behind his critique of American and Western ideals of freedom.[80] What comes out intensely is that here Barraclough reacted less as a historian and more as a citizen, a citizen who felt offended by the notion that the Allies who had just fought courageously German totalitarianism at its most consummate and dangerous form could be seen as the originators of totalitarianism. Butterfield's first reaction to the Barraclough–Ritter dispute was recorded in a letter to Michael Oakeshott on 15 June 1950. With characteristic caution he expressed the view that: "the Germans ought to be left to work out their own history and to do their own reflection of their experience and that if things are working properly in this direction they ought to be producing a kind of history which we in England would not like. Some of them may be doing something more sinister than that, and I should be sorry if that were the case with Gerhard Ritter".[81] However, after he went deeper into the matter, it became apparent that his own misgivings did not focus so much on the substance of Barraclough's critique as on the form and tone he used. Hence on 20 July 1950, he admitted that "personally, he and some Germans, would differ from Ritter on certain points", but the real problem resided elsewhere. He was worried lest "the mode of Barraclough's attack" was contrived to "alarm English public opinion" and "ginger up the indignation of the victor power against the kind of history which contemporary Germans are producing". He considered Ritter "an impressive person and an interesting mind – a man who has altered his views in interesting ways, though he does refuse to throw overboard the whole Germanic tradition". Besides he thought that an attack against a personality who "held a kind of presidential position amongst German historians" would "injure the feelings of a great many of the historians whom we over here have valued" and further increase alienation between the two intellectual communities.[82] If Ritter enjoyed a high prestige among his colleagues it was because he had successfully cast himself into the role of resistant connected to the Friburg Circle of Carl Goerdeler and was allegedly arrested by the Gestapo on account of his involvement in the 20 July 1944 plot to assassinate Hitler.

In the wake of the unparalleled level of destruction and death wrought by Germany, historians were confronted with one agonizing choice. The wisdom of reforming or abandoning German historicism is the single most important question exercising their minds. When Northern Ireland erupted, Irish historicism already embattled in the past, plunged in its most profound crisis yet and it is then that the possibility of its abandonment crept into the minds of some Irish historians with the same burning and guilty intensity it did with German historians in the post-war era. Strangely enough, it is also then that the question of the origins of this late conflict began to hold the stage and led some historians to expound arguments which were not always, strictly speaking, historical. Hence, the notion of *Sonderweg* is all the more intriguing, as it seems to have spawned an Irish equivalent. Father Francis Shaw who was not a historian was the first to speculate along those lines. Although one can doubt his motives, one has to admit that Shaw succeeded in capturing something of the dilemma that the Easter Rebellion subsequently posed for all the political traditions in Ireland. By imagining 1916 as a multiple wound inflicted on the body of Ireland with ongoing "psychological" or "spiritual" complications he certainly inaugurated a most dramatic theme in the Irish historical debate. For with this trope was for the first time postulated the idea of a linkage between the 1916 Rebellion, the partition of the island, the Civil War of 1922–1923, the repudiation of the men who fought and died during the First World War – and if one follows the argument to its logical conclusion – also the outbreak of the Troubles in Northern Ireland in 1968. Here the Rising is conceptualized as the cardinal starting point of a revolutionary skidding off with truly tragic consequences for the future of the nation.

It foreshadows and contains *in nuce* the explosion of a series of confrontations that proved fatal for national unity. Thus despite its Catholic bias, it would not be wrong to say that this article, represented a landmark in the history of ideas insofar as it did not shirk from gauging the impact of the insurrectional logic of 1916 on the future of democracy in Ireland; 1916, it forcefully suggested, has caused an imbalance in the heart and the soul of every Irish person. Its rhetoric has opened perilously an era of perpetual revolution and sown the seeds of discord in the deepest recesses of the collective subconscious. In prophetic accents, Shaw declared:

> The sword, it would seem, is never as clean a weapon as we are sometimes led to believe. Wounds may often fester for a long time ... The resort to arms in support of the separatist doctrine in 1916 inflicted three grave wounds on the body of the unity of Ireland. The first is the wound of partition. Already in 1916 the threat of secession in the North was very strong ... The second wound is the wound of the Civil War of 1922–3. This bitter strife between Irishmen who were brothers and had recently been comrades in arms was a consequence, if not an inevitable one, of the Rising of 1916. The extremist teaching of Tone and Mitchel could brook no compromise: it dictated a choice of a separatist republic or nothing. It had won the day in 1916 and it was still strong enough in 1922 to drive men to civil strife ... The third wound on the national unity will continue to fester until the injustice, which causes it, is removed ... I refer to the many thousands of Irishmen who fought and died bravely in the First World War and are yet virtually without honour in their own land.[83]

In his zeal to prove his republican credentials, Patrick Pearse invented a noble ancestry by identifying with T.W. Tone. However this identification proved deficient for historians in some important respects. Following symbolic patterns that were visible in other parts of Europe as well, Pearse included Catholic imagery in his defence of Irish separatism. But the artificial coupling of Republicanism and Catholicism, two forces that were at best uneasy bedfellows and at worst outright enemies, was problematic and this rhetorical embellishment begged more questions than it answered. Hence his appeal to Catholicism later opened a Pandora's Box for generations of historians and commemoration committees. This fictitious identity between an oppressed religion and an oppressed nation suitably eluded the embarrassing fact that the marriage had been one of strategic convenience and toleration and not love. Equally it dodged the fact that purists in both camps had dismissed the notion of a common purpose and opposed the idea of an alliance. Wolfe Tone, the founder of the United Irishmen, was one such purist. His patriotism hid a visceral anti-Catholic sentiment he overcame only through his vision of an Irish brotherhood rising above all divisions and unanimous in its desire to break the British yoke. As an Irish carrier of a putatively ecumenical Enlightenment, who had sought and obtained the support of revolutionary France, Tone could not imagine any compatibility between Catholicism and Republicanism because for him these words were by definition immiscible. Pearse, on the contrary, saw Catholic mysticism in a more utilitarian spirit; it was a tool which, if astutely handled, could carry profound echoes in the collective psyche and enlist on a much greater scale people's sympathy for the cause.

Another purist on the other side of the fence was precisely Father Francis Shaw. His hostility towards Anglo-Irish Republicanism was a modern-day expression of the Church's long-standing doctrinal and institutional objection to a French Revolution which had calculatingly planned to eradicate Catholic clericalism. And in Ireland, opposing the French Revolution meant opposing the United Irishmen and all its latterday derivatives. Hence the equation of patriotism with sainthood, or the idea that one ought to be ready to sacrifice himself for his country the way Jesus did to save mankind was sacrilegious arguably because Jesus' action promised only spiritual and not material freedom. However, Shaw was not merely offended by a cavalier appropriation which twisted the message of the Gospel. What bothered him more was the danger, forever present, that Irish Republicanism might supplant Catholicism in the affections of the people and level an attack on the institutional power of the Church.

That his revisionism had an ideological taste was also evinced by his anxiety to pre-empt the accusation, usually thrown by Republicans, that the Church had been opportunistic and collaborationist in its dealings with the Crown. It is then only half a surprise to discover that this ideological burden drove him to impose his own preconceived and narrow "canon". He forgot the tragic consequences of Britain's social and economic policies and most significantly emptied the conflicted social composition of Irish nationalism so as to present it as an Anglo-Irish affair, foreign to the sensibilities of and irrelevant to the needs of the common people and a false religion which had to be resisted in the name of the true one, Catholicism. Furthermore, his retrospective search for an origin to the "chain of error" pushed him in a maze of self-contradiction. On the one hand, his knowledge made him appreciate the fact that by 1916, partition was strongly on the cards. He wrote that in choosing to attack Britain instead of Belfast which was the real stumbling block standing in the way of Home Rule, the separatists had implicitly recognized the reality of partition. The Ulster Unionists were adamant that they would not even accept a modified form of Union in which there would be a lesser Home Rule because they feared that democratic advances since 1800 would eventually tip the scales in favour of the majority. On the other hand, Shaw's antipathy to Pearse made him overstate the extent to which the Rising was responsible for deepening the chasm between North and South.

When in 1966, he confessed the Church's objection, the doctrinal one, the other one was better kept silent, the editorial committee of *Studies* that had commissioned his article deemed its tone was not appropriate for its inclusion in a commemorative edition. The Irish State was then preparing itself to celebrate with pomp and pride the fiftieth anniversary of the Easter Rebellion, unencumbered by philosophical doubts about the legacy of what was generally recognized as the great turning point in modern Irish history. It was finally published in 1972 when the outbreak of sectarian violence in Northern Ireland caused a trauma in the hearts and minds of all. Other writers in the 1980s and 1990s took up a similar line but this time the emphasis was no longer on deviation but rather on a continuous thread of latent fanaticism. Sean Cronin perceived a direct line unfolding from the Split after the Treaty to the start of the military campaign of the Provisional IRA in Northern Ireland. Nationalism in Ireland had encompassed many contradictory forms that could have been reconciled only by the skilful use of ambiguity. He concluded with a series of linked characteristics showing the chameleon nature of Irish nationalism. It went: "from democratic theory to Jacobinism, from constitutionalism to revolution, from comprehensive nationality to sectarianism, from French republicanism to seminarist gallantry, from Marxism to near-Fascism".[84] In the *Irish Times*, Kevin Myers wrote about 1916: "I maintain it was a deplorable thing, with deplorable consequences since. It was a triumph of anti-democratism and militarism over democracy and civicism, of evil methods over peaceful ones". He argued that virtually everything to do with this event was horrible, from the homicidal manipulation of its preparatory stages, through the carnage and agony of Easter Week, to its hideous aftermath.[85] By intimating that the IRA is the most authentic incarnation or "the cutting edge of Catholic nationalism" as Cruise O'Brien put it, a number of historians and commentators not scrupulous enough in their style and conclusions exposed themselves to criticism. They were accused of overstressing the negative elements of nationalism instead of underlining its positive attainments. They were then predictably accused of being anti-nationalist, counter-revolutionary and apologists of the colonialist adventure. If negative excess, under the form of a dormant chauvinism, racism or fascism, has indeed always been integral to Irish nationalism, then one is likely to infer that it is a very imperfect instrument given its dangerous leanings.

Surprisingly enough, this endogenous paradigm was something shared by both Irish revisionism and postmodernism. For a time those reductionist and nihilistic tendencies were present in both schools granting the fact that Irish Nationalism unlike Marxism was still far from being declared dead and buried. Those tendencies were however harmful because they played right into the hands of those who wanted to stigmatize them as reactionary. Postmodernists were indeed prone to believe that the dismal deterioration of Marxism into outright terror had proved that domination was inevitable and that all efforts conceived in order to resist it were susceptible to spawn more monstrous forms of oppression and more alarming forms of servitude. Likewise if domination and oppression were inherent features of Irish Nationalism then all those who praised its virtues and intended on challenging contemporary forms of power like globalization and capitalism thanks to it, did nothing more than implicate themselves further in the imposture of this theory. For the theory, despite claims to the contrary, was not an emancipating one but one secretly designed to invent more irrevocable forms of oppression. The Gulag is not a deviation from Marxist theory but a product of its own logic. Equally, the Irish Civil War of 1923–1924 and the violence of the IRA are not accidental instances of a veering off from an origin that remained pure but intrinsic products of the logic of Irish nationalism. Furthermore by presenting the violence of the Provisionals as a natural upshot of the ideology that gave birth to the Irish State, the 1916 Rebellion becomes infected with this violence and soon nothing redeemable can be found in it. It is the epitome of irresponsibility and evil. The next step in this reasoning is to dabble in with the conclusion, as did Conor Cruise O'Brien, that it is a conceptual category that one should dispense with altogether for its faults outnumber its qualities.[86]

5 The clash between the new historians and the Bureau of Military History

On 21 January 1986, Ronan Fanning gave a formal lecture in UCD during which he said: "The psychology of Irish historians as it evolved in the thirty years after 1938 ill-fitted them for research into the history of the Irish revolution. They shared the political sensitivities of their generation and, even had the records been available, they were not temperamentally disposed to seize upon the role of physical force as their chosen subject of research".[1] In holding this opinion, Fanning was closely echoing that of F.S.L. Lyons who wrote in 1971 that the civil war was "an episode which has burned so deep into the heart and mind of Ireland that it is not yet possible for the historian to approach it with the detailed knowledge or the objectivity which it deserves".[2]

The author would contest this assumption. It is a moot point whether the "new historians" were as reluctant to dissect the Irish Revolution and delve into its failures and paradoxes. There is indeed evidence to the contrary. To illustrate this one needs to look at their original initiative to build an oral archive and the consequent conflict which occurred between the historians and the Bureau of Military History after they teamed up to bring the project to completion. On 5 January 1943, Dudley Edwards, then Professor of Modern Irish history at UCD, drew up a memorandum on behalf of the Irish Committee of Historical Sciences in which he stressed the need for "a scientific collection of the oral evidence of the Irish people regarding the history of the last one hundred years". Displaying a healthy scepticism of history based entirely on official sources, he wrote: "Official records and newspaper reports are notoriously misleading. This will readily be appreciated if it be remembered how insufficient and inaccurate would be any account of the Irish revolution (1916–23) if based exclusively on existing documentary material".[3] Such a survey should be carried out by a "body of trained historians", with the Committee acting as the "organizational nucleus". Edwards had broached the issue with the Taoiseach, Eamon de Valera, in December 1942 and was asked to send a proposal to the government. In January 1945 the President, Sean T. O'Kelly, wrote to Maurice Moynihan, Secretary to the Department of the Taoiseach, advising that records be collected by a private commission which would work without publicity, and whose membership would be selected carefully "so that its work might not be hampered or perhaps rendered useless by the refusal of vital witnesses to collaborate with it".

On 10 October 1945, Edwards asked G.A. Hayes-McCoy to act as convenor of the Sub-Committee on Military History. Hayes-McCoy who then was an official at the National Museum accepted enthusiastically the invitation and his reply shows how frankly buoyed up with excitement he was by the potentials of this idea: "I don't imagine that posterity would forgive us if we neglected the opportunity ... Don't schemes like these, and the Davis centenary business, make you very conscious of the fact that we are such a young nation in many ways and so very anxious to prove our birthright? But they are all sound ideas and good will come of them".[4] He had himself visualized a catalogue that would have listed the material already available in the National Museum, the National Library as well as "the contents of that mysterious repository, Army Archives" and he hoped that this initiative would convince the British Authorities to disclose their own records, "which must tell half the story".

On 3 April 1946, Edwards invited some leading names of Government and opposition to a meeting designed to envisage plans for future work in Irish history.[5] As a result of this meeting, a number of prominent historians, including Edwards himself, T. Desmond Williams, T.W. Moody, Richard Hayes, Florence O'Donoghue, Gerard Anthony Hayes-McCoy, P.S. O'Hegarty, James Carty, J.H. Delargy, Denis R. Gwynn, James Hogan and Sheila G. Kennedy, joined together in an Advisory Committee to give technical advice to the civil servants hired to interview people about these decisive events. Herbert Butterfield was also invited to express his opinion on the Bureau and the quality of the work it was carrying out. After Butterfield's visit, the Director of the Bureau, Mr McDunphy, drafted a report in which he emphatically assured that the historians, including Butterfield, were satisfied with the evolution of the work, despite initial apprehensions at having a Government department directly engaged in the project. McDunphy remarked that Butterfield had expressed "doubts" regarding "the possibility of a biased selection of witnesses" but on that point too he persuaded him that "the Bureau was not erring".[6]

Yet this demonstration of goodwill failed to impress and sway Butterfield into relinquishing his philosophical principles. Asked around the same time by the Rev. A.W. Blaxall to give his opinion about the appointment by the South African government of a historical research committee to write the "real" history of events that led to the outbreak of hostilities between the Boer Republic and the British Empire in 1899, Butterfield voiced his deep distrust of official history. He doubted whether any government would in the long run invest in a kind of history which operated to the detriment of the party or the people or the nation that they purported to represent. If he conceded that governmental support might initially prove essential, especially when as in the case of Ireland the country was in the process of reclaiming itself and the organization of its historical activities was perceived as an indispensable means to it, he still remained sceptical of the outcome of such collaboration. Furthermore those cooperative endeavours smacked of self-serving orthodoxy, which "made it more difficult for a new outlook or for unwelcome revelations to make their way in the world". He added: "I have warned some of my Irish friends that at any rate I foresee difficulties in the future in respect of plans similar to the one which your letter describes. This kind of support on the part of the state may contribute something to the development of historical science at a given point in the story; but I think it is going to have its dangers sooner or later".[7] During a broadcast on Radio Eireann, on Sunday 30 October 1955, the Minister of Defence, Lieutenant-General Sean MacEoin, reiterated the autonomy of the Bureau:

> Although the work of the Bureau is financed by the State, no member of any of the Governments during whose terms of office the Bureau has operated, has, at any time, tried to influence in any way the selection of witnesses or the nature or form of evidence to be collected, or has seen or sought to see any of the material collected. In that respect, the Bureau has, since its inception, acted and continues to act as an independent body, in no way affected by political affiliations, past or present, and concerned only with the objective recording of facts.[8]

If we except Butterfield's own account, the impression given here is of agreement between the historians and the Bureau. The Bureau accepted the remit and limits of its role; the historians acknowledged the sincerity and good faith of the Bureau. Everything was progressing smoothly to the satisfaction of all the parties involved. However, the first historian to voice misgivings about the method used in the gathering of the information was Florence O'Donoghue. In his view, the work was hindered by a glaring absence of co-ordination between the material already available and the pace of research on the ground. This led to duplication of work, waste of time, effort and money, and an inevitable slowing down of the process of collection. To make things worse, the fieldworkers lacked the attuned historical sense that would enable them to detect and separate the important from the unimportant. He confided to Edwards that the investigative system in force was dangerously faulty and needed to be refined if anything worthwhile was to come from all this effort: "I have seen enough to say that the work in the South is proceeding so slowly that no member of the Advisory Committee will live to see its completion if it is continued on the present lines".[9] This picture is at odds with the one offered by the Director. Still more worrying was that the Bureau and the historians did not define a balanced historical record in the same manner. What qualities should enter into its composition? Or even what form the Chronology intended to be attached to it should take in order to be of use to the reader?

O'Donoghue believed that in the interests of impartiality, the fieldworkers had to show discrimination and acumen if they were to build a complete picture of these events, and they had to distinguish pertinent information from the trivial. But he soon realized that the civil servants were deficient in these indispensable qualities and the random and patchy methodology was not conducive to the development of this skill. He also contended that the Chronology would be of value to future research only if it patiently removed the prejudices of the past. In contrast, the bureau defined its function too literally to serve the interests of future history. As Edwards had put it in a letter to the Director, his only concern was to create an impression of great efficiency. To do this, he was prepared to build up a vast collection but allowed no consideration of what future historians might need. Rushing to amass material without a prior precise idea of what could secure the confidence of future historians was, in his opinion, preposterous and a sure way of corrupting the initial objective. Disapprovingly he concluded: "What is uppermost in your mind is that you must prevent anything being said to the members of the Bureau which might impair your authority and this is of more importance than giving the members of the Bureau that contact with trained minds".[10] O'Donoghue objected to the conception of a Chronology that recapitulated the unilateral views of any single party or intellectual authority, in this case those of the press.

On 14 March 1951, in a letter to McDunphy he argued that the Bureau should not capitulate to its unsuspectingly inaccurate and mendacious reports but seek to give the facts "fairly and impartially". To do otherwise, meant that the Bureau "lends its authority to" and "perpetuates" its errors; errors in large part unavoidable given that it was severely hindered by scarcity of information from one side of the conflict and propaganda from the other. Intractable, he protested: "No matter how you disclaim responsibility in a foreword you cannot in fact shed it".[11] It was not normal that "in only one solitary case" was "a named member of the Irish Forces given his military rank". The failure to provide more systematically this information implied that the Bureau adopted the offensive notion that "the national military forces from 1913 to 1921 were not an Army at all, but merely an armed gang".[12] Angrily he remarked: "You do not of course thereby diminish the stature of these officers; you diminish the stature of the Bureau".

But the Director was categorical in resisting any such careful trimming or grafting of the Chronology. He countered that "it was not proper for the Bureau to assume the right to determine where the truth lies" in cases where there was ostensible conflict of evidence. And by way of validation, he retaliated: "The Chronology has been studied and used by many distinguished people whose national records are beyond reproach, and none of them has suggested, as you have done, that it is biased against the IRA or any other manifestation of the national will to freedom".[13] On 12 January 1960, O'Donoghue's fears were confirmed. Apparently, Padraig Colum wrote a biography of Arthur Griffith in which the Chronology prepared by the

Bureau was quoted several times. Not only did this constitute in his opinion a breach in the policy of non-access – later imposed on the entire collection – which heightened his suspicion that the Bureau was guilty of double standards, but he also noticed again that:

> Items taken from contemporary newspapers, particularly when they referred to IRA activities, were often quite misleading in the form in which they were given. Unless one understood that all they represented was the effort of some harassed reporter twenty miles from the scene, to scratch up some kind of story for his paper, whatever he wrote being subject to editorial mutilation so as to avoid the wrath of the censor, one could not assess these at their true value. Now I fear they will be quoted, as they are quoted in Colum's book, as the gospel according to McDunphy.[14]

To O'Donoghue, method was central to the accomplishment of this great idea. That's why he proposed that the oral evidence be used in a strategic manner. The witness statements had to be directed towards filling the gaps the documents would have disclosed, together with supplementing and elaborating the information contained in them. This tactic demanded the following of two steps in a specific order. First, the taking of oral evidence could only begin when a substantial number of documents were brought together; the only exception allowed was when the oral evidence could be lost through death of the witness. Second, it implied that the investigators who set off to interview had already thoroughly digested the available documentary information relating to a period or event and assessed judiciously its reliability. On 2 March 1949 during a meeting of the Advisory Committee, he was invited to present personally his memorandum of 27 January 1949, in which he pleaded for the adoption of this method. T.W. Moody immediately supported it because "it contained three principles which were sound historical research practice". Moody added that "he was ashamed to say this Committee had approved a proposal of the Director's which was in direct conflict with one of them. It was quite clear to him now that they should reverse that".[15] O'Donoghue had been working as a member of the Bureau since 1 January 1947. He was a key figure in launching the project and had applied unsparingly his military knowledge to set out with precision its logistics. As a man incidentally caught between two rival worlds, the Military and State Authorities on the one hand, and academia on the other, he had played a vital role in defusing mutual suspicion, smoothing out violent personality clashes, and keeping the cooperation going for the sake of a scheme he regarded as crucial for the future of Irish history.

On 4 February 1948, Fianna Fáil suffered defeat at the General Election and from March 1932 was replaced by a coalition government led by J.A. Costello. On 7 April 1948, O'Donoghue was notified that his appointment would be terminated in two days "in the interests of 'economy in the Public service' and to make room for surplus army officers". Brooding over this shocking and depressing news he wrote: "It is the hardest blow I have received since all my dreams and plans for work for Ireland were shattered by the Civil War".[16] On 19 April 1948, he noted down:

> After another almost sleepless night I concluded it would be as well to let a few more responsible people protest. I wrote to Michael Costello and gave him the facts. Patrick McGrath had voiced the matter in the Dail on Sunday, but of course got no satisfaction. I'm sorry he did so. I knew nothing of his intention, nothing can be done that way and it only tends to give the thing a political complexion, which I dislike. Patrick's intentions were the best of course. But he is not the man to tackle this.[17]

On 6 May 1948, Edwards advised him to join the Advisory Committee "on the grounds that [his] knowledge both of the difficulties of the actual work and of the manner in which it was being muddled by McDunphy would be invaluable to the Committee in trying to prevent the project becoming a total loss".[18] Two days later O'Donoghue had a conversation with Michael Costello, which he later recorded in his diary:

> His interpretation of the position was more alarming ... The present Government did not want this job done in the way I would do it. They thought that too much was being made of the military side of the period. What were needed were a few good biographies, which could incorporate all that was necessary of the sordid details of the fight. The most urgent of these were one on Collins and one on Kevin O'Higgins (Beaslai being now no longer regarded with favour). As Hogan always had similar intentions to do such biographies his opposition had been spiked. I could not be controlled to do the job in a way that would suit this programme therefore I had to go. Archer was the ministerial advisor in the matter, and Archer knew me too well to make the mistake of thinking I could be diverted from an honest effort to record the truth. The whole thing was governed by the proposition that historically no credit must be given to anyone who was on the anti-Treaty side in the Civil War – no matter what their earlier services may have been. The economy aspect was of course mere camouflage ... No one would be appointed who was not a 100% Fine Gael supporter.[19]

But the most suspect thing of all was the confidentiality clause. This measure was initially construed in a limited sense. It was for those who wished that no part of their statement would be disclosed during their lifetime. But as it transpired this measure was swiftly imposed over the entire collection and automatically drew in all those interviewed regardless of whether or not they had expressed such a wish in the first place. The Advisory Committee had not been informed of this change of policy. Dismayed by the news, the historians reacted all with a mixture of disbelief, disillusionment and derision at this ludicrous clause. A letter from Edwards to Hayes set the tone: "Is one to gather from paragraph 8 that the proposal is to maintain some official as 'caretaker' at 26 Westland Row (the address where the Bureau offices were located) until the last man who claims to have been an eye-witness, no matter how youthful a one, to the events before the end of 1921, has departed this life"?[20]

Nevertheless, these men did not surrender without an honourable fight. On 14 February 1958, O'Donoghue wrote:

> I have always felt that indiscriminate tying up of this material is in fact inimical to the purpose for which the Bureau was established ... Whatever case may be made for denying ... use of the witnesses' statements, no case whatever can be made for impounding original, contemporary documents, which would be available if they had not been given to the Bureau.[21]

He had himself entrusted to the care of the Bureau a number of original documents, some his own, and some he had obtained from friends. He chose to do so on the assumption that they would before long become accessible. So he was incensed when he realized the full import of the original promise of confidentiality. On 29 April 1960, O'Donoghue detailed to Edwards the outcome of his interview with the Minister of Defence. He impressed on the Minister that Patrick Brennan, the Secretary of the Bureau, had confirmed that segregating the documents from the statements without infringing on the confidentiality promise would present no problem given that these were filed and boxed separately. This was an argument for releasing the documents which apparently contained no harmful intelligence material.[22] In a memorandum to the Defence Minister, Kevin Boland, Edwards and Hayes-McCoy explained:

> Our disquiet arises mainly from the fact that a cloak of secrecy which at the beginning covered statements made to the Bureau under a promise of their being regarded as confidential has been so extended that it now covers the entire collection and apparently precludes all examination of the material until the final work of writing begins. The material held on safe deposit is, we understand, all regarded as confidential, whether, in fact, a pledge of secrecy was originally given in respect of it or not.[23]

The imposition of this harmful proviso meant that the material could not be subjected to an indispensable review. No interim examination of the collection could render the entire endeavour useless because the fear was that "on the eventual breaking of the seals, the information contained in the material might be found to be incomplete". Under such scenario, "it [would] be then too late to fill in the gaps". Finally they asked that: "The whole position of the Bureau collection be reviewed by the government, ... consideration be given to the organization of a full survey by competent persons of the whole collection with a view to the supply where possible of information found missing and deemed necessary for the future work of the compilation of the written record".[24] Not surprisingly, the Defence Minister declined to negotiate. The government was not going to budge; in order to deflect criticism and forestall repeated requests they used the argument that they and the opposition were agreed.[25] James Hogan thought the decision unfortunate because "the contemporary documents formed the really reliable part of the collection from the historian's point of view", and foolhardy since it blocked the "weeding out of tendentious and false statements". Deeply sceptical about the soundness and logicality of this official move he claimed: "It would be rather a paradoxical result of all this gathering of historical material if it made the writing of the history of the period not only more difficult but postponed it for another generation".[26]

In fact, Hogan was perhaps not so surprised when he learnt the news of the disappointing outcome of this collaboration because he had in his more mercurial moments more or less predicted it. Already in November 1945, as soon as he heard of the ambitious plan, he had seen fit to play the part of devil's advocate and sought to rein in Edwards' enthusiasm: "Your proposals for the collection of oral material is novel and full of fine possibilities but when undertaken by a select body which would really be the organ of the State is liable to the gravest abuses. It might work out in the sort of propagandist history in which similar institutes in the USSR have been specializing".[27] Sheila Kennedy opined that "any artificial barrier calculated to interrupt controversy will be deplored" by future historians. What is more she was sure that the need for this protection was blown up because "revolutionaries are by nature extroverts [and] the vast majority of those who made statements have no desire to shun publicity".[28] Needless to say, those historians felt betrayed and indignant. They were frustrated at the curb on their influence and the lack of transparency of the Bureau. Edwards reminded his colleagues that the Advisory Committee could only tender advice to the Director. It had no control over the Bureau nor did the members of the Bureau normally attend its meetings. They were truly ignorant of what was happening since the Committee had, outside the Director's progress reports, no other information verifying that the work was being conducted in a competent fashion. There were no data to show whether any area or period was fully investigated; no evidence that existing material had been appraised to enable effective coordination between the control office and the field workers to decide whether any particular question required further coverage. He emphasized that in arranging for analogous work on the history of the First and Second World Wars, the British Foreign Office had handed over direction to trained historical students. On the basis of this example, he advised a reinforcement of the Bureau with university graduates. He was adamant that if this advice was ignored no useful purpose could be served by maintaining the Advisory Committee because, as he put it, "it was unpaid, it was impotent, and many of its members considered that on the existing basis it was condoning a deception of the public".[29]

After the Bureau's work was terminated on 31 December 1957, Edwards, still plagued with doubts, wrote to the Minister on 23 January 1958, asking what was going to happen to the material while reminding him that the Advisory Committee considered that "the most competent custodians would be the officials of the National Library of Ireland". He was informed it would be placed in the custody of the Department of the Taoiseach, confirming Edwards' fears that the historians were trapped in a situation where they had lent their reputations to an initiative in which they never had any real voice. A similar note of despondency was struck by Richard Hayes, then Director of the National Library, when, on 10 February 1958, he learnt of the final destination of the documents:

> The government's decision … does not surprise me – it is what I expected. It means, I presume, that they are now "State documents". What does it matter now what you or I think; I am regarding "you" and "I", when I say that, as members of the Advisory Committee which has ceased to exist since the winding-up of the Bureau. And even if we were still functioning, I fear we would be going outside the terms of reference under which we were set up.[30]

On 14 February 1958, Hayes replied to Edwards' appeal for further action by stating, "I think we can do nothing and I have no time to bang my head against a blank wall. Incidentally the material collected seems to me to be of so little value that I do not mourn the loss".[31]

The evidence put forward thus far may convey the false impression that the historians who cooperated in this project agreed on essentials. True, there was a common grievance about the manner in which their serious objections regarding method and policy were intentionally side-stepped. There was a fear too that the slipshod and haphazard fashion in which the information was gathered had damaged beyond repair the initial vision and the prospects of a sound modern Irish historiography. Their hopes to write as soon as possible an authoritative narrative of the Irish Revolution to counter inaccurate versions and assist Irish education were cruelly dashed by the State's embargo. They were also furious that they should receive only passing mention and all the credit go to the State when through the agency of the Sub-Committee on Military History set up by the Irish Committee of Historical Sciences they had been the true architects of this original idea. McDunphy explained the "obstructionist" moves of Edwards, O'Donoghue and Hayes-McCoy by the fact that "the establishment of the Bureau was resented by many of its members as an encroachment on their preserve and, from the very outset, they endeavoured by every possible means, either to get control of the Bureau, or to bring its work to naught".[32] But underneath a common disappointment lurked sometimes opposite epistemological and political assumptions which derived from a gap in generation and experience and were bound to colour assessments of the intrinsic value of oral history as well as expectations about its results.

James Hogan, Professor of History in University College, Cork, born in 1898, nine years older than Moody and eleven years older than Edwards, and a man caught in the vortex of Ireland's most morally exacting chapter, first as a member of the Irish Republican Brotherhood, and then, as a Free Stater attaining high rank in the National Army, found it difficult to espouse the cause of an objective history. Nor did he believe the times called for objectivity or a retreat to the ivory tower. As the Irish prototype of the anticommunist crusader of the 1930s, and the pro-Michael Collins *engagé* intellectual who watched at close distance attempts from the Old IRA and the Irregulars to topple the fledgling Irish State, for which he felt an almost paternal solicitude, he felt goaded into defending a very authoritarian type of democracy. His anxiety to protect the new state from subversion led him to become a founding member of the Blueshirt movement and its theoretical backbone and to flirt with continental fascism as represented by Mussolini, Salazar and later Franco. Something drove him to oppose Nazism, however, and to compare it incisively with communism. But unlike some secular continental voices who became famous for their heartfelt denunciation of communism in the 1940s and 1950s, Hogan was unapologetically Catholic. Faced with what his pessimistic temperament imagined as the imminent collapse of Christian civilization, he became convinced that only a corporate and vocational system based on Catholic social philosophy could arrest it.[33]

Hogan was therefore less emotionally equipped to embrace objectivity as a personal creed than were men like Moody and Edwards, who being younger, found themselves more sheltered from the painful events of the revolutionary years and the Civil war. When Hogan heard about the creation of the Irish Catholic Historical Committee in 1951, he did not disguise his pleasure and his belief that: "It was high time for Catholic Ireland to turn to its history and not to leave the materials and their interpretation to secularists or even opponents of Catholicism". He commented, "this does not mean that I am advocating a sectarian approach to history but rather that I do not believe in so called neutral or scientific history".[34]

In 1958, a certain scepticism for the real potential of oral history or the empirical method or both forced him to confess his doubts to Edwards:

> If the Bureau had confined itself to collecting documents from all possible sources – that would indeed be a very valuable work, but by getting people of all kinds to write down their recollections … a premium was put on the temptation to tendentiousness, self-glorification, partisanship and the actual manufacture, conscious or unconscious, of all kinds of exaggerations, distortions, not to speak of falsehoods. I cannot help feeling that this collection may intervene between the historian of the future and the actual facts as they happened.[35]

On 16 January 1947, Sheila Kennedy laid bare to O'Donoghue her apprehension that the methodical and carefully planned co-ordination of material might give the false impression of "a well-regimented, unified [Republican] movement". The re-invention of the past out of an "academic passion for order" was even more tantalizing in view of the unspoken desire to "lend dignity" to it by portraying the struggle for independence as "the work of an orthodox army with a G.H.Q. initiating, controlling and directing the activities of every unit throughout the country".[36] In his effort to restore her confidence in oral history, however, O'Donoghue showed accidentally insufficient awareness of the ways in which method, itself coloured by opinion, can unobtrusively colour evidence. Typically therefore his response begged this disturbing question and revealed he had more guileless faith in the possibility to get to the facts with the use of a sound technique than Kennedy did:

> There was no uniformity of military policy or tactics, no uniformity of method, of armament, of control, or even of estimation of the general situation facing the volunteers. G.H.Q. did little more than act as a brake, and as a medium for the exchange of ideas in the late stages of the struggle. These are facts, and I conceive it to be our duty to record them in such a manner that there can be no possible misconception by the historians who will some day have to assess the worth or otherwise of our work. Some widely cherished myths will, of course, be killed, and most of the romantic legends that have been snowballing for twenty-five years will not survive. I believe it to be still possible to get the facts; and if we build them up methodically and fully from their base in each separate unit of the organisations, the resulting picture must inevitably show the true state of affairs.[37]

In "Getting Our History Put Straight" written for the *Sunday Independent*, on 28 April 1946, Patrick Sarsfield O'Hegarty (1879–1955) agreed with the scientific spirit of the new school of Irish history: "Historical judgment of a lasting nature on the Insurrection and the Treaty will not be possible until a later generation, far removed from any of the prejudices, inhibitions, and lack of perspective … can sit down and consider the whole period from the death of Parnell to the Treaty calmly and judicially and on the facts". He also concurred with its visionary approach when he warned against capitulating to the mood of civic lethargy that the Civil War had bred and urged all to remember that although "We are still suffering from the effects of the split of 1922 [because] it broke up the whole spiritual mould of the Sinn Féin movement, cheapened and materialised the remnants and discouraged the best people in it", those negative feelings would pass and posterity would be eager and grateful to discover, if such evidence was collected, "the least fact about the lowliest participator in the movement".

However, unlike the new school, O'Hegarty's petition for this kind of collective work was not devoid of political motives. The documentation to be collected was all important because it could disprove the socialist analysis of the 1916 Rising espoused by British publicists "who once attributed it to the Dublin strike of 1913 because they were prepared to accept any fantastic explanation which could prevent them from having to face the unpleasant fact of an Irish National Insurrection". He also looked with favour upon anything that could shatter the illusions of "our own social ideologists" who "are constantly interpreting the Rising in the light of this or that post-insurrection ideology" in a bid to prove that James Connolly was a social reformer, that the Proclamation was intended to commit Irishmen to "some particular brand of land ownership and control" and that the ultimate goal of the leaders was a Workers' Republic, and he added: "that term being used in its current unsavoury, bloodstained, and post-Lenin sense".[38]

As early as 23 November 1947, in the same newspaper, Edwards forthrightly accused the Fianna Fáil administration of harbouring totalitarian proclivities, as it was reluctant to devolve power and trust the knowledge of specialists. In an article entitled "Fianna Fáil and Frankenstein", he rebuked the government for emulating Soviet Russia by entrusting the work to civil servants while camouflaging it to the public eye by adding a committee of historians who were powerless to do anything to advise. He concluded: "It remains to be seen whether this work will have the slightest value except to lull the old warriors into accepting pathetically the legend that a civil service file is a passport to immortality".[39] Two later articles written by Edwards, one in 1952 and another in 1954, eloquently showed that all was not well in the Utopian world of mutual cordiality and industriousness that the Press, the Bureau and the Government were trying to present to the Irish public.

In the first article, "The historian, the civil servants and the records of 1913–21", published on 25 October 1952, Edwards described the Bureau as a firm where shareholders did not have a right to expect "dividends" and had to feel pleased with a vague promise that the beneficiaries will be their grandchildren. He joked that "the audit will take place when they are dead and have been given paupers' funerals". If the children of the heroes wanted to tell their stories too, theirs would also be put away to avoid awkward questions from being asked in their own lifetimes. The same tactic could deal with "troublesome and crotchety civil servants and army officers".[40] Edwards was not afraid to scoff at the righteous and patronizing attitude of the Bureau. The tone used through the whole length of this article is one of at once controlled, savage and incisive irony.

Edwards hinted that the Advisory Committee was fully aware of what was at stake, or what went on behind the deceptive manoeuvres, the public contortions, the policy contradictions and the ingrained anti-intellectual propensities of the director. With unforgettable mordacity, he showed he could read McDunphy's mind, as he pretended to prefer political intelligence over history because the former was more useful "for building up and breaking down narratives" whereas the latter "produced the smug graduate who was not easily adapted to practical work" and irksomely "more concerned with the interpretation of documents than with their construction". Evidently one could not dispense with the historians altogether, if only because with them "constantly at his elbow", he had an invincible pretext for "depending upon his political intelligence officer".[41] To Edwards the ultimate test of the Bureau's final product was to come when the official publications edited by American, British, French and Russian historians provided a direct challenge by the quality of their own separate work. He deplored that the natural suspecting glance of the Irish was too often cancelled out by their intimidation at the hands of authorities. But he trusted that while the Bureau could easily "afford to snap at Irish sceptics" it could never do so at foreigners even if "belief in the authority of one's seals and signatures" lulled "the critical faculties of the highest officials" and "expression of commendation uttered by a distinguished foreign visitor [Herbert Butterfield]" did more harm than good.

Again, he sought to fend off his cynicism with the wishful thought that directors could not be indifferent to "a deluge of posthumous ridicule", that they were human after all, just like "dictators" were, and this made them sensitive enough about their reputations to be "far-seeing" and try to "avoid the condemnation of posterity". None of this blinded him to the fact that cold reason dictated the decision to give the job to the civil service which could usually be "depended upon to be methodical and persistent even if it rarely dared to be imaginative or over-intelligent". He urged investigators to show intelligence in dealing with witnesses. The pitfalls were many and caution had to be the rule for all but "the egotists and the impulsive". Among these were inaccuracy in reminiscing, loyalty to comrades, fear of self-contradiction, and a too ready acceptance of the myth of a happy and successful revolution. Against all these dangers, the investigator who was worth his job, had to apply adequate tests and critical deduction, otherwise, protested Edwards, "the rule of secrecy [was] but a cloak for inefficiency, the lack of opportunity for public cross-examination or professional criticism a means to perpetuate a gigantic and expensive bluff". Since cross-examination was not a possible, he was recommended to act sometimes as devil's advocate by inviting people to speak off the record, in order to gather some insight into the sympathies, apathies, dependability and balance of those interviewed. However in any case, those interviewed should not be permitted to answer solely the questions they want or to "frame them in accordance with their prejudices, honest or otherwise, or in a fashion suitable to their vanity". Edwards concluded by underscoring the ontological barrier which separated the State from the historical profession: "Bismarck once said that he was composing two separate accounts of the same incident, one for posterity and one for his own private use. The alliance between the historian and a state servant is necessarily an uneasy one. 'No man can serve two masters'. Of the civil servant who would be a creative historian, it must be demanded, again and again, that he should testify his belief that the state can do no wrong".[42]

In the second article, "Ireland's Historical Trial" published on 23 October 1954, Edwards seemed anxious to dissociate himself on behalf of the entire Irish historical profession from the shallow, facile and mawkish pronouncements of the bureau's officials. Nor did he approve of the paternalistic and overbearing attitude of the government in this whole matter. He insisted that even if historians were to take an interest in the final product of the Bureau's work, the simple application of the canons of historical criticism would ensure that: "No reputable historian will take sworn statements made twenty five years after the event at their face value. Instead, they will proceed to do what their opposite numbers do today – no doubt in some more expert way – they will consider those sworn statements as evidence for what people in 1947–1954 thought of events in 1913–1921".[43] Furthermore, he feared that the bureau had overstepped its authority when it decided to stay in "existence until every living person whom it is possible to reach has been asked to express anything they know if it is considered they have matter of importance to record on 'every piece of evidence about Ireland's history' between 1913 and 1921". This was going "beyond the proper competence of a body set up to deal with 'military history'". Clearly here we are led to believe that he suspected the government had pounced on this pseudo-anthropological initiative perhaps not so much in order to facilitate the search for the truth but more to pre-empt it by taking control and thus rendering redundant any other independent and idealistically inspired investigation. By incorporating it in the official channels of the State, the government certainly defused the potential of a project it could now oversee both financially and logistically. Equally clear is Edwards' anguished realization that by recruiting the State's financial help the historians had bartered their idealism and the high standards of their craft.

Retrospectively, his indignation at this patent infringement on the rights of knowledge by the State is somewhat puzzling because when in the 1940s he floated the idea of a State-financed Dublin Historical Institute in the hope of securing better resources, Hogan had warned him against the dangers of contamination of research by political causes and the more burdensome monetary pressures that this arrangement would have authorized.[44] In the 1970s, apparently a similar idea was resurrected by Moody and Williams and it was greeted with the same equanimity and reserve this time by Butterfield.[45] Furthermore in a letter to Aubrey Gwynn in March 1946, Edwards had himself acknowledged such a possibility, although at the time he did not think this risk was a strong reason for not seriously weighing up the plan. With undeterred passion he declared:

> On the whole question of state control I feel it difficult to be patient with an attitude which implies that the people who have been building up a tradition in Irish Historical Studies would for one moment consent

to dictation on the interpretation of history. If the State wants to hold the financial pistol to the historians' heads it can do it in very subtle ways if it likes. How did the autonomy of the university protect Mac-Neill in 1916? A mere institute will not be the end of the totalitarian state's interference. Totalitarian France in 1946 flings the Secretary General of the International Committee of Historical Sciences out of his job in the university and the president of the American Council of Learned Societies and a Professor of Balliol, Oxford condones it for he was a collaborationist. Let us try to be practical for once and admit that our objections may be valid ones but we have not yet stated them. For those we put forward as governing our views are easy to be resolved once they are put up.[46]

Edwards' steadfast intervention in the oral archive plan should be seen in the context of a personal life-long commitment to rouse consciences to the urgent need to organize national archives. It is fascinating to see such an early manifestation of a preoccupation that grew greatly with time. In 1971, Edwards, in a recurrent plea to "rescue the records" even those deemed the most trivial, defined historical evidence as being "the people's papers". He insisted that archives were no longer "confined to Governments and Institutions" and that the term could equally "be used of the collection preserved by the most insignificant individual". The function of history did not consist in writing mere propaganda as in the times of Napoleon where no one appreciated the value of a scientific history, especially not Napoleon himself who "sneered at history as the agreed lie" but "to please society by answering questions and by studying the current issues". The prerequisite for this was the preservation of "irrefutable evidence".[47] In his wish to balance out conventional political history with the voice of the people, Edwards echoed the views of his illustrious teacher, Eoin MacNeill. In the 1940s in a radio talk given on the "Preservation of Records during War", MacNeill decried the narrow focus of such history because it brainwashed people into accepting submissively to kill and die for the interests of a state: "It used to be thought by historians that everything was trivial except the achievements of statesmen and military chiefs. That sort of history is still thought good enough for schoolbooks. Its practical results on the mentality of people are written in blood and devastation".[48] This commitment to the people and their experience, one must emphasize, was just one principle of a culturalist philosophy; a philosophy deeply rooted in an astonishingly eloquent and commanding anti-Hegelianism. As the best representative of a noble cultural nationalism, one which never bowed to the fallacies of racism, and a founder of the Gaelic League, MacNeill was disconcerted by the ubiquitous State-adulation to which all his compatriots had succumbed; an enthralment all the more bewildering as their ancestors "the Gaels never entertained the least glimmer of State-worship, or of the glory that filled its ardent devotees". Although he invested all his energy to prove the rich individuality of the

Irish nation, he was never duped by the notion in vogue at the time that the State was its best custodian and its only vehicle. If to the German historicists the State was benign, to MacNeill it was the epitome of evil, selfishness and the cause of internal fracture.

On 25 November 1922 he declared: "Too much State, hypertrophy of the State, is the disease of the modern political world. A grandiose Statism was the cause of the Great War and all the little wars that have followed it, including two in Ireland". He scorned the condescending attitude of those "Antipathetic writers on Irish history, among them not a few whose stand-point is more or less patriotic" who "laid it to the charge of our forefathers, as a sort of crime or moral delinquency, that they failed to rise to the con-ception of an Irish State co-extensive with the Irish Nation". Besides the assumption behind this attitude was scientifically groundless given that "our claims to political autonomy have never been based and could not have been based on Ireland's having existed in former times as a state. They were based and rightly based on the existence of an Irish nation throughout the ages of Irish history".[49] While he conceded that some "organic cohesion" was lacking in the ancient Irish nation and that this made it vulnerable to the aggression of "a centralised external enemy", he rejected the doctrine that put "centralised government" on a pedestal and turned "passion" for it into a "national virtue" or "indifference" to it into a "national vice". He denounced the importation on Irish soil of this alien way of thinking and the damage it was causing in the Irish mind by instilling the spurious principle that "the State is a thing of transcendental sacrosanctity, for the sake of which the people should be ready to perish and, if they are not ready, should be made to perish at the hands of the truly virtuous". And he warned that "even without malice aforethought, the State is apt to be insidious".[50] One must not underestimate therefore that Edwards was trained in this strong anti-totalitarian tradition, it was inscribed in his intellectual make-up and it almost certainly shaped his political and historical vision. This outstanding episode in the development of professional Irish history is also very impor-tant in another respect; it demolishes the myth of revisionism's epis-temological naivety. There is a widespread misconception which holds that the first generation was more enthusiastically inclined towards political history and did not view with much favour or seriousness social and cultural history. J.J. Lee wrote :

> The *Irish Historical Studies* concept of a source was itself largely a product of a particular concept of history. History was essentially the study of institutions, mainly political and ecclesiastical, rather than of society or of mentalities. Sources were therefore narrowly defined. The type of source material already beginning to be widely used by some continental and American scholars, even in the study of political history, much less the type of sources used by social and economic historians, remained largely a closed book to this mentality.[51]

Here again empirical research belies this notion. The enthusiastic and earnest involvement of the "new historians" in the construction of this oral archive shows unmistakably that it is not so much that the new school was dogmatically opposed to the use of social, local and oral evidence, but more a case of this evidence having too long remained unavailable. When this information did become available and held the potential of opening new and exciting options for research, mainly by offering the unprecedented opportunity to counterbalance the picture given by official sources (which by nature carried a strong bias) the Government decided against its release. It is also likely that in their combined efforts to reverse this prejudicial state of things the historians were hoping precisely to anticipate such posthumous accusations of methodological narrow-mindedness.

As this remarkable incident shows, the new historians were not much impressed by the wobbly consensus of the first decades after independence. Nor did they feel any obligation to cultivate its allegedly benign lies or genuflect at the shrine of the new political entity. This artificial consensus rested on a consoling myth propagated through the channels of public education. This myth focused only on the external enemy, Omnipotent, Formidable Perfidious Albion, described separatism as a deep-rooted impulse emanating from the soul of Ireland, and the outcome of the struggle as a foregone conclusion. Its most remarkable feature was the all too conspicuous absence of any mention of the internal "adversaries" of the Irish Revolution. Undoubtedly its purpose was to dim the atrocious memory of the Irish Civil War of 1922–1923 but also the perhaps more disquieting and haunting memory of this other civil war avoided "in extremis" by partition in 1920. For it was feared that these two memories, if revived, could irremediably dilute the logic of Irish nationalism and undermine the foundations of the State. For instance, Frank Gallagher's mental powers of alchemy are so strong that his narrative verges on denial. Instead of being this life-shattering event which calls at least for some serious meditation on the anomalous shifting of ends and means, the Civil War is air-brushed out of the national psyche by subsuming it into the old struggle against the familiar foe. There is something poignant about this wishful thinking when in all seriousness Gallagher declares:

> The conflict is written of and spoken of as a civil war. In the mere physical sense it was that, but more deeply it was simply part of the age-long effort to make Ireland free. It was a continuance, not a new thing. It was 1803 after 1798 in a new form, a much harder form, calling for courage of a special order. Those who would not submit were many, the majority of the General Headquarters Staff, a majority of the Commandants in the field, the great majority of the Volunteers, and I believe a majority of the people too. For there was never a popular vote on the Treaty. That there was is one of the fictions that have been accepted as history.[52]

The "new historians" must have been all the more anxious to update the revolutionary era given the reality of a continual overbid for republican legitimacy on the part of the old Pro- and Anti-Treaty camps. This battle lasted well into the late 1950s and was conducted by literary spokesmen whose mission was above all one of vindication, especially when they feigned objectivity and good faith. The release of an oral archive on these events was no doubt close to their hearts because it gave them the unique chance to expose the misrepresentations of both sides and also maybe thanks to a restrained narrative, to initiate a repairing of the social fabric, torn apart by years of recrimination and resentment. The disagreement between the Bureau and the Advisory Committee is the embodiment of two separate philosophies on what is conducive to reconciliation. The historians' wish to break the silence rested on a philosophy based on truth. It represented also a wager on the virtues of this truth, "better to know what happened, and who did what than not". The State's decision to impose an indefinite sequestration was clearly founded on another opinion, that silence and not truth was the vehicle of unity.

Why the government choose to add a rider to an objective that could have been truly pioneering, nullifying its original designs, is doomed to remain a mystery. Nonetheless a hypothesis can be advanced. Lest this sound too conspiratorial or Machiavellian a view, there is definitely a paradox at the heart of these developments. Would it be wrong to say that notwithstanding the government's claim to have enforced austerely this confidentiality clause solely for the sake of the people who put their trust in them, or for the noble cause of the welfare of the nation, this decision was motivated by more prosaic motives too? After all, the Civil War and its brutality still loomed large in memories. True the terms of reference of the guidelines deliberately excluded statements concerning the Civil War.

This archive was however, predominantly oral and as such had about it an inescapable human waywardness or whimsicality that a formal cut-off point could not control. Some of those who submitted their memories of the events of the war of independence would have most certainly alluded to the traumatizing experience of the Civil War as well. Names would have been mentioned; prominent personalities directly or indirectly discussed, judged, if not incriminated. Some of this narrow partisanship would perhaps have crept into the written statements and the transcripts and coloured the general picture. So it is not unreasonable to ask whether the Minister of Defence found himself under pressure to protect the reputation of certain personalities? As Laffan has perceptively remarked:

> For many decades the Civil War continued to be a sensitive issue, and some of its survivors remained powerful; to examine their earlier careers might be unwise. Democratic Irish governments, which imprisoned and executed rebels who took arms against them, sometimes preferred not to be reminded of their own rebellious origins.[53]

The Civil War did lie like a time bomb threatening to blow up the whole undertaking. It was perceived as an annoying constriction and was a source of endless foreboding for the "new historians" and the government alike, although for opposite reasons. McDunphy was touchy about allegations that the Bureau was not entirely neutral in its pursuit of records. In August 1955 he noted: "From time to time I have had to answer charges, usually in the form of veiled innuendo, that the Bureau had been set up for the purpose of producing a history biased in favour of one particular party; a suggestion which I had immediately countered and repudiated".[54] Florence O'Donoghue who had invested all his energy and detailed knowledge of Volunteer organization in the South for the building of this historical compilation, was acutely aware that he was about to tread a mined path that demanded of him the utmost sensitivity. A confidential memorandum sent to the Irish Committee of Historical Sciences on 24 July 1945 assured that:

> Major O'Donoghue fully realises that any history written now must be produced with considerable discretion or it will result in controversy or hurt the feelings of persons mentioned or their relatives. For example, when writing the article on Tomás MacCurtain in the February issue of An Cosantóir, he was inclined in the interests of history to raise the question why MacCurtain and Terence McSweeney, as soon as they became aware that arms would not be landed in Kerry because of the loss of the "Aud", did not change the plans for attack in Easter Week in Cork which had been intended entirely to deal with the reception of the arms; to raise such a question might be regarded as reflecting on the judgment of the two leaders and might cause pain to their families, therefore he did not raise it. He equally realises that a historical record to be complete must deal with the opposition to the movement in Ireland and therefore with Irish individuals, but he sees that in most cases it would be highly undesirable in the writing of history to touch on points in which Irish persons who are still living or recently dead would appear in a bad light.[55]

James Hogan expressed his keen interest in the project given his status as the "only professional historian now left who was actually in the military movements from 1915 to 1921", but warned that the Split "which ran right through the military movement" called for the "greatest circumspection, care and objectivity". This is why he opposed the idea of governmental bodies directly choosing the future collectors because there was a danger that people who were politically motivated would have controlled the work of collection. His solution was to include on the controlling committee as many as possible of those who actually supervised the military movements during these years. The Treatyites and Anti-Treatyites needed to be represented equally because no single party had the monopoly of Truth or Right and Hogan regarded with distrust the decision that nominations by

Thomas Derrig, Sean MacEntee, Kevin Boland or Frank Aiken should automatically take precedence over those of Richard Mulcahy, Sean MacMahon or Gearoid O'Sullivan who had similarly played an important role in the military movement from the beginning to the end. Firm in his principles, he continued: "If any attempt is made on the part of the State ... to establish a monopoly in the collection of military records, I shall feel it my duty to oppose it and I have no doubt that Richard Mulcahy will take the same view. I will resist any attempt to vest the control of such an all important undertaking in the hands of the State, that is to say, in the hands of the ruling party, which, it is to be remembered, has its roots in a civil war".[56]

Over the years, Irish revisionism has been arraigned for being overly fixated on facts. Facts can turn into a hindrance when there are too many because they drown the central meaning of the Irish historical experience. However the moral rationale behind this empirical "fixation" is overlooked. Facts were to lay the foundations for a mature understanding of Irish history and the conditions for a real reconciliation among Irishmen of all stripes. The historians imagined a social cohesion this time predicated no longer on silence, the suppression of unpalatable truths, the exclusion of the Ulster or Southern Protestant or the muzzling of dissenting voices inside the nationalist family, but instead on the therapeutic virtues of the truth however unsettling it might be. Willey Maley has argued that by invoking the spectre of physical violence, revisionism wanted to censure the dissenting voices of those who sympathize with Irish nationalism. Its inadequacy is that it is a reaction rather than a response to violence and that is why it is concerned as much with concealing as with healing the wounds of Irish history. That is also why it has a tendency to dissolve conflict into consensus.[57]

Clearly this statement is non-historical and a distortion of the unfettered and audacious spirit at work in revisionism from its beginnings. As it transpires through their handling of the oral archive dispute, historians were devoted to establishing the best conditions conducive to an authentic dialogue inside Irish society. They were not interested in consensus. They wanted to divulge the truth in all its petulance and cantankerousness, even if this meant forcing Irish people to face the suffering they had inflicted on each other in the name of sacrosanct or lofty ideals. Theirs was a job of reactivation of differences, and transformation of dissent into something admirable and respectable. If there were ever a desire to manufacture a phoney consensus in Ireland one would more likely find it not among historians but on the side of the political elites. Indeed, despite seemingly insurmountable ideological differences, Fine Gael and Fianna Fáil would both come to appreciate in due course the virtues of silence or induced public amnesia. With the experience of governing with the threat of irreconcilable extremists hanging over them, each party had to use tactics which were perhaps justified politically but forever deprived them of a high moral ground. Fine Gael did not want things to be stirred up for fear that its authority be challenged by those who opposed the Treaty and saw the Free

State as an imposture. Fianna Fáil it did not want to be reminded of a major anomaly at the heart of its ideology, which was responsible for sending many courageous Irishmen straight to their deaths: the fact that in 1922 the oath of loyalty to the King was presented as the ultimate act of betrayal of the Republic, something no true Republican could ever surrender to, and yet only five years later, faced with the prospect of yielding real power, de Valera swallowed his pride and took the oath by dismissing it as an "empty formula". No one was more aware of the impending discredit in this opportunistic volte-face than de Valera himself when in April 1948, summoned as a witness in the Sinn Féin funds case, he hijacked the legal proceedings for his own benefit by expatiating on how he and his supporters managed to enter the Dail without taking the oath.[58]

In 1936 during a Fianna Fáil meeting in New Ross he proposed that a historical commission of enquiry be set up to examine independently and scientifically the sequence of events leading up to the Treaty and the start of the Civil War. This is an unambiguous hint that de Valera was obsessed with the verdict of history and the indictment that he, more than any other high-profile figure inside Sinn Féin, by doing too little to stop defiance in the Army was responsible for the dramatic drift towards civil war. There are thus grounds to think that de Valera and his associates would have felt some trepidation at the idea of an independent investigation into the origins of the Civil War. After a meeting with the Taoiseach on 13 June 1946, O'Donoghue received the impression that: "while he would appreciate and welcome the technical assistance of persons like Edwards, control and direction should be in the hands of old army men".[59] If he saw a benefit in wooing and winning the favours of the historians, he also guessed that their role had to be circumscribed as their kind of history would certainly have disinterred too much embarrassing information and thrown the mud too widely.

The evidence also suggests that Fianna Fáil, the party with the longest record in power during the lifespan of the Bureau, must have felt itself to be on the horns of a great dilemma. On the one hand, they probably saw a golden opportunity to appear publicly confident in the favourable verdict of history as well as high-minded, ground-breaking, equitable in their willingness to extend an invitation to their opponents to give their version of events and finally honourable in their decision to finance this risky business. Would we be assigning ignominious intentions if we said that Fianna Fáil was hoping to capitalize by showing that the "slightly constitutional" party had now become fully democratic? Would we be unreasonable if we supposed that de Valera wanted to give the lie to Richard Mulcahy for whom Fianna Fáil could never "safely be left unwatched"?[60] Surely men who assist the ideal of historical truth with such fair-mindedness cannot be the assassins or anarchists of Cumann na nGaedheal propaganda. They wanted all to believe they were paragons of democratic virtues who were prepared to let the sharp light of science illuminate a dark moment of history. So all the necessary steps had to be taken to ensure that they would earn the trust both of Fine Gael and the voters. On the other hand a contrary impulse, the fear of exposing the turmoil and scarring frictions inside the Republican camp, especially after 1923 when de Valera succumbed to the comforting bosom of conventional politics, possibly forced them to police more and more tightly the method and the final product.[61] In the end, the opting for silence by deferring all engagement with the collected information, after years of dithering on how to carry out a project bristling with difficulties, is the best testimony to the feeling that regardless of their aura of martyr and their perceived moral advantage over the winners, even the losers stood more to lose than to gain from any disclosure. It is clear that any attempt to probe objectively into what was from the beginning not just a simple war of independence but the story of a people profoundly divided in their loyalties and interests between Protestant and Catholic in Northern Ireland, Castle Catholic and Protestant Nationalist, Irish Parliamentary Party and Sinn Féin, Irish Republican Army and Royal Irish Constabulary, Pro-Treaty and Anti-Treaty in the South, would have destroyed the convenient myth of Britain's extraordinarily evil manipulation of the Irish.[62]

That's why the proposal of a documentary and oral reconstruction of the Anglo-Irish war was always bound to be also an oblique invitation to explore the reality of Irish internal disunity. It is worth recounting this exemplary avant-garde attitude of the "new historians" because it does convey something of the innate suspicion of those intellectuals towards the state and of their resolve henceforth to adopt a critical position vis-à-vis all invocations of *raisons d'état* and considerations of party image. At some point it must have dawned on them that the whole venture might degenerate into a public relations exercise on behalf of the Government, that perhaps this was all along the Bureau's calculation and that they were simply solicited to give it a veneer of objectivity, integrity and prestige. Hence their resentment at having their names associated with an enterprise shorn of its originally innocent and open-minded intent. Would they have put their opposition so strongly to the way the Bureau was impairing the creation of a reliable historical record to the Minister of Defence and to the Press if they had themselves been prone to feelings of cowardice and weakness? Is it not more realistic to suppose that if they shared in these feelings, they would have adopted the ostrich's tactic of burying its head and ratified the work of the Bureau irrespective of how flawed they found it to be? The consistency with which the most eminent voiced his dissatisfaction is evidence of his refusal to debase the standards of professional Irish history, let an opportunity for collective catharsis be lost and silence the truth for the sake of a few reputations or ephemeral political susceptibilities.

There is thus, serious evidence against Fanning's contention of the reluctance to embark upon a study of the Troubles on grounds of political prejudice and emotional vacillation. The quarrel between the Advisory

Committee and the Bureau of Military History proves rather that the new historians deemed themselves professionally and emotionally mature to confront head-on the implications of the contradictions, errors and failures of the Irish Revolution. Their determination to bring all this information out in the open signalled that they believed the Irish people were adult enough to assimilate history's tragic lessons and sublimate the pain of the Civil War into a new wisdom. It is far from sure that, given the opportunity of seizing this new evidence, they would have chosen to postpone this vital experience of national soul-searching.

Part III

The Great Famine

The crisis of representation and the limits
of empirical history

6 Weaknesses in ethnographic method

It is estimated that during the Great Famine between 1845 and 1850 one million people died of hunger, fever and disease and another million emigrated. The accounts of the Famine in the nineteenth century bore eloquent witness to the interpretative rivalry between the theory of classical political economy and the theory of Irish separatism. It was predictable therefore that they would propose opposed views on the causes, the scale and the consequences of this catastrophe. However, what is striking is that these two competing histories also present discursive similarities. Hence both discourses subsumed the Famine under a teleological perspective either of progress or liberation. Isolated as a unique moment, the Famine had become what the opposed parties wanted it to be; for some it confirmed historical continuity and represented a necessary stage of the evolution, for others it denied it and epitomized a radical break with the past.

Once immersed in this exorbitant indoctrination, the awesome challenge facing Irish revisionism was to retain some distance from these two formidable discourses. It had to allow their value systems enter in its estimations to deepen understanding of how this event happened while being careful not to be unduly influenced by their smooth or suave rendition of the facts. In 1817, the Reverend Thomas Malthus came to a deduction terrible in its simplicity: "The land in Ireland is infinitely more peopled than in England; and to give full effect of the natural resources of the country a great part of the population should be swept from the soil".[1] In 1848, Charles Trevelyan said with no compunction that the Famine presented "a great opportunity offered by an all-merciful Providence".[2] Trevelyan was the Assistant Secretary to the Treasury and could use this naturalizing speech to refuse important famine relief at the height of the catastrophe and impress the contention that intervention would inhibit the forces of the market. In 1598 Edmund Spenser declared: "Until Ireland can be famished, it cannot be subdued".[3] Irish Nationalists saw the Famine as the last stroke of evil inspiration of Britain and took Spenser's declaration literally, as an admission of criminal premeditation. The prediction of a violent transformation, to which was added a sinister resonance by the word "famished" seemed to have been fulfilled by the Famine.

It all happened as if Nature had granted the wishes of British power, showing thereby that God approved of the imperial mission. In the nineteenth century, British educated opinion caricatured the Irish as incurably indolent and primitive. The dominant opinion was that congenital weaknesses rather than colonial oppression had caused economic retardation. This debility coupled with agrarian rioting and a pattern of abortive rebellions confirmed Ireland as ungrateful and impervious to any beneficial incursion of progress. Resistant to the ideology of progress, Ireland became this obstacle that had to be rooted out if a noticeable change in the Irish temperament did not happen. Thus in 1839, Thomas Carlyle repeated the imperative of coercion: "The time has come when the Irish population must be improved a little or exterminated".[4] The economist Nassau Senior wrote a masterpiece of distortion in 1849 in which he presented assistance as the real problem.[5]

The belief that one should let the situation take its natural course attained the heights of philosophical wisdom so much so that many intellectuals hardened their hearts to the sufferings of the Irish people, persuading themselves that to act otherwise would have run contrary to the laws decreed by nature. Ideological constraints had thus indubitably increased the probabilities of the disaster. Extended over a period of five years, the sums distributed by Westminster represented only roughly 0.3 per cent of the annual gross product of Great Britain. The historians, Joel Mokyr, S.J. Donnelly and Cormac O Gráda contrasted the lack of generosity of the British Government throughout the Famine with their eagerness to spend almost £70 million a few years later in an "entirely futile expedition in Crimea". Anticipating objections O Gráda argued that this comparison between arms and food was neither odd nor marred by anachronism since the opponents of governmental policy had also used it as a convincing argument.[6]

The attitude of the government was indeed criticized by many decent people who could not understand how in a time of peace, one could leave the famished to die in the name of the principles of political economy. An acknowledged fact is that the export of grain and meat never stopped during the Famine, even when human losses reached a frightening number. However, historians have found that grain and food exports were greatly reduced in the 1840s. The post-revisionist opinion has also stressed that even in a situation of maximum productivity with no exports the shortage of food caused by the failure of the potato crop could not have been compensated by the grain harvest. Emigration and hunger had been recurring features of the nineteenth century and the lack of food variety and the dependency on the potato rendered the rural population vulnerable to this catastrophe. Directly rebutting the assumptions of Malthus and Spenser, Joel Mokyr and Cormac O Gráda have proved that Ireland was not the victim of overpopulation. Roy Foster has argued that to put an end to exports during a famine was an unfamiliar notion not only for the region of the British Isles but also for the rest of Europe.[7] The organization of relief, in the form of the government purchasing food for distribution, required the adoption of powers that no contemporary government possessed, and inevitably caused violent resistance among the farming classes. Foster, however, admitted that "fundamentally, relief was up to government initiative; and this, in the long run, was not up to the challenge".[8] Later he qualified his initial relativist reading in another essay in which he closely examined the ever-changing nature of the Union and the ambiguities and eccentricities that accompanied the Unionist Government since 1801.

He saw the Famine as emblematic of the dissonance between the theory and the practice of the British–Irish connection. Thus, he admitted that the British Government were guilty of double standards for discounting the full import of the Union or defaulting on their constitutional obligations: "Here, the theory of the Union should have worked to the Irish advantage; by spreading the burden and the cost on to the private rates and public revenues of the largest possible unit, the united Kingdom. But the practice was exactly the opposite: Ireland paid, or did not pay, county by county, and people died like flies".[9] Graham Davis opined that the world's richest nation responded with culpable inefficiency and a degree of "moral distancing".[10] George Boyce claimed that the Famine was not unique, the government was not influenced by racist feelings and it was unreasonable to expect ministers to have done more, after all, he insisted, "early Victorian government was not in the business of providing state support on any considerable scale, and certainly not enough to cope with the Irish famine; the age of *laissez-faire* was not the age of the welfare state".[11] The opinion that a decision must be reliant on established norms and precedents leaves one with a feeling of dissatisfaction because it tends to make too many allowances for the government. Its passivity is explained away with outwardly cant excuses such as because there were other famines before the Great Famine of 1845–1848 or because such practices of direct intervention in the economic sphere were not common or even because the famine had not affected all the country identically, the British Government could not weigh up its gravity and work out immediate solutions.

To put it differently, the acute fear in certain quarters was that the general direction of revisionism, by recounting too closely the cultural and structural context of the nineteenth century, risked endorsing, rather than critiquing, the jaundiced portrayal of Ireland by imperial economists. Similarly, by laying too much emphasis on the weaknesses of the Irish economy then, historians forgot to unearth the original causes behind them. In 1849, in a letter to Trevelyan, the Quaker Jonathan Pim observed "the Government alone could raise the funds, or carry out the measures necessary in many districts to save the lives of the people".[12] And as the studies by O'Sullivan and Lucking showed, within thirty years, in another part of the British Empire, within the lifetimes of many of those involved in the implementation of famine policy in Ireland, famine policy did change. An active scheme of prevention was launched, fine-tuned and proved successful. O'Sullivan poignantly remarked that it was not unusual for the Irish Nationalism of the late nineteenth century to wonder sometimes what Ireland's fate might have been if the country had been conquered by another empire. He himself concurred with these sentiments when he declared that the "history of famine policy within the British Empire showed that this was an unusual Empire among Empires: the British Empire was an Empire capable of shame".[13] Here the own-sakeist method is found inadequate and is challenged by a new generation of experts. The principle that one should study the past on its own terms, by engrossing oneself into the system of political criteria of other times so as to grasp their alien logic and avoid the temptation of judging situations with modern criteria, is here demolished on its own ground. For it is proved that already then, influential personalities reacted to this desperate situation on the basis of humanitarian impulses comparable with those invoked during the twentieth century. Terry Eagleton defined ideology as "the naturalisation of culture" or as a "device" which transmutes history itself into a "seamless evolutionary continuum", endowing every event, phenomenon or institution with all the "stolid inevitability of a boulder".[14]

The dull and neutralizing certainties of political economy could not however convince Irishmen that there were not strong racial connotations behind British attacks on the rural culture and economy of Ireland. These racist undercurrents confirmed them in their opinion that the Famine amounted to genocide. The man who demystified the providential explanation was John Mitchel. Unveiling once and for all the artifice of the naturalizing discourse, he made this important clarification: "The Almighty indeed sent the potato blight, but the English created the Famine".[15] But in his visceral indictment of British rule Mitchel did not content himself with lifting the naturalizing veil of imperialist ideology; he also invented his own teleological fiction in which the Famine became the sinister symbol of colonial history and the proof par excellence of Ireland's victimization in the hands of a callous oppressor.

In his introduction to *The Jail Journal*, Mitchel masterly produced a version of Irish history in which all the elements were subordinated to a diatribe against English tyranny. From Cromwell down to the 1848 uprising, all was depicted as a catalogue of oppression. As Patrick O'Farrell put it, "his withering prose created an unforgettable image of the Famine as starvation in the midst of plenty".[16] It was the etched yet not entirely authentic memory of huge starvation while Ireland was compelled to send its surplus produce to feed England. Mitchel claimed that the Devon Commission of 1843 had nothing fortuitous about it. Far from being an innocent initiative it was a villainous design to rid Ireland of its surplus population. What was set down in the Commission report in 1845 as a straightforward analysis of the size of holdings and the need to make them more economically viable, albeit in the interests of landlords and strong farmers, he read as a conspiracy to annihilate the cottiers and the labouring poor.

Mitchel wanted to prove that the idea of surplus population had become axiomatic in English political circles prior to the Famine and that the Famine provided a superb opportunity to carry out this "clearance": "The potato blight and consequent Famine placed in the hands of the British Government an engine of state by which they were eventually enabled to clear off not a million, but two millions and a half of the surplus population to preserve law and order in Ireland (what they call law and order) and to maintain the integrity of the English for this time".[17] The charge of genocide was not without weight as it had a fictional precedent. It revived Jonathan Swift's infamous satirical essay *A Modest Proposal* in which he recommended the eating of babies as a cure to overpopulation. As hinted by O'Farrell, the genocide thesis had irresistible accents because it lifted the tragedy to the status of high drama, with "villains" in the highest political places bustling about to engineer a monstrous plot capable of causing "racial extermination, emigration and big land clearances in the interests of economic principles and power".[18] The Famine became the real face of British domination and the catalyst for the resurgence of nationalism.[19] It was also the incontrovertible proof of the failure of the Union. It provided late nineteenth-century separatism with the undeniable claim that the British Government was incompetent or worse indifferent to the interests of the Irish. S.J. Donnelly stated, "The evocation of mass starvation and forced emigration became part of the attack on the twin targets of landlordism and British government developed by Parnellite nationalism".[20] This social catastrophe, so the argument went, could never have happened, had there been an Irish parliament, accountable and responsive to the needs of Ireland and its people. In the light of this tragedy the Union appeared wholly negative and it seemed tendentious to attempt its rehabilitation.

Terry Eagleton averred that this was however the outcome of a new history which flinched from looking at fundamental causes. This history concentrated only on the effects of the property system and stopped short from engaging in a radical critique of it. Eagleton condemned this conservative disposition and its too naïve acceptance of the naturalizing rhetoric with which the Famine was apparelled. It concealed a fraudulent aspect because it described the property relations imposed in nineteenth-century Ireland as normal. The typical gesture of revisionism, according to him, was to take these property relations for granted, to postulate these as some impassable horizon, and then to argue the toss within these constricted limits. By doing this, Irish historians re-enacted the mental habits of the Victorian economists who assumed that the structure of capitalist relations fell beyond the bounds of criticism. Thus he insisted, "Much of the historical debate over the Famine was thus loaded from the outset, secretly governed by what it dogmatically excluded as a legitimate topic of enquiry".[21] Given those property relations, the Famine became inevitable once the potato crop failed; yet what demanded attention was that there was nothing inevitable or unyielding about the relations themselves. So Eagleton was not being only polemical when he protested that Irish historians were quicker to pounce on the naturalizing stratagems of nationalist mythology instead of being more alert to their own naturalizing habits of mind. It is sensible to ask whether revisionists trusted too much the historicist method in their treatment of the Famine. There is indeed a danger in it for in his concern to contain the excesses of judgement the researcher can hamper his critical capacities. In their introduction the editors of *The Great Famine* declared:

> The timidity and remoteness of the administrators in the 1840s may irritate the modern observer who unhesitatingly accepts the moral responsibility of the state to intervene in economic affairs in a time of crisis. But it needs patience to realize that what is obvious and uncontroversial today was dark and confused a century ago to many persons of good will.[22]

Certainly there is truth in this statement and this method can be rewarding when one tries to fathom the incapacitating hesitations and the mistakes of the ministers, how and why the situation got perilously out of control. But can it not also turn into an excuse for the lack of vision and courage of these officials? An historian who uses only this method can be on a slippery slope. The rights of the workers in the big factories at the start of the industrial age as well as the rights of the tenant farmers in the rural world all have been gained thanks to a persevering battle against tradition. The critique of this tradition was and is still the cornerstone of progress in Europe. Nothing of the sort would have been accomplished if everyone had genuflected at the feet of industrialization, capitalism and economic *laissez-faire*. Understanding a different age should not amount to surrender to its prejudices.

The dethronement of a superior morality, the refusal to appeal to Justice or Reason as countervailing forces against the logic of economics or the logic of the state is problematic. If the historian always forbids himself the use of these universal anchors to form a more detached judgement, the institutions, conventions and norms of the past could soon pass for natural phenomena to endure submissively regardless of how brutal they have proved to mankind. Furthermore once his suspecting glance is crippled, the historian is reduced to being a mere chronicler of crimes, robbed of his most precious gift, that of ripping apart the veil of fatality and becoming through a polyvalent method an active agent of change. As he reflected on the world caught in the maelstrom of the Great War, J.H. Sheenan blamed Georg Hegel for the impasse. In a letter to Edmund Curtis, the renowned Irish mediaevalist historian, he disclosed his estrangement from colleagues who were at ease with the inbuilt passivity of German historicism:

> Beaven, with whom I am in many respects strongly in sympathy, prides himself upon being no philosopher, accepts political institutions and interstate animosities as ultimate facts, which it is useless and silly to criticise, and in general takes a historical rather than a philosophical

point of view. Perhaps he is wisest after all. I have my knife into political philosophers, because while emphasizing the impossibility of dis-
severing the individual and the state, they mostly talk as though states
themselves were absolutely instated individuals, each free to pursue its
own ends without regard to those of any other. Hegel is the worst
offender.[23]

Yet Eagleton's attack is not fully justified either. In their preface, the
editors approved of James Connolly's diagnosis. They cited his provocative
aside that "No man who accepts capitalist society and the laws thereof can
logically find fault with the statesmen of England for their acts in that awful
period".[24] Connolly was infuriated by the hypocrisy of those Irish politicians
who rushed to denounce the passivity of the English Establishment and yet
did nothing during and especially after the Famine to reform this unfair
system. They also stated that their reading was very similar to his, once
Connolly's position was shed of its Marxist dogmatism:

> In the ultimate analysis, the picture that emerges from modern research
> has much in common with James Connolly's sketch in *Labour in Irish
> History*. We may reject his attempt to force the picture into a doctrinaire
> frame, but we must recognize with him that the evil spirit of the Great
> Famine was the history of Anglo-Irish relations in the very widest sense
> over a long period.

Why then did this wisdom seem wasted somehow? Was it not because
Irish revisionists targeted this injustice only in the abstract, as if that system
had no face and was not represented by an elite? This critique also seemed to
disallow itself by its reluctance to judge the decisions of those who benefited
from this unjust system. Nobody is responsible because everybody is. The
problem, would reply an activist, is how do you fight an omnipotent
system? One needs to start from somewhere, and even if it is unpalatable to
the historian who may think his job is simply to describe what happened
with as much precision as possible and not to arrogate himself the status of a
hanging judge, he needs to follow through the logic of his critique and
identify those groups whose policies made the plight of the labouring poor
in Ireland worse by condemning them to a sure death or exile. The first
demographic and economic analyses did succeed in correcting the distorted
picture of the Famine spread by nationalism and colonialism. Still, as Eagleton underlined, there was a harmful tendency in early revisionism to confine
itself to the passive reporting of the structural shortcomings of the nin-
teenth-century system and a reluctance to linger on the causes of these
faults. Moreover, by trying to neutralize the impact of this disaster in the
name of moderation, it risked falling into the trap of condoning.

These blinkers imposed on the historian a unidirectional gaze and forbade
him from looking backwards, into more essential causes, such as the exist-

ence of a vindictive economic status quo bolstered by an ideology which tolerated massive eviction, emigration and death on a large scale in the name of the balance of the market forces. Compelled to debate within the terms imposed by a rigoristic historicism, the discourse of the historian soon found itself in a state of collusion with the colonialist discourse as everything he observed, he refuted, judged and evaluated solely in relation to time, place, context and environment. For with this system, he is taught to discover, not whether the government was right or wrong, but how their attitude was historically conditioned and their action inherent in the dialectic of events. Eagleton concluded:

> Most historians are unwitting positivists, wary of what Hegel called the power of the negative, reluctant to grasp what happened in the light of what did not. They are also, commonly enough, ethical relativists in practice if not in theory, given to exculpating some piece of historical inhumanity on the grounds that one could have expected nothing more high minded of the age in which it occurred.[25]

Cormac O Gráda thought that Irish historians were "a rather conservative bunch".[26] Yet he also conceded that an academic representation of the Famine posed a considerable stylistic challenge, which was bound to act as a deterrent. Indeed the issue remained so emotive that any attempt at balance always risked being read as an extenuatory pretext. This went some way to explain why "the historiography of the Famine had been muted", and why the *Irish Historical Studies* journal, then five decades old, had carried only half a dozen contributions on famine-related topics. As for the record of *Irish Economic and Social History*, O Gráda noted it was no better since it had failed to carry a single piece on the Famine since it first appeared in 1974.[27]

The Famine is perhaps best conceptualized as the site of a conflict between intentionalists and structuralists, for no other event of Irish history raises as much the sensitive questions of coherence and intention. This becomes apparent when one looks at the objections raised against the book of Cecil Woodham-Smith. Woodham-Smith was no academic historian but she was an impressive researcher whose work was based on previously unused archival material. Her book, *The Great Hunger*, published in 1962, became an instant success with the public and the elite, notably with Eamon de Valera who paid her the honour of attending the public lecture she gave at Trinity College in late 1963.[28] Its one outstanding quality is that contrary to revisionism's recoil from venturing down the path of original causes, it described at great length the system of property relations which oppressed all the farming class. She wrote: "All this wretchedness and misery could, almost without exception, be traced to a single source, the system under which land had come to be occupied and owned in Ireland, a system produced by centuries of successive conquests, rebellions, confiscations and punitive legislation".[29] This assertion may sound simplistic or demagogic but it had at least the merit of examining the brutal functioning of the system, and how the poor peasants caught up in it, were turned, in the words of Eagleton into "labouring instruments and fertilising mechanisms, in a kind of savage Swiftian reductionism utterly out of key with the legitimating idioms of cultural idealism".[30] It insisted on the pernicious role of the middleman, the absenteeism of the landlords, the non-fixity or insecurity of the tenures, the outrageous subdivision of land, the enormous competition for land and the extravagant increase of the rents, the fact that the tenant could be evicted at any moment without any compensation even when he had improved the state of his holding. It was a devilish parody of a system that conceded no right to the tenant farmers and every right to the landlords and its lack of fairness only betrayed its shameful origins in a massive enterprise of purposeful depredation. Although a good friend of Cecil Woodham-Smith, R.D. Edwards was not blind to the weaknesses in her approach:

> How will Cecil Woodham-Smith tackle the Famine? It seems a safe bet that she will tie it to a few personalities – administrators, landlords, and gombeenmen. There will also be a chance to enliven the generalization that Ireland has in consequence bedevilled the good relations of Britain and America. In the last resort, this is in danger of not being history. The pouncing upon the conspicuous personality and the vivisecting of him may create a caricature (sic) and impose upon him a type that is only partly illustrative ... There is also the danger of accepting some contemporary thesis such as that of the Economist that the landlords were to blame.[31]

Edwards noticed a propensity to inflate the importance of the English minister and impute culpabilities too rashly. When she reasoned, "all this wretchedness and misery could, without exception, be traced to a single cause" – the land system, F.S.L. Lyons retorted "that phrase a single source betrayed an attitude of mind which was not, in the deepest sense, historical!"[32] He then took issue with the excess of confidence running through her narrative. He readily acknowledged her remarkable powers as a descriptive writer but could not help confessing disappointment at how overly smoothly her narrative ran. It was "limid as a pool is limpid". It lacked "depth" or "awareness"; "that lurching, nagging uneasiness, which is the hall-mark of the true historian", and warns him that "however prolific his sources" are "there are still problems to be solved and much that remains untold." He was, however, on firmer ground when he criticised her representational style. Yet Lyons was not being totally consistent here since in 1957, he too saw fit to elaborate on the existence of an underlying determinism: "We can see now that the Great Famine was a logical consequence of a vicious system of land-holding, a pitifully backward agriculture, and a social structure which invited disaster".[33]

7   Theoretical underpinnings and their impact

From its beginnings, Irish revisionism faced methodological doubts. To find inspiration and put flesh on some of them the founders of the new school came into contact with the finest minds during their training in England and invited them to address the meetings of Irish historians in Dublin. Herbert Butterfield is the most recognized influence. However, another as important was Michael Oakeshott (1909–1990). Oakeshott was invited to supply the opening paper to the first volume of *Historical Studies*, published in 1955. There are in Edwards' diary repeated notes on Oakeshott's book, *Experience and its Modes*, published in 1933 and on a lecture called "The activity of being an historian" he gave at the Second Conference of Irish Historians. In his own paper called "An agenda for Irish History, 1978–2018", and read before the Irish Historical Society, on 10 January 1978, Edwards approved of Oakeshott's own-salicism and especially his departure from the quest of origins.

The reminder of how misguided was the search for origins was unpleasant, granted Edwards, until historians remembered what empirical research had taught them; mainly that the documentation on "origins" found in archives was never disinterested and therefore could not be trusted. Increasing familiarity with the archives made historians develop a fine-tuned awareness of how self-serving and loaded was the claim of origins on the part of administrators. The likelihood of them succumbing to this temptation was so strong that Edwards compared it to original sin because they constantly felt the need to find ways of strengthening their reputation in the eyes of the people they represented. Thus as a result of this ploy, one could find an administration basing its documents on fabrications or statements not taken from contemporary documentation, but linking through artifice its activities to those of a comparable institution in the past. He insisted that historians were no mere archivists, because contrary to the latter, they were expected to possess a deepest knowledge of the circumstances which drove an administration to engage in telescoping. Only a rigorous critical appraisal of sources could protect historians from face value acceptance of the administrator's declarations concerning his material.[1] In *Experience and its Modes*, Oakeshott explained why the search for original causes was a red herring:

Explanation of change in terms of general causes implies that a single historical event may be abstracted from the world of history, made free of all its relations and connections, and spoken of as the cause of all that followed it ... And when events are treated in this manner, they cease at once to be historical events. The result is not merely bad or doubtful history, but the complete rejection of history.[2]

Oakeshott regarded enquiry into "origins" with suspicion because this activity led one to read the present into the past and thus assimilate the past to subsequent events. Such "practical-mindedness" looked to the past to supply information about the "cause" or the "beginning" of an already specified situation: "governed by this restricted purpose, it recognises the past only in so far as it is represented in this situation, and imposes upon past events an arbitrary teleological structure". This method rested on a preconceived logic since "instead of provoking the enquirer to discover the manner in which one concrete situation was mediated into another, it provoked him merely to an abstract view of the past appropriate to the abstraction he has chosen to investigate".[3] This was a warning that all revisionists were to heed in the following years.

Transposed to the reading of the Famine and the Union, this caution against telescoping radically changed the manner in which these processes and phenomena had been conceptualized by traditional historians. The Union stopped being singled out as an irredeemably evil concept, which almost mechanically caused the Famine. The Famine ceased being this genocide brought about through the Machiavellian alliance of the landlords and the British Government. Of course, the system of property relations remained an ominous contributory factor, but instead of being conceived as an absolute cause from which every other tragic occurrence unfolded, it was demoted to the role of fertile ground, thereby mentally freeing historians to look for other "contributory factors".

This enabled them to explore with more depth what it takes to create a famine and to apportion blame in a more careful manner. Revisionists were no longer satisfied with Woodham-Smith's assertion that "the primary object of the Union was not to assist and improve Ireland but to bring her more completely into subjection",[4] but sought to register the gap between intention and actual outcome. These new readings complicated Irish history, made it less "hospitable" or "habitable" because to paraphrase Foucault, they robbed the "sovereign consciousness" of the illusion of controlling again all that had once eluded her. More significantly, these readings were provocative because they underplayed control and calculation and foregrounded underlying determinism, to the point whereby the Famine came to be seen as an unavoidable ecological disaster.[5] Theodore Hoppen stated that the Famine could not have been anticipated: "This, indeed, was part of the trouble, and explains much about both the nature of the popular reaction and the manner in which the government responded to the catastrophe".[6]

However, more recent studies carried out by post-revisionists such as Peter Gray[7] and Christine Kinealy[8] have revived the old "intentionalist" opinion that the British Government was guilty in its handling of the Famine. Perhaps wisdom resides in the awareness that the trap always beguiling the historian is the tipping of the scales too much in favour of one paradigm to the detriment of another. In his review of *Historical Studies*, in 1958, Edwards' first impulse was to praise the scientific principles laid down by Oakeshott:

> Now this attitude to history might appear to restrict the activities of historians. In actual fact it makes their interests more exciting; within a more limited field they are obliged to be much more careful in what they say, and if they keep to their own rules, if they do not seek for the origins of movements, or attempt to trace cause and effect, they can gain a knowledge of the past far more coherent than has ever been achieved previously. It will be a past divorced from the present, which would otherwise be condemned in the future.[9]

Yet, strangely enough, he was also to voice oblique misgivings about them in other journalistic interventions. In his review of Mary Bromage's *De Valera and the March of the Nation*, he confessed his suspicion not only for the way in which de Valera saw the role of historians but also in a more tortuous fashion for the minimalism prescribed by Oakeshott. We know from other articles written for the *Leader* around the same time, that he was no admirer of de Valera. He thought his policies were parasitical and an encumbrance to youthful energies. He declared de Valera guilty by association: "History said Napoleon is the agreed lie. To Henry Ford 'history is bunk'. Are we to assume that great men fear the adverse verdict of history and try to pre-empt it by casting doubt on its validity before it is even recorded?" Napoleon feared the negative verdict of a trial process he could not control; so, he wished to discredit the enlightening potential of history. De Valera must also fear the verdict of Irish historians, which is why he is so anxious to define proper history as a "chronological conspectus of events in a particular context" and reduce their role to that of mere archivist. His assertion that "it was not for historians to express opinions on matters outside the recorded events" should not be taken at its face value – declared Edwards – because it is not a plea for objectivity:

> In this, perhaps, Mr. De Valera has more professional opinion upon his side than he may know. Such an austere critic as Prof. Michael Oakeshott has laid it down that the historian should not go beyond "what the evidence obliges him to believe". Moreover, as far as he does so he immediately transforms himself into a political propagandist or a fallible prophet. Moreover, even if he keeps within the limitation defined by Oakeshott, the historian need not expect acceptance. His

own intellectual limitations may not be proof against wilful thinking and certainly not against those of hostile critics. The association between politics and history writing in Ireland has, of course, created a special problem in the past and political personalities may be pardoned if they tended to take up the attitude of a Napoleon or a Henry Ford.[10]

There is irony here not least in the startling pairing of de Valera and Oakeshott. Although Edwards granted that in the politically saturated climate of Ireland it was tempting to reduce the role of historian to that of annalist, it is not sure that he himself was satisfied with such demotion. Certainly obtaining the correct facts was a necessary step, especially when one remembered that "the most non-revisable position in history is that of the individual who has escaped the record of the annalist for then he will be consigned to that bottomless pit where all the forgotten foregather and where all are forever non-entities".[11] Yet, on Sunday 24 May 1959, in the aftermath of the UCC Irish Conference of historians, Edwards articulated again his doubts for the sort of history advocated by Oakeshott: "The Walsh-Cobban thesis deserves application. Historians should go beyond Oakeshott employing their expertness to select. Significance and comprehensiveness are needed or history becomes a mere technique. Not Namier but Gibbon and Macaulay in the hard thrusts of a creative act. Written as we would speak it especially if we are inhibited Irish or self-conscious timid intellectuals".[12]

These doubts are effectively the counterpoint of his reluctance to dismiss entirely the nationalist interpretation of the Famine. Repeatedly, he showed that his scepticism targeted not only the certitudes of the nationalist history but also those of the revisionist history. On 9 September 1952, he confessed feeling "a little depressed at the dulling effects of academic discipline". He feared that the excessively technical style of the coming volume would neither attract the attention of the press nor appeal to the public. Summing up his doubts, he wrote: "The logic of all this – and Desmond T. Williams agrees – is that the historiography of the famine will have to state the real (as opposed to the administrative) position".[13] In a similar vein, although the narratives of John Mitchel, William Carleton and Liam O'Flaherty were heavily flawed, some intangible yet real quality about them unfailingly aroused his respect and led him to believe that these works had "at least an equal right to be taken for history" and could not be impetuously discarded. On 11 September 1952, a contrary impulse led him to cogitate on the enduring impact of the Mitchel–McHale story for it had proved "as effective on the next generation as the depositions story on the post-1641 world" and "had probably more effect on the writing of Irish history than the Young Ireland nationalism which really acted as a medium for translating Irish ideas (often wrongly) for foreigners".[14]

Willy Maley declared recently: "An appreciation of complexity around questions of language and representation is not a strong point in revisionism."[15] This declaration is false. Language and representation were central issues for Moody and Edwards when they were absorbed in the gigantic task of rethinking the discipline. On 18 February 1963, in a letter to Moody, Edwards deemed it in the interest of *Irish Historical Studies* to "avoid the type of contribution which tends to be uncritical just as much as we do with the overcritical. In this instance, the two are very close friends".[16] This fretting over language and representation was at its peak when the volume on the Famine was in preparation.[17] Edwards was painfully aware that in the haste to provide an antidote to the nationalist version, the revisionist version could become "cold", "dehydrated" and be detested by the public. He remarked that although the genocidal thesis of John Mitchel was false, its attraction lay in that it conveyed with unforgettable compassion the feelings of the people trapped in this apocalyptic event.[18] Remarkably, Edwards anticipated the sort of criticism that would be made of Irish Famine historiography later. After reading E.C. Large's *Advance of the Fungi* early in 1952, he brooded:

> I begin to feel that there is real danger that the sections of the specialists will fail to convey the unity of what was clearly a cataclysm in the Butterfield sense. The modern Irish of the countryside are largely predestinarian. Was the famine inevitable? And was the belief in its inevitability a factor which has tended to strengthen a tendency that one can well believe was always an Irish belief? I doubt if I can answer either but the need is to ensure that at least in the final result the Famine book will contain some attempt to see the explosion as a whole, mark its beginnings and indicate its short and long term limits. Neither politics, relief, agriculture, emigration (not to say history or folklore) can bring this out. It requires a careful assessment of the cumulative factors and a demarcation of how they became explosive. This will also answer the question of responsibility, so unhesitatingly laid at England's door by John Mitchel.[19]

That the unconventional format and the subdued tone of the new volume might ignite the fury of those who quantified patriotism only according to the degree of indignation they detected in someone's voice was a real concern not only to Irish historians but also English historians. Kitson Clark felt called upon to defend the reputation of his Irish counterparts against all slurs by insisting that "the authors are Irishmen; they clearly and rightly feel very strongly about the catastrophe which their forefathers suffered". Yet, the book was "admirable" precisely because their Irishness did not overly interfere with "the exacting demands of the idea of objective scholarship". He concluded: "To confront old and bitter legend with objective scholarship and critical judgment is one of the hardest, as it is one of the most useful, tasks of a historian; but in history moral responsibility is not everything, we want to know how things happened and why things happened".[20]

The most serious prosecutor of Irish revisionism who dwelt on the weaknesses of the *discontinuiste* method was Brendan Bradshaw. He claimed that Butterfield's influence on Irish historiography had been negative because the scientific criteria he expounded had given the illusion that one could produce a "value-free" history and the adoption of this faulty procedure had vitiated the entire output of the school.[21] Revisionism, charged Bradshaw, disclosed its thorough inadequacy when it neglected "its own 19th century version of a holocaust". Between the mid-1930s and the end of the 1950s, only one academic study appeared on the Famine.[22]

When a second brief analysis appeared, thirty years later, yet another strategy was deployed to distance the author and his readers from the bleak and disconcerting reality. This distance was achieved by assuming a clinical tone and by resorting to sociological euphemism and clinometric digressions. The result was to desensitize the trauma.[23] In the light of this report he concluded: "In short, confronted by the catastrophic dimension of Irish history, the discomfiture of the 'new school' is apparent".[24] A method which denied the historian recourse to value judgements as well as access to the kind of moral register capable of conveying human tragedy could only lead to bad history. This was so for two reasons; first because it filtered out trauma, and second because it overlooked the social function of history which resided, and here Bradshaw paraphrased Butterfield, in mediating between the actuality of the historical experience and contemporary perceptions of it.[25] This mediating function acquired a particular urgency when, as in the case of Ireland, communal memory retained such a keen sense of the catastrophic dimension of national history. He conceded this function was not intelligently fulfilled by stoking the memory of hate and bitterness through the melodramatic rehearsing of past wrongs. However, nor was it beneficial to conspire to remove the pain by using stratagems to minimize and sanitize. He stressed the need to convey a past that was both true and compassionate. Furthermore, this past had to be especially attentive to the propensity of the historical process for turning the most adverse human situations to constructive purpose yet without watering down tragedy. This second statement is important because it is precisely what Irish revisionists did in their treatment of the Union of 1801. Bradshaw argued that in *The English Man and his History* Butterfield had backtracked on his earlier advocacy of a value-free, own-sakeist history.

Writing in the darkest days of the Second World War, Butterfield did ponder the utility of "a sublime and purposeful unhistoricity", that is, of the deliberate recounting of a past known to be "conveniently and tidily disposed for our purposes".[26] Bradshaw snatched at this irony to argue that by remaining stuck in the pseudo-scientific mould laid down by Butterfield in his youth, Irish revisionists had ignored the implications of his later volteface, and this mistake would not be a cause for worry if it had not severely stymied the understanding of the Irish historical experience. The value-freeness claimed by revisionism was not impartiality but negative bias. Negative bias under the form of an invincible scepticism targeting the torchbearers of the separatist cause proved eventually no more resistant to distortion than positive bias.[27]

Still, before one lets the soothing and morale-boosting effects of public history work marvels on the collective psyche, perhaps one needs first a proper scientific history. In his desire to redeem the much-maligned Whig history, Bradshaw forgot important considerations and even ventured a little too far. He argued that the traditional faith-and-fatherland view of Irish history was salutary for the soul, a benign legacy, *"its wrongness notwithstanding"*.[28] The fact this statement was uttered by a professional historian of the early sixteenth century added to the feeling of absolute bewilderment for he appeared to regard an official history cluttered with Manichean myths as the true purveyor of meaning because the implication was that facts were too disparate, discrepant or dissonant to mean anything really worthy of attention.

However, imaginative recapture is not just a mimetic operation. It is also bound up with the discovery, analysis and inclusion of new facts in the overall equation. Here the suggestion seemed to be that one could dispense with the good assiduous task of documenting the past because the right questions had been answered already and further research would surely spoil the sweetness of a consoling story. Ultimately this came down to a denial that technical history when pursued with a measure of integrity, could and did fulfil an irreplaceable function. More worrying still, this depreciation of technical history ignored its two most fecund qualities, its critical estimation of documents and its deliberate effort to get behind the conscious representations and the limited horizons of historical actors. Michael Oakeshott defined the good historian as someone who "translates", "simplifies", "adds to" and "contradicts" the documents "if he thinks they are not telling the truth". His task is not just "sympathetic re-enactment" It is "to understand men and events more profoundly than they were understood when they lived and when they happened".[29] "Historians" as Eric Hobsbawm, Britain's most distinguished Marxist historian said, "are professionally obliged not to get it wrong – or at least to make an effort not to".[30] This obligation not to get it wrong is how the majority of Irish historians define their craft, and that is why Bradshaw's statement provoked such commotion. Revisionists also believed that wrongness proved a terrifying ferment of confusion and hate in the past. Public history begged entirely the question of Irish disunity. Internal discord, one must recall, was as much a historical reality as the desire for freedom from the British yoke. To drive the point even further, in Ireland, the very idea of freedom assumed conflicting emotional meanings, a deep-rooted clash in the experience and interpretation of crucial events, and finally it entailed opposed political expectations. Internal disunity was such an omnipresent, all-consuming reality that de Valera was forced to announce in September 1939 that the twenty-six counties would remain neutral in the impending Second World War. The document that started the European Conflict was a unilateral British guarantee to defend Poland.

To bring Ireland into war over a unilateral British commitment would have spelt trouble for the leadership of Fianna Fáil, but more dangerously, it would have split the country with a majority against being aligned with Great Britain. One must recall that loyalties were about to be seriously tested and old animosities on the brink of being revived again by the IRA's declaration of war on Britain some months before with a series of bombings in London and the collaboration of some of its elements with the Nazis. Faced with the prospect of a renewal of sympathy for the IRA, the "double game" policy of de Valera, official espousal of neutrality with secret support of the Allied war effort, notably through his assurance that he would not allow Ireland to be used as a base for attack on Britain and the clamping down on the IRA, did adequately capture something of the fine ideological subtlety of Irish public opinion at the time. The majority was anti-fascist, yet the memory of past wrongs and persecution in the hands of Britain made a segment reluctant to accept the *bona fides* of British imperialists as champions of the anti-fascist struggle and to allow the British Government the use of Irish ports. Neutrality meant the Irish would not be a mere pawn in a war between rival imperialist powers. On another level, it was an attempt, justified and clever, to forestall the unleashing of the still smouldering passions of the Civil War. In Ireland, public history could not act as social cement the way it did in England during the wartime crisis, not only because it had been a strong contributory factor in the clash of interests and ideals between Nationalism and Unionism but also because it had lent a hand in the banishment of dissenting voices inside the nationalist family. Bradshaw is indifferent to the plausible notion that revisionism may have been driven not by banal ideological reasons but by a genuine yearning to restore social unity. The negative bias he attached to it also applies to him and to all those who have a stake in overlooking this ethical dimension.

Irish revisionism proposed to make sense of a deeply divided people. It believed in the ratiocinative virtues of true historical knowledge. If people could be brought to see with what calculation their elites had manipulated their emotions, then maybe this process of education could, with time, lessen the intensity with which they still engaged in their present conflicts. Bradshaw has slightly identified the limits of own-salicism but he is too partial to admit that it is to revisionism that we owe the merit of having placed on the agenda the peoper function of history in a divided society. He refuses to contemplate how it represents an authentic Irish self-critique at its infancy, the first faltering yet steadily balancing act of coming to grips with the reality of Irish discord and its aggravating effects in the historical quicksand. Nor is he even remotely attentive to the fact that revisionism correctly spotted the need to break away from the discourse of identity to which Irish history had been acquiescent way too long to be able to perform its therapeutic and pedagogic role. One should not forget that before the 1930s the history offered to the public had a strong autobiographical slant because it was told by men who had fought for the separatist cause, were eager to justify themselves and misguidedly wrote on the principle that history in its totality was a mere continuation of their personal experience. Collective history was reduced to being solely the horizon of their own conscience. By prising out the fissiparous character of Irish opinion, the new history showed its daring and democratic face because it denounced the caricatures of the truth drawn by Unionism, Nationalism, Pro-Treaty and Anti-Treaty and conceded value to those politically incorrect voices that were suppressed. Furthermore, the portrayal of revisionism as an exercise in pure impartiality is debatable because it does not square at all with Edwards' approval of Macaulay. It is not clear how much he actually approved of this nineteenth-century English historian who had, one must stress, impeccable Whiggish credentials both in politics and in epistemology.

The evidence does suggest, however, that Edwards had noticed in Macaulay's style of history something gripping and swaying. In characteristic fashion, Macaulay claimed the Whig party could be credited with most of the remarkable progress that English society had known since the Stuart era. He was the typical nineteenth-century English intellectual, proud of his country's achievements and viewing English political institutions as the solid rock on which this colossal strength was built. From this supreme confidence in the state of perfection of the present conditions grew the assumption that the central theme of English history was the steady development of these benevolent institutions. He searched the past for precocious flowerings of the parliamentary spirit. He also established the forces that had been conducive to progress and those that had impeded it. He passed moral judgements on personalities of the past, with James II in the role of the principal villain and William of Orange, the principal hero who had rescued Englishmen from Catholic absolutism.[31] In other words, Macaulay displayed all the questionable attributes of Whig history that Butterfield and Oakeshott had stigmatized as unhistorical and unhelpful to the pursuit of the truth. Yet this did not stop Edwards from appreciating certain qualities about his work. Finally, there is indication refuting the portrayal of Butterfield as a "value-free" historian. Already in *The Whig Interpretation*, the seeds of doubt were sown. Even in the "austerity of youth" when he was composing his first treatise, Butterfield showed no sign of being a "narrow-minded academic puritan". Nor was there any symptom of a lack of tolerance and imagination, as it was again alleged.[32] What shines through those pages is no single-minded zeal in the superiority of Rankean history, but a searching mind which if not yet ready to throw overboard the conventional boundaries of knowledge, was at least prepared to recognize the limitations of empiricism. In it, he recognizes that a history without bias, a history that is partial to nobody, can be the dullest of things.

He is too astute not to discern how "the mind that too greatly strives to be an open mind" can end up being "featureless" or even how a writer who is dominated only by the fear of saying something wrong, can stifle his creative energy because he is labouring under too many repressions. There is too much of an "entrenched, self-liquidating antinomianism"[33] about him for him to forget the paradox that "impartiality is truly impossible, and that the appearance of having achieved it, is only the greatest of all illusions".[34] The historian's duty is not "to whittle himself down to a mere transparency" but rather to mediate between his subject matter and his reader. This process of mediation involves creativity and is a "venture of the personality" in which sympathy is crucially summoned up to neutralize the desiccating effects of an intellect which can be too mathematical when it is focused on a scientific end.

In direct contradiction to the premise of empiricism which holds that the only truth worthy of the name is that recovered from the facts, he conceded there was a knowledge which came with the sharpening of insight and imagination and these qualities were vital if the historian was "to catch the overtones in history and in life as well as touch the human side of his subject".[35] The most often commented work of Butterfield in Edwards' diary is *George III and the Historians*. There is evidence that Edwards tried to understand the theoretical problems raised by Butterfield's objections against the Namier School. Butterfield's analysis focused on the alleged plot by George III to subvert the constitution and re-establish absolutism. The Whig historians expounded the thesis that George III, who was inspired by wicked principles in the nursery, had set out to break the perfect English constitution.

In *Structure of Politics at the Accession of George III*, Sir Lewis Namier blasted this legend by showing that George III's system of government differed little, if at all, from George II's. Butterfield was pleased with neither of these interpretations for he believed that the Whig orthodoxy had distorted the actual picture out of partisanship and the Namier orthodoxy had added to the confusion in the name of scientific stringency.[36] The Polish-born historian, Sir Lewis Namier personified exact and unbending empiricism in England. He eschewed all speculation, denied any transcendental dynamic to history and did not believe in the primacy of ideology. Namier frontally attacked the "Whig interpretation" of British history which depicted eighteenth-century politics as a struggle between the forces of freedom and constitutionalism, led by the Whigs, and the forces of absolutism and royal power, led by the Tories. Namier downplayed the role played by these ideologies and upgraded the competition for power, money and influence through patronage and kinship networks. The political crisis was not caused by ideological clashes but by the disruption of these networks after the new King took power. George III's own beliefs and principles accounted for nothing in the confusion that followed. Richard Evans remembers that in the 1960s the response to this "scholarly achievement" was almost unanimous with one historian cheerfully saying, "Namier perhaps has found the ultimate way of doing history. If Namier had his way, all controversies would cease, and we would know as much historical truth as is humanly possible".[37] However, Namier's diehard positivism lacked the impeccable standards of integrity that were commonly associated with this practice. It was later discovered that in his anxiety to exculpate the King, he had been quite selective in his use of evidence and pruned his quotations from the sources to serve his argument.[38]

Surprisingly enough, it was Herbert Butterfield, who had fervently urged historians to tear apart the Whig straightjacket, who in the 1950s complained already that Namier had "taken the mind out of history" in his reduction of conviction to the operation of individual self-interest.[39] Butterfield did not think that the uncritical acceptance of Namier's new orthodoxy represented an auspicious sign because history was above all "a realm in which trust was the enemy of truth, and all critical standards were in peril if one was required to believe Ranke because Ranke was a reliable man".[40] Too much obsequious approval could turn a whole field of study into "the monopoly of a group and a party, all reviewing one another and standing shoulder to shoulder in order to stifle the discrepant idea, the new intellectual system, or the warning voice of the sceptic".[41] Furthermore, he dismissed the neat distinction between facts and ideas which provided the technical, structural and scientific foundations that underpinned Namier's type of analysis. In their actual effects mental projections were as significant as material phenomena that is why he urged historians "to remember that what men imagined the situation to be, what they dreamt or felt they were out to do was an actual dimension of the political events that were the object of study". He accused the new school of being carelessly "neglectful of this dimension which political conduct possessed, too neglectful even of those glimpses or leakages of purposeful policy, which occurred in the documents they were actually using".

In a similar vein, he thought, "they were over-contemptuous about the writers on politics, too supercilious in their treatment of Bolingbroke and Burke and too blind to the part which such literature might have played in actual life and in the political development of society". Given his credentials as an anti-Whig historian, his conclusion was surprising and damning: "Here is an interpretation of history which, through an anxiety to avoid being hoaxed, through an understandable desire to avoid the mistakes of the doctrinaire, is in danger of refusing to realise the operative force of ideas".[42] Underneath the harangue against the Namier School, Butterfield's intervention was a plea for moderation, because "just as one could be too doctrinarian even in one's anti-doctrinarism, one might be too wilful in one's emphasis on the wilfulness of history and the caprice of time".[43] He argued that the Namier School had gone too far in the atomization of structure in so far as it gave the impression that reason and purpose did not impact on the world and that the narrative possessed no coherence at all. An exchange of letters between Edwards and Butterfield indicates that Edwards sought to reconcile structural analysis with political narrative by pinpointing elements of complementariness to Butterfield. On 9 January 1958, Edwards wrote:

> Your appeal for narrative history to preserve that essential story of interplay of actions and accidents demands a two-dimensional study, if not

indeed a multi-dimensional one. For the Namiers, the bald sequence of events, duly analyzed, should precede the higher history of Butterfield and of Labrousse, quoting him in the context in which you cite him. Scientific mechanics should release more Butterfields to write more books like *George III and the historians*. Would the Oakeshotts hold with this use of the word scientific?[44]

On 24 January 1958, Butterfield replied:

> I agree that the bald sequence of events, duly analyzed, should precede the higher kind of history, but I think that the Namiers sometimes consider their work as the end-product of all historical endeavour, and they imagine that their positivistic method has brought them the final conclusions, which means that they see the political situation and the political structure too little in terms of ideas … Certainly, where political action is concerned I do not think people can talk (as I know some of them do) of actions as though they were independent of ideas. I rather agree with you that if an injection of Butterfieldism could cure it might of course, alternatively, kill.[45]

Butterfield's book was ambitious and original but it was dismissed as an "unfortunate piece of controversial writing, and best forgotten" by one reviewer in the *Times Educational Supplement* in 1958. Edwards was sufficiently intrigued by the complex methodological problems that Butterfield raised in his critique of the new consensus and annoyed by the sight of this wall of intolerant placidity that greeted the book, to write a letter to the editor on 9 January 1958 in which he launched his own offensive against the arrogant reviewer:

> Professor Butterfield has made it clear that the actions of the court after the accession of the young King provoked a first-class constitutional issue. He asserts the methods of the Namier school obscure this if indeed they do not blind themselves to the evidence because of their reluctance to deal with "ideas and purposes". Prof. Butterfield seems to fear that if the blindness of research workers is not subjected to treatment, the disease might spread so that historians and reviewers could reject the inconvenient truth. Your reviewer may not wish to trouble himself further with this work, but has he a right to condemn publication as being "controversial" and "difficult to comprehend", or even to assume "the general reader and the bewildered schoolmaster" is no better than he should be. But, as Prof. Butterfield insists that if the Namier school prevail, history will cease to be of value for political education, the "bewildered schoolmaster" should at least be given the chance to make up his mind whether to abandon teaching history.[46]

The research disease whose spreading Butterfield wanted to check and we must stress here that Edwards shared Butterfield's apprehensions, was an attitude that carried too far the reaction against ideas, and "against the sort of history which was woven at least in part out of men's conscious aims and purposes".[47] The excessive atomization in structure ran the risk of turning the whole history of mankind into a "tale told by an idiot". No matter how sidetracked by successive developments an intention may seem, the researcher must keep exercising a presiding mind over this forest of details because the view under the microscope conveys the misleading impression that the statesman is a bundle of contradictions, without cohesive purpose and with a readiness to drift with wind and tide. But it is "an occupational disease" to imagine that only details matter, or that they are all of equal importance. Beyond the ironies of circumstance, there is a larger course of history in which agency, either as mental projections, successful or aborted initiatives, actions even if thwarted, dissemination of myths geared to produce a desired shift in collective consciousness, does translate a real play of competing ideologies.[48] Historical research, by definition, should not cause desolation or puzzlement. If it does so, it is because the historian has been so mechanically scientific, so literal in his obedience to empiricism that the system has predictably failed him, defeating the purposes of science itself as well as the imperative of political education. It is intriguing to see the man who wrote of the need for a higher attention to detail, a synchronic treatment of past situations in order to uncover the unlikenesses from one age to another and opposed telescoping, arguing henceforth for a position which appears to be the opposite. His structuralist angle, vital according to him, if one is to dig up the true uniqueness of situations and the meandering workings of a historical process instead of assuming the intervention of some direct agency, never eclipses his belief that ideas, while never remaining static in their import, do percolate down the centuries through a palpable work of transition and mediation.

Given the theoretical subtlety of Butterfield's thought and his incontestable influence on the opinion claiming that the progenitors of the new history were puritanical empiricists becomes increasingly difficult to sustain. Evidence suggests that at least Edwards had taken on board Butterfield's warnings against excessive positivism and structural atomization in *George III and the Historians*. Most likely Edwards had not yet made up his mind about what represented the most suitable method. He seemed to weigh the strengths and weaknesses of opposed methods and be torn between contradictory impulses. More important still is the fact that Edwards was not alone among Irish historians in supporting Butterfield against Namier. On 24 January 1958, Desmond T. Williams informed Butterfield: "That a lot of people outside now realise what those inside formerly knew, and I quote Michael Oakeshott, Theo Moody, and Hugh Kearney (an unusual triumvirate) – that Namier's position is by no means generally accepted and that there are serious doubts about the quality of his approach".[49] As we have seen, Butterfield, contrary to Bradshaw's allegations that he had back-pedalled from his youthful fanaticism by qualifying his "impoverished" empiricism, was in fact as early as 1931 engaged in the effort to build a mature and balanced definition. Thus, Bradshaw's suggestion that Butterfield led his Irish disciples astray is a gross oversimplification of the epistemological stance of both the master and the disciples. Conor McCarthy claimed recently that Butterfield and Namier were "methodological allies".

But if we care to step behind the curtains we realize that this affinity rests on tenuous grounds. McCarthy expatiates on the conservatism of Namier to drum in the notion that Butterfield and the Irish historians were also by virtue of association guilty of the same conservatism. He wrote: "Irish revisionism is inherently negative and breaks up the national narrative. But in these features, it is wholly analogous to the description of Namier's approach: the empiricism, the distaste for nationalism, the assault on 'mind' or consciousness".[50] However evidence suggests not only that Namier's empiricism and Butterfield's empiricism stemmed from a different political sensibility but also that the fathers of Irish revisionism were thoroughly opposed to the lengths at which Namier had pushed the anti-Whiggish method.

What emerges from the revisionist treatment of the Famine is a demotion of the cataclysmic view in favour of an interpretation highlighting the transitions of the historical process over the long run. Roy Foster noticed the methodological change. While the nationalist reading described the Famine as a watershed, an absolute turning point precipitating new conditions such as demographic decline, large-scale emigration, changes in agrarian patterns, and new economic policies, and above all justifying the institutionalization of Anglophobia amongst the Irish, the revisionist reading, on the contrary, tended to moderate its real impact by showing that the economic and social processes that it supposedly set in motion were already visible before the outbreak of the disaster. That said, Foster immediately added a caveat by insisting that the Famine did accelerate these trends to such a degree that they became qualitatively different.[51] Thus, the adoption of a long-term approach dampens the exceptional character of the event. The eschatological impression of a defining moment with a "before" and an "after" is here qualified and the historian must seek elsewhere than in the economic and demographic trends if he wants to convey the unique character of this event. This is the direction which the post-revisionist generation of researchers appears to have chosen.

Far from abandoning the notion of the exceptional character of the Famine, they have registered and translated the frustrating gap between its empirical remnants and its unfathomable silences. Without in the least giving up the arduous task of documenting why and how it happened, they have nonetheless arrived at the deduction that the empirical method is not equipped to existentially make sense of an occurrence with such macabre consequences. Luke Dodd caught the mood of the new generation when he declared: "An understanding of how the famine is experienced is fundamental to an understanding of its causes and effects, but this past experience cannot be meaningfully retrieved by historical discourse alone. It requires a methodology which combines the tangible and the intangible".[52] In 1979 J.J. Lee also underscored the limits of empiricism in the face of an event whose facts could not all be retrieved: "Discussion about whether the Famine constituted a watershed often seems to take for granted that we know what happened during the Famine. We don't".[53] James Donnelly explained why one could not be sure of the number of people evicted during the Famine years and its immediate aftermath: "The police began to keep an official tally only in 1849, and they recorded a total of nearly 250,000 persons as formally and permanently evicted from their holdings between 1849 and 1854".[54] Cormac O Gráda's words echoed those of Donnelly: "Evictions and clearances are an important part of famine history, but confusing and incomplete statistics make estimating their number difficult".[55] Mary Daly wrote: "Both pre-famine and post-famine eviction levels appear to have been relatively low".[56] She claimed that eviction was never part of government policy; yet, she omitted to say that the Government did nothing to prevent evictions.

The number of evictions given by Daly comes to three and a half thousand families in 1846, six thousand in 1847 and nine and a half thousand in 1848, whereas that given by Tim O'Neill is of about seventy thousand to eighty thousand between 1846 and 1848. For W.E. Vaughan, the number adds up to seventy thousand families for the entire period 1846–1854. O'Neill, according to O Gráda, "implies that the number of evictions in 1849–1854 was only half that in 1846–1848". In other words, O'Neill's estimate of evictions over a three-year period is four times higher than Daly's. As Colm Toibin stresses, the plausibility of her argument, which seems to be to play down the importance of evictions and refuse to blame landlords or government, depends on the accuracy of her figures. O Gráda has expressed serious doubts about the accuracy of those figures and Daly's circumspection if not evasiveness on the issue of responsibility. The role of government, writes Daly, should "perhaps be seen in a more sympathetic light than it is generally regarded", since "it does not appear appropriate to pronounce in an unduly critical fashion on the limitations of previous generations". The Treasury is absolved of any wrongdoing with the remark that "greater sympathy with the Irish case would not have automatically guaranteed a dramatically reduced mortality".[57] If Daly's figures are incorrect, as O Gráda suggests, and if eighty thousand families, perhaps as many as half a million people, were thrown out in the streets in the three worst years of the famine, then, as Toibin says, the role of eviction in the aggravation of the catastrophe is central. What crystallizes here is a major difference between revisionists and traditionalists. The former vacillate when they must deal with responsibilities and hold that it is unreasonable to incriminate on the basis of incomplete knowledge of facts. The latter are impatient with this diffidence and factual obsession and retort that one does not need to dispose of all the facts to establish a number of indubitable truths, such as, the food exports and the evictions were never completely interrupted despite the report that thousands of people were dying. Two conceptions of the truth are clashing here; one driven by an empirical reflex, at times too timorous and futile because certain facts are destined to remain unknown, another driven by an ethical obligation, at times too moralizing and Manichaean.

There is after all, a hard core of injustice in Ireland that cannot be denied. Ireland was colonized. The natives were dispossessed of their land. In the nineteenth century, a horrible famine swooped down on the country, decimating a great number of the population. When this tragedy unfolds, the country is under the control of England. The Union, however, does not translate into systematic and concerted action to relieve the suffering of the people. This hard kernel always has its place in the recesses of popular memory. To goad memory, to stir up the acrid taste of injustice, to rake up pain and humiliation is the role of the demagogue and he usually does it skilfully. It is then that the emotional valence of myth takes over and imposes its distorted meaning on a complex event. So the mere descriptivism to which one has taken good care of removing any suggestion of larger or less obvious forces of determination, is susceptible to beg important questions. Why did the British, with an unreasonably high number of executions, deliver the Irish people into the hands of Sinn Féin? Why did they so badly interpret the popular mood that was initially hostile to the rebels, and upset the fragile equilibrium? One could surmise that they too, instead of showing intelligent statesmanship, fell right into the trap set by Pearse and repeated an old relational pattern, that of the imperial power punishing an indigenous insurrection. During forty years, instead of seizing the opportunity of cementing the constitutional foundations of the Northern State by giving a fair deal to the Catholics, the Unionist Party chose to persist in the monopoly of power and the endorsement of discrimination and in so doing gambled away its existence. In 1969, it read prematurely in the Civil Rights demonstrations a will to destroy the state. Could it be that it also felt the compulsion of a "Pavlovian" reflex? These questions are difficult. However, what one guesses already is that a history deprived of any theoretical equipment or conceptual finesse, entirely confined to chronicle, cannot go far in its heuristic effort. This was one of the objections raised by Irish theorists in the 1980s. Generally, they deplore a history which is only factual, exempt of any higher meaning. Conversely, Irish historians scorn a history devoid of facts. Hence, Edwards was dumbfounded by the claim that one could be opinionated without having a sufficient knowledge of what had actually happened:

> The experience of examining matriculation leaves one divided between
> the belief that Irish history should be done away with as an entrance

subject or one should attempt a school book within the near future. The bleakest aspect about any attempt to make candidates think is that they show so clearly their readiness to write and express opinions while they have not enough basic fact upon which to ground their views: until the claims of faith and fatherland are done with there can be no surprising objectivity. And once more one can see the need to end the imaginary divide of partition if the idea of Ireland is to survive.[58]

This difference echoed Eagleton's ironic rebuke of postmodernists. He compared them to inhibited students who could not articulate an opinion until they had all the details of a situation.[59] The detection of a falsehood does not require access to information. The search for total truth is, argued Eagleton, just a bugbear, which relieves one from the obligation to face the implications of the blatant injustice he is witnessing. One does not need intuitive access to Platonic Forms to be aware that apartheid is a regime which leaves something to be desired or, in the Irish situation, that the continuation of a system of property relations which concedes no right to the tenant and allows the practice of arbitrary evictions in the midst of a famine is a criminal action since it sends people right to their deaths.[60] Cognitive vagueness is no sufficient reason for throwing in the sponge and concluding that truth is ultimately unattainable or the task of determining responsibilities trivial and juvenile.

The wariness towards official conceptions of truth transpires in the reticence of some revisionist treatments of the Famine. Both postmodernist and revisionist imaginations carry a suspicion for histories which claim a privileged access to truth, or a monopoly on it, and dismiss inconvenient information as irrelevant. Both suspect that behind such overweening claims, there are hegemonic intentions that if left unbridled, can rob the individual of the freedom to decide alone what the truth is. By the start of the 1990s the post-revisionists set about revising some of the conclusions of the revisionists, coming back, this time with more analytical rigour, to a traditional position. Hence, if between 1950 and 1970 historians have used a style of exposition which erased the trauma and verged on whitewashing in their over-scrupulous efforts to refrain from supporting the genocide thesis, this latter reappeared in the 1990s almost with a vengeance. Anxious to underline how much the consensus on the Famine has evolved since the first revisionist analyses, O Gráda wrote: "We have come a long way from 'revisionist' claims that the Famine was just a regional crisis blown out of all proportion by nationalist propagandists, a mere catalyst of long-term changes already in train or inevitable, or a tragedy which no government could have done more to alleviate".[61] Still, although O Gráda and Donnelly have recognized the responsibility of the government, they have not done so by throwing a blanket accusation, which covered and explained everything that ever happened. The responsibility of the authorities, although aggravating, was not erected into an absolute cause from which every tragic development of the period unfolded. O Gráda's conclusions are more balanced and have the merit of separating the inevitable aspects from the avoidable ones, notably the passivity of influential sections of the Establishment. A general shortage of food is not a necessary condition of mass starvation. It takes yet the conjunction of two other factors.

The first is a high level of poverty, preventing the peasants from purchasing what food is available. And the second is the refusal of the authorities to transfer the food to them through political means, relying instead on the regulatory forces of the market. These market forces, according to O Gráda, can be seen as operating through a system of legal relations such as ownership rights, contractual obligations and legal exchanges. This means that the policy of non-intervention in the economic sphere sanctions non-interference in the functioning of these property relations even if they are a priori unjust and potentially criminal. He adds: "The law stands between food availability and food entitlement. Starvation deaths can reflect legality with a vengeance". He concedes that a simple arithmetic calculation shows that the Famine could not have been avoided only on Ireland's resources. Nevertheless he insists that the lack of generosity from the rest of the United Kingdom guaranteed and worsened the outcome. No government, Whig, Tory or Repeal, could have insulated the Irish poor against the effects of the potato blight. An excess of mortality was the inevitable result of a massive shock in the rural economy, but it is undeniable that the unsound policy of the government intensified the extent of the tragedy. The *laissez-faire* ideology, respected with religious fervour by all contemporary politicians, stipulated that free markets would naturally cure the shortages caused by the blight whereas a policy of more systematic public relief risked perpetuating the problem. O Gráda concludes: "The final irony is that when these ideologues played fast and loose with people's lives they did so not out of genocidal intent, far from it, but from a commitment to their own vision of a better world".[62]

If the revisionist interpretation tends to overemphasize the inevitability of the Famine, O Gráda singles out three major factors: an ecological accident which could not have been predicted, an ideology ill-geared to save lives and mass poverty. Cultural theorists have also contributed to the re-thinking of the Famine by showing, often with a good measure of insight, the limits of the empirical, own-sakeist method when applied to this event. To this extent, they have been instrumental in dispelling complacency by raising difficult ethical, political and methodological questions. They have exposed the dangers of relativism and induced higher sensitivity for the representational challenges involved in the reconstruction of traumatic experience. Christopher Morash declared that the Famine represented "the great abyss of modern historiography, the black hole around which so many narratives of Irish history circled, but into which it seemed relatively few historians had entered".[63] Eagleton remarked that if the "Famine stirred some to angry rhetoric, it would seem to have traumatised others into muteness. The event strains at the limits of the articulate, and is truly in this sense the Irish Auschwitz".[64] Revisionists would most certainly reply that this comparison means little in historical terms. By definition, comparisons are problematic. But they are even more so when as in this case there are so many differences in the nature of these two events; differences in premeditation, culpability, scale, contingency, circumstances, necessity and time. For this reason, it is doubtful whether this comparison can help the work of historical elucidation. To equate the Famine with the Holocaust is to devalue both. One needs to know everything there is to know about the Famine as well as everything there is to know about the Holocaust if one intends to get at the bottom of the significance of these events. If historically this comparison means little, why does Eagleton put it forward? Two hypotheses can be advanced here. The first, the most cynical one, is that Eagleton does it for purely political reasons, to claim that the Irish like the Jews have a special monopoly on human suffering. The second, a more redeeming one, is that he voices a sincere postmodern concern. In the light of his negative opinion of postmodern philosophy, this is a rather surprising discovery.

This second hypothesis seems more legitimate since these two events, with their debilitating core of trauma and silence, do raise the problem of the limitations of conventional modes of academic representation. The chasm separating the disembodied precepts of all political theories, here those of the Aryan Race and of English economic *laissez-faire*, and the vulnerability of the human body, is a theme truly haunting postmodern imagination. Another similarity is that in both events, Reason is complicit with the abject evil. In the Famine, harrowing reports of starvation and death are rationalized in the name of political economy. In the Holocaust, the Third Reich carries out its murderous enterprise in the name of an *indo-germanique* science proclaiming the superiority of the Aryan race, and Reason, methodical, operational and industrial is shamelessly enlisted to guarantee the enormity of the crime.

Finally, in both events, Reason stands righteous even though it has turned into an instrument of evil, got the better of the feelings of brotherhood and even of the obviousnesses of common sense.[65] Thus, if the pairing of the Famine and the Holocaust appears at times so irresistible, it is because both have a core that remains unfathomable and irretrievable. In his search for the reasons why the Famine continues to haunt Irish imagination, Eagleton made a crucial point: "Part of the horror of the Famine is its atavistic nature, the mind-shaking fact that an event with all the pre-modern character of a medieval pestilence happened in Ireland with frightening recentness".[66] Yet one cannot ignore that on a strictly historical level this comparison has something tendentious if not offensive. Indeed, it becomes problematic when one cares to look without sentimentalism at Ireland's inadequate response to Europe's greatest trial that was Nazism and the persecution of the Jews and allows the real facts to sink in one's conscience.

This is what Michael Longley, Gerard Delanty and Conor Cruise O'Brien urged Irish people to do.

Hence, in a speech in U.C.C., Delanty regretted that Ireland had not participated in the collective remembering of the Holocaust and the defeat of fascism and insisted that Ireland like the rest of Europe was aware that the fate of the Jews was sealed. Conor Cruise O'Brien declared: "We shut the doors, knowingly and deliberately. All of us, Britain, the US, France, us, everyone. Our only defence, as Ireland, is that we were no worse than the others. That is quite true, but it is hardly enough to entitle us to that high moral plane we so often claim for ourselves". Delanty concluded: "Instead of a probing of unexamined consciences on the extent of Irish anti-Semitism and … pro-Fascist sympathy, we have had the grotesque attempts to promote the 150th anniversary of the Irish Famine as an Irish Holocaust". Longley pertinently asked whether in 1945 it would not have been impossible, even offensive, to commemorate the 100th anniversary of the Famine in some of the politicized ways in which it was being conducted in the 1990s. And he wondered whether this type of self-pitying and wishful escapism was not an evasion of responsibility for a recent painful past.[67]

8 The claims of memory and critique

If it can record the fatal hesitations at official level, the scale of the actual outlay to meet the famine and the growth in the public relief system, own-sakeism can also evade questions which are immediately relevant to Irish society. If the historian follows it too rigidly he may abdicate some of his duty, which is to ask how and why the present came to be what it is as well as to underscore the missed chances in the past that could have led to a different present. The following passage shows that the editors of *The Great Famine* were aware of this methodological hurdle:

> The famine problems were approached from the limited viewpoints here described because the state in that era had a different view of its positive responsibilities to the community; but that historical conclusion must never be allowed to obscure another equally important one, namely, that in the mid-19th century the rulers of Britain lost an opportunity to carry through a programme of reform which might well have influenced the future course of Anglo-Irish relations.[1]

Christopher Morash retraced with the curiosity of an archaeologist the steps that led to the making of *The Great Famine*, the volume that provided the arguments for the prosecution case of Irish revisionism as a value-free practice.[2] Based on a close reading of Cormac O Gráda's new introduction to the book, Morash drew attention to the signs of a tension in early revisionism. We are now all accustomed to the trite contention that Irish revisionism stands for a clear-cut separation between fact and myth supposedly because these are conceived as arch-enemies.[3] However, a close look at the making of *The Great Famine* does not corroborate this. If Irish revisionism was empirical in its initial impetus, it was not nonetheless theologically opposed to the appreciation of other truths whose strength did not reside on the accredited facts of a tangible reality. If *The Great Hunger* and *The Great Famine* represent the two extremes in the field, then O Gráda identified a point of reconciliation by stressing the qualities of both genres. In defence of *The Great Famine*, he claimed, "curiously, perhaps, there is very little of the work included here which has been superseded", except in the area of the pre-Famine economy. However, he could not suppress the feeling that it is "as dry and cold as a Blue Book".

However, the two books "nicely complemented each other", the former "more scholarly, more analytical, more dispassionate", while "the world-wide and enduring success of that more evocative study [signalled] an opportunity lost by professional Irish historians". "Evocative" is habitually what an empirical style fails to be. The editors of *The Great Famine* were apparently conscious of this weakness when they invited Roger McHugh, Professor of Anglo-Irish literature and drama at UCD to write an essay on the Famine as experienced from the point of view of an Irish oral tradition. If this volume was designed to stand for a rigorous historical practice, then the presence of McHugh's essay was in Morash's words a curious and "telling anomaly embedded in *The Great Famine*". The evocative force of McHugh's essay was inseparable from the plurality of small narratives it contained and from "its problematisation of the concept of historical truth". McHugh wondered whether orature could "supply anything more than a vague and distorted outline to place beside the clear picture presented by the historian". Still he was somewhat nonplussed to discover that, "the truth which [he] had tried to piece together from scattered oral accounts was not essentially different from the truth derivable from the [official and journalistic evidence]". McHugh had just identified a paradox because the similarity he referred to was not simply one indicating an equal validity between these two orders of truth, but rather one revealing an eerie convergence between the British official perception and the victims' perceptions. Trying to make sense of this strange coincidence, he wrote:

> If more amorphous, its peculiar personal and local flavour communicates its own special reality and it has an objectivity and a detachment which perhaps seems strange, until one reflects that the history of the famine was indelibly printed upon the lives of our forefathers, that to them it was an accepted fact and might be recalled as a great and ruinous storm might be recalled.[4]

More to the point, the surviving evidence uncovered a religious explanation of the potato blight, which was annoying because it ran parallel to the racial prejudices of the British elite.[5] It was ironic that in a contribution designed to underline the gap between folk memory and scientific history, the former seemed to qualify Mitchel's allegation that the Famine was the fault of the British government. Oral evidence showed that the people on the land believed the very abundance of the crops in good years had made them careless of their good fortune and wasteful of the Lord's generosity. They scarcely knew what to do with their surplus potatoes and wasted them. Such waste created a foreboding of retribution, and as famine spread over the land, it was assumed a scourge from God, a punishment for the abuse of plenty. Clearly here, the researcher's expectations were disappointed and this odd finding said something positive about the validity of the ethnographic method in historical research. From the outset, two orders of truth are welded together: the voice of the historian, "clear and precise", conveying an impression of cool rationality, which is imperceptibly destabilized by another voice "vague and distorted" and heralded in McHugh's conclusion as: "the truth, heard from afar, of the men and women who were caught up, uncomprehending and frantic, in that disaster". Hence, from within the volume that became synonymous with impeccable empirical history, Morash and O Gráda glimpsed the disruptive presence of other forms of knowledge whose value resided neither in their clarity nor in their analytical insight, but whose very existence intimated the relativity of all historical knowledge.

Over the last twenty years, the post-revisionist debate on the Famine has shown growing sophistication, especially in the decision to think of subjective and objective truth no more as antinomic but as complementary poles which is desirable to associate through dialogue. Christine Kinealy's *This Great Calamity* is just such an example of the effort to combine the facilities of both scientific and popular truth. Her argument takes on a narrative form but it also heavily relies on quantitative and econometric tools of analysis. She rejects Mitchel's thesis of a calculated and racist act of genocide but she also dismisses the lacklustre or complacent assertion that suffering was inevitable and could not have been relieved to a greater extent. She provides her own answer to what O Gráda calls "the conundrum glossed over by Edwards and Williams" and A.T.Q. Stewart expresses this as: "The English may not actually have caused the Famine, but it was never possible to explain why the richest and most powerful empire in the world was unable to avert its worst consequences".[6] Kinealy challenges the revisionist tradition dating from Raymond Crotty in the 1960s and exemplified, most notably, in the 1980s with Roy Foster. Her analysis focuses on the administration of the Poor Law in Ireland during the Famine years. She looks at the way relief policies were implemented and at the reaction of the British authorities, which she finds "patently inadequate". She argues that the "challenge posed by the Famine could have been met successfully and many of its worst excesses avoided, had the political will existed". She concludes:

> There was no shortage of resources to avoid the tragedy of a Famine. Within Ireland itself, there were substantial resources of food which, had the political will existed, could have been diverted, even on a short-term measure to supply a starving people. Instead, the government pursued the objective of economic, social and agrarian reform as a long-term aim, although the price paid for this ultimately elusive goal was privation, disease, emigration, mortality and an enduring legacy of disenchantment.[7]

Thus if the new experts have abandoned Mitchel's thesis of genocide, they have all the same retained the charge of moral neglect: the failure of a great imperial power to feed its people in time of dire want. Graham Davis is not afraid to ask: "If the Famine had struck Cornwall instead of Cork would appropriate measures have been taken to prevent starvation and death?" Davis' oblique warning seems to be that there is no limit to the rationalizing power of the mind, that one should use this intellectualizing inclination with circumspection and sometimes trust more one's instinctive judgement, which here points to the evasion of a constitutional, moral and humanitarian duty. In the 1990s, researchers were haunted again by the problem of adequately representing the pain and human loss. It is at this junction of the debate that the problem of representation was met by a move towards theorization by a younger generation. Morash decided to apply the theoretical support of Jacques Derrida's *Spectres of Marx* to convey the unspeakable nature of this event. The figure of the spectre becomes a usual metaphor in nineteenth-century literature testifying to the inadequacy of language when confronted with the *différance*, or a dimension of truth which does not easily comply with linguistic rules. Because by definition a spectre is neither soul nor body while at the same time owing to both, it contains a disproportion, an asymmetry which speaks of man's ethical compulsion. It is what never stops stirring the feelings of the survivors and their descendants. Nagging, harassing and granting no respite, it is, declares Derrida, a reminder of the responsibility to bear witness.[8] Together present and absent, the ghost tells us that we will never be fully able to master and overcome the trauma of the Famine through language and the conventional theories of knowledge.

"One does not know", Derrida writes of the spectres which haunt the texts of Marx "not out of ignorance, but because this non-present present ... no longer belongs to knowledge. At least no longer to that which one thinks one knows by the name of knowledge".[9] The figure of the spectre is at once that which obstinately resists saying, and yet demands to be said, as much a "phantasm of the brain", as "an object of dread and terror". Like the "ghost of Hamlet's father", it looks at us with "an absolutely unmasterable disproportion".[10] No Famine sufferer is simply himself; each individual, comments Morash, conjures up the presence of the countless others who are absent. The simultaneous presence and absence of these others whose number is unaccountable turns the Famine into something unrecoverable. Morash draws attention to the fact that researchers in the field are always obsessed by the impression of a shortage of writing even after the publication of at least eight new texts in the single year of 1995. Variously explained as a case of collective neurotic repression or a proof of the failure of revisionist historiography, there is a tenacious feeling of incompetence in the face of the Famine "which its spectral language tells us may never be written away, or else written away only at a cost". Morash concludes:

> A substantial part of our experience of the Famine will continue to be one of disproportion, asymmetry, of responsibility accompanied by the compulsion always to say something more. This will be a difficult

recognition for any Irish historiographic practice (revisionist or otherwise) whose project ultimately relies upon the horizon of stable, knowable past. It will mean replacing, or at least supplementing, ontology with what Derrida calls "hauntology", those yet unrecognised forms of knowledge, which are at the margins of language, but are nonetheless in it.[11]

As Frederic Jameson explained, society faces a paradox. On the one hand, it cannot afford to forget the dead because to let them lapse into oblivion is an act of such impiety and irresponsibility that it would most certainly germinate its own retribution. On the other, a degree of forgetting is felt as vital because to remember the dead can assume a neurotic form and merely feed a sterile repetition. What is required here is a commemorative practice, which is both ethically imaginative and intellectually regenerative. Grappling with these implications, Morash ends up renouncing the discovery of a proper way of relating to the dead or a correct version of the past, and urges instead for the nurturing of a spectral and critical knowledge. By choosing to buttress his point of view by referring to Derrida's *Spectres of Marx*, Morash is being tactical. His objective is to belie the accusation that original analysis founded on a principle of deconstruction and dissection of national memory is either reactionary, unavailing or worse still, a violation of the rights of memory. His choice cannot be reduced to a fortunate coincidence in the imagery since *The Spectres of Marx* is to this day the most overtly political book ever produced by Derrida. The ghost is the symbol of the victims of history, a word used in its larger meaning to include all those losers, deviationists, dissenters, "might-have-beens", men and women who backed the wrong horse, and were consigned to the dust-heap of history by Leon Trotsky. Derrida perceived two worlds; that of ontology where Truth, History, Being, Consciousness, Origin all assume a rock-bottom or incontrovertible reality and that of *hauntology* where all the defeated alternatives and ideals (an unmistakable allusion to Marxism) haunt the living and cast a perpetual doubt on their decisions and assumptions. For him, attending to these spectres was a political gesture, signifying recognition of their rights and demanding responsibility, justice and a certain idea of impartiality. The decision to recover the Other is a major principle of any credible historical practice originating from Europe's liberal tradition and is, as we have already seen, the most pronounced characteristic of Irish revisionism.

An acute difficulty confronts the researcher studying the Famine; he must walk a tight rope between the impulse to sanitize it and the impulse to succumb to it. If he were to sanitize it, he may repeat the prejudices of English classical economy or collude with the racism of colonialism. If he were to succumb to it, he may mimic the prejudices of Irish separatism, and overlook of its contradictions. One of these is that the commitment to social justice found limited support in the emerging Irish nationalism of the post-Famine era. The danger that in committing either "sin" he may miss an important element of the truth is here equally present. Thus if historians want to obtain a more rounded truth, then they need to spot the distortions intrinsic to these discourses. To this end, Morash recommends a dismemberment of these discourses inspired by Michel Foucault's method. Like Foucault, Morash proposes a historiographic genre, which deliberately refrains from thinking directly about the Famine in order to concentrate solely on the narratives invented and clustered around the event. He describes the event as it is recounted in these narratives without unduly bothering about its foundations in reality and truth. In keeping with Foucault's basic philosophical premise, Morash views discourse as a privileged vehicle of control and highlights how the discourse of the Famine allowed one to diffuse under cover opposed ideological messages. He shows how truth is sometimes the product not of cognition but of power, and how a dominant discourse can emerge out of a field of competing discourses in order to defy or buttress the foundations of a regime:

> In the living skeletons and spectres that materialise repeatedly in the pages of Famine writing, we see a discourse of the Famine taking shape, with its own particular vocabulary. Like all such discursive formations, it owes much of its appearance of truth to repetition, a revenant effect in which the repeated reappearance of a word or phrase begins to look like corroborative evidence. Once repetition has established a phrase or image as a fact of discourse, it is no longer confined to the texts in which it originated, and it enters a promiscuous public sphere where it can be appropriated by other discourses, other narratives.[12]

In any case, those phrases or images never surface or circulate in the intellectual atmosphere as innocent pursuits of the truth, as the logocentric tradition imagined it. Traditional historians are usually hostile to the methods of critical theory because in their view they place too much emphasis on the texts and ignore agency. Not always grasping the utility of this intensive dissection in their impatience to recapture the "real" or the "truth", they have suspected theorists of devising cunning ways of distracting the researchers' attention from what really matters.

The role of the historian is to celebrate man's capacity for resisting oppression and to preserve intact the memory of this resistance. They see post-structuralist theory as a sign of intellectual decrepitude, political conservatism and of the defeat of Western thought. Under a display of false erudition, the theory overshadows or minimizes the fact of oppression. Old-style Marxists in particular would argue that all theory is bankrupt once it ignores experience in favour of discourse, dissolves agency into *textualité* and replaces social commitment with nihilism. For instance, Brian Palmer declared: "Critical theory is no substitute for historical materialism; language is not life ... Left to its own devices, post-structuralist theory will always stop short of interpretative clarity".[13]

E.P. Thompson explained that authentic experience cannot be superseded and declared his intention to rescue the old artisans from "the enormous condescension of posterity".[14] Traditional historians do not want to be reminded that texts can be concealing screens interfering between them and the past, that they have multiple meanings or agendas and that the act of decoding them involves a heavy input of their own subjectivity at several important levels. However, the Irish situation is anomalous since, with the exception of Brendan Bradshaw, it is the cultural theorists, especially those of the now defunct Field Day movement who initially reacted to the "linguistic turn" and the revisionist method much in the same way as did traditional historians. For a long time, when it came to the protection of truth – the moral lesson of the Famine, the soundness and decency of the separatist cause and the integrity and courage of the 1916 leaders – many of those specialists put forward the same old logocentric arguments. Conversely, it is the revisionists who have been more heedful of the warnings of postmodern theory against the illusions or logocentrism, receptive to the ambiguities and uncertainties of truth, alert to the authoritarian and coercive force inscribed in its commandment, and conscious that truth is as much a construction designed to yield power or smother awkward questions as a value retrievable for reason through a critical analysis of documents. It is also the revisionists who historically have shown acute discomfort toward the production of a mimetic truth abnormally glued to the discourses of Nationalism or Unionism, invented a method that produced an "alienation" effect and set the conditions for the recovery of a truth that was no longer complicit with either of these political forces. In other words, revisionists are the first postmodern critics of Ireland.

However, the revisionist treatment of the Famine does not invite a completely confident verdict. One cannot dispel the feeling that by trusting too much own-sakeism, early revisionists have tilted their judgement in favour of the ideology of *laissez-faire* and forgotten to counterbalance this picture with the powerful critique emanating from contemporary English radicals. What this mistake tells us is that the Famine more than any other event of Irish history necessitated a combined method, one which would have employed both distance and proximity as cognitive tools and therefore avoid the excesses latent in each of these approaches.

When Derrida announced, "there was nothing outside the text", this declaration became instantly for many historians the rallying point of the defence of history. Of course this phrase does not mean that there is no identifiable past outside the texts or that the wars, colonial oppression, religious and racial persecution, concentration camps, or the Great Famine are literally texts with no origin in or bearing to an extra-linguistic, reality. In *Telling the Truth about History*, three American historians riposted that "in final analysis, there could not be any postmodern history" because a transparent knowledge of the world was the only basis on which to establish the truth: "If postmodern theories are taken seriously, there will be no reason for a tran-historical or transcendental interpretation, and human beings will have no immediate access to the world of things and events".[15] To observe, the historian must have an Archimedean point from which to survey the whole evidence. However, Derrida, Foucault and Lyotard did not think that historians ever stood on this lofty perch. A proof of this is that Irish historians have often written within the constricting limits of an ideological nation, a nation which has first excluded the Catholics, then the Protestants, and then again all the deviationists who were opposed to the orthodox republican line. Historical writing does not produce discursive effects that loyally translate an instant relation to actual events and conditions. Without a critical analysis of this discursive production, historians can fall prey to these illusory effects and simply convey semblances of the truth and not the whole truth that is usually a lot more complicated and sinuous than the biased documents that survive time.

Traditional historians saw the attack against the totalizing discourse as a depoliticizing act when in fact it was intended as a radical effort to renew the work of critique. The French philosophers encouraged historians to create a mode of writing which would prove more resilient to the cultural prejudices of the subjects studied. In 1984, during an interview with Richard Kearney, Jacques Derrida rejected the accusation of nihilism. Deconstruction, he explained, did not mean that language only referred to itself:

> It is totally false to suggest that deconstruction is a suspension of reference. Deconstruction is always deeply concerned with the "other" of language. I never cease to be surprised by critics who see my work as a declaration that there is nothing beyond language, that we are imprisoned in language; it is saying, in fact, the exact opposite ... I totally refuse the label of nihilism that has been ascribed to my American colleagues and me. Deconstruction is not an enclosure in nothingness, but openness towards the other.[16]

The postmodern objection to a mimetic truth is based on the belief that truth indeed matters a great deal and that historians must become more guarded with authoritarian renditions of it. A priori, the Irish Famine seems to be an event that needs no theoretical support to speak of itself. Starvation, death, disease, poverty, and a suffering humanity, appear to require no spokesman. Anyone with a reasonable degree of compassion can imagine such terrifying experience. Common sense also supposes that its tragedy would be a powerful deterrent to any propagandist manipulation because of a moral imperative. Yet, it is precisely these two assumptions that the revisionist findings on the Famine have belied. In *Making Memories*, Christopher Morash explains the frontier that separates literary representation from empirical history built on statistics. Whereas empirical history seeks total representation, narrative history by definition excludes an important amount of data in favour of a small selection and that is why it heavily depends on the tropes of synecdoche, metonymy and metaphor.

For this reason, literary representation is purveyor of meaning only when we understand it as part of a semiotic system composed of an archive of other texts, each carrying its own particular interpretation on what and why it happened. No text is pure or autonomous. Every appearance is a reiteration, and every occurrence is a recurrence. Nevertheless, instead of feeling handicapped by the limitations of literary evidence, Morash adopts an epistemological relativism akin to that of postmodern theory since for him these limits are simply an example of "the fundamental inadequacy of all the paradigms of understanding; whether they are rational, romantic, political, religious or millenarian and of the perpetual inadequacy of all subsequent paradigms".[17] Lyotard argued that all the great theories of knowledge, be it Marxism, Structuralism or Empiricism, in order to forge the illusion of their authority depended illicitly on a presupposition which is refutable and cause "an internal erosion of the principle of legitimacy". About *Libidinal Economy*, he wrote that the book was a testament to "the dizziness that can take hold of thinking when it becomes aware of how groundless all the criteria that are used to respond to the requirements coming from the law, are".[18] Each type of history, historicist, empirical, structural, or cultural, contains aporias because no method can alone penetrate all the reality of the past, nor supply all the answers we seek from the evidence. Thus, the *discontinuiste* method favoured by the revisionists presents also antinomies and weak points and fails to address adequately certain more imponderable aspects of the Irish Famine. By the same token, Morash's analysis does not suppose a rigid hierarchy of paradigms. Narrative history and empirical history are equal in their validity as they are equal in their deficiencies. Lyotard held that science is just as much a set of narratives as any other discourse, but that it refuses to admit this, bent as it is on maintaining its superior status in Western culture.

Generally, the method it uses to prove a point is based on the research game – "Not: I can prove something because reality is the way I say it is. But: as long as I can produce proof, it is allowed to think that reality is the way I say it is".[19] What we have in such cases is not so much proof as "adequacy" between theory and experimental results. In the past, science has gained legitimacy by the very same tactics habitually associated with political discourse, repetition and ritualism, and this Lyotard offers as evidence that science did not deem itself strong enough to rely only on its rules of proof, verification and falsification to establish its authority. It is doubtful that revisionists would endorse Lyotard's levelling. To do so would amount to self-liquidation, at least that is the way some historians would look at it. Given that ideology has been their target they would be distraught by the relegation of their work to the rank of opportunism or escapism, not so much out of selfish indignation or hurt pride but because they would see in this a sabotaging of a courageous initiative and the reactivation of ideologies that have bred unmitigated hatred and disaster on the island. The effort to contain the encroachments of ideology and to get to the bottom of its magnetic power has led Morash to concentrate on a key purveying text of Irish nationalism, the canonical *Jail Journal* of John Mitchel. Morash thinks that the power of this text to influence the mind is due to its unique structural quality which conjures up a total identification between the narrator and the events he describes: "The general history of a nation may fitly preface the personal memoranda of a solitary captive; for it was strictly and logically a consequence of the dreary story here epitomized that I came to be a prisoner, and to sit writing and musing so many months in a lonely cell".[20]

Mitchel says that his personal life-story is synonymous with the history of Ireland; when his captivity puts his life on hold, historical time stops. This structure of identification applies to the whole of the journal since he brings the history of Ireland outlined in his introduction to a halt at the point at which he leaves Ireland. The rest of the journal, written while he was a "solitary captive" in a "lonely cell" is severed from the processes of history. This Mitchel recognizes when he laments, "there is more Irish history, too, this month, if I could but get at it". Cut off from history as a living, evolving reality, Mitchel has to rely increasingly on his memory; a memory that in time replaces history for "impressions of the past grow vivid as the soul shuts itself from the present". Lost in his memories, Mitchel leaves history in a state of "suspended animation" and everything happens as if it is forever 1848 and the Famine has never ended. Reflecting on the impact of this text, Morash concludes:

> It is possible to imagine a member of an Irish migrant community (particularly a member of a first generation community in the 19th century) encountering such a textual suspension of history, and finding it emulates their own experience of Irish history, suspended at the moment of departure. For such a reader, the text would create an illusion of authenticity validated by experience; its claims to truth would be difficult to question.[21]

The originality of a discourse of identity consists in its capacity to suspend real history, to erase the pastness of an event, here the Famine, and therefore instead of exorcising it, keeping it as lifelike, vivid and traumatic as when it was first experienced. The Famine not only happened; it continues to happen every time one reads Mitchel's text. With such a formidable power, the *Jail Journal* was bound to have a disproportionate influence on the manner in which reputed nationalist historians perceived and narrated the Famine. Patrick O'Farrell thinks that Mitchel's opinion on the Famine as a deliberate act of genocide is the all-encompassing hypothesis behind several studies. It has defined the parameters of the works of Canon J. O'Rourke,[22] Charles Gavan Duffy,[23] P.S. O'Hegarty,[24] Cecil Woodham-Smith,[25] Robert Kee,[26] Thomas Gallagher[27] and even Christine Kinealy.[28]

The contribution of postmodernism to the historiography of the Famine, often through the medium of Irish literary criticism, is that it has brought into relief what nationalist history tended to forget: the opacity and unreliability of evidence. However, this presentiment was present in early Irish revisionism too. Since, history and literary criticism have begun to explore in earnest the potentials of a more conceptual history, interested as much in what actually happened as in how this event was subsequently represented. The new historiography is also more conscious of the processes of authentification of literary representations as well as of the textual strategies employed to naturalize literary representation as memory. Finally it is more cognizant of the incongruities; fact that images are not safe windows providing access to an unquestionable truth, but rather "open structures", "mutable", "pliable" and susceptible to being "appropriated from a range of ideological positions" including a priori diametrically opposed positions. For instance, the images of the walking skeleton, grass-eating man and dead mother all have acted as signifiers of famine before the 1840s.

"When we recall", as Morash enjoins us to do that "Edmund Spenser used these images – which we have seen used by nationalist writers – for the very un-nationalistic purpose of proving that the native Irish were little better than animals, we are given an indication of the ideological mutability of such images" and of the strange collusions between colonialism and nationalism. It is because they attest to a profound need to have real memories of the Famine that those textual strategies are so efficient. Yet, the quest for real memory risks being seriously sabotaged if one is not sufficiently alive to the fact that no narrative of the Famine is ever pure. In fact, a close critical analysis never fails to reveal that every Famine text partakes of other discourses, whether it is militant nationalism of the John Mitchel school, social policy as propounded by the Catholic Church in Ireland, or imperialism and capitalism as defended by English economists. Thus we must see how the Famine is appropriated or hijacked by those other interests to further their own cause and unless we want to be manipulated by their intentions, we must show a heightened critical sense during the analysis of fictional and evidential representations. Finally Morash concludes with a remark which could serve as an ultimate argument for a reconciliation between the critical imperative of a revising project and the ethical imperative of a memorializing project since both fulfil a pertinent function, express a natural compulsion and for this very reason deserve from scholars equal attention and respect:

> The need to bear witness stands opposed to the need for analytical criticism; remembering opposed to dismembering. Yet, both needs have legitimate claims upon our attention which any attempt at coming to terms with the legacy of the Famine amongst the Irish Diaspora, ignores at its peril.[29]

The new historiography has come to terms with the impasses of rudimen-tary empiricism and reconciled the opposite imperatives of remembrance and critique. Henceforth it knows that facts given their limited number in cases like the Famine cannot easily seal fractures. Nor does it harbour any longer illusions about the potentials of empiricism when confronted with an event whose core of human suffering defies our familiar mental categories. To compensate for this crisis of representation it has turned to the insights of theory and availed itself of its eccentric method. This method privileges the hermeneutical act and this translates in a healthy curiosity for the valence of the Famine for Irish separatism, and the disquieting parallels between the metaphorical language of imperialism and that of nationalism. It is conversant with postmodern sensibility for researchers are more inclined to see why there is no "hors text", how the Famine, contrary to some naïve expectations, does not escape this rule and how all its representations are involved in the pragmatics of a given ideological discourse. It shows it has integrated the principle articulated by Jean-François Lyotard according to which:

> We are always within opinion. There is no possible discourse of truth on the situation. In addition, there is no such discourse because one is caught up in a story and one cannot get out of this story to take up a meta-linguistic position from which one could dominate the whole. We are always immanent to stories in the making, even when we are the ones telling the story to the other.[30]

Part IV

Master narratives

Discarding of historical thinking?

9 The epistemological and philosophical position of Irish revisionism

It is a cliché to say that the Irish use their troubled history as a weapon to invest their faction with legitimacy and deny legitimacy to their opponent. What is overlooked is how history can provide a safe haven, a refuge from the hazards of negotiations and compromise. It also promises a surrender of responsibility in the present deadlock. If the Protestants cannot be trusted because of the cruelty of the Cromwellian invasion in 1649 and the injustice of the Penal Laws of 1695 or because they smothered the enlightened democratic spirit of the 1798 Rebellion, and persecuted Catholics out of their jobs and houses in 1893 and 1912 and gerrymandered local electoral boundaries to prevent Catholics from voting, then one has a stronger excuse for caricaturing them as rapacious, bigoted settlers bent on annihilating natives and their culture.

Equally if the Catholics cannot be trusted because they massacred Scots and English settlers in Ulster in 1641, or because they displayed a slavish loyalty to the Pope and obeyed the "Ne Temere" papal decree on mixed marriages in 1908, or refused to amend a Constitution which lay claim to the territory of Northern Ireland and turned the Irish state into a theocratic regime, or finally because they condoned the terrorist campaign of the Provisional IRA, then one has a stronger case for essentializing them as dangerous irredentists who are bent on coercing a noble tradition of freedom of conscience into submission. These arguments are used repeatedly to mock the professions of faith in democracy and ecumenism that are regularly vented by each side. But more subtly this annexation of a serviceable past represents another way of shifting the onus for initiative and calculated gamble in the present situation away from one camp and onto the other. It puts the party at whom all these accusations are hurled in a vulnerable position, in a state of irremissible guilt where no later action, no matter how charitable, can make the least difference to the verdict. One could go a step further and argue that the more expressions there are of goodwill and a desire for conciliation, the more likely is suspicion to be aroused. The more heroically reality contradicts the colonialist antagonism the more automatically it confirms it in the brainwashed minds of the people.

It is no coincidence if the Anglo-Irish Agreement of November 1985 was interpreted by both sides as a treacherous manoeuvre plotted to thwart their opposed objectives. For Unionists, Hillsborough was the first step to absorption into a United Ireland and the cunning mechanism by which they were to be expelled from the United Kingdom. It portended the end of the Union. For Ultra-nationalists, it tightened the shackles of partition by bestowing upon it a spurious legitimacy. It foreboded the end of the republican dream of completing the revolution. Its in-built ambiguity made the document dynamite: each party discerning in it the materialization of their worst nightmares. And yet this agreement represented a fresh departure and a wholly new experiment. It was revisionist even sceptic in spirit since both the British and the Irish governments admitted for the first time that nothing constructive could be achieved unilaterally. A certain cravenness is thus concealed behind the argument of history.

More worrying is when scholarly conclusions endorse historical determinism. The Ulster historian A.T.Q. Stewart who studied the psychology of the belligerents wrote that only some "mysterious form of transmission from generation to generation" could explain the recurrence of older patterns of conflict.[1] However, in the same passage, Stewart denounced this instrumental use of history: "To the Irish all history is applied history and the past is simply a convenient quarry which provides ammunition to use against enemies in the present".[2] This determinism which in the 1980s and 1990s coloured British journalism, literary criticism in Britain and Ireland and even some historical analyses is however dubious for it lent Northern Ireland a definite ring of self-exoneration. What's more, this blanket argument obscured another truth, maybe more important; that contemporary battles may be the real driving force, the real reason affecting why, what and how a people choose to remember or forget. There comes a time when all of us both in the conduct of our personal lives and in our civic duties have to stop using history as an excuse, a means of escaping difficult challenges. Propagandist manipulation in a war situation, the stirring up of chauvinistic emotions, intimidation, even blackmail are ploys that no man may be invulnerable to. However, these do not define nor sum up his mind. Man is endowed with a power to resist, to dissent, to break the vicious circle of repetition and bring about real change and it is this ability that makes history so engrossing and riveting.

This statement may sound like a platitude and yet it has often been a beleaguered notion which has serious implications for the way in which men appraise the potentialities of the political realm and tackle intractable conflicts. Europe has entered the aporia of the postmodern condition. This aporia is understandable when one recalls that it was in Europe that the two antagonistic experiments of humanistic universalism and the quest for absolute difference were acted out. Ireland struggled with the quandaries of both. Not being able to make up its mind as to which offered the most durable way of cementing the foundations of the idealized nation and solving the riddles of its history, it has sought, somewhat guilelessly to integrate both. These efforts were not successful.

Two scenarios have usually arisen out of these. Either Romantic National-ism, the more charismatic of these two bedfellows would outshine the enlightened spirit of equality. Or else the fusion between these two equally arrogant acolytes would distil the most lethal alchemy. The competition between them is not over yet either in the political realm or in the intellectual domain despite the thriving of radical trends which claim to have transcended their archaism. But these are not easily defeated. They are tenacious, pugnacious and seem to have insinuated themselves in most eccentric ways into the historiographic disputation. In reality, they are the subtext. To discern them, one has to decipher carefully the arguments and criticisms launched from each camp.

Under the veneer of an esoteric debate, Irish intellectuals have been rehearsing a very old play, the first staging of which happened around the time of the French Revolution. On Irish soil this ancient dispute reached its climax with the Cultural Revival at the turn of the nineteenth century when the prospect of impending autonomy galvanized minds into defining a coherent Irish identity. But the construction of a national identity turned out to be an arduous task in a land where discord assumed almost a ubiquitous form. Partition, seen by militant Nationalists as a mischievous plot visited on Ireland by the English enemy, was first and foremost the transposition in the realm of polity of a profound rift, the jagged and ugly silhouette of which would simply not recede into the past. The proximity of violence and the precariousness of all the constitutional settlements tested in Northern Ireland since, have ensured the persistence of this dispute in some edulcorate and tortuous fashion.

In its attack on Irish revisionism, a certain literary criticism rambles on about the primacy of structure without regard for this breaching ability of the mind. This explains why in its interpretations of Irish history it draws so heavily from postcolonial and post-structuralist theory even though in its use of the latter it is quite selective. Its argumentation disguised under convoluted and disheartening layers of theoretical jargon can sound intimidating. But it is no more than a pre-emptive rhetorical technique, a technique whose workings can be unravelled and queried with the aid of proper philosophical insight and aplomb. Conversely in its embrace of universal humanism, its social idealism, and its *discontinuiste* method based on a rejection of deterministic and teleological horizons, Irish revisionism gives the impression of being infused with a more optimistic view of man as with it the mind still remains the overruling authority. In *The Defeat of the Mind*, Alain Finkielkraut rehabilitates the philosophical innovations of the Enlightenment and argues that the latest offshoots of Western thought reveal they have looped backwards into the theoretical armoury of French theocratic discourse. The social positivism originating from the Counter-Revolution, that which had as main exponents Auguste Comte and Saint-Simon openly acknowledged its debt to what it itself baptized "the retrograde school", and especially to Joseph de Maistre who was the leading figure. The social theories that became fashionable from the 1950s and 1960s onwards such as structuralism and post-structuralism unwittingly colluded with the fatalism and cynicism of French reactionary thought:

> Animated by their passion of the past, German Romantics and French Theocrats accomplished no less than a real epistemological revolution. Their hate of modernity engendered a radically new conception of man. Their nostalgia inaugurated in the sphere of knowledge a mutation of which we are still largely dependent. These relentless reactionaries are inventors in spite of themselves. In their fury to take man down a peg or two, they discovered the unthought-of that worked within him and founded human sciences. And even though the traditionalists left relatively early the political and intellectual scene, it was the philologists, the sociologists or the historians who immediately took over and came out in favour of the *Volksgeist* in the debate between the two types of nation. Henceforth it was not the ideologues but the scholars who declared that the social contract was a fiction, because, outside society, there was no autonomous individual.[3]

A certain Irish cultural theory is now complicit with the same political tendencies. In both cases, one notices that all universal and immutable values, be they philosophic or epistemic, such as Man, Truth, Objectivity, are debunked. All hope of a social healing in the uncovering of an overarching historical truth cancelling the truncated and mendacious versions of the Unionism and the Nationalism is suspected of harbouring hegemonic propensities which need to be fought at all cost and their thrust neutralized. In its insistence that no one can jettison its cultural burden without going astray, Irish cultural theory has taken over the arguments of the retrograde school. It revives the same philosophical tradition.

On the contrary, in its refusal to resign itself to the fatalistic verdict on the clash between Protestant and Catholic, revisionism, apart from the notable exception of F.S.L. Lyons, proceeds from a more optimistic philosophy, one which includes in its estimations the notions of individual freedom, prerogative and journey. In its worldview, man can always see and reach beyond the structures which oppress him and engage in a dialogue with his ancient enemy in spite of all the differences that habitually separate them. The disagreement can also be approached in terms of idealism and materialism. Irish critics, those of the Field Day school especially, have heavily inclined towards a materialist conception of culture whereas Irish revisionists have espoused an idealistic conception. Generally, social theory oscillates inadequately between a vision of reality that is over-materialistic, where all creative impulses are considered chimerical and a vision of reality that is over-idealistic, where the insidiousness or stealthiness of power is underestimated.

Sadly, not many analyses focus on a theoretical synthesis of those polarities or reveal something about their degree or manner of interaction.[4] Thus the philosophies of man underpinning Irish revisionism and Irish traditionalism do capture a portion of truth, but it remains disempowered or emasculated because for a long time each denied the insights and intuitions of the other, often out of bad faith, sheer misunderstanding or even disciplinary snobbishness. Any serious study of the historical process would reveal a continual tension between determining factors and instances of courageous initiative. It is this tension, this dynamic which supporters of determinism evacuate with all the dangers, moral, psychological and political, involved in this facile gesture of evacuation. An awareness of the determinations to which we are all prone to fall victims is indeed necessary if we want to avoid the trap. But a theory which buries human drive and mettle under the crushing weight of social, historical and unconscious determinations and denies man the power to free himself from these is damaging if not specious. Most Postmodernists would dismiss this argument as a liberal-humanistic cliché often employed for the wrong reasons, that is, to buttress further the hegemonic drives of the bourgeoisie or those of the imperialist West. But where would be the inspiration of a theory which declares that man is dead or a puppet actuated by forces beyond his control, that his capacity for creative dissent equals zero because power constraints not only his actions but also coerces insidiously his psyche until it becomes a mere echo of these mighty ideological forces?

Hence, a Marxism engaging with the reality of determination is useful, but a post-Marxism which cannot see beyond the workings of determinism has defeated its original aim and become an encumbrance. Raymond Williams made the same point: "A Marxism without some concept of determination is in effect worthless. [But] a Marxism with many of the concepts of determination it now has is quite radically disabled".[5] Nor was it unusual to hear in the 1990s that an Irish human condition was a liberal illusion and that a more objective truth about the past could never flourish because critical thought had been and still was imprisoned in colonialist categories. This opinion holds that the native and settler dichotomy is still very much a reality in Northern Ireland and any attempt to define the problem otherwise is denounced as sophistic. Terry Eagleton describes nineteenth-century cultural idealism as a hypocritical philosophy and belittles its devotees as men who either suffered from bad conscience or were trying to capitalize from historical amnesia:

> The problem in Ireland was that the mantle of liberal disinterestedness descended, *faute de mieux*, on those displaced upper-class spirits whose self-interested stake in cultural pluralism was occasionally all too palpable. A class, which had so dismally failed to provide political leadership, was now largely offering itself as a band of cultural commissars, hoping to fashion a refurbished selfhood for Ireland out of their

own crisis of identity … Yet it could not pass entirely unnoticed that if the forefathers of the colonial class in Ireland had been a little less intent on undermining the native culture, their emancipated sons and daughters would have needed to busy themselves rather less with restoring it.[6]

Eagleton's judgement is not devoid of truth. However it remains safely glued to the dichotomic mindset and cannot appreciate the unforeseen and beneficial effects of the combined efforts of those liberal aficionados on the cause of Irish nationalism. The rough importation of the colonial paradigm on Ulster is sometimes the academic equivalent of the self-serving retreat into the past used by the belligerents to justify their lack of progress in the present and waffle on in an endless zero-sum game whose result is to enervate the most generous expressions of diplomatic ingenuity. This inflexibility ignores that the models created by Frantz Fanon and Albert Memmi were never as simplistic and rigidly prescriptive. Recent developments inside the field of postcolonial theory suggest indeed otherwise as new studies have with an authentic curiosity shifted their focus from Fanon's revolutionary activism to the hitherto overlooked wealth of information buried in his clinical meditations on the psychic effects of colonialism.[7] One example of how the contrary impulses of impeccable scholarship and conservative temperament could blend in the same mind and have unanticipated effects can be glimpsed in the vicissitudes of the nineteenth-century historian William Edward Hartpole Lecky (1838–1903). As Roy Foster astutely wrote, Lecky is the example of an unintentional *trahison des clercs*. A balanced interpretation of the history of Ireland, one which would treat at once with realism and even-handedness the fateful blunders and misdeeds of all the parties involved in the Irish imbroglio, presented a formidable challenge to the historian as Lecky well knew for he saw it:

> So steeped in party and sectarian animosity that a writer who has done his utmost to clear his mind from prejudice, and bring together with impartiality the conflicting statements of partisans, will still, if he is a wise man, always doubt whether he has succeeded in painting with perfect fidelity the delicate gradations of provocation, palliation and guilt.[8]

Thus it should not come as a surprise if the prescience of this statement sprang as much from theoretical as from burning topical concerns. In 1892, Lecky wanted to disprove the unrepentant imperialism of *The English in Ireland*,[9] because he feared that J.A. Froude's distortions by their very exaggeration would bolster the case for Home Rule. The overthrowing of the landlord class conspired through the unholy alliance of the Fenians, the Land Leaguers and the Home Rulers which Lecky interpreted as embryonic signs of popular democracy and socialism, foreshadowed the collapse of Irish society into chaos. Yet he remained enough of a pragmatist to predict that the cause of the Union and the chances of the negotiation of a *via media* between Southern Unionism and Irish Nationalism would be further damaged by overt expressions of racial superiority and arrogance by the colonizer. What is remarkable about his *History of Ireland*[10] is that it betrayed the intentions of its author. It is famous for having convinced W.E. Gladstone in 1886 to examine the practicality of Home Rule for Ireland. If it cannot be denied that at the critical moment Lecky's latent conservative tendencies got the better of him and he became a troubled defender of the status quo, there still remains some recalcitrant elements about him such as a faith in objectivity, his relativism, both in doctrinal and political matters, his federalism, his repugnance to the worship of force as the incarnation of right, and his compulsion to defend the unpopular viewpoint, which almost against his will combined to erode the legitimacy of colonialism.

Those features may be trivial to those critics who think of the colonialist machine as an unassailable road-roller which crushes all tenacious or original thought stirred by philanthropic or scientific considerations, yet they are bound to acquire more importance if they are articulated by more than one individual. They also become more conspicuous when Lecky's heretical unionism is compared with Froude's unadulterated imperialism. Froude loathed everything Irish and justified the Penal Laws on the numerical threat of the barbarian natives; Lecky was a nationalist whose ascendancy patriotism spurred him to prove in a most proficient way the moral and constitutional invalidity of the Act of Union. Froude was an unapologetic imperialist whose mind, in the words of Lecky, "singularly lacked gradation" and gave free rein to his racist prejudices. Lecky was a historian who believed that "the truth of a historical picture lies mainly in its judicial and accurate shading" and fought a relentless battle against himself to attain an honourable degree of impartiality. Froude was a propagandist who never dreamed to question the righteousness of the ideology of the White man's burden whereas Lecky was an open-minded thinker whose vehement conservatism had lost some of its coarser and jagged edges as it came into contact with new ideologies originating from the continent.

His dilemma puts him in the category of the "hybrid" as it was coined by the postcolonial theorist, Homi Bhabha;[11] a man whose perspective on politics is ambivalent because by virtue of his "liminal" position in the colony, the straddling of a border, he has assimilated facets of both the dominant and the dominated culture. Donal McCartney touched upon this hybridity when he named Lecky "an intellectual hermaphrodite", because one side of his personality always cancelled out the other. As a historian who esteemed above all objectivity and empathetic imagination, he was exposed to the native's point of view in a way he might never have been if he had remained on one side of the border; a pure Anglo-Irish Unionist landlord. He thus espoused the cause of Irish independence as an absolute while protesting more and more angrily against the form it was taking in the late nineteenth-century. He personifies the ambiguity hidden in the heart and mind of all those men who refused to contemplate until it stared them in the face the inevitability of the choice between "going" Irish or "staying" English. His biographer said as much: "Lecky's tragedy was to be born and to grow up neither Irish nor English at a time when his Anglo-Irish landlord class were being forced to make a conscious choice between the two".[12] F.S.L. Lyons also conveyed something of the curious position of the Anglo-Irish when he explained that their dilemma took a quasi-schizophrenic proportion because they were continuously torn between their country of origin and their country of settlement: "Their tragedy was that, hesitating as they did between two worlds, they could never be fully accepted by either. To the English they came increasingly to seem an anachronism, to the Irish they remained an excrescence".[13] In the 1990s a radical form of postcolonial theory emerged which sought to correct some of Frantz Fanon's observations into the colonial situation. This version gave a portrait of the colonial relationship that was less mechanical and above all more plausible in ethnographic and historical terms.[14] Hegel, Marx, Sartre and Fanon's yearning for a transformation of society through revolution was sidelined as Utopian and replaced by a vision in which subversion was presented as a more efficient form of agency. His most famous exponent, Homi Bhabha, feared lest conventional postcolonialism had glossed over the themes of ambivalence and fragmentation of identity that truly characterized the dynamics of the colonial encounter. Bhabha believed that research should direct its attention not just on how a White and Western culture imposed itself upon a Third World culture, but also on how colonies, despite their political disempowerment and economic disadvantage, responded to this aggression by inventing acts of cultural survival through linguistic strategies. But his most contentious argument had yet to come. He described the area around the border as a "liminal space" or a site of conflict. Reality there was infinitely more unpredictable and intractable because it was a shifting space where no absolute monitoring was possible and where all kinds of dangerous conversions, changes in alliance and intellectual and political cross-fertilizations could happen. These phenomena rigorously occurred in both directions and this set in motion an irresistible withering of the coherence of colonialist discourse.

The myth of the colonialist mindset is that it can maintain iron-clad identities; forever entrenched and staring at each other in absolute enmity and suspicion. However, Bhabha thinks that these colonial identities are always a matter of flux and agony because the border created mysteriously a desire to transgress it and discover for oneself what human experience lay beyond it. "It is always", writes Bhabha in an essay about Fanon's importance for our time, "in relation to the place of the Other that colonial desire is articulated".[15] Both antagonists unconsciously envy each other's position. The colonizer, because he feels guilty and is ashamed of the injustice perpetrated in his name, especially if he happens to be a man of the left who is genuinely appalled by the crude triumphalism and the dehumanization of colonialism. The colonized, because understandably he dreams of the day when he will outwit and beat the colonizer at his own game and force his will upon him.

Therefore, in sharp contrast to the vision of a programmed universe where even resistance is anticipated and contained, where colonizer and colonized are hermetically sealed off from each other for all eternity as if they belonged to different species, Bhabha shows how subversion, a less manageable situation than resistance, grows within the cracks of the structure. If this hypothesis is brought to its logical conclusion, indeterminacy is in the wings and the imperialist agenda in all its assumptions and illusions is in a state of imminent discredit and collapse. Whereas before colonial discourse was perceived as immovable, bombastic and hegemonic, now it is described as neurotic, guilt-ridden and self-defeating. More to the point, the weight of analysis, like the turn of postmodern and revisionist hermeneutics, falls on the obstacles to the materialization of a theory. The most problematic implication behind Bhabha's discovery is that the sabotaging of the imperialist mission happens not so much from without but rather from within its own ranks, as it were. Sedition is here presented as a condition generated by the dominant discourse itself as the hybrids, the minority who is stranded between two countries, exposed to the powerful magnet of another ethos, lose their certitudes and the confidence which come with them and are necessary assets if they want to defend their position in a system of organized injustice.[16]

It is palpable that Lecky's contradictions are an apposite illustration of those recent theoretical cogitations. Terry Eagleton is not blind to this ironic twist in Irish history when he writes: "What began life as an attempt by Protestant patriots to discover common ground among the Irish ended up as a weapon in the hands of those out to dispossess them. The Anglo-Irish had helped to give birth to their own gravediggers, and not for the first time: Irish nationalism, after all, had been their idea in the first place".[17] It is undeniable that the "new history" has paid a respectful attention to the long-term and startling effects of this Anglo-Irish "cognitive dissidence" as is called in psychoanalytical jargon the capacity to transfer oneself in the modes of thinking of an intellectual opponent. One reason why it did so, a reason often overlooked in the politically saturated climate of the 1980s and 1990s, is simply because of its methodological bend.

History and sociology, including other theory-based pursuits, function on the basis of different methodological premises as the German scholar Wilhelm Windelband originally noticed it. Sociology is a monothetic discipline because it seeks to develop a general theory and therefore tends to gloss over differences. History is an idiographic discipline because it tries to isolate and understand the unique, the distinctive and the exception in a situation that appears otherwise analogous to others. Guided by this imperative, history is naturally impelled to notice all event, phenomenon or process which do not obey the rules of the schema, escape the narrow limits of the system, and discard the truth advanced by the theory. The move in this direction is predicated on the belief that the heuristic element, what will enrich knowledge, lies dormant in those odd aspects and effects which contradict the predictions of theory. George Boyce hinted at this epistemological priority: "This is not to say that nationalism should be relegated to a less central role in Irish history. Rather, it is to urge that nationalist writing that simplifies the tradition, ignores its variety, sets aside its own internal disputes and contradictions, can hardly be said to amount to historical thinking at all".[18]

Anti-colonial theory as expounded by Albert Memmi insists that the colonial situation is about dealings occurring only at the level of two peoples. The style of colonization does not depend on one or several generous and enlightened individuals. Instead the will of any such liberal-minded person counts for nothing because, whether or not he accepts colonialism, the machine is so powerful that it will remain unruffled by his indignation, qualms, guilt or even defection. It is this colossal structure which assigns his place in the society and nothing he could say or do would change the fact that he belongs to the oppressor group and is condemned to share his fate as he shared its fortune.[19] Memmi held that the two casualties of this omnipotent system are the belief in the oneness of the human condition in all latitudes and the feelings of fellowship and compassion that stem from it. Besides the contradiction in the desire to escape mentally from a concrete situation while continuing to live its objective relations cannot forever be borne. To be coherent and credible this liberal would have to relinquish all the privileges of his special status. Logically a man who is of settler descent but opposes colonization must be ready to contemplate his own downfall. Yet it is precisely this step he cannot find in himself the courage to take. To accept with no trace of resentment a logic and a fate that will lead to one's sacrifice, even if it is on the altar of justice, is a little too much to ask of one's imagination. For this very reason, Memmi assumed that the moment of "syntony" between settler and native never happened. Politically, the colonizer of left-wing sympathies is an aberration. His utterances betray only legislative vagueness and impotence. Intellectuals of the Left, even communists, unconsciously share the assumptions of a colonialism they reject in their conscious political actions.[20] Certainly Memmi's remarks on the psychological deadlock caused by the settler's entrapment in a system, although designed for his own benefit, carry conviction and Lecky's late conversion from youthful nationalism to mature unionism seems to bear them out.

And yet Irish history, in the choices of some personalities of the Anglo-Irish tradition, dramatically disproves the idea of men always recoiling from espousing an ideology that is inimical to their interests. We are all accustomed to the habitual inventory of Protestant names, men such as Jonathan

Swift, Henry Grattan, Robert Emmet, Thomas Davis, Isaac Butt or Charles Stewart Parnell who belong to the national pantheon because they have advocated the right of Ireland to govern itself freely. Often the suggestion behind this trite argument is that if Protestants were once nationalist, they can with some wheedling and baiting, become so again. In Ireland it is the Protestants who first invented nationalism. That it should be so is no surprise given that Catholics were for a long time in their great majority disfranchized. And yet one cannot help being astounded and fascinated by a fact which belies the hypothesis of a structure whose tremendous pressures, internal and external, are supposed always to triumph of the isolated and avant-garde wills of a few individuals. The suggestion here is not that the Protestants were deliberately conspiring to their displacement out of buried suicidal tendencies. Generally, the "new historians" have not been blind to the material calculations behind the political and culturalist initiatives taken by these personalities at various junctions of the past. They have persuasively shown that by embarking on a patriotic policy, this minority did not go "native", but defended its own interests and the British Empire through the untrodden route of legislative autonomy and appeasement of the Catholics. It is as true of Edmund Burke's protest against the Penal Laws and his aborted efforts to write and champion a more objective account of the rebellion of 1641,[21] of Henry Grattan's pursuit of legislative autonomy, of the Volunteer movement of the eighteenth century[22] as it is of men like George Petrie and Samuel Ferguson who devoted themselves to the revival of Gaelic studies.

The objective instead – as in Bhabha's contention – is to give an inkling of the bungling that can happen unawareness to its watchdogs even in the most omnipotent power machine. It is also to stress that the ineradicable ambivalence of these men, regardless of their subjective estimations and rationalizations, has produced unforeseen long-term effects which they never intended or were even emphatically trying to obviate. S.J. Connolly said the same thing when he wrote that recent research had emphasized: "the extent to which patriotic rhetoric could mask vested interests and the pursuit of political power".[23] However true this is, it is grotesque and reductive to suggest that the cultural idealism of the Anglo-Irish was merely a cloak concealing covetousness for power. Subscribing to this opinion would amount to a repetition of the witch-hunting gesture of the *Catholic Bulletin* or the economic short-sightedness of a primitive form of Marxism whose soundness historians and theorists of the second half of the twentieth century have not stopped querying. The *Catholic Bulletin* argued that this minority could never be or act like true Irishmen because an ethnic fate loomed over their minds. W.B. Yeats, Horace Plunkett and George William Russell were guilty for all eternity only because they were the descendants of a caste of despoilers. Just as Maurice Barrès rejected the autonomy of Alfred Dreyfus' mind, the Jewish officer who was wrongly accused of espionage, so the extremist *Catholic Bulletin* disparaged the innovations and counsels of the

Anglo-Irish as alien to the Gaelic ethos and a threat to true Irishness. Barrès thought it was pure folly to see Dreyfus as an independent mind because he was impervious to the stimuli of land, honour and flag that impacted emotionally on the French. Likewise Edouard Drumont thought Dreyfus' supporters took too much at its face value Dreyfus' claim to be loyal for "one cannot improvise himself into a patriot, one is so in blood, in marrow".[24]

Likewise, in the hysterical effusions of the *Catholic Bulletin*, the Anglo-Irish were a "mongrel upstart" and the Agricultural Co-operative movement was a mere "carrier device" invented by "its astute promoters" to "plant a pet poison propaganda, usually found in close association with moral putrescence and pagan filth".[25] Thus, the "constructive policy" of these men was rubbished because it "had many aspects of dishonesty, conscious as well as unconscious".[26] The belief that despite their professions of loyalty these men were potential traitors derived from the principle laid down by Maurice Barrès: "We are not the masters of our thoughts. They do not arise from our intelligence. They are ways of reacting which mirror very ancient physiological dispositions".[27] This explains why it was not so much the self-proclaimed deprecators of Irish culture like J.P. Mahaffy but the constructive unionists like Horace Plunkett and especially the Anglo-Irish nationalists like George Russell and W.B. Yeats who aroused the frustrated anger and self-feeding suspicion of the fanatical revivalists. Despite their enthusiasm and ingenuity, all generously spent on the cause of a wholesome and prosperous Ireland, these Anglo-Irish men did nothing but betray the place where they spoke from, this duplicitous anti-Ireland, whose real intention was to jeopardize the foundations of the Gaelic nation. Or to use Margaret O'Callaghan's metaphor, they were wolves in sheep's clothing who were conspiring to insinuate themselves once again at the top of the pile.[28]

Evidence of a rejection of the dualistic colonial model and the awareness of a volatility along the dividing line abounds in the "new history". Conor Cruise O'Brien wrote: "The root-relation between Protestant and Catholic in Ireland is one between settler and native. Yet the vegetation sprung from these roots is complex and intertwined. Frantz Fanon's stark, Manichean contrasts between the coloniser and the colonised, though suggestive, are too simple for the situation and for most others".[29] Roy Foster explained how the colonial nationalism of the Ascendancy proved more undermining than their exponents had initially intended because sometimes, as in the case of Jonathan Swift, it "was couched in terms of an appeal to natural as well as historical rights; principle was asserted rather than precedent". And Foster shrewdly observed that this "raised [one] implicit difficulty: the argument from principle implied inclusiveness of all Irishmen, however much the theoreticians of colonial nationalism might strain at it".[30] George Boyce threw into sharp relief the insuperable contradiction at the heart of the Ascendancy's claim to be the heirs and guardians of the Gaelic tradition when he remarked:

It was all very well to claim that Irish constitutional theory could be inherited by the Protestants; but how could they regard themselves as the legitimate heirs to that "respectable and free nation" that enjoyed the benefits of freedom before the coming of the English? How could they claim any kind of real or legal descent from the Native Irish and Old English whose power they had destroyed and whose property they had taken? How, in short, could they call themselves the Irish nation?[31]

The fiction that the Anglo-Irish were the Irish nation could be sustained, clarified Boyce, only because of the effectiveness of the Penal Laws: "Since the Catholics were obliterated politically, they could also be obliterated from the minds of most Irish Protestants".[32] Yet he refused to be flippant about the involuntary service the Ascendancy rendered to native nationalism in the long run. The "bold assertion of Ireland's historic right to independence", the "willingness of Henry Grattan, and of many of his followers to admit Catholics as their fellow-Irishmen (albeit not at the expense of Protestant power)" and the "assertion that a self-governing Ireland would be a prosperous Ireland" all this "stirring nationalist rhetoric" provided an ideological arsenal against imperial Britain, and imposed a certain standard from which too-obvious deviations became unacceptable.[33] Or in the words of Boyce this model became "the minimum demand for every Irish nationalist, and the maximum demand for many of them, a symbol of nationhood even for those whose ultimate aim was separation". For these two important reasons therefore, the political strategy of the Protestant nationalists "could not be [simply] dismissed as a smokescreen thrown up by an alien and predatory colonial ascendancy".[34] Elsewhere Foster stressed that enthusiasm for antiquarianism and historiography did not necessarily lead to conversion to nationalism in the minds of such different scholars as John O'Donovan, Eugene O'Curry and George Petrie. Yet, their discoveries did lend a hand to its fortunes by creating "a currency of thought that familiarized the Irish with shamrocks, wolfhounds, round towers, the cult of Brian Boru, and the image of an ecumenical St Patrick".[35] Likewise, Boyce came to the conclusion that the rediscovery of Ireland's cultural and political heritage that began thanks to the initiatives of Protestants was "to start their country off to a destination which was to prove their own undoing".[36]

This hypothesis of the involuntary benefaction on the part of the colonizer of the tools of nationalist struggle is surely provocative and was at first hazarded in the pioneering work of the sociological historian, Benedict Anderson. *Imagined Communities* showed how the spread of print greatly assisted a strange phenomenon of collapsing of the important differences between "Creole" or colonial nationalism of the late eighteenth and early nineteenth centuries and the European nationalisms that blossomed between 1820 and 1920. Anderson wrote: "The independence movements in the Americas became, as soon as they were printed about, 'concepts', 'models', and indeed 'blueprints'". From the start opposite tendencies "jostled one another chaotically" as when the Argentinian San Martin decreed that certain aborigines be identified as Peruvians or when the Venezuelan Bolivar opposed a law issued by Madrid to specify the rights and duties of masters and slaves on the grounds that a Negro revolt was "a thousand times worse than a Spanish invasion". But the "printed word" had the magical power "to wash away" the latter fact almost at once, so that, "if recalled at all, it appeared an inconsequential anomaly".[37] In the Americas, North and South, the men who rose against the metropolis were not all democrats and altruists since some of them were – as in the case of the Thirteen Colonies – slave-owning agrarian magnates. In fact a key factor initially spurring the drive for greater autonomy was the fear of native uprisings.[38] In a biography on Edmund Burke in which he set out to prove the contested Irishness of his hero, Conor Cruise O'Brien adopted a similar line of reasoning. He argued that Burke stood a real patriot to the end, especially when he opposed Grattan's Parliament and the Volunteer movement in the 1780s. The agitation for legislative autonomy spearheaded by Grattan and Flood had alarmed Burke because it headed in the direction of the breaking of the connection with Britain and the setting up of an independent Irish Protestant nation.

As it turned out, this event was averted by Britain's decision to retain substantial control over the Irish Executive and indirectly over legislative processes also. In 1783 a more radical tendency appeared among the Irish Volunteers who put pressure on Grattan's parliament to widen the franchise so as to include the middle classes. The apparently liberal gesture of entitling some wealthy Catholics to vote, provided they met the required property qualifications of the new franchise law, was not, insisted O'Brien, as generous and disinterested as it sounds, for out of this proposed reform only three hundred to five hundred Catholics would have been enfranchised; thus ensuring that the Irish parliament would have remained either exclusively or overwhelmingly in Protestant hands. O'Brien concluded: "The people whom the Hervey proposals really aimed at emancipating were middle-class Protestants. These were generally more enthusiastic for the 'Protestant nation' than the landlords were, and their representation in the Irish parliament would have increased the pressure for real independence for that nation".[39] If this had happened, Catholics would have found themselves perpetually trapped in a position of subaltern with no chance in the future to recover and exercise their fundamental political rights as a numerical majority. Certainly O'Brien's argument is provocative because it contradicts the old nationalist belief, expounded in the works of such Nationalist historians as Eoin MacNeill or P.S. O'Hegarty, that the extraordinary events in the 1780s were the unambiguous sign of a primordial and embryonic unity between Protestant and Catholic, the revolutionary potential of which was defused by the imposition of the Act of Union.

With unforgettable incisiveness O'Brien exposes the illusions of Irish nationalism and the emptiness on which rests its claim to an uninterrupted separatist consciousness going back to medieval times: "In 1982, Charles Haughey's Government happily celebrated the bicentenary of a parliament into which neither he nor any of his colleagues would have been admitted, and for which none of them would have been allowed to vote. The reason why Nationalists idealise Grattan's parliament is that the British Government got rid of it in 1800".[40] O'Brien's conclusions are indicative of the use of a *discontinuiste* method, which is based on distance, both conceptual and temporal, and is the hallmark of revisionism. In this respect the latter functions on historicist principles that were in actual fact revitalized in the writings of the French Postmodern philosophers. Like postmodernism, Irish revisionism thinks that each field of history has its own incidence and that history is this sum composed of heterogeneous elements which is improper to yoke together by a dubious postulate of continuity.

This *discontinuiste* approach is also similar to the structuralist techniques used by ethnology. To purge the past of all present-day imperialism, Irish historians do not unwind the thread of time; they break it and teach their readers not to look in eighteenth century colonial patriotism for the origin of twentieth century separatism. Contrary to their habitual vocation which was to bring out the memory of the past, they now shield it from the grip of the citizen; they underscore the caesura separating them, thereby frustrating any desire to project onto the past present concerns. Finally, they dissolve the supposedly solid bases of a fictional kinship that served to endow the Provisionals with legitimacy. In *Archaeology of Knowledge*, Foucault pondered how the status of discontinuity had changed with the arrival of the "new history". Formerly discontinuity was both a known fact and the unthinkable. It was the raw material which offered itself to the eye of the historian under the form of conflicting decisions, statements and accidents and for which the spontaneous response was to avoid, minimize and efface the excess of illogicality so that the illusion of continuity between all the facts be kept alive.

Discontinuity used to be "this stigma of temporal dispersal that the historian had to remove from history" but now it has become a fundamental of historical analysis. It is a deliberate operation, an active tool instead of something the historian receives in spite of himself from the information he has to deal with. It is also the outcome of his description and no longer what has to be purged through synthesis. Henceforth the historian sets out to discover the limits of a process, the reversal of a movement, the moment of derailment of a circular causality. Where previously discontinuity was conceived as an obstacle it has now become a practice. It is integrated in the historian's method where it no longer assumes the role of external fatality that one has to reduce but that of operational concept that one uses to hone one's powers of penetration. This leads to a change in perception as it is no longer the negative of a hypothesis, its reverse side, its failure, the limit of its capacity, but the positive element, which determines its object and validates its analysis.[41] It is the archetype of internal critique, Sean O'Faolain (1900–1991), a man who from a tender age was immersed in the culture of the Gaeltacht, joined the Irish Volunteers and fought on the Anti-Treaty side in the Civil War and thus came from the very womb of the republican tradition who pioneered this unorthodox method. Luke Gibbons later accused him of "strategically shifting the blame for the ultimate failure of the Revolution from external sources – British imperialism – to inherent deficiencies in the native tradition".[42] Indeed, in 1938 O'Faolain made the provocative claim that the Old order of the bardic society was not so much destroyed by colonial oppression as by its inability to adapt itself to new conditions. Chained to its memories of prestige and its aristocratic contempt for the poor it let the opportunity of becoming their intelligent mouthpiece pass it by. He wrote: "How much the plebs lost is impossible to say. They do not make many appearances in the annals of the old Irish world ... Hypnotized by the Past, yet never fed by it ... they might have become, but for Daniel O'Connell, picturesque appendages of England".[43]

In 1988 Louis Cullen showed that Daniel Corkery, Prof. of English at UCC and a dominant figure of the Gaelic League, did not really understand the Gaelic poems he was praising in his *Hidden Ireland*.[44] Bradshaw and Whelan had repeatedly reproached revisionists of gliding over the "subaltern" or "colonized" voice that a close study of Gaelic sources would surely excavate; the belief being that it is there that the convincing proof of a continuity in the separatist conscience would be found. But when Louis Cullen, "the most influential interpreter of the 18th century" set out to decipher closely this poetry, his conclusions disappointed and angered Bradshaw because they weakened instead of strengthening the idea of an indomitable Irish mind surviving in a state of instinctive and indefatigable rebellion. Corkery read those poems as an authentic mirror to the experience of poverty and marginality of all the Irish people and on this misapprehension he spread the principles of homogeneity and continuity which were later annexed by nationalist history. Yet Cullen's more extensive and attentive reading yielded an accidental richness of social detail which convinced him that the poetry did not reflect the lifestyle of the poor peasants but that of a Gaelic elite composed of affluent farmers and small nobility.

Cullen did not see continuity between the aristocratic feelings of alienation and resentment and the social agitation that manifested itself here and there after 1760 and was couched "the union of mind between the big house and the cabin". After all, argued Cullen, Gaelic society also comprised poor and rich and this literature with its core of vague nostalgia and disembodied injustice sat awkwardly with the concrete claims of the agrarian secret societies. The poems of Munster and Ulster did not aspire to revolution but to restoration of the old regime. Cullen conceded that defeat cancelled at least superficially social differences. Still it only hid and did not cement let alone heal those divisions. Because he read the poets' dramatic evocation of loss literally, Corkery assigned the same intentions to the poor and rich classes when in actual fact the poetry disclosed nothing of the material conditions of the poor or of the degree and form of their politicization.[45] The "cumulative error" present in the *Hidden Ireland* betrayed Corkery's enthusiasm for the success of the Gaelic League and the rise of Sinn Féin. As these events unfolded, cultural revivalists like Hyde, Dinnen and Corkery protectively coated them with layers of historical necessity and a compelling way of going about it was to engage in a fervent quest for Gaelic origins. These men read in those poems what they wished to read: the hopes, the grievances and the separatist will of their contemporaries. This discovery does not question the intrinsic worth of those sources nor does it categorically undermine the theme of a buried or silenced Irish mind. But it certainly alerts one to the discomfiting truth that not even those type of sources escape the most fundamental epistemological rule of empirical practice: no source, no matter how authentically it seems to reflect a dead reality, is a transparent window and all of them must be handled with vigilance during the philological and deciphering act.

The depth and continuity of a separatist consciousness is the crucial question that has opposed traditionalists to revisionists and it is also on this issue that one can see profiling itself with sharp clarity the clash between two different methods. The English historian Steven Ellis feared lest the Whiggish tendency of early modern Irish historiography with its "concern" to uncover "a pre-history of Irish nationalism" had "pre-jug[ed] the issue of the island's separate development in the late middle ages".[46] Ellis contended that the notion of a progressive erosion of the English colony thanks to the extraordinary vitality of Gaelic culture represented a classic example of the trap against which Butterfield had warned the historical profession and into which fell all those historians who were convinced of having found in the evidence what they secretly and most ardently wished to find. He questioned the appositeness of the anthropological concept of acculturation and described the reality being observed as a process of slow adaptation by which settlers simply adjusted to the particular demands of a frontier life while maintaining their separate English identity and their loyalty to the Crown. Ellis did not thoroughly oppose the idea of acculturation. Rather he insisted that this phenomenon had happened in both directions. Because Bradshaw tended to ignore the influence that minorities like the Normans and the Scots had in the creation of Irish cultural identity, he deemed his remarks strangely unilateral and for that reason partial. Echoing Benedict Anderson, Ellis contended that separatism was too strong a word to adequately describe the rhetorical gestures of opposition and mobilization emanating from the old English settlers against the crown administration during certain moments of political crises. For him this reading betrayed just a projection deriving from a nationalist system of reference. On the contrary, Bradshaw insisted on the relevance of the conceptual tools of acculturation and separatism in this situation and robustly opposed the notion they were anachronistic perceptions. Moreover, he feared that the effort to establish an inviolable barrier between the intellectual climate of the present and that of the past had obscured rather than elucidated its dynamics described. In his opinion "separatism well described an important current that developed within the political consciousness of the colonial elite in the late medieval period".

Hauling out his "academic shillelagh" – his own metaphor – he took "a few swipes" at the rejection of a Gaelic consciousness before 1600 as nothing more than "an optical illusion". "Gaelicization" was not a modern political implant but a process "rooted in the historical sources", he averred.[47] That a clear distinction operated between the colonists and any other regional sub-group is indicated by the contemporary designation which applied to the Old English community the qualifying epithet "by blood", thus setting them apart from the normal English "by birth". Territory was not the only separating factor. With it came the consciousness of a constitutional differentiation. The colony represented a territory which was annexed to the English crown and not to the English kingdom and the colonists were acutely sensitive to this difference. And this was reinforced by political separation since by virtue of its unique constitutional status, the colony was endowed with its own institutional system; thus enjoying a form of devolution of power which was unheard of in other dominions of the crown.[48] When revisionists attacked the traditionalists for imposing inflated continuities between the modern Irish nation and its historical predecessors, Bradshaw retorted that the revisionists had with equal zeal and exaggeration depicted the "past as a foreign country". The challenge of Irish historiography was – according to Ellis – to find an interpretative framework which would do justice to the respective contributions of the natives and the settlers equally. Instead, the continuous exclusion of the English dimension and the insistence on the medieval English being Anglo-Irish and not English, their overriding ideology separatism and not loyalism and the English–Gaelic interaction producing no anglicization and no English revival, but only an uninterrupted gaelicization fortified by the experience of English oppression amounted, Ellis declared, to a complete repudiation of the past.[49]

The method Ellis advocates is no different from that of Lévi-Strauss, who sought to counter the most deleterious aspects of the mystique of history with the edification of a historiography capable of internalizing the ethnologist's approach, which sees all things from a remote distance since he tries to observe a tribe's customs as if he came from another planet. To behave as if everything human is alien is crucial because it is only this coefficient of strangeness which can prepare one to rid oneself of prejudices dragged from education, culture and convictions.[50] Ellis' method is also, as he himself admits, heavily indebted to Butterfield's definition of historical practice. Indeed, Ellis wants to convey the "unlikenesses between past and present" and awakens one to the possibility that by systematically "magnifying the similarities between one age and another", by "haunting for the present in the past", one can ride "after a whole flock of misapprehensions".[51] Butter-field was convinced that more often than not when a historian tumbled upon a "root" or "anticipation" of the twentieth century it was just an illusion as the past represented "a world of different connotations altogether" and he needed to use all his powers of critical resistance if he was not to be pulled by the powerful "magnet" of "misleading analogies". In keeping with this intuition he declared the entire project of origins-seeking bankrupt and warned that those who persisted in looking for roots too narrow and deep were doing so at the high risk of determinism and telescoping. The misleading analogy against which Ellis was fighting in his disagreement with Bradshaw is "conceptual anachronism". One can define it as a corrup-tion of the use of modern concepts in historical narratives. It occurs when a historian, struggling to recapture the past, and often well aware of a concep-tual gap between past and present which hinders accurate description, ends up clumsily imposing a concept from the present; thereby distorting a past reality.

Revisionist method is also founded on the effort to retrieve the historical moment in all its potentialities and to a certain extent Ellis' analysis is also inspired by similar motives. In the words of Roy Foster, the "new historians" have "tried to break up the seamless construction of narrative incident which was presented as the story of Ireland" and set out "to analyse the moment, rather than simply follow the flow".[52] An example of this can be tasted in Paul Bew's argument. Bew claimed that the displacement of the old Irish Parliamentary Party signalled the demise of the middle ground in Irish poli-tics and this had disastrous consequences for the future of the North. Con-ceding that by 1914 partition had already been ratified by the Government of Ireland (Amendment Bill) on 23 June, he nonetheless thought that the 1916 rising and their leaders' professed support of Germany greatly strengthened the Ulster Unionist bargaining position with the British State. His opinion was that Redmond's support of the British war effort had been designed to ensure a maximum leverage for the nationalists when the final arrangements for the north-eastern "excluded areas" were sorted out. It also aimed at promoting better relationships with Unionism and thus opening possibilities for a future unification. This whole strategy was sabotaged by the Rising. As a direct result of this, the Unionists were placed in a much stronger bargaining position on account of their unconditional support of Britain during the war. Bew added: "History, of course, can not be rewritten but it is worth acknowledging the cost of the choices actually taken in 1916".[53] Thus Bew refutes the idea of the inevitability of the split between Ulster and the twenty-six counties and suggests that nationalist Ireland would have been satisfied with a limited form of Home Rule government. One need not agree with Bew. The exposition of his argument is designed rather to show this radical reopening of historical vistas that is evinced by this method. On a more theoretical note Roy Foster elaborates what is implicit in Bew's interpretation: "[Revisionism] is quite simply a desire to eliminate as much as possible of the retrospectively 'Whig' view of history, which sees every event and process in the light of what followed rather than what went before; the effort to get behind hindsight. Along the way, many simple assumptions need to be questioned".[54] It would seem that synchrony is experienced as a more authentic order because it penetrates the incommensurability of situations and circumstantiates better the multitude of reasonings, intentions and fantasies that men project onto the future hoping or betting on their materialization. This order is more human because it denies omniscience and shows the limits of man in comparison to the innumerable factors of history. Conor Cruise O'Brien explained why synchrony presented also a higher degree of heuristic potential:

> Historical speculation is often called futile, because it is of its nature unverifiable. Speculation is not futile if it helps us to reconstruct the possible universe which great men strove to bring into being. We are only too liable to regard our being in the universe of "how it actually turned out" as conferring on us some kind of advantage in retrospect. The advantage is illusory; our knowledge of "how it actually turned out" is in reality a block to our comprehension of a historical figure in action; his primary characteristic is precisely the lack of that knowledge which distinguishes us.[55]

Unfortunately, the synchronic angle is not devoid of limitations. Deprived of the special power of hindsight, it can lead to a history where every event is arbitrarily regarded either as a fortunate or unfortunate accident. Equally it can lead to a history where every event is superficially diagnosed as rational or irrational. These labels, these lapidary and peremptory judgements are not useful to historical understanding. Dramatic events like the Easter Rising or the First and the Second World Wars are rarely just accidents; they are often only the tip of the iceberg. They are immensely complex occurrences heavily influenced by past relational antecedents and obeying to a subterranean logic. While it can be enthusiastic and optimistic in its wager on the future, the revisionist school is no less austere and intransigent in its attitude to theory. It tends to regard it either as a lazy shelving of reflection or as an exonerative ploy. A succinct look at its epistemological starting point reveals that it wants to contain the invasion of theory; the manner in which postcolonialism, Marxism, Nationalism and Unionism have with impunity encroached upon the rights of a complex history. It resists its impositions and strictures because they preclude the finding of other heuristic routes. It denounces the facile comfort and the surrender of responsibility that is promised by the refuge into the certainties of theory for all those minds who cannot find the courage to take up the challenge of knowledge. Contrary to other intellectuals, Irish revisionists took into account the yawning gap between prediction and reality and in this regard their profile was typically postmodern. The revisionist phase in Irish historiography bespeaks a greater vigilance for the dangers of tautology and for this reason it is, as Tom Dunne says, a local exemplification of a mainstream international current which has increasingly come to view theory as a major impediment to real elucidation.[56] Roy Foster understands why "faced with the complications and confrontations of Irish history, where axes and whetstones lay conveniently to every hand", the temptation always beckons the researcher to "simplify the story" by "adhering to one big idea". Yet he still believes that "the prescriptive and dismissive imposition of frameworks taken straight from one theoretician or another, irrespective of context or temporal conditions, can illuminate very little and may obscure a lot".[57]

To give an example, revisionism does not agree with the systematic importation of postcolonialism to the study of Irish history. Part of the reason why it does not is because Ireland's colonial profile does not correspond to that of the Third World countries, some of which were only heavily colonized during the nineteenth century, as in the case of Algeria. In fact by the end of the nineteenth century Ireland had already recovered a great deal of economic autonomy and was in the throes of an agrarian and social revolution, even though this should not be understood in a truly radical sense. Liam Kennedy claims that differences of degree are of paramount importance between countries that present otherwise similar superficial trajectories. To threaten an opponent with a fist and push thousands of Jewish children in the gas chambers are both acts of violence, equally deplorable, but the difference in degree renders the two acts incommensurable and therefore in a sense incomparable.[58] He maintains there never was a war of liberation in Ireland of the scale of the liberation wars waged in the countries of the Third World. The struggle of Arthur Griffith and Michael Collins bears only a small resemblance to the mass uprisings and the bloody reprisals that occurred in Algeria, Vietnam or Cambodia. The events that took place in Ireland at the turn of the twentieth century resemble more a process of secession on the model of the separation of Belgium from Holland before the mid-nineteenth century or on that of the secessionist tendencies of Scotland. His refutation of colonial theory proceeds on the basis of abundant statistics that show the gap between the theoretical model and the socio-economic profile of the country at the time of the crucial events. When he compares the rates of gross national product, of literacy and of child mortality on Ireland on the eve of independence with those of the Third World countries, he notices significant differences that are difficult to ignore.

In the light of this statistical information which clearly shows that previous historians had not paid adequate attention to the evolving relationship between England and Ireland in its political, economic and social aspects, the partial failure of nationalism to materialize over the whole territory looks less like an aberration. So why is colonial theory used if Ireland does not fit in the category of the Third World countries? Kennedy is adamant.

Ultra-nationalists use this paradigm to modernize their traditional rhetoric. It gives it a gloss of erudition by suggesting an abusive identification that is not borne out by the facts. We need not agree with the more political conclusions of Kennedy. On the other hand, those remarks do bring into sharp relief the methodological barrier between traditionalists and revisionists. Where the first display a tendency to make light of facts that speak against the theory, the second want to emphasize their salience. Kennedy dislikes that: "the assertion, often peremptory, has become a cheap substitute with which one can avoid the empirical search for proofs". He also thinks that the burnishing and polishing of the memory of victim both among Nationalists and Unionists has served as an excuse for ignoring the rights of the minorities in their midst. The only healthy way out of the impasse of a history continuously tampered with by the ideologues is the introduction of a comparative European approach.[59] If revisionism dissects sternly without batting an eyelid the phenomenon of repetition of repressive patterns by the independent indigenous power, it is because it thinks that postcolonial theory used as the main explanatory principle veers towards an eclipse or overshadowing of this issue. Indeed, postcolonial theory states that the colonial machinery is so implacable that its logic is eventually internalized and repeated by the native authorities.

Seen through these lenses, the oppressive and reactionary behaviour of the new state towards its own ethnic and social minorities represents neither an aberration nor a scandal but is simply the obvious sign of the ferocious efficiency of colonialism which perpetuates its conditioning of human beings even after its actual departure. Here, the faults of the new society convey only alienation and defacement in the hands of a foreign power. As a result this society is absolved from all its faults because it is the colonial system that has shaped her in this harmful way. Seamus Deane has said it in a manner that leaves no room for any doubt. All nationalisms turn out to be exclusivist, racist and doctrinarian because they are an accurate copy of the imperialisms that had oppressed them. Thus, "the point about Irish nationalism, the features within it that have prevented it from being a movement toward liberation, is that it is, mutatis mutandis, a copy of that by which it felt itself to be oppressed".[60] Bill Rolston's self-serving use of theory is even more revealing of an intention to find mitigating circumstances for Irish nationalism: "In failing to recognise that all nations are social constructs, and that the nationalism of colonised societies in part mimics that of imperial societies, revisionism in Ireland implies that Irish nationalism is somehow unique and somehow uniquely culpable".[61] At first sight, the argument put forward by Deane and Rolston is irrefutable. The repetition of old structures is a problem widely acknowledged by revisionists. As Stephen Howe put it:

> The basic claim that Irish nationalism in many respects resembled the
> imperialism against which it ranged itself, is hardly as original as David

Lloyd, (Seamus Deane or Declan Kiberd) make it sound: historians like Paul Bew, utterly opposed to (these writers) in their methodological, disciplinary and political presuppositions, had already observed as much in relation to the new culturalist nationalism of the later 19th century.[62]

This phenomenon of repetition of old relational patterns and the failure to implant revolutionary initiatives is in fact a concern typical of the post-modern intellectual and features extensively in the revisionist literature. In 1907 and 1913, Belfast and Dublin witnessed unprecedented labour strikes that for a while gave the impression that the start of the twentieth century was to be different, an era no longer dictated by the old divisions but characterized by the new confrontation between the industrial bosses and the workers. Yet, despite a promising radical phase, this battle was furtively swallowed up in the obsessive debate over the national question by conservative nationalists and ecclesiasts. They presented the socialism of Connolly and Larkin as yet another underhand attempt on the part of the British to reinstall their hegemony in Ireland.[63] This observation prompted the following comment from Oliver MacDonagh: "Ireland never had a revolutionary theory; what it had, was a mere insurrectionary theory". Insurrectionary theory by nature soon "congeals" and this explains why it never evolved "secondary or tertiary fermentation". He concluded: "The repeated casting of fresh foreign yeasts into the tun over more than sixty years has had no apparent effect beyond that perhaps, of demonstrating the incompatibility of the two".[64] The French Revolution affects only super-ficially eighteenth-century Ireland because it is still the site of an indomitable contest between the Forces of Reformation and Counter-reformation. Ian McBride has shown convincingly that a big part of the 1798 Presbyterian Radicals' attraction to the new French order lay in the vowed obliteration of Catholic "superstition".[65] In the writings of Voltaire, Diderot and Alembert, the teachings of the Catholic Church were merci-lessly lampooned and pilloried and the Church itself was presented as the greatest obstacle to the propagation of the ideas of the philosophers. Irish Presbyterians could and did seize this dogmatic aspect of the French Revolu-tion to dissimulate their sectarian leanings. They retorted that by suppress-ing Catholic "ignorance", the Penal Laws actually furthered the project of the French Enlightenment.

A foreign theory was here hijacked to buttress the sectarian practices of Irish society.[66] In a dispiriting assessment of post-revolutionary Irish society, Ronan Fanning declared: "In many respects indeed, it is continuity rather than change which was the principal characteristic of independent Ireland and it was easier to dispose of the statue of Queen Victoria than erase Victorian mentalities".[67] Obsession with severing the constitutional link with Britain was so devouring that while it galvanized all the minds it also exhausted all the energies so much so that no administrative, eco-nomic or social experiments were mooted between 1922 and 1932. Nowhere is this feeling of *plus ça change plus c'est la même chose* more disturbing than when old revolutionaries learn to excel in conservative speech and practices. The Treatyites defend the new regime and become the new oppressors. The beautiful dream of unity is forsaken in the hidden pages of the Boundary Commission. Civil war hardens conviction in the rightness of the Treaty. That Irishmen had killed Irishmen to defend it "reinforced the inhibitions of Free State ministers against tinkering with, let alone dismantling, the treaty which they had fought [for] and won".[68] The irony reaches its peak when it is de Valera himself, the man who led the opposition to the Treaty, who this time in his defence of the *Treason Bill* in 1939 outshines in legalistic rhetoric. The idyllic and dreamlike clarity of the exhilarating beginnings is replaced by a darkness which engulfs conscience. The Irish discover that the iniquitous phenomenon of repression can have an Irish face.

On 3 June 1968 Jacques Derrida declared: "I do not believe in conclusive ruptures, in the oneness of an epistemological break, as it is often called nowadays. Breaks always re-inscribe themselves inevitably in an old cloth which one must continue unpicking, endlessly".[69] This was a very untimely or out of key declaration given that in 1968 philosophical fashion lauded Louis Althusser; his break from the anthropocentric interpretation of Marxism and the political mood announced total revolution. In the *Ends of Man*, Derrida invites us deeper in the elliptical contours of his thought:

> A radical shaking cannot come from the outside. But the logic of all relation with the outside is very complex and surprising. The strength and efficacy of the system, precisely, transform regularly these transgressions into false exits. To say nothing of all the other forms of *trompe-l'oeil* prospects into which such a displacement can become trapped, inhabiting even more naively, more tightly than ever the inside that one proclaims to have deserted.[70]

This awareness of the futility of the revolutionary break calls for a deconstruction of the traditional logic of the break in order to understand the vampirism of the system, its monstrous capacity to devour the break, to cramp it ineluctably in an old mould. Such a strategy eventually calls into question the radical temporality of the revolution. What renders necessary the deconstructive gesture, according to Derrida, is the prohibitive and self-defeating nature of all radical breaks. The era of modernity: a century of disparaged hopes and failed revolutions have forced the postmodern school of philosophy to confront the one unfathomable mystery of the history of humanity. Why have the revolutionary projects never managed to loosen up the grip of the old master without further tightening the bondage of mastery? In the postmodern sensibility, the break becomes therefore but the illusion of having reached a threshold, an illusion that is made only too apparent by the reappearance of political oppression under other guises.

Everything happens then as if escape was at once plotted, anticipated and precluded by the very logic of revolutionary break. Thus both postmodernism and revisionism are intrigued by this sobering and frustrating repetition of old patterns of behaviour. Roland Barthes once observed: "History never secures the uncomplicated triumph of an opposition over another opposition and in the meantime it often discloses unimaginable outcomes, unpredictable alliances".[71] Nonetheless, the use which Irish traditionalists have made of this awareness of a problem leaves a lot to be desired. British imperialism is, since Irish nationalism was almost in a congenital manner compelled to mimic it, the one that eventually deserves to be condemned. This reasoning remains safely fastened to circularity. Without the pernicious influence of England, Irish nationalism would have blossomed into a truly egalitarian and freeing movement. For a long time the nation embodied moral triumph, a vindication of the inalienable right of all peoples to be free of foreign domination. It was a source of endless pride, an anchoring value from which men drew comfort especially at moments of crisis. It is this ethical origin of the nation and the images of political and spiritual vacuum that its abandonment conjures up which stops traditionalists from admitting that Irish nationalism is by nature restrictive, homogenizing and repressive and is therefore as Colin Graham put it, intrinsically a monolithic elision of multiplicity.[72] Graham's thesis deserves attention. His belief is that instead of restating Irish nationalism in its old style radical terminology, recent postcolonial theory has the potential to demolish the habitual assumptions and political rationale of Irish nationalism. His conclusions are interesting because he notices a surprising rapprochement between Irish revisionism and the theory as articulated by the Subaltern Studies Group in India. What both schools have in common is the notion that the nation after independence soon turns reactionary by stifling the voices of the minorities trapped inside its borders. There are bound to be limits of course to this rapprochement because to carry it further both schools would have to overcome an important epistemological barrier. Indeed, each uses a different scientific language.

Revisionism's refutation of myth and ideology is carried with reference to facts, statistics and specifics whereas recent postcolonial theory is by definition sceptical of all such positivism when it is not downright suspicious of it and has a tendency to credit ideology with an omnipotence that no researcher can hope to steer clear of. In his final comment, Graham writes: "The knowledge that these accusations will inevitably flow to and fro between revisionism and cultural theory, has meant that revisionists have not read theory with enough attention" and perceptively he adds: "The reverse, of course, may also be true".[73] Therefore, if initially postcolonial theory offers valuable insights on the relationship between colonizer and colonized, in the antediluvian manner it has been applied by theoreticians in Ireland, it threatens to go awry by providing covertly Irish nationalism with extenuating circumstances. It seems to promise a perpetual exoneration most conspicuously from the mistakes of Irish nationalism but also in ways that have not been enough underlined from the mistakes of Ulster unionism too. It is this quibbling logic that the revisionist school has astringently criticized. Francis Mulhern captures well what is so problematic about this way of thinking. What one must never lose sight of, he insists, is that Irish nationalism has by and large succeeded in its most important economic and political objectives. It forced the withdrawal of the imperial power from most of the island; it unambiguously recovered all of the confiscated land for the benefit of Irish farmers and secured, by the late forties, a stable, neutral republican state. Ireland presents none of the structural devastation, political chaos and tribal strife that are habitually observed in Third World countries. This report leads him to conclude:

> To describe the culture and society thus created as "postcolonial" is either platitudinous or – more interestingly – tendentious ... To represent the history that actually unfolded, the accomplished colonial fact, as the defining crux of Irish culture today – three generations after Independence – is tantamount to suggesting that indigenous propertied classes and their politico-cultural elites are not really responsible for the forms of exploitation and oppression they have conserved or developed in their own bourgeois state, and that radical social critics must acknowledge a continuing, mitigating "national" ordeal. The name for this is postcolonial melancholy. Its political implication, like that of any nationalism prolonged beyond its validating political occasions, is confusionist and, at worst, reactionary.[74]

The postmodernist school flirts with political nihilism for its post-lapsarian wisdom predicated on a vision of the introjection of power by man, prevents him from imagining a space exempt from domination. It is more hazardous to conjecture on the political message of the revisionist school since its function is primarily to find out what happened and why. But if one looks at the revisionist phase of the 1980s, one is prompted to think it is abnormally conscious of the conceptual millstones that men drag around their necks and for this reason it inclines towards pessimism too. But idealism is there too and it is manifest in its espousal of a liberal humanist ethic and its faith in the didactic value of its work of rectification. Revisionism is just like postmodern theory terribly conscious of the insidious forces clotting the human mind, but unlike postmodern theory, somehow it never embraces the notion of the thorough indoctrination of man. It would seem to baulk at this conclusion perhaps because it suspects that in this latter are hidden the elements of a manacling to a determinism harnessed ultimately to whitewash since it conveniently succeeds in avoiding the question of the separate responsibility of both Nationalism and Unionism.

Irish revisionism has refused to yield to a view of the human being as totally imprisoned by external conditions. True, the proper balance between man on one side and collective forces on the other is sometimes precarious and the danger of encasing man in structures of overwhelming power is still there, most conspicuously in the work of F.S.L. Lyons. Then again, when all is said and done, its methodological bend shows a prioritization of the element of human inconsistency and whimsicality, notably in its exploration of political and social non-conformity and what Roy Foster, borrowing a phrase from Beatrice Webb, has called the "treasuring [of] exceptions". It is no coincidence when Foster campaigns for an Irish history that pays as much attention to the Castle Catholic or Catholic Unionist as to the nationalist Protestant. His guiding principle, as he told Peter Gray, consisted in "tracing ambiguities, paradoxes and complications in social and historical developments", with the result that it led him to stress that "to be Irish living in the island of Ireland can be variously analysed, identified or felt without making you any less Irish for that".[75] It seems then that there is a great misunderstanding between theorists and historians in Ireland. The revisionist reluctance to think about totality which is regarded as a dubious non-political or neutral stance playing right into the hands of the status quo arises rather from the intuition that to absorb automatically into a totality can amount to a fudging of responsibility for the decisions taken by the leaderships since independence. It is not a coincidence if the revisionist method insists so much on the differences, is anxious to take apart, to fight the mixing up, the jumble, the short-cuts, the telescoping and to dismantle the identity discourse and reveal the desire for justification hidden underneath. It is founded on this major idea of separation and this will to separate is a demand for clarity. By refusing to encourage the spread of an approximate theoretical, analogical and mythical discourse, by hunting down the reductive tendencies which torpedo the materiality of facts in the name of a symbolic truth deemed superior, revisionists insist on the recovery of the very rights of history.

But they do even more. If they try to extricate history from these contaminations, it is because they understand that the blossoming of a critical truth requires each party implicated in the Irish entanglement to come to terms with its own mistakes and history as a discipline must help all to become fully aware of their share of blame. On the other hand, the discourse of identity amounts to a rhetoric of exculpation and is an evasion of individual responsibility. The character of Cain in the Bible is, writes Emmanuel Lévinas, the double inventor of crime and mythology. After his murder of Abel, he cries out: "Am I my brother's keeper?" and like the sly man who wants to fend off accusations, he forgives himself by trumpeting his faith in God. "The keeper of my brother isn't me, it is You, You our Father to us both, who has endowed me with the evil penchant, and who hasn't stopped, as you could, my criminal action".[76] Cain refuses separation because he wants to escape judgement. To better relieve himself from the burden of his sin, he absorbs the human in the divine and gives the Eternal an absolute power over the universe. The entire political thought of the twentieth century is reliant on the logic of Cain and the history of Nationalism and Unionism in Ireland is no exception to the rule. The last century is indeed littered with crimes committed in the name of a God or in the name of a Historical Reason or a Universal Theory supposed to inaugurate an era of peace, freedom and equality. What matters is the end which will restore the Good in society. If in the meantime, we resign ourselves to getting rid of the obstacles that separate us from this holy aim by killing if such course of action proves necessary, then this decision constitutes only half a homicide since it is driven by a noble cause. It is what Albert Camus called the "Logical Crime", the one explained away by calling upon the philosophies of liberation.

By dint of invoking God, by dint of blindly following a theory, the man who kills succeeds in effacing from his conscience the consciousness of committing a crime. Thus rationalized, the emotion triggered off by any such crime is also correspondingly tamed and the road is then open for the proliferation of crime. Because it strives to "untie all those knots that [traditional] historians have patiently tied", and "breaks into pieces anything which enables the consoling game of identification",[77] revisionism conducts its own brand of deposition and discrediting of Cain's discourse. Beyond the imperative of cognition it is also a radical ethical impulse which informs the *discontinuiste* method. It refuses to collude with specious alibis like the principle of the moral obligation binding a people to their ancestors because it knows that they are guileful language games to justify claims or crimes perpetrated under circumstances of completely different power relations. Because it exposes the illogicality of such alibis, declines to shield political traditions from the clinical light of dissection and denounces the justificatory reflex, revisionism has set in motion a disenthralment of Irish society. Given that truth has no political sex and no single group holds a monopoly of it, revisionists do not hesitate to pit it against their own tribe. The Provisional IRA have always prided themselves on being a movement of national liberation similar to the Organization for the Liberation of Palestine or the National Liberation Front of Algeria and above all a direct descendant of the Irish Volunteers before the Split even though their immediate origins and precise circumstances differ from these armed groups. By claiming such popular pedigree, they purge themselves from their anti-democratic aspects and grab a legitimacy they do not deserve. There is no conflict of interest which is not first and foremost a fight for denomination. In a democratic culture where power changes hands more rapidly, the outcome of many struggles depends on the name one honours things with. To dictate one's law is to impose one's vocabulary and conversely to whittle away at a language monopoly by succeeding in imposing some other vocabulary is, whatever weak position one momentarily finds oneself in, to gain an advantage in the race to final victory.

This is even truer for a jurisdiction like Northern Ireland where the very structures and practices of power have deplorably failed to meet the minimum consent. For a long time, instead of existing for reasons of its own, the Northern Irish conflict is indeed caught in the mechanics of a disguise which intends to locate it at the level either of the Third-World liberation struggles or the heroic epic of the Irish war of independence in 1919–1921. In this latter comparison, the name it uses to baptize itself converts the present into the past and history into pure mythology. Events are doomed to mimetic repetition; contemporary actors do nothing else but lend their bodies to ghosts. Ulster stages once more a play that has already been played. Hence, Unionist politicians, especially the Reverend Ian Paisley have tried to model their actions on those of Craig and Carson in 1912. Thus in 1990, the Official and Democratic Unionists portrayed their opposition to the Hillsborough Agreement of November 1985 as a reconstruction of their ancestors' resistance to the third Home Rule Bill even if they diverged on the question of the precise nature of the legacy or the exact allocation of individual roles.[78] The forefathers of Unionism, we are told, faced a dilemma, a dilemma all the more terrible for being immutable and ad infinitum experienced down to this day. In Frank McGuinness' play, *Observe the Sons of Ulster*, Kenneth Pyper the only survivor is a soldier who reminisces examples of love and brotherhood in the midst of a suffocating fear and the obscenity of the war and proclaims in cryptic undertones that ancestral hands have the power to exert a control from beyond the grave. In April 1991, the journalist Dick Walsh wrote that the era of government beyond the grave was over and backed up his wish by quoting Thomas Paine, the English radical theorist who had given his active support to the French and American revolutions. He fiercely believed that "the vanity and the presumption of governing beyond the grave was the most ridiculous and insolent of all tyrannies".[79] He added: "I am contending for the rights of the living and against them being willed away and controlled and contracted for, by the authority of the dead".

Walsh's remarks were directed at the Republicans who claim continuity between their aims and those of Pearse and Connolly. Sinn Féin have always arrogated to themselves the title of only upholder of the principles of the Republican Founding Fathers; those who, contrary to the bunch of coward, compromising and "by and large unprincipled careerists", stood faithful and unswerving in their tenacity to make the dream of one nation–one territory, a reality.[80] Hence, in both ideologies, legitimacy is coveted in a very selective and artificial use of history. With this chapter I hope to have shown that if the first stage of revisionism can be described as empirical in its attitude and method, sceptical to theory while at the same time being infused by theoretical concerns, the second stage has slowly but confidently erected upon the debris of the demolition of the old nationalist and unionist ortho-doxies, a new conceptual framework. This original structure heavily influenced by ethno-methodology is founded on one major theme: no historical and cultural construction or overarching concept when subject to a work of deconstruction transcends time.

10 The revolution comes under revisionist scrutiny

The Irish revolution and the French revolution have both gone through critical reappraisal and emotional divestment. A researcher too long immersed in the Irish debate runs the risk of picking the blindfolding habit of thinking like an insular and forgetting that despite its insularity, this country is unusually bound to the continent by common preoccupations. What at first glance denotes a parochial character conceals just under the surface more universal accents. Kevin Whelan does not agree with this opinion. He thinks the revisionist project has speculated solely within the constraining limits of an English historiographic tradition. It has remained hermetically closed to developments which took place in France, the country that was the host of the most original experiences in the field of historiography all throughout the second half of the twentieth century.[1]

These innovations were represented by the Annales School and historians like Bloch, Febvre, Braudel, Le Roy Ladurie and the very polemical François Furet. This chapter contests Whelan's opinion. If the influence of English historiography on Irish revisionism and the latter's engagement with it are undeniable, it does not mean that Irish historiography has remained stuck in a crude empiricism. Although it may be true that in terms of theorization, Irish revisionism cannot yet claim the same level of confidence, the situation cannot be described as archaic. One detects an analogous methodological turn and remarkable thematic affinities, especially in the revision of the revolution. Historiography both in Ireland and in France has been influenced by the linguistic turn taken by the human sciences. This translates in a greater emphasis on discourse. Whereas in the past, traditional historians saw political language as the reflection of deeper social and political forces, now their postmodern successors have argued that truth was never so simple essentially because language was not a neutral tool in the rendition of the past but a potent factor shaping and often distorting the very reality it described. Since social reality could only be penetrated through the deceptive veils of linguistic representations, those representations had to be conceived as key objects of enquiry for the historian.[2] The ambition behind this chapter is to underscore how Irish revisionism has, like its French equivalent, moved away from a logocentric tradition by reversing conventional interpretative techniques and looking at evidence with a more sagacious gaze; as a field of discourses where ideological interests compete to gain control of the hearts and minds of the society.

In *1916: Revolution or Evolution?* F.X. Martin adopted an approach remarkably reminiscent of Furet's method in that he sought to underscore elements of both continuity and break in the 1916 Rebellion. It is important to stress how innovative this method was because usually Marxist and Nationalist historians would simply content themselves with assuming that the Revolution did represent an absolute break intervening at every single level of reality and were not unduly concerned by those facts that conflicted with this hypothesis. In France Georges Clemenceau declared that it was a "bloc"; an inseparable unit whose tightly woven fabric could not be unpicked without threading bare the rich tapestry of the Republic itself. The revolution had come to represent a monument around which the entire nation was summoned to defend the honour of the Republic. In such a context, the role of the historian consisted in corroborating the self-justifying legend of the Third Republic.[3] Self-justification and apologia through the medium of official commemoration and control of historical teaching in schools had been central strategies of both the Cosgrave and de Valera governments after taking power in 1922 and 1932 respectively. To better secure the compliance and assimilation of disaffected opponents inside or outside the nationalist family, this exercise ostensibly had to be conducted in a spirit of appeasement and reconciliation. However, this was far from easy as no single event or hero in Ireland could truly represent all factions and elicit the same degree of respect.[4] Like their French counterparts, Irish historians were enlisted to support the official historical narrative. Unsurprisingly, their stories of Ireland presented remarkable evasions, inconsistencies and omissions.

Hence, under the patriotic pen of Frank Gallagher, the 1798 United-Irishmen Rebellion, Robert Emmet's uprising of 1803, the 1916 Easter Rising and the Civil War became one single struggle for national liberation. Referring to the letters of famous personalities who were executed during the Civil War, he wrote: "These are not the letters of '98 men or of Emmet's time or of 1916. These are the letters of 1922 and 1923, the same continuity, the same pride in death for Ireland, the same unquestioning service to Independence".[5] This telescoping had started a lot earlier with Patrick Pearse who, anxious to justify his insurrectionary plans, wrote: "It will be admitted that Theobald Wolfe Tone is a separatist. He is The Separatist".[6] Until the end of March 1916 he would claim that Tone had been "the intellectual ancestor of all the modern movement of Irish nationalism".[7] Refusing the imposition of this *continuiste* principle on the historical process, the "new historians" have spent a great deal of time on documenting the differences between 1798 and 1916. George Boyce,[8] Tom Dunne,[9] Louis Cullen[10] and Marianne Elliott[11] have all shown that T.W. Tone and Patrick Pearse were the product of two radically different socio-political and ideological contexts and for this reason their nationalism could not be of the same nature.

Their method vividly brings to mind that of Furet who was the originator of this new conceptualization. Instead of treating the revolution as a "bloc" (chunk), and endorsing such telescoping, he insisted on the need to distinguish three "revolutions", none of which necessarily entailed any of the others. Echoing Alexis de Tocqueville, a nineteenth-century belletrist but not a trained historian, he argued that far from heralding a new era, the revolution was instead a continuation of earlier structural tendencies and that the centralization of state power it had accelerated had been apparent already under the reign of the Bourbon monarchy.[12]

A critical history of 1789 or 1916 must therefore start out from the intuition of a conceptual problem rather than from the nebulous consciousness of the participants, with their illusion of a break, or their desire of being an origin. If the historian lifts this theme of a break out of the past without using the insights provided by a structural and conceptual analysis, the revolution becomes a pure origin in the present, "a mechanism that justifies the present by the past, which is the hallmark of teleological history". For Furet, de Tocqueville did not write a more Rightist history of 1789; rather he courageously undertook its first sociological analysis; one that examined "objectively" "the real content" of the revolution.

François Furet, who was a member of the History Faculty at the eminent *School of High Studies in Social Sciences*, had launched a systematic critique of those Marxist historians, Jean Jaurès, Albert Mathiez, Daniel Guérin and Albert Soboul, whose analyses had dominated for a long time the spirit and the direction of research on 1789. The image of the revolution profiling itself from his revision was singularly different because as it was explained by Michelle Vovelle, it refuted "the notion of a rapid change in history: in one word the very idea of revolution". It was a non-teleological approach; one which attacked telescoping and showed an event of such magnitude could not be reduced to a single cause. The monist interpretation, averred Furet, did not derive from actual scientific induction but from a prejudice, nourished and cherished by socialist thinking of Marxist obeisance. This rigid determinism reduced important phenomena to mere froth under which was purportedly submerged the real economic reason. In this study Furet emphasizes the limits of crude empiricism, a tendency, not limited to Marxists, to take at face value the statements of historical figures and to regard these as many windows into the truths of the past. If however he chooses to direct his epistemological animus against Marxists it is because he deems that these historians in particular should have known better. After all, Marxism had always displayed a healthy dose of scepticism for empiricism. Marx himself declared once: "men who make history do not know the history they are making". To forget their impotence they "simply rationalise their role through mental representations".[13]

The historian's job was precisely to subject these mental representations to critical evaluation. The failure of the Marxists to do so, their naïve identification with Jacobinism when they naturalized 1789 and portrayed "the most mysterious aspect of the French Revolution as no more than the normal result of circumstances and as a natural occurrence in the history of the oppressed"[14] revealed a major inconsistency in method. Habitually, in their explanation of economic and social conditions, they had shown conceptual finesse, and structural and long-term analysis. But they did not apply the same method to the political events themselves and fell into a narrative, positivist mode of which the main drawback was that it could never fathom the enormous upheaval caused in the realm of culture by the invention of democratic language. He cut to the bone when he asked: "In fact, one wonders whether it is a great intellectual achievement for a historian to share the particular image of the past that was held by the actors in the Revolution themselves, and whether it is not a paradoxical performance for an allegedly Marxist historiography to take its bearings from the prevailing ideological consciousness of the period it sets out to explain".[15]

In Ireland, Vincent Comerford criticized the teleological bend of popular and academic views of the revolutionary era. The shrinking into a series of inevitable stages leading all towards a presumed objective that is the present situation is contradicted by the meandering and unpredictable quality of the past. The teleological prism puts the seal of finality on the evolution of the nation-state. Yet outside myth, there is no ostensible reason to believe that all the great events of Irish history had a single meaning or that the entire universe laboured to give birth to a United Kingdom of Great Britain and Northern Ireland or an Irish Republic of twenty-six or thirty-two counties. These teleological lenses carry a dangerous implication in Ireland for it is felt that only the recovery of Ulster, at whatever human cost, could create a durable utopia.[16]

The rejection of teleological horizons is also at the heart of J.C. Beckett's work. In *Confrontations*, he explained that to validate this hypothesis one needs not only to overlook evidence but also to invent some that is not there, thus by essence the teleological reflex violates the truth. Linking twelfth-century resistance against the Anglo-Normans to twentieth-century opposition against the Black and Tans is not only fallacious it also "reduces most of what happened during the intervening period to a meaningless jumble of events" and "obscures the true significance of the union period" when it does not simply "deprive it of any significance at all".[17] The writing of history is influenced but not governed by the end towards which it moves. The process teaches us more than the outcome. The real history is a lot more complicated than the story of a long war between the Gael and the Gall: the unflagging struggle of an imperishable nation to expel the invader.[18]

In *Modern Ireland*, Roy Foster declared: "The scenario for 1916 was created almost entirely by another extraneous event: the First World War, which set off within IRB circles a reaction almost Pavlovian in its dogmatism. An external war created the necessary conditions for a rebellion against the British Government, even one that had put a Home Rule Bill on the statute book".[19] The Republicans alleged that it happened because the

British government was preparing to renege on its promise or because it was showing too many signs of propitiating Unionism. The Nationalists maintained that it was a logical outcome of the Cultural Revival started in 1891. Revisionism breaks with all those explanations and starts out from an epistemological position which does not believe anymore in the possibility of identifying mechanical causalities in the muddle of human affairs.

By choosing the cause which a priori is the most superficial and chronologically the closest to the event, Roy Foster asserts that the indeterminacy of the historical field renders illusory any hierarchical construction of the past according to a scale of importance. Indeed, who can say with certainty that the rebellion would still have occurred without the outbreak of the Great War or that its impact would have been as decisive on the British Government without the aid of this extraneous factor? Would the sense of threat to the British Empire have been of the same degree and prompt the same harshness in the form of a high number of executions? What can be asserted with confidence is that Irish revisionism has registered the convulsions caused by the fall into disuse of the deterministic model of historical explanation.

By advancing other causes than those habitually offered to explain the Famine, the 1916 Rebellion, or as we will see later the opposition of the protestant working class to Home Rule, revisionism indicates that it has taken its distance vis-à-vis the monist explanations defended by Marxism and Nationalism. Is the 1916 Rebellion a revolution, an absolute dropping of the existing political outlook, including the improvements begotten from this outlook or is it, regardless of the claims made by the revolutionaries, more a completion of the work pursued by the Irish Parliamentary Party and the Land League? F.X. Martin preferred to regard the Rising as the crowning point of a long period of radical renegotiation of the relationship between England and Ireland. Break is included in his estimation but reduced in his scope to a psychic, symbolic and ideological level.

Immediately, two dissonances emerge and, contrary to previous reflexes, the revisionist refuses to discount what is in urgent need of an explanation. If the historian still resorts to the writings of the leaders, it is this time in order to highlight the discrepancy between their speeches and actual reality. Hence, when Pearse writes that bloodshed is a purifying action, that the nation seeing in it the ultimate horror has lost its manhood, and that slavery is a lot worse than death, tyranny and slavery have, strictly speaking, ceased in Ireland. At the start of the twentieth century, every Irishman has the right to vote, can become a member of the civil service, enrol in the British Army and enjoys all the advantages common to all the loyal subjects of the Crown.[20]

Tom Garvin noted an astounding irony in that the Great War ushers in an unmatched wave of prosperity for the farmers and the cattle merchants and these men begin to see assets in the British connection that the separatists certainly do not want to hear of.[21] Once landlordism was destroyed

"The 'agrarian motor', which the separatists had hoped to use to move their own rather different cause along, began slowly to run out of fuel".[22] He came thus to the conclusion: "It is arguable that, had the 'accident' of the First World War not intervened, the Irish Revolution would have died by the mid-20th century without realizing its objective of complete separation".[23] Furet had praised in the work of de Tocqueville the effort to distance oneself from revolutionary rhetoric. Good history eschews the simple reporting of the utterances and actions of participants. It steps back from the heat of contention, brings concepts to bear on the events and sees beyond the illusion spread by revolutionary ideology. The other dissonance is that the circumstances, which could justify a resort to violence, are concretely absent. The regime would have to be tyrannical. And one would have to ensure that all the other means available to end this tyranny are effectively exhausted. Finally there would have to be some proportion between the evil caused and that to be removed by the revolt, a serious probability of success and a widespread approval of the community. The fulfilment of these conditions is evidently dictated by democratic logic. But the justification invoked in the writings of Pearse defied the "neat syllogisms of the logician or the detached declarations of the theologian".[24]

Partly because it was itself conspiratorial, the separatist mind was prone to detect the handiwork of crafty intrigue in the expressions of generosity of the British Government. All this redistribution of power and land in favour of the Catholic majority was an abominable trap; "the Irish were being flattered with chains of gold". The intention was to arrive at their subjection not by the old coercive measures but this time by seductive tactics. The idea was to bring "Paddy" to a point where he would consent with good grace to his own enslavement. England was purchasing the souls of half of them and intimidating the other half. For the separatist mind, the problem lay in the fact that the concessions granted by the English Parliament were being doled out as many privileges and not as the inalienable rights of a distinct people. Of course, the separatists were not completely wrong as is testified by the debates conducted inside the British Establishment and the English Unionist Party around that time. Unionists were obsessed with finding a means of persuading the Irish to abandon Home Rule. Historians now know that the Land Act of George Wyndham was not conceived by his inventor as an end in itself but as a means of "euthanasia of Home Rule" or of "killing Home Rule by kindness".[25] Liberals were also divided on the question of the real nature of Irish nationalism. Granting that it derived from social oppression, where was the assurance that it would end with it? However, if Irish nationalism were not a derivative but an absolute, then the stratagems devised by Wyndham would be found derisory sooner or later.

The insurrection was, asserted Nicholas Mansergh, the moment of truth for a Unionism that had always declined to credit the authenticity of Irish nationalism.[26] All those who had never envisaged the seriousness of the separatist claim had to resign themselves to this new truth staring them in the face. Republican separatism had not been a bluff just as the Unionism of the Ulster Protestants had not been a bluff either. Pearse's writings and speeches installed a high symbolism at the centre of political action: one that by definition rejected the possibility of a *via media* between the interests of the Empire and those of Ireland. Revisionism has tried to diminish the appeal of that symbolism. In the treatment of the 1916 Rebellion, the actors' subjectivity no longer organize or dictate the search for the reasons behind their action. The "new historians" have stopped taking the revolutionary discourse at its face value and unearthed a maximum opacity between its official claims and the objective meaning of the event. They have ceased portraying the revolutionary mind as the natural outcome of oppression or discontent and shown that the invocation of a historical necessity hides an anxious desire for validation. By highlighting the gap between the republican discourse and the actual conditions prevailing in Irish society on the eve of the rising, they have drawn attention to what Furet called "the perpetual overbid of the idea over real history".[27]

The revisionist mode of critique is highly attuned to the ironies; the fact that the scandal of oppression burst onto the historical stage when this oppression had actually started subsiding. The revolution put an enormous strain on those who were caught up in its whirlpool and revisionism has delved into how the unreasonable desire to submit history to the exigencies of a work of art has severely tested human bonds and loyalties bringing many to the brink of destruction. In the dominion of symbolism, it is infallibly man who suffers the most because he is beaten into shape to fit in the constraining limits of an ideal projection. Ideological overbid is guilty of causing an imbalance, a hypertrophy of the human heart and imagination. Man is in the grip of an irrational faith in the illusory power of revolution. This illusion pushes him to stretch situations beyond what is materially feasible and salutary for the collective interest. The traditional interpretation of the Act of Union is encapsulated in the indignant statement made by Arthur Griffith, the leader of Sinn Féin in 1902: "The Act of Union was at the time of its passage and has been since declared by independent Irish lawyers and statesmen to be a nullity, a usurpation and a fraud".[28] P.S. O'Hegarty wrote: "There is no doubt that it was conceived in treachery and carried out in corruption and that it was constitutionally illegal".[29] This statement is not entirely false but by accepting too literally the opinions of the politicians who immersed in the fight for separation, painted a black and white picture and were bent on convincing the people that the Union had been a total liability, nationalist historians like O'Hegarty were sabotaging the process of knowledge.

Directly contesting this view, George Boyce argued that it is the Union, however paradoxical this may seem, that made it possible for the Irish nation to regain a foothold, to recover its self-confidence and fortitude after the humiliation and decline it had suffered all throughout the eighteenth century. It is the Union that facilitated the emergence of a native leading class. And even if the 1916 generation was opposed to everything that the Union stood for, its rampant mercantilism and its bourgeois, complacent and too provincial mindset, the fact remains that it became the first beneficiary of the political and social transformations that the Union brought about.[30]

Oliver MacDonagh saw the Union not so much as a total evil than as a series of miscalculations. It was the sad result of a set of real fears, that of a French invasion, a republican revolution, the possibility of a social levelling up or of what a frightened tenantry or a hysterical and embattled leading class could both do in a moment of mutual terror. This act was a relief against pressures emanating from all sides, a sort of safety valve to avoid catastrophe. Yet, in MacDonagh's estimation, what is most remarkable about it is how it contributed to the progressive erosion of the Unionist position between 1815 and 1914, an intriguing fact which had been completely neglected by nationalist historians. If the miscalculations underlying the Act were serious, the abandonment or the disintegration of the tacit agreements behind it were an even more astounding development. The latter is so significant that it pushes the new historian to see in it the "defining" or "principal" theme of nineteenth-century Irish history.[31] For the Protestant nation, the first guarantee of this contract was the continuation of their monopoly over local government, public services, liberal professions, higher education, landownership and the system of order enforcement. Yet, in all those areas, the Protestants powerlessly witnessed their inexorable displacement. The act of Union marked the transfer of all administrative responsibilities to Westminster. From 1815 a new definition of public service began to emerge in England, one which increasingly took its distance from narrow political imperatives and was founded on the principle that the State should be a neutral tool to adjudicate amongst the competing claims of opposed interests. The policy of widening the right of vote was dictated by conditions specific to England and was extended to Ireland because, given its integration in the system, it was impossible to exclude it from this measure. Instead of the usual telescoping which suggests that nothing of significance happened before 1880 and the intervention of the Land League, MacDonagh adopts a *longue durée* view and shows that changes in the balance of power between Catholics and Protestants had began much earlier, as early as 1829 with the Catholic Emancipation Act which gave some wealthy Catholics the right to sit in Parliament. The architects of the Union could not imagine initially the long-term implications and administrative effects of this law. But it meant that British values and criteria were sooner or later applied to Ireland; leading to an irrevocable change in its social and political landscape.

Roy Foster chose also to ponder over how ambiguous and eccentric the Union was. The nature of the law, so logical in principle, proved to be in practice contradictory and complicated. Bad government and poverty formed part of the picture but where the Union functioned correctly, it also paved the way for its own dissolution.[32] For instance cultural revivalists were convinced that the disappearance of the Irish language would chain psychologically and for eternity the natives to the conquering power. And yet it is this very phenomenon, so often deplored, which helped the fortunes of nationalism. Anglicization led to superior levels of literacy, revolutionized the means of communication, and allowed the spread of a highly politicized culture through regional newspapers, all essential steps to the flourishing of a separatist consciousness. Nowhere do MacDonagh or Foster deny that economic exploitation was central to the designs of the British but their curiosity pushes them to elucidate what escaped the control of the leadership, what it had not foreseen. It is a profoundly ironic reading surveying the gap between initial intentions, exploitation in the guise of a benevolent integration, and the outcome, a situation which slowly smoothed the way for Catholic supremacy. Revisionism, French and Irish alike, claims that the actual redistribution of power and land had begun under the old system, the Union of 1801 in Ireland, the Old Regime in France, and that strangely it was facilitated by it. The old system had connived with the new forces towards its own extinction. Certainly, the "new historians" have stressed the innovative elements of the revolution and are conscious of a caesura in time intervening at once at a political and symbolic level. But they have also persuasively proved that in other more fundamental respects, the historical process of the revolution is one of continuity.

In the French case, 1789 extends, consolidates and brings to a higher degree of perfection the administrative state and the egalitarian society whose development is the accomplishment of the old monarchy. In the Irish case, 1921 becomes the crowning point of the administrative, agrarian, electoral and legislative reforms whose development is the accomplishment of the Union. Both historiographies agree to say that the central role, when it comes to the actual transformation of the socio-economic disposition, is played, in France, by the administrative monarchy, and in Ireland, by the administrative Union. The first empties of its living substance the order of hierarchical society.[33] The second dissolves the eighteenth-century system of property relations and paves the way to the democratization of agrarian society, first of all by proclaiming illegal a number of unjust practices, and then by legislating equitably the relations between landlords and tenants and eventually by enabling the purchase of the land by the native farmers. Foucault once wrote: "people know what they do; often they know why they do what they do; but what they do not know is what does what they do".[34] Irish revisionists have shown that the Union, conceived in order to reinforce Britain's control over Ireland, had the exact reverse effect. Seamus Deane was quick to find fault with this new interpretation: "The nationalist rejects revisionism because it is an institution that reproduces as history a form of knowledge that denies the atrocities of colonialism in order to defend the state as the outgrowth of colonialism rather than the achievement – however flawed – of nationalism".[35]

Deane may have a point. But one can also derive another conclusion from this new reading. The accomplishment of Irish nationalism is perhaps all the more exceptional for having succeeded, through an assiduous, skilful and efficient propaganda, in defeating the hidden dynamic of the Union, which had the effect of mollifying the hostility of important sections of Irish society to its existence. Moreover to argue that the British did not know what they were committing themselves to with the Union, that it revealed a misleading mechanism forever more shackling them from arbitrary action and betraying their rationale of domination, does not mean one is passing a moral or political judgement in favour of the Union. One can be in principle opposed to the Union, its underlying motives and important aspects of its operation and still recognize a degree of uncertainty, instability and slipperiness in the period it opened. Revisionists avoid humanizing the Union and choose to see it instead as a process because they think that humanizing it is the best way of ruining all chance to comprehend more profoundly its logic. Reification and objectification are here tried out with the object of attaining a truth which goes beyond conspicuousness. Of course, it is a non-teleological, non-catastrophic reading which severely upsets the Hegelian presupposition of an omniscient rationality at work inside history to which Nationalist discourse subscribes.

11 The concept of totalitarianism
Comparison and its pitfalls

It was Hanna Arendt who first used the concept of totalitarianism with the object of referring to the disquieting similarities between Nazism and Communism.[1] This equation between Nazism and Communism promised many fascinating insights but was also fraught with insuperable problems. It is no surprise if Arendt's *Origins of Totalitarianism* met so much opposition among European intellectuals when it was first published in 1951.[2] It was almost blasphemous to suggest that two ideologies, whose antagonism for each other had just been sealed by the blood of millions of people, could be subsumed under the single word of "totalitarianism". These concepts could only be conceived as perfectly watertight or immiscible.

Ernst Nolte and François Furet were the first historians to agree on the need to break this taboo. The suggestion of analogies is an immensely problematic issue for all historians who want to summon up the singularity of truth without watering it down. This is compounded by the fact that comparability can also be invented and imposed. What one needs to keep in mind is that nothing that has so much explanatory power, like comparison, in truth another form of reduction, is ever going to be harmless. The central issue of the *Historikerstreit* in Germany was whether the Holocaust had a claim to special horror in the annals of twentieth-century barbarism or whether it could be compared to other atrocities, especially Stalinist terror. Uniqueness is perceived as a crucial issue even though one could argue it should not be so because the killing remains horrendous irrespective of whether or not other regimes committed mass murder. German revisionists, especially Ernst Nolte, argued that if Auschwitz is admittedly dreadful, but dreadful only as one specimen of genocide, then Germany does not have to carry an infinite burden on its shoulders and can still aspire to some normality, acceptance and trust from the international community that no one denies to perpetrators of other massacres, such as Soviet Russia.

But if the Final Solution remains incomparable, as their opponents have insisted, the past may never be worked through, the future may never be normalized and German nationhood may remain forever tainted. The philosopher Jürgen Habermas accused revisionists of normalizing the Final Solution. The accused retorted he did not understand the scientific stakes of free historical research. For Habermas, revisionists, such as Andreas Hillgruber and Klaus Hildebrand, were neo-conservatives who through their tendentious interpretations licensed a general mood of surrender of collective responsibility.

Equally, in the Ireland of the 1980s it was not unusual to hear a similar sort of repartee. Theorists derided the outmoded historicist method of the revisionists and were appalled by conclusions which remained divorced from larger moral and political ramifications. Revisionists retaliated their opponents did not understand the *raison d'être* of historical scholarship. This was a dialogue of the deaf. Yet both sides had the intuition of something very important indeed. Historians had sensed the urgent need to reform a tradition and an identity. Theorists were eager to point at the dangers intrinsic in this exercise of reappraisal. Both sides had voiced a valid concern that needed to be addressed intelligently. Moreover revisionists openly doubted the capacity of outsiders to estimate the validity of their findings. They also fumbled when it came to confront head-on the real substance of the accusations thrown at their faces. One response was to define the word "revisionism" in its most literal sense and deny that there was a problem at all. Hence for Roy Foster revisionism was an inappropriate label, devoid of any real meaning given that all professional historians were by definition revisionist.[3] He also pressed his belief that a historian could be revisionist and yet continue to espouse nationalist convictions.[4] Ronan Fanning chose characteristically to stress the difference between fact and myth while yet avoiding the deeper implications behind "revisionism": "In its simplest sense, it merely means re-ordering or revising our knowledge of the past in accordance with such new evidence as we may unearth".[5] What is somewhat disconcerting about these statements is that they seem unaware of the slippery turn taken by similar historiographic experimentations on the Continent. They do not acknowledge that there can be sometimes a fine line between revision and negation. It was in 1963 in *Fascism in its Epoch* that Nolte first made an original contribution which sought to throw light on Nazism by replacing it in its contemporary European context. European Fascism, as embodied in the nascent French reactionary movement of *Action Française*, Mussolini's blossomed autocratic rule and Nazi dictatorship, was the conceptual structure chosen.

This bold approach accomplished several impressive intellectual tasks at the same time. It defended the notion that Fascism was a coherent and logical movement that had prevailed in different parts of Europe in various degrees. It related Fascism to its political enemies that were Liberalism and Marxism and argued with success the validity of the comparative method. Moreover far from collapsing the differences apparent in these three types of Fascism, Nolte rigorously emphasized them. A key concept in this first book is transcendence. According to Nolte's hypothesis, Marxism brought to a climaxing point the transcendence of modern society that had already begun with industrialization and the era of revolution. Because it unreasonably promised dissolution of the economic constraints of capitalism, it pushed transcendence to a dangerous vacuum. From being a creature defined by family, village, workplace and national loyalty, man became radically autonomous, unencumbered by these traditional roles. Yet this freedom came with a price: existential loneliness. Nolte argued, as had other conservatives before him, that the weak individual was not prepared to stand so completely stripped of the fabric of anchoring roles that had been intellectually constraining but spiritually nurturing. Fascism entered history with the one purpose of comforting man: to help him fight back the anguish of being free and without mooring values. Thus viewed, Fascism became a reaction to extreme transcendence; it was a programme of counter-transcendence and for this reason could not fully emerge until after the Russian Revolution. And yet, as Furet did not fail to notice, if Nazism was indeed an extreme reaction to transcendence, it betrayed its rationale and spirit when it fought its enemies, Bolshevism and Judaism with these very weapons: industrialization and modern technique.[6]

However, Nolte's subsequent writings reveal aspects that are more problematic. Since Nolte has deviated noticeably from his original thesis by claiming that Communism and Fascism are less radically opposed doctrines than twin creations of the industrial and bourgeois revolutions – two revolutionary choices to counter the uprootedness of the liberal age.[7] In 1986 in "The past that will not pass away" Nolte pushed the comparison between Russia and Germany to an extreme which was abhorrent. This time his thesis was that the atrocities of the Russian Civil War had directly inspired Hitler's Final Solution. He deemed the following question "permissible": "Did the National Socialists carry out an 'Asiatic' deed only because they regarded themselves and their kind as the potential or real victims of an 'Asiatic' deed? Wasn't the 'Gulag Archipelago' more original than Auschwitz?"[8] Here Nolte effectively succumbed to the mechanics of exculpation for he was no longer content with just advancing the irrefutable idea of a chronological interconnection between the Russian Revolution and the rise of Nazism. He, from then on, proposed a causal or reactive explanation. Nolte wanted us now to believe that the Nazis feared that Soviet terror would be inflicted on Germans, and that the Final Solution was a sort of preemptive defence. Here the Gulag precedes Auschwitz in the strong sense; it is the original blueprint from which the Final Solution derived, against which the Third Reich reacted in a kind of frenzied manner.

One must stress here that François Furet did not endorse this new interpretation. If initially he was supportive of efforts to explore thematic similarities, the common hatred for the bourgeoisie or the ways in which each ideology fed itself on the fear that the spectre of the other aroused – as this was evidently harnessed to full effect for recruitment purposes – he refused to go down the dangerous path opened by Nolte. His opinion was that Nazism had a cultural "endogenous" core, a "prehistory", as it were, independent of Marxism, existing already before the war of 1914, under the

Republic of Weimar, that was in danger of being overlooked in such an ambitious comparative structure. Furet was prepared to defend the utility of comparison but not one that collapsed completely the unique or autonomous features present in each force. He had welcomed the concept of totalitarianism because he deemed that a communist movement that was trying to conceal its hideous reality from the eyes of Western opinion had too often exploited the obsession with Nazism after the Second World War. The menace of Nazism and the fact that the Red Army played a crucial role in its defeat seem to confer, as Furet wrote, "a certificate of democracy to Stalin, as if anti-fascism, definition purely negative, was sufficient to guarantee freedom".[9]

Thus, if the educational nurturing of the painful memories of the crimes committed under the Third Reich has fulfilled the useful role of warning for humanity, its downside is that it has also inhibited for a long time the analysis of its startling affinities with its main rival, Communism. Fascism and especially Nazism were subject for so long to such a categorical condemnation and were, understandably so, the object of such loathing that this mood prohibited any objective critique into their origins. Moral rejection prevented one from discovering to what extent their popularity in the 1920s and 1930s was conditioned by the perceived and inflated threat of Communism. Moreover, during the Cold War, the pairing of Communist and Nazi crimes was always in danger of being dismissed as a tool of anti-communist propaganda cooked up by America in spite of the fact that it was a theme haunting already a few important writers of the 1930s. Hence, the ban on engaging in any critique that could boost the confidence of anti-Communist propaganda induced complacency if not a condoning of Stalinism's abuses in many writers of the Left. For all these reasons, the breaking of the taboo was a good thing.

Still, interdependence did not amount to absolute identity and Furet was concerned that Nolte out of a hurt patriotism had pushed the comparison to conclusions that were logically untenable. If he agreed with Nolte to say that there was effectively a reactive element to Fascism both in its Italian and German form and that it was reacting against Russian Communism, he refused to stretch this argument too far and reduce Fascism solely, as Nolte did, to a by-product of Communism. By overplaying the reactive aspect, Nolte implied that Nazism had no separate pedigree despite the ample evidence that it was rooted in German Romantic Nationalism and preceded the October 1917 Russian Revolution.[10] Maier concurred with Furet when he explained: "To compare two events does not entail claiming that one causes the other. Comparison is a dual process that scrutinizes two or more systems to learn what elements they have in common, and what elements distinguish them. It does not assert identity; it does not deny unique components".[11] Moreover, Nolte's thesis was weak in yet another respect; the evidence for the possibility that the Nazis obtained exaggerated reports of Bolshevik reprisals during the Civil War was indirect at best and occasionally flew in the face of known records. And the only direct quotation on which Nolte relied to allege the impact of such reports derived only from 1943. On the contrary, there is direct evidence that Hitler was already discussing euthanasia programmes, the concept of life unworthy of life, as early as 1935. This indicates that Nazi murders had their own momentum. Since, Nolte has qualified considerably this fantastic hypothesis. He denied that he meant the Bolsheviks intended to exterminate physically the bourgeoisie. The obliteration of the bourgeoisie involved, presumably, its definitive removal from the spheres of power and the nationalization of enterprises: but in no way a physical annihilation. Nevertheless Nolte still held that Hitler had just gone from ascribing class guilt to ascribing biological guilt. Apparently only the latter required physical extinction. The Gulag Archipelago is more original than Auschwitz because Soviet terror provided an example for the architect of Auschwitz, not the other way around. Now it is important to underline that Nolte is not a denier in the strong sense of the word, the way David Irving[12] and Robert Faurisson[13] are. He is too sophisticated in his theoretical articulation to be bracketed with such names. Nevertheless, his example does show dramatically how conceptual experimentation, if not controlled, can become a Trojan Horse to tendentious apologetics or even denial. It is easy to imagine how the revisionist arguments of Nolte can be appropriated by a denier to convey his message while camouflaging his repugnant pedigree by adorning himself with all the trappings of scholastic integrity. The German case has provided us with enough food for thought to look at the Irish historiographic debate this time hopefully with more profitable distance and from a fresh angle.

The German case exemplifies the aberrations into which comparison can degenerate. The Irish debate is also awash with comparisons. The question that is relevant here is whether these have improved the intelligibility of the past or else spread a contagious ambiguity or a general fuzziness that has camouflaged the issue of individual responsibilities. The opinion of this author leans towards the latter proposition. If it cannot be denied that the comparisons offered did reflect a certain amount of truth, they also overshadowed other truths, perhaps more disquieting and in more urgent need of elucidation. No comparison is politically neutral or innocent. It usually is a relatively reliable indicator of the ideological position of the writer. If it is not rigorously controlled, it can almost surreptitiously, against all authorial intentions, become a tool in the service of mitigation or even downright falsification of history.

Michael Oakeshott, the man who influenced the fathers of modern Irish history and can rightly be hailed as an epistemological purist, so reticent he was of the encroachments of theory on history, had this to say about the incompatibility between analogy and history: "Whenever the historian is presented with an apparent identity, not merely are his suspicions aroused, but he knows that he is passing beyond his own presuppositions". He added: "The institution of comparisons and the elaboration of analogies are activities which the historian must avoid if he is to remain an historian".[14]

In Ireland the most innovative form of revisionism came from the Marxist school. Like its continental counterpart old-style Marxists or Nationalists distrusted it for the same reasons. Hence for Anthony Coughlan it is merely an "Establishment socialism", instilling profound conservative instincts into the next generations and conspiring to sap the subversive potential of the theory through a strategy of cooption. Way too detached, dogmatic and esoteric to solve the Northern Irish conundrum, its real driving force was to contain the formidable challenge that Marxism put out against the Capitalist West. Its method revised key concepts of the classical tradition and trumped up a new apologia for conservative political practice by using an impeccable left-wing terminology. Coughlan is indeed convinced that its political thrust has been to provide a double apologia: one for British intrusion in Irish affairs and one for the reactionary intentions of Ulster Unionism.[15] Because he is not prepared to concede any validity to this neo-Marxism, Coughlan lapses into a form of metaphysics where all explanation is reduced to the workings of betrayal and conspiracy.

Coughlan's comment strongly suggests that this withdrawal of the Left is a sign that the enemy has crept into the Marxist camp and that some gullible souls have capitulated to its lures and deceptions. Those who waste their time interpreting instead of changing the world have become laughable puppets or mere pawns in the enemy's game. Those who dare question the theory are potential renegades. Coughlan's mind anticipates in self-critique the first signs of desertion. It is a disaster waiting to happen. To own up to a possible mistake is to help the forces of reaction, to lose the advantage. It would be convenient to repeat the denigration and impatience of Coughlan and retort that there are no serious grounds for his concern and that his intellectual position simply smacks of paranoia. It is a much more cumbersome process to identify fragments of truth in it. Irish revisionism has quit the dichotomic Cold War frame of mind. It is bound up to the epistemological principle that a theory ought to be regularly re-appraised if it is to avoid atrophy and lose touch with reality. It has decided to take the gap between theory and reality seriously and try to narrow it. Although Marxism failed in its prescriptive dimension, it could not create a united Irish working class indifferent to the enticements of the elites or to the fate of the national question, writers such as Bew, Patterson and Gibbon remained confident that the theory retained still a rich critical and analytical potential. Their objective was to recapture this potential in order to understand what went wrong and point to new possible directions. In *The State in Northern Ireland*, they declared the imminent death of Irish Marxism and to find the reasons for its premature end, they carried out a sort of autopsy. Since James Connolly, the Left has inexorably regressed. The membership of the party has continuously decreased since 1945 and no political strategy has been so far rewarding. Contrary to the Southern bourgeoisie, which has steadily been shedding its chauvinism and confronting its past mistakes, the Left has still not freed itself from the stifling embrace of nationalism.[16]

They argued that Connolly's interpretation has overshadowed fundamental factors of the historical equation. The assumption that local conditions in the North were an aberration and thus could only be artificial and temporary ruled out any serious scrutiny of the Northern Irish state. This ban on the State as a permissible and valid subject of research hindered the realization of the exceptional character of the economic, social and political parameters of Ulster. None of the fathers of Marxism, Marx, Engels or Lenin, deemed Ulster an abnormality remarkable enough to merit a separate investigation; the only bizarre aspect about Unionism was its stalling effect on the victory of Home Rule. For it was never imagined that Unionism could forever thwart the irresistible march towards independence. Such an opinion pre-empted all effort to understand its origins, its obduracy and above all the mechanics of hegemony, or what was identified as "Tory Democracy". James Connolly never recognized the plebeian element in Unionism or the material grounds behind Unionism. Hence he once said: "There is no economic class in Ireland today whose interests as a class are bound up with the Union".[17] This myopia was the derivative of an obtuse economic view of the national question. It assumed that neither the bourgeoisie in the South nor the bourgeoisie in the North were sincere in their espousal or opposition to Home Rule. Their respective mobilization was a sham. This whipped up conflict hid a sinister desire to divert the working class from its real interests and squander its socialist revolutionary energy. Connolly was indeed convinced that: "The question of Home Government, the professional advocacy of it and the professional opposition to it, is the greatest asset in the hands of reaction in Ireland, the never-failing decoy to lure the workers into the bogs of religious hatreds and social stagnation".[18]

Yet crude economism, the belief that developments on the political front reflect precisely developments on the economic front, that this latter always precedes the former and that in no case can the former operate autonomously, that is to say, politics as a mere epiphenomenon of economics, was disproved by Antonio Gramsci and even by Lenin. Strict economism postulates that history is impelled by a necessary movement, independent of the human will, derived from the continual growth of the productive forces. Capitalism is seen as heading inexorably towards crisis and collapse as the contradiction between the forces and the relations of production become greater. But Gramsci's years of activism and the failure of the Left in Italy made him question the accuracy of this postulate. He suspected that this mechanical determinism tended to promote a passive attitude of waiting for the inevitable economic collapse and this discouraged the adoption of crucial political initiatives by the Labour movement. If the Italian Socialist Party failed to give the kind of leadership required in the revolutionary upsurge of 1919–1920, it is because it clutched tightly at the economic illusion, Gramsci believed. Wrongly convinced that as the contradictions of capitalism grew, the people in their entirety would spontaneously arise and sweep the Socialist Party into power, the socialist leaders did not orchestrate a shift in the balance of forces through the building of a broad alliance between the working class and the new social forces originating from among the peasants and the urban petty bourgeoisie. Instead they allowed these forces to be mobilized by Mussolini's Fascist party, leaving the Labour movement isolated and ensuring a popular basis for the ultimate triumph of Fascism.

These observations drove Gramsci to reverse the classical theoretical schema: political forces [superstructure] precede the economic forces [basis].[19] In fact Lenin had already emphasized the importance of the political when he explained that the working class should not limit itself to a trade unionist or corporatist action but seek alliance with the peasantry. For he thought that only such cooperation could change the balance of power and create a hegemonic force capable of engaging in a democratic struggle against Tsarism. If it is accepted that capitalism does not contain within itself some intrinsic quality, which propels it towards inevitable collapse, one logical conclusion is that the outcome of any economic crisis depends on the conscious actions of men, that is, on political interventions. In 1917 the Russian working class gained political power because, under Bolshevik leadership, it unified under a single movement the massive popular struggles of the Russian people, of the oppressed nationalities and of the workers.[20] Gramsci's original input to the theory was his elaboration of the concept of hegemony which had been pioneered by Lenin. Influenced by Machiavelli's definition of power, Gramsci contended that the ruling class usurps power through a combination of coercion and ideological conditioning: by creating subjects who willingly submit to its control and introject its value-system. Conditioning is more insidious and subtler than force. Finally, following a reasoning which Bew, Gibbon and Patterson seem to have adopted, he claimed that an ideology is not to be judged by its truth or falsity but by its efficacy in binding together diverse social elements, and in acting as cement or as an agent of social unification.

One notes with Gramsci's revision a shift in the meaning of hegemony; initially it was a strategy for successful revolution, later it becomes a conceptual tool which throws light on the means by which acquiescence, consensus and class alliance are manufactured for the benefit of the ruling elite.[21] Thus the hypothesis of an innate revolutionary drive in the proletariat had already been qualified by Gramsci's observations. For no matter how paradoxical it was, facts proved that workers could be equally susceptible to opposed ideologies. Their conscience was dual; one half was indebted to the elite and complicit with its will, another half had some potential of dawning into resistance: yet this was by no means a foregone conclusion. Indeed, the Italy of Gramsci had shown clearly that the working class had to be won over single-mindedly to the cause of Labour, and that it was not by resting on their laurels that the Socialist leaders could hope to contain the manipulative interventions of the capitalists. On 9 August 1913 Connolly could confidently write: "Despite their diverse origins, the workers of Ireland are heirs of a common spoliation and sufferers from a common bondage, the watch-words or rallying cries of the various parties, led by the various factions of our masters, are but sound and fury, signifying nothing to us in our present needs and struggles; it is no longer a question of Celt against Saxon or Catholic against Protestant".[22] Thus, he was convinced that a reminding of cross-ethnic exploitation through the medium of a Marxist education would suffice to see through the fomenting of sectarian hatred. His whole outlook on both past, present and future had as bedrock the principle of false consciousness as Marx defined it. In *German Ideology* (1846) Marx and Engels explained that ideology was a false consciousness; fictitious representation of the world that the dominant class invented to impress the legitimacy and necessity of its domination on the masses and to hide from them their real condition.[23] They declared: "We must take care of this history since ideology reduces itself either to an erroneous conception of history or to a complete disregard of that history".[24] In his turn, Connolly held that Unionism misrepresented the true instincts and interests of the Protestant working class. Their mobilization against Home Rule was "stage-managed" by ruling-class manipulation of Orange prejudices underneath which was the desire to thwart the emergence of a united plebeian movement. However, in the Irish situation, the concept of false consciousness proved inadequate in several respects.

The writers of *The State in Northern Ireland* questioned its appositeness because they discovered that Orangeism and trade union militancy were, contrary to Connolly's assumptions, by no means mutually exclusive. Where Connolly rested his reasoning on the notion that Labour activism had the power to cancel out Orangeism because the former was natural and the latter was artificial, Bew, Gibbon and Patterson made instead the discovery that these two elements had coexisted and reinforced one another in the past. Apparently Connolly failed to grasp the complexity of the Orangeist phenomenon. Since the 1860s an independent form of Orangeism which articulated at once a visceral anti-Catholicism, proletarian concerns and strong democratic anti-landlord and anti-oligarchic sentiments had challenged the Protestant bourgeoisie. Hence, ironically enough, the notion of bourgeois manipulation of the Protestant masses in the service of ulterior economic interests was not at all a discourse invented by Connolly. It was already a familiar theme of the political imagination of the Independent Orange Order that was created in 1903 and was able to win considerable Protestant working-class support. The interpenetration between Orangeism and militant populism for all these years unambiguously showed that instead of being a threat announcing the future disintegration of Unionism, a limited sense of class awareness could actually assist it in its fortunes.[25] This was surely a situation, which defied the neat strictures of classical Marxism. The intensification, the endorsement and harnessing of sectarianism by the Unionist leadership and the employers owed much to a deteriorating economic conjuncture and to the necessity to stave off the electoral inroads of independent Orangeism and Belfast Labour, argued the revisionists.

This is why, by the beginning of 1920, faced with a situation of growing unemployment in the engineering and linen industries and a large number of demobilized soldiers still out of work, and a Protestant working class more dissatisfied than ever, the Ulster Unionist Labour Association gave the conflict inside the Protestant bloc a sectarian twist by scapegoating the Catholic minority. It ascribed the root cause of unemployment to the alleged "peaceful penetration" of Belfast industry during the war by "tens of thousands" of Catholics from the South and the West. Indeed, the Unionist Establishment felt so threatened by the growing appeal of independent Orangeism and the socialist movement among the Protestant masses, that for the first time, it not only acquiesced in the expulsions from the factories of Catholics, Socialists and Belfast Labour members, it also justified them – in sharp contrast to its attitude to previous expulsions in 1893 and 1912.[26] Unmistakably, the entire logic of Connolly's interpretation is founded on the principle that Marxism is not itself an ideology, that it stands outside ideology, and that its *raison d'être* is to denounce all manipulation and indoctrination through an appeal to the values of rationality and objectivity. Hence if Protestant workers were imparted with knowledge in Ulster's hidden radical history, their common sense would be stimulated and they would realize that: "The Irish Catholic was despoiled by force, the Irish Protestant toiler was despoiled by fraud. The spoliation of both continues today under more insidious but more effective forms".[27]

Clearly what transpires here, especially when we contrast Connolly's wilful rationalizations with the astringent interrogative spirit of the Irish revisionists, is that adherence to a strict economism and an evolutionist Marxism had precluded any serious engagement with the identity of Ulster Protestantism and the structural divisions that underpinned it. On the contrary, these neo-Marxists identified the weaknesses in Connolly's interpretation and decided to adopt a conceptual approach, which hinged no longer on external pressures, but on internal pressures, that is to say, on developments inside the Protestant bloc. To explain the rationale behind this conceptual structure, they wrote:

> The major strand in the Unionist viewpoint has the merit of stressing the dominant importance of forces inside Ireland. That of the Nationalists has the value of stressing the role of an important external force – even if British policy is accorded a unity it did not always possess. However, a persuasive analysis of the situation cannot be produced simply by supplementing these strands. For in fact both Unionist and Nationalist accounts share a common deficiency. They do not pose the connection between the formation of the Northern Ireland State and the class relations inside the Unionist or the Nationalist blocs ... The action of external forces was effective only in so far as it fused with forces thrown up by these relations.[28]

The focal points in this conceptual choice are the shifts in the balance of power inside the Nationalist and Unionist blocs and the way these influenced the character and evolution of the Northern Ireland State. The book claims to be poised between two unhelpful extremes: "In the context of efforts made either to demonise the system rather than understand it (the labelling of NI as an apartheid state) or alternatively to whitewash it, we present this extended interpretation which, unlike so many others, at least has the merit of a substantial acquaintance with the archives".[29] The value of this study is to have scanned in minute detail the hegemonic strategies (such as the invention of a "Labour democracy") inside the Unionist bloc. The argument is outstandingly original because its starting point is no longer just the external pressures emanating from Southern Nationalism or the British Government, but the internal tensions inside the Unionist camp together with the imperative of preserving Unionist unity to ensure the defeat of Home Rule. The writers' objections to previous analyses are that their conclusions have tended to be too "abstract", "moralistic" and "uninformative". Moreover, none of them could clarify why the state took such peculiar form, why Craig felt compelled to insist upon its Protestant character long after any Republican threat had receded and above all why no effort was made to give a fair deal to the Catholic minority in order to cement the democratic foundations of the state and deflect the threat of a more profound constitutional change. To answer those questions demanded to "trace and identify the connections between class relations in the dominant social bloc and their effects upon the state".[30] Yet it is true that this argument had also inescapable political repercussions whether this was intended or not in the first place. Even the careful conceptual choice adopted here presented problematic aspects that were bound to be criticized. Indeed it could be retorted that this new method connived to mitigate the responsibility of the state by depicting it as more benign, because overall less deliberate in its discrimination against the Catholics. By postulating that sectarianism took more the form of an expedient tool for the Unionist leadership which it harnessed only or mostly when it felt that its hegemony was faltering, the writers seemed to dispute the major argument, defended by Traditional Irish Marxists, that the Northern Ireland State was intrinsically evil, therefore beyond the power of any political reform in the future. This issue of whether or not the state was reformable had been at the centre of all the political discussions inside Irish Marxism since the outbreak of the Troubles in 1968, for the young socialists that had gathered forces under the banner of People's Democracy were convinced of the futility of reforming the state and had conducted a campaign in favour of its violent overthrow as a precondition to the creation of true socialism in the region.

For instance, according to Eamonn McCann, the democratic deficit and the opposition of the Unionists to the smallest reform rendered inevitable a frontal attack on the state: "The machinery of government could not operate democratically. It was not designed for the job. So the fight for a democratic

Northern Ireland was always likely to become a fight against the state itself. The 'national issue' was going to be posed. The only question left open was: by whom and in what form"?[31] But this was not the opinion of the revisionist Marxists. The latter were more inclined to believe that the issue of the illegitimacy of the state or its failure to garner any ostensible cross-community support had become in fact a red herring which was delaying the initiation of real socialist politics.[32] Worse they thought that the pursuit of Socialist goals by Republican means, the violent destruction of Stormont, with the Socialists lending their tactical support to the IRA, could only trigger a reactionary backlash among the Protestant workers and seriously compromise the chances of a future rapprochement inside the ethnically divided working class. Meanwhile if the most dangerous and irksome pressure was the internal one and the Unionist leadership felt obliged to outdo electoral opponents in sectarian overbid to retain its hegemony, then one should be forgiven for deducing the unpalatable idea that maybe, after all, Unionism did not need so much the prodding or the provocation of Irish nationalism to do all the undemocratic and questionable things it did against the Catholic minority. Maybe – and this seems to be one of the indirect deductions of this book – there was a hard core of anti-Catholic sentiment inside grass-root Orangeism that predated the Home Rule Crisis, had its own momentum, and was shaped by its own mythical and cultural view of the world.

This leads us to the conclusion that the thesis put forward by these writers has at least the advantage of not dwelling disproportionately or dubiously on the reactive character of Unionism and in this aspect alone it displays a methodological and political restraint that was conspicuously lacking in the historical pamphlets of another group of revisionists, the British and Irish Communist Organisation. Hence the argument hinging on the pressures supposedly coming from the Southern and Northern Nationalists is weak because, "the summer and autumn of 1922 appear to have marked phases of retreat from support for even peaceful forms of resistance in the North"[33] and the Belfast Catholic stance of non-recognition of the regime was not automatic. Nor does the evidence suggest any outright or principled rejection of the idea of involvement in the Security Forces. Rather it indicates that participation in the B-Specials was conditional on "a cessation and reversal of the expulsions of Belfast Catholics from their jobs and homes".[34] The overwhelming impression, one gathers, is that "the Belfast Catholic attitude to the Northern Ireland State was a product of a specific conjuncture of events rather than simply the expression of a deep-seated ideological attitude". Finally the writers came to the unconventional conclusion that "on balance ... the nationalist pressure was [not] sufficiently coherent or united to explain *ipso facto* the form of the state".[35]

This emphasis on meticulous scholarship, one capable of warding off both the dangers of whitewashing and moralistic condemnation, no doubt revealed a faith in objectivity and in conceptual experimentation which contrasted vividly with the sort of political and theoretical nihilism in fashion on the Continent and in Ireland at the time. The Marxism of Bew, Patterson and Gibbon was in fact influenced by Althusserian structuralism since it claimed that the only means to recover the critical potential of Marxism was to disinter its scientific origins;[36] to unearth a less anthropomorphic and purer form of the doctrine before it began to dilute itself with the welcoming inside its theoretical boundaries of the concept of the nation, which in the Irish context, led James Connolly to identify the cause of socialism with that of bourgeois national liberation and its pointless militarism. Thus revisionists maintained that "the great unfulfilled need of Irish Marxist politics is a scientific analysis of Irish society". To set up these propitious conditions, Irish Marxism needed to detach itself from bourgeois ideology and emphasize its proletarian content. This entailed an accentuation of its distinctive features rather than a systematic underestimation of these in favour of what it shared with petty-bourgeois thought.[37]

12 Revision, deconstruction, semiology

Similar methods?

Insolent and imbued with a Nietzschean wisdom, revisionism has dwelt on the unheroic and vulnerable facets of the revolutionary character and shown that instead of being this god-like figure inspired by immaculate and unselfish motives, he was fallible, contradictory, prone to uncertainties and for this reason as much acting as acted upon by various determinations. More precisely, revisionist procedures bear the hallmark of Derrida's deconstructionist tactics. One notices an overturning of critical oppositions. Hierarchies have been reversed and the second term, habitually seen as negative, deficient or derivative is now privileged. Derrida held that Western philosophy has always sought to subordinate this second term because it distrusted it, and continuously depicted it as the enemy of the *logos* (word), logic and reason. Sensing that its power was subversive, it tried to contain it and prevent it from diluting, attenuating and bleaching out the "Truth".

By choosing discontinuity, difference, ambiguity and irony as heuristic tools, revisionism has also done its share in the erosion of what Derrida called logocentrism; the illusion that voice, consciousness and subjectivity gave a privileged access to the "truth". The choice of those tools indicates that revisionists know how arbitrary and unreliable the language they deal with all the time when they study historical documents can be. They realize the instability of the meaning embedded in them. Revisionism has shown that nationalist history was not an impregnable intellectual edifice because it was riddled with cracks that were unwisely or rashly sealed. It was a discourse saturated with discordant voices that were deliberately silenced. Far from being a flawless *positivité*, revisionism asserts that a hidden umbilical cord has always chained it to doubt. Like Derrida's deconstructionist method which consists of dismantling metaphysics from within, revisionism brings pressure to bear on the most brittle links of the chain, for, on reflection, one discovers that it has always been fissured to such a degree that all efforts since its birth have been geared to draught-proof, camouflage or deny its contradictions and illogicalities. Revisionism invites us to pay more attention to those areas of doubt whose importance were glossed over or downplayed because they muddled the clarity of the chiliastic vision of nationalism. It is a recuperative history whose speculative search for the truth rests on a symptomatic or interstitial reading of the evidence. Jean-François Lyotard likened postmodernism to psychoanalytic therapy whereby hidden meanings in Western cultural history are brought back to the surface, thus breaking a cycle of repression.

He explained: "The 'post' of 'post-modern' does not signify a repetition but a procedure in 'ana': a procedure of analysis, anamnesis, anagogy and anamorphosis which elaborates an 'initial forgetting'".[1] Georges Duby noticed that postmodern history tended to approach evidence no more like a magnifying glass through which one gained access to the past instantly but more like the brush-strokes used by the painter to achieve a certain effect. With this technique, the most interesting evidence is that to be found in what remains unsaid, in what a period has omitted to disclose or discover about itself.[2] In the Irish case, the recovery of forgotten voices that were censored by separatism resemble photo negatives conveying precious insights into the motives and fears of the Easter rebels and the hidden logic of the Rising. Unsurprisingly, these testimonies are subversive because they remove the illusion of inevitability. They are the *pharmakon* (poison or cure) – Derrida plays on the ambiguity of the word – or the "undecidable" because they stand both inside and outside Irish nationalism. They are inside it since these men belong irrefutably to the nationalist family and they are also outside it because they criticize it, casting doubt on the purity of its ethics. As such, they represented a threat to the Republican cause and that is why a nationalist history set on buttressing the foundations of the new state, silenced them. Derrida held that deconstruction was more insidious and formidable than downright revolution because the *undecidables* did not content themselves with simply opposing a discourse. On the contrary, these discrepant or incongruous elements spread confusion in the structures of binary oppositions because they play all ways and refuse to choose, either by leaving or espousing totally the lines of the doctrine. Their power of subversion is superior since as internal cells, they possess the knowledge that is required to attack a tradition on its own ground, at the level of its own rhetoric and concepts. Hence the undecidable that is not pinned down is dangerous because if it is judiciously harnessed and its disruptive play intensified, it has the power to shake the core by sending a terrible tremor through the entire structure.

Revisionism has challenged the identitarian dichotomies identified by colonial discourse by showing that these only very superficially reflected the quality of human contact in the past. And in doing so, it has also queried the wisdom of the *either* versus *or*, or *us* versus *them* rationale of extremist nationalism; thereby proving that it is both in spirit and method deconstructionist. Like no external critique could ever hope to do it, deconstruction implacably exposes the lacunae and lies of a tradition, revealing that despite claims of moral or scientific authority, all traditions lack analytical, conceptual and ethical finesse, and are guilty of wrong-headed dogmatism. Thus none of them are worthy of the admiration and the worship they inspire. Julia Kristeva explained: "The semiology is the site of aggression and subversion of the scientific discourse within this very discourse. It demystifies the exactness and the purity of scientific discourse".[3]

François Furet nimbly made the difference between external and internal critique perhaps because, as an erst-while communist activist who in his mature years confronted squarely the blunders of his tradition, he struggled existentially with the emotional and political demands entailed in the latter. In indicting the USSR or China, the Right has no need to adjust any part of its heritage and can simply stay within the bounds of counter-revolutionary thought. Whereas an internal critique is bound to inflict more intellectual and psychological "wounds" and be more taxing because the Left must face up to facts that compromise its beliefs, which are as old as those of the Right. This is why – insisted Furet – the Left was loath to face up to such facts, and why, for a long time, it would rather patch up the edifice of its convictions than look into the history of its tragic mistakes.[4] In his turn, the political scientist Alan Finlayson has decided to avail himself of the potential of a political outlook founded on deconstruction in his effort to defuse conflict in Northern Ireland. He insisted:

> We must not seek to establish a middle ground, find commonality between communities or push for parity of esteem. Rather the task is one of deconstruction. Firstly it is to deconstruct the traditions in question. By deconstruction I mean precisely showing that each is dependent on that which it excludes and that each is dependent on a contradictory and empty logic. Rather than think of each "tradition" as equally legitimate we should demonstrate that each is equally illegitimate.[5]

In *Writers and Politics*, published in 1965, Conor Cruise O'Brien wrote:

> This is an age of propaganda; all of us who work with words are awash with propaganda, our own and that of others, open and covert. One can hardly fail to have – unless one has ceased to be moved by any human cause – what J.B. Yeats called "a touch of the propaganda fiend" in one's own writing. And yet one also feels the need for an effort of decontamination, the elimination of lies, not merely of one's political enemies but also of one's political friends and – a more difficult and longer-term task – of one's own. One can come to feel that this effort of personal intellectual survival is a tiny part of the human effort of survival, in which intellectual integrity must remain an essential element. My own guess is that the liberation of the communist world and of the poor world, from their crude forms of mendacity, will have to proceed from within and the liberation of the Western world from its subtler and perhaps deadlier forms of mendacity will also have to proceed from within. From the other side, we can hear a few writers, Poles, Russians, Hungarians and others, busily chipping away. Our applause can neither encourage nor

help them. What might help them would be that, from our own side also, should be heard the sound of chipping.[6]

The prescience of this statement is remarkable since the Eastern bloc's chipping from within was to achieve its astonishing revolution a quarter of a century later. Besides the remarkable similarity in the language, the words "chipping" and "decontamination" presenting undeniable Derridan accents, it is the exhortation to expose the lies and even more so, the advice to carry the critique of a tradition from within, which convey most convincingly the idea of an identical purpose behind both the revisionist and the deconstructionist projects. During a conference organized by the Irish Association in November 1998 whose object was to assess the future in Northern Ireland in the aftermath of the Good Friday Agreement, the journalist Eoghan Harris argued that the work of critique should first and foremost be turned to one's own side, mainly for two important reasons: there is already enough work waiting inside one's camp and this approach is also the best chance one has of gaining respect in the opposite camp. Conor Cruise O'Brien grasped precociously the appositeness and potential of this unorthodox method. Paying homage to his tenacity, Harris stated that paramilitary violence on both sides blatantly revealed the shortage of tolerance and compassion inside and between the two communities. The very fractiousness of these organizations indicated that critique, especially internal critique, had yet to become acceptable. With the true zeal of the converted, Harris stressed the need for Nationalists to fall in love with the Orange culture and empathize with its plight. Reconciliation is an agonizing labour of the soul, which demands that each man gathers within him the spiritual resources to open himself once again to the feelings of solidarity or compassion. He needs to make room inside him for a glance which is Other, fearsome, disturbing, and that is probably what Cruise O'Brien tried to express when he compared his conversion to Unionism to a real "existential metamorphosis".[7]

In 1977 at Trinity College, T.W. Moody gave a valedictory lecture during which he encouraged historians to persevere in the war of liberation against the servitude of myth. Opponents later brandished the speech as the essence of all that was wrong with the revisionist school. They pounced at the hardheaded "moralizing" tone, fulminated against the facile separation between myth and fact, and carped at Moody for adopting an epistemological puritanism that gave him the "moral high ground", allowed him to arbitrate in disputes and dispose in a gesture of arrogance of the discursive communities which still treasured those myths. His theoretical ignorance was an abomination, not least because it gratified shamelessly his hubris. Now allegations of the sort do jar especially when one cares to remember that as a member of the Broadcasting Authority in the 1970s he was unflagging in his plea for more open and direct dialogue between belligerents. When R.T.E. journalists ran into serious trouble with Minister Gerry Collins for flouting the principle that debarred advocates of violence from putting their opinions across, he pluckily sided with the mutinous because Ireland "needed more, not less, real communication". Hardly a trace of wrong-headed dogmatism here! Moody was at heart an Ulsterman. He was deeply affected by the tragedy that had beset his beloved province since the outbreak of the Troubles in 1968. He recoiled as much from the violence as from the complacent posturing which demonized the perpetrators. His heart was too involved for him to be casual, overbearing or censorious and he would almost certainly have found such accusations tasteless. A committed and sometimes stern pragmatist as well as a marvellous educationalist, he guessed that academic truth was just a clanging and hollow cymbal unless men were given a chance to taste its complexities undiluted and frankly. His choice for a free broadcasting was also sound Socratic advice; men must wrestle with their own and each other's assumptions, prejudices and fears before they can give birth to a more lasting truth. So was Moody's memorable speech utterly devoid of theoretical flair? A good starting point is to draw out how he disables the power of those myths on the imagination.

Superficially Irishness seems to be an invariant, indisputable and unproblematic concept. It means Gaelic, Catholic and Separatist. And yet until the end of the seventeenth century, the Old English gave their loyalty equally to the Catholic Church and the British Crown. When he singles out a time when Catholicism and Loyalism were harmonious, he subverts the notion of an immutable and quintessential Irishness as the Irish-Irelanders narrowly defined it. Orangeism – we are conditioned to believe – arrived on the stage of history just to protect Protestantism and its ideal, civic and religious freedom through the destruction of the divine rights of Kings and its replacement with constitutional monarchy. But Moody is concerned to show a less publicized and less spectacular side of the story. William of Orange who became King William III of England in 1689 was the leading spirit of a European Coalition, the Great Alliance, formed to resist France's onslaughts, then under the reign of Louis XIV. In this European War it was not primarily a conflict opposing Protestants to Catholics, for amongst his allies were the King of Spain and the Pope himself, Innocent XI. Louis XIV had taken the defence of the Catholic king, James II.

The war between the two kings in Ireland which took place between 1689 and 1691 was the outcome of the confluence of three sets of rivalries: between James and William, the dethroned king of England and the man who succeeded him, the Great Alliance and France and finally the Protestants and the Catholics of Ireland. The famous victory of the Boyne on 1 July 1690 marked in the Europe of the epoch above all the victory of the Great Alliance. By isolating an episode when Orangeism entered into a coalition with Catholicism, he loosens in the mind the throttle-hold image that made of Protestants and Catholics eternal enemies. Strangely enough Moody's fight against myth coheres with Roland Barthes' semioclastic operation. In *Mythologies*, published in 1957, Barthes argued that myths drain things of their memory and social origins. They also placate frustration and

smooth out the rough edges of material competition. The illusion is forged
that the world is perfectly limpid, with no contradiction, no conflict and no
complexity. Human actions are depleted of their political dimension and
transformed into indisputable and neutral facts. He contended that the
founding actions and myths of a nation were integral political gestures,
social constructs derived from a specific situation and tailored to match and
further the interests of the bourgeoisie. The dissemination of this agnostic
view of life caused people to retreat from the world of action and lapse into
submissiveness, preventing them from realizing that society's patterns were
reversible and perfectible.[8] In his conclusion, Moody declared:

> If "history" is used in its proper sense of a continuing, probing, critical
> search for truth about the past, my argument would be that it is not
> Irish history but Irish mythology that has been ruinous to us and may
> prove even more lethal. History is a matter of facing the facts of the
> Irish past, however painful some of them may be; mythology is a way of
> refusing to face the historical facts. The study of history not only
> enlarges truth about our past, but opens the mind to the reception of
> ever new accessions of truth. On the other hand the obsession with
> myths, and especially the more destructive myths, perpetuates the
> closed mind.[9]

Historical inquiry is not only a cognitive endeavour but also an exercise,
which makes a claim on our subjective and emotional resources. Moody is
not just alluding to factual truth here but also to a superior kind of truth, a
more charitable and humane one which gladly accepts to stretch its limits
and be challenged by other samples of existential fear, suffering and injustice. Clearly this statement can hardly be isolated as representative of an
empiricist mindset. The importance of facts is stressed but not argued in a
vacuum. Technical history is defended not merely on the strict ground of its
intellectual benefit but on virtue of its spiritual enriching of the mind; a
mind which as a result becomes less judgemental and more attuned to the
need for empathy. The disposition required to understand imaginatively
new truths, which is here celebrated by Moody, stands in diametrical
opposition to what Robert Ballagh, an opponent of revisionism has to say on
objectivity. On 21 May 2001, he wrote mockingly in the *Irish Times*:

> Sir, – I was intrigued by the comment of my friend David Norris that
> my article on the "suicide [hardly a neutral assertion] of Bobby Sands
> was totally one-sided", as if this in itself was a fault. It seems to me that
> all views and opinions by their very nature are one-sided and to attempt
> anything else defies reality. The folly of so-called "revisionism" was
> founded on the attempt to construct objective or disinterested history.
> In Ireland the result of this was simply to replace nationalist versions of
> history with anti-nationalist interpretations, frequently camouflaged

with the mask of supposed objectivity. *Homo sapiens* is a creature with a single perspective. You have to look elsewhere for alternative models – for example the chameleon, with its revolving eye-sockets, has the capacity to look in two directions at the same time![10]

Revisionists like Brian Walker[11] and J.C. Beckett[12] among others have followed Moody's advice and set out to dissect the myths of nationalism and unionism by recalling the exact environment that led to their production and consumption. Barthes' principal target is the middle class. It is interesting to notice that it is also the target of the proto-revisionist Sean O'Faolain and the object of investigation of historical revisionism especially from inside the Irish Marxist School. Roy Foster summed up the views of many revisionists when he wrote: "But Larkin himself was to find (like Sean O'Casey and other Irish socialists) in the 1920s that the new dispensation of national independence would be very different from a socialist New Jerusalem: nationalism not only absorbed pre-war social radicalism, but apparently negated it".[13] In 1943, in the *Stuffed Shirts*, O'Faolain dismissed the 1921 revolution as a middle class putsch and lamented that what "came out of the maelstrom" was not a "society" but a "class". He added: "The Gaelic League sold itself to politics, became vulgarised, and forgot its true cultural function. Worst of all, the Labour movement hastened to cash-in on self-government and threw ideas and idealism overboard: so thoroughly that when I, myself, interviewed the present leader of that Party in January 1934, he refused to admit that his party was 'socialist'". Tom Garvin's opinion on the Irish middle class's infatuation with separatism is not exactly flattering either. "Its politics", he argued, "was a class-derived emotionalism rather than an organized set of political ideas".[14] The semioclastic and the revisionist projects display both the same impatience with the way collective representations, and obtuse common sense, and a fossilized version of history attire reality with an illusion of natural. Both are impelled by a wish to remove the apparent fatality clouding situations and reinvest reality of its historical limits. Both want to show that the function of myth is to turn an intention into nature, a contingency into eternity. It was through the idea of the nation, insisted Barthes, that the haemorrhage of the word "bourgeois" was made possible.

If for a time when it helped to depose the aristocracy, the nation was a progressive concept it had now become regressive because its function was to reject the minorities it ruled non-native or unassimilated.[15] Purposeful syncretism is a method designed to win the electoral support of those minorities. Indeed no other group of intellectuals has been more conscious of this hegemonic tactic in Ireland than the revisionists who have devoted so much attention to the exploration of the theme of capture and annihilation of socialist objectives by middle-class nationalism. Hence David Fitzpatrick[16] and Michael Laffan,[17] to name only two, have illustrated in their work the gigantic and protean force of Irish nationalism in the midst of challenging situations and its uncanny capacity to absorb social dissent. Fitzpatrick has stressed the continuities that underlay the dramatic period of the revolution. Where in a climate of revolutionary effervescence one might expect to see a deep disruption in the material, make-up of a nation, Fitzpatrick came to the disheartening conclusion that "once the revolutionaries had completed the *revendication* of three-quarters of their country, those satisfied with the terms of the Treaty proceeded ostentatiously to imitate the institutions which they had worked so hard to overturn". The new institutions were designed not by "iconoclasts but by ingenious copyists"; inexorably "imitation drove out enthusiasm". The shift from Home Rule to Sinn Féin was not accompanied by radical change in the countryside. Political bosses changed their banners, but there was no real revolution in Irish minds. Sinn Féin itself resembled the old nationalist movement to a striking degree. Both were marked by what Fitzpatrick exotically termed "vampirism", the urge to suck in all other manifestations of popular initiative and by the struggles for domination of local factions.[18] This vampirism was tactical because the Sinn Féin leadership found itself confronted by the same bewildering questions as the Irish Parliamentary Party (IPP) leadership did before it. How would Sinn Féin cope with the conflicting traditions of agrarian agitation, the Labour struggle and the defence of the Catholic community against outsiders that demanded political embodiment? How much freedom would the party's successors have to mould their revolution as they wished?[19] The strength of Fitzpatrick's study resided in the fact that he was able to show in detail and considerable panache the mechanics of hegemony.

Laffan identified the same inexorable logic. Sinn Féin's interventions in labour, agrarian and other social problems were not designed primarily to help the underpaid or the landless, but to defuse that radical energy. Sinn Féin followed an established tradition. Its predecessor, the IPP, had feared that British remedies for Irish grievances might blunt the demand for Home Rule. That is the reason why when faced in its turn with the outbreak of agrarian unrest in 1918–1920, in Galway, Clare and Roscommon, Sinn Féin's response was to dampen rather than arouse or even channel this social radicalism, and "they stumbled, reluctantly and hesitantly, into efforts to contain it".[20] Barthes, the Marxist felt offended by a bourgeoisie who endlessly absorbed through mythological methods a whole humanity who did not possess its economic and social status and whose only means to experience it was by imagining it. He feared this escape into unreality came at a high price for the working class because it impoverished its political consciousness. Lucid he declared: "The excitement of collective imagination is always a cruel exercise, not only because the dream converts life into providence, but also because the dream is poor and is the proof of an absence".[21]

But perhaps the most original part of his thinking was his dynamic definition of revolution. Indeed nowhere did he suggest that the proletarian revolution retained forever a superior moral status or founded an eternally irreproachable social practice. On the contrary, when the Left stops being synonymous with questioning and change, then the myths of the Left settle and the road is open for a distortion and an inversion of reality in every way similar to that effected by the myths of the bourgeoisie. Both semiology and revisionism are constructivist techniques for they stress the contingent, open-ended nature of processes and dynamics – especially those conventionally seen as fixed. Particular constructions may present a "reality" as static, immutable or inexorably unfolding in a given direction, but the recognition alone of the constructed nature of the reality we perceive suggests that things could be different. Constructivism, thus understood, is subversive because it seeks to restore politics and agency to a world often presented to us in such a way as to render it rigid and unyielding. Julia Kristeva concurs with Barthes on the vital requirement not to confuse revolution with nihilism. In the last two centuries, more often than not, political revolution meant just forgoing retrospective questioning in favour of a straight rejection of the old so that new dogmas could take its place. Men who had reconciled themselves to the false stability of new values held the spirit of nihilism. But not only is this stability illusory it is also a totalitarian death trap. Totalitarianism is the result of a collapse or retrogression of revolution into what is precisely its betrayal.[22] If in the Irish situation, revolution is understood philosophically, as a never-ending process of interrogation, then revisionists are undoubtedly the true revolutionaries. Since they are the ones who have unveiled the ideological abuse behind the dream of the revolution, and have not hesitated to expose the gap between what ought to be and what is, their work remains a powerful antidote against all political nihilism, by which we mean the suspension of critique in favour of the cult of some hollow-ringing values, not borne out by reality.

In the 1960s Barthes launched a prodigious theoretical offensive against the objective pretensions of historical narrative. In *Historical Discourse*, he demoted the discipline to the status of ideology and even fantasy and added that its corollary concept, objectivity was a myth invented by Western bourgeois society.[23] All the same, in the light of the similarities in sensibility and method we have just underlined, we would be justified in thinking that he may have shown more curiosity for a historiography whose principal targets were the political myths of the Irish bourgeoisie.

The revolution of Easter 1916 was a cathartic moment when a link presumed natural and imperishable between England and Ireland was suddenly thrown back into question. It was an adventure designed to expose the naturalizing stratagems of imperialism and the profound alienation and disaffection between two countries that the paternalistic munificence of England at times was only trying to hide. To shake Irishmen and women out of their stupor, and end their indoctrination, Pearse countered with a myth he knew would not fail to carry profound emotional echos inside the collective subconscious – that of the martyr. By replaying the original self-sacrifice of Jesus in the name of absolute and untradable values like honour, dignity and freedom, he made an unforgettable statement; that life could be death and death could be life. Yet his choice of myth may have concealed another motive; the desire to find a good alibi for the anti-democratic and precarious path he was about to tread. Thanks to this myth, Pearse purified his action of any residual doubts and problems.

One such problem was the 1873 constitution of the Irish Republican Brotherhood which stipulated: "[It] shall await the decision of the Irish nation, as expressed by a majority of the Irish people, as to the fit hour of inaugurating a war against England".[24] The supreme council did not formally commit itself to an insurrection until the beginning of 1916, but even then it was taken without setting a precise date.[25] Clarke and MacDermott manipulated the constitution and bypassed the supreme council of the I.R.B. They were determined to use the I.R.B. for their own insurrectionary ends just as the I.R.B. had used the Irish Volunteers after having infiltrated them by occupying key positions. This small minority set up a military council which remained outside the control of the supreme council and managed to hide its plans both from the executive committee of the Irish Volunteers presided by Eoin MacNeill and the supreme council of the I.R.B.[26] The underlying rift was at once moral and strategic. The majority wanted to avoid the military failures of 1848 and 1867. But those men had decided to go into action irrespective of conditions and consequences. Maureen Wall was the first historian to have uncovered that 1916 represented not only an attack against English rule and the Constitutional Nationalists but also more problematically a coup within militant republicanism. This was a disconcerting finding because it punctured the myth that the 1916 rebellion had its legal underpinnings in the solidarity and common purpose of all Irish people. The reflections that those early conclusions inspired in the next generation of revisionists were often a lot more sceptical if not downright negative. Paul Bew stated, "The Irish party was smashed thanks to a successful coup, quite without a shred of democratic legitimacy". The Rising bequeathed the unsavoury notion that "it was right, not only to die for, but to kill for Irish nationalism" and tersely he added: "Most citizens of the Republic do not like to contemplate the current application of this idea in the North".[27] Roy Foster joined Bew in the belief that political extremism was a red herring, preventing one from grasping the real realities in a political impasse. Hence he thought that "the idea that violence was the realistic response" was "unhistorical", and what is more "unrealistic" because "the easy solutions that were posited, by their very nature, denied the real conflicts and ignored the basic conundrum". He defended his opinion by offering two concrete examples:

> As in the nineteenth century, those who embrace solutions which rely on violence are inevitably shifting the ground and identifying an easier enemy than the one who really constitutes the problem. This applies just as much to draconian British governments as to visionary republican nationalists. It is equally true of Gladstone invoking martial law against the supposed "village ruffians" who provoked land agitation in

the 1880s, and of the 1916 rebels preferring to attack a British government that had put home rule on the statute book, rather than take on
the Ulster Volunteer Force that was actually blocking its way.[28]

No doubt the revisionist who devoted the greatest amount of attention to
the dissection of political violence is Conor Cruise O'Brien. In 1978 he
declared his intention to "dismantle" the "structures" of "legitimation of
violence". If violence was tolerated or condoned it was because it was regularly justified by pseudo-historical allusions uttered by influential figures.
But what made this phenomenon so "oppressive" was the "frivolity" with
which the legitimation of violence was conducted; the "refusal to see that it
was legitimation" and that legitimation perpetuated the lie and prolonged
the conflict in Northern Ireland.[29] All reasons for a resort to violence "had to
be capable of being established and defended on rational grounds", and
always with due respect to specific circumstances if it was to carry any moral
force. Anyone who justified violence "by playing on the emotions, by obliq-
uity, by scientism, by appeal to tribal self-applause and atavistic resent-
ments" was just involved in a political game. Here again O'Brien's method
bears strong resemblance in expression and in spirit with the way Derrida
defines his own method; "I believe in the need for the dismantling of
systems, I believe in the need for the analysis of structures so as to find out
how it functions when it works and when it does not work, why the structure cannot close itself. It amounts to a *destructuration* in order to undo the
structural layers within the system."[30] The Irish philosopher Richard
Kearney intuited the effects of deconstruction on Irish history: "The translation of this textual strategy of deconstruction into political terms has radical
consequences for our inherited ideologies. All totalising notions of identity
(imperial, colonial, national) are to be submitted to rigorous scrutiny in the
name of an irreducible play of difference".[31]

Born in 1917, O'Brien is one of the most outstanding historians of the
second generation of revisionists. He is a daring and pithy voice who has not
flinched from engaging in theoretical analysis of intimidating questions like
the role of the intellectual in polarized societies, the intrinsic nature of
nationalism, political violence, the rhetorical stratagems of its justification,
and the locus of responsibility for it, while bringing his impeccable historical training to bear on them. He is the son of Francis Cruise O'Brien and
Cathleen Sheehy. His father was agnostic, a man of the Enlightenment as
he liked to present himself. His mother was a Catholic who endured the
pressures both social and psychological when after her husband's untimely
death she decided to honour Francis' wishes to educate Conor in a non-
denominational but of mainly Protestant ethos school. Being steeped in an
environment where ethnic and religious difference was a daily reality
sparked off in him a sort of dual vision which proved a unique benefit for the
man who was to become the most uncompromising and redoubtable critic of
his tribe. In his own admission Sandford Park School gave him an emotional

distance not only from Catholicism but also Nationalism. As the orphaned boy grew into a questioning and unconventional adult he not only embraced this apartness but sharpened it into an ever more precise scalpel for the dissection of the mental processes of his society. He studied modern languages and history at Trinity College where he also did a PhD on Charles Stewart Parnell and his political machine under the supervision of Theo Moody. *Parnell and His Party, 1880–90* was immediately recognized as a major piece of scholarship for its superior control of documentation and argument and for bringing the light of scholarship to pierce one of the most obscure and puzzling episodes of modern Irish history. In 1977, O'Brien asserted that the separation between good and bad nationalism was tenuous because even "under the most benign definitions of nationalism" there was some hidden degree of "aggression", "the legitimation of persecution" and "the old doctrine of the superiority of one's own nation". He believed that the governing propositions underlying Irish nationalism, the principles that Ireland is the whole island of that name, and that the nation which once filled the whole island must expand to fill it again, were a falsity and had to be challenged because their logic was leading straight towards civil war. What's more O'Brien went a step too far for most Irish nationalists when he charged that those propositions whether stated in a coaxing or coercive manner were inherently imperialistic. The coaxing method by trumpeting good will and a desire to educate the Ulster Protestants into seeing the error of their ways was just another "form of colonization which aims at the assimilation of the conquered".

If one cared to look underneath "the obtuse and apparently high-minded discourse" one realized that "the Irish Catholics, through the nationalist logic of 'unity', are led to assume, towards Ulster Protestants, the same role which Britain assumed towards Irish Catholics". The coercive method simply expressed with the full force of forthrightness what was deeply felt by the majority, mainly that Ulster Protestants were settlers in a land all of which rightly belonged to the native Irish and the only choice they had was either to stay on the terms dictated by the majority or "clear out". The first method is here to "mask the uncomplicated drive of nationalist aggression" whereas the second method even though denounced is also calculatingly "exploited".

By provocatively pairing off nationalism and imperialism O'Brien not only hit a raw nerve but also introduced a theme which at the time was unheard of inside Irish intellectual circles. Before this moment there had been a common assumption that Pearse's Left was superior to Carson's Right. The interests of the oppressed community were superior and more legitimate than those of the Empire and its supporters. The oppositions seemed unambiguous and impassable. And yet history showed repeatedly that those oppositions were not stable, they moved all the time, switching sides with one another, assuming an angelic face and a monstrous face by turns. Edmund Burke, the great Irish thinker of the eighteenth century had guessed an important truth which the twentieth century was to learn at a very high cost to mankind. He urged "wise men to apply their remedies to vices, not to names, to the causes of evil which are permanent, not to the occasional organs by which they act and the transitory modes in which they appear" because "the spirit of wickedness transmigrates".[32] O'Brien heeded his hero and became the first to explode this fatuous Manichaeism by pushing under the nose of Nationalists the desolate spectacle to which this sort of fundamentalism or dull wittedness had led. Evil was stealthy, omnipotent and tremendously resourceful and versatile. As for Good, it was too narcissistic to remain modest and vigilant. Categories were porous and Irish nationalism could secrete poisonous germs which were as lethal as those secreted by British imperialism. The fact this happened on a smaller scale and on a smaller stage did not make it any less worse or any more excusable.

His first intimation of this sponginess of conceptual categories burst onto the academic stage when he delivered a lecture on William Butler Yeats, entitled "Passion and Cunning" at Northwestern University on 29 April 1965. Conor caused a real pandemonium when he suggested that the incomparably beautiful metaphors Yeats invented were not solely the product of his creative imagination but expressed also his hope that the Fascists would win in Europe. The strength of O'Brien's argument derived from his use of an historical epistemology on an audience which may have counted the most brilliant literary scholars but was nonetheless innocent on the Irish Blueshirts movement and more generally on the appeal which the corporatist ideal exerted in the 1930s. Furthermore, O'Brien devastatingly showed that Yeats' ideological flux, or what D.H. Akenson called the continuous flooding and ebbing of his latent Fascism, dated back at least as far as 1903; thereby destroying the counter-hypothesis that his flirtation with it was just a passing affair.[33] Unfortunately, this interpretation was a veritable dragon, hard to control, bristling with dangers; which showed their problematic face only gradually and intermittently. John A. Murphy, the man who guessed those dangers and in his robust individualist fashion told O'Brien to stop dancing away from them, was also ironically a historian who had moved close to his position. So in 1978, Murphy, who had saluted O'Brien's courage for annoying the ultra-nationalist "yahoos", also showed he was not hypnotized by him. Hence he felt that the politically inspired revisionism that O'Brien personified had offered no constructive answers and its tone increasingly "pedantic and supercilious" had "diminished the force of the message he wished to convey".[34]

Put another way, the power of his flagellating incantations had receded and was now roaring like a terrible engine running on empty. For him, O'Brien betrayed all the signs of having been hoaxed, as it were, by the Provisionals' deceitful claim to be the heirs of 1916 into forgetting all the density of the past. If he came to the unfortunate deliberation that Irish nationalism was intrinsically malign it was because he was acting more and more like a politician with a crusade, frantically bustling to bring about a desired shift in public opinion, and thinking less and less like a historian. It was essential, judged Murphy, to bring history again into the equation and he did so by recalling its first axiomatic principle, that no two historical periods are identical. The 1916 rebellion was the initiative of romantic nationalists whose elitism was founded on the plausible claim that in their day there was no democratic avenue to express the separatist aspiration. Furthermore their action was given democratic endorsement in the 1918 general election. Their violence was countervailed by a "chivalrous, even a quixotic concern for the lives of civilians and the nobility of the cause", a mind-set which was worlds apart from the terrorizing methods of the IRA who felt no compunction in killing large numbers of civilians. On the contrary the IRA were Ulster Catholic Factionalists or Hibernians arrayed in the noble mantle of republicanism who after thirteen years of so-called military campaign had not come close to receiving a similar mandate from the Catholic minority they purportedly represented.[35] But Murphy's distinction, however unimpeachable it was historically, carried also its own vulnerable spot, and in this it betrayed the Achilles' heel of scholarly revisionism in general. It assumed that if given all the facts and niceties of contexts, and if submitted to the proper intellectual stimuli, public opinion would appreciate the difference between a rebellion against the rule of a foreign power and the use of the gun to force one million people to accept a destiny they had always despised and feared and thus it would withdraw its active or passive support to the paramilitaries.

In other words, Murphy appealed to their reasoning selves, assuming this would suffice to produce a shift in feeling. O'Brien on the other hand did cut through some historical complexity, did ride roughshod over certain facts, especially when after 1974 he became convinced of the imminence of a civil war in Northern Ireland. But in rejecting the old segregation between good and bad nationalism he raised naggingly the more elusive issue of collective responsibility and may have impressed their emotional selves and prompted a searching of the hearts that perhaps proved more decisive at the time. Still there are aspects in O'Brien's reflection which remain problematic. One of them is perhaps that his intransigent gaze began to rest disproportionately on the mistakes and excesses of Nationalism with the result that little was heard from his mouth about the equally disastrous mistakes of Unionism. In his autobiography O'Brien explains that the object of his unflagging loyalty has been not the Union but the Protestant people.[36] He is no dogmatic ideologue and the entire *raison d'être* of his action has been to defend not a principle but a people physically threatened by the IRA. Presupposed in this statement is that the people and politics are not the same thing. And one could garner examples of working class Protestants who radicalized by Marxism have temporarily declined to lend their support to the Unionist ruling elite or of liberals who would have no truck with the sectarian fundamentalism of Ian Paisley and gladly marched with Catholics under the banner of the Civil Rights Movement in 1968. Yet the history of

Northern Ireland has also shown with perhaps more regularity the victory of hegemony. Its most sensational vindication is the formidable mobilization of Protestant workers who in tandem with the Unionist leadership imposed a general strike to oppose the Council of Ireland in the Sunningdale Agreement of December 1973. No one is more aware of this immovable feature in the physics of the region than O'Brien himself who has devoted a very considerable part of his intellectual activity to refute the artificial dichotomy between confessional identification and politics on both sides of the divide and show how deeply and ominously they have intertwined in the past.[37]

And yet under the pressure of events, O'Brien's analyses seem to lose their historical sophistication and become disturbingly weighted. Hence the paradox that the people he feels obliged to defend out of an irreproachable humanistic impulse are not completely innocent either as he is well aware himself. Because in their majority they have condoned practices which were unfair and contemptible of the democratic *exigence*, and because those were imposed in their name and to protect their interests, they also partake in a collective responsibility which is not easily ignored. Furthermore, in affiliating himself to a unionist party out of solidarity for this beleaguered community and in respect for a humanity which is equal to others, he affiliates himself, whether he intends or not, to an ideology and a power whose own democratic record leaves a lot to be desired. His commitment to the Union in the name of a people besieged by the IRA omits something important and rings almost like a contradiction in terms because the Union, especially under the Stormont regime, has excluded whereas humanism by definition includes. His final political decision seems to negate his humanistic motivations. Murphy did tease out accurately the hidden temptations in O'Brien's reasoning when in 1978 he rebuked him for descending into a sweeping anti-totalitarian position which was unhelpful because it too quickly identified nationalism with irredentism thus rendering unacceptable the mere articulation of a unity aspiration, pointed the finger only and unreasonably in one direction, and in so doing ran the risk of "becoming a stalking-horse for an assault on nationality itself".[38]

In 1969, O'Brien wrote a masterful piece of criticism on Albert Camus in which he took up again the same haunting theme of the collusive character of political categories although this time on a different setting and with different categories. O'Brien suggested that Camus was what Albert Memmi called a reluctant Left-wing colonizer, trapped in the aberrant position of advocating a *humanitariste* romanticism when this philosophy smacked of provocation and was intolerable to both factions in Algeria, the pied-noir settlers and the native Muslims. He also maintained that Camus shared unconsciously the colonialist prejudices he rejected in his conscious political commitments. Hence when Camus denounced the violence of the FLN and erected into a principle his refusal of negotiations with them because he feared it would lead to an Algeria, granted, free from France, but under the tyranny of the most implacable leadership of the rebellion and the expulsion and humiliation of over a million pied-noirs, his position amounted in fact to a support for the repressive methods of pacification employed by the French government. Camus – declared O'Brien – is in the thrall of the French Algerian myth. He is an admiring candidate to the humanistic and rationalistic oratory propagated by French education and his fiction registers the ambivalence and the ideological contraction of a life lived in the insecurity of the frontier. In short, despite his socialist and democratic professions, Camus is at a deeper level a settler. O'Brien's critique was remarkable not only for its marvellous command of literary detail but also for its empathetic rendition of Camus' dilemma. While the work was placed under the microscope to lay bare Camus' conflicting pulls and hidden contradictions, Camus the man surprisingly retained his dignity despite O'Brien's opinionated search for the colonialist syndrome in him.

Although O'Brien made it clear that he believed Camus' final choice to have been wrong politically, he still appreciated the inner struggle Camus endured and it instinctively aroused his respect. While the *bien-pensants* of the Parisian intelligentsia had watched for any opportunity to shred him, O'Brien's Camus was fallible but also courageous, hard-pressed and wrestling with daunting questions. He wrote: "Yet we must recognize that it was to Camus, not to Sartre, that the choice was presented in a personal and agonizing form: that Sartre's choice, even if it was the right one, came relatively easily, whereas Camus' choice, wrong as we may think it politically, issued out of the depths of his whole life history".[39] O'Brien also conceded another important merit to Camus, that of having "explored with increasing subtlety and honesty the nature and consequences of his flinching" from the realities of his position as a Frenchman of Algeria.

Ironically, twenty years later, O'Brien would tread down the same path as Camus did. He became the arch-rival of the IRA and consistently opposed negotiations with them, declared himself in favour of the Union with Britain, became the defender of the Ulster Unionists and argued that those settlers had the right to resort to the same secessionist principle as the Nationalist majority. In addition, he counterpoised the legalistic and historical arguments of territorial and electoral gerrymandering, discrimination, and in international law, the majoritarian definition of self-determination which made it notoriously reluctant to concede secessionist rights to minorities, inside newly independent nations used to deny legitimacy to Northern Ireland, with another argument. That argument is simply that those reasons do not justify in any way the terrorizing methods of the IRA. Two wrongs cannot make a right. Violence ought not to be fought with violence. One reaches this rather unsettling conclusion, mainly that Camus' colonialism is dormant, his predicament and incoherence a reflection of his status as a "casualty of the post-war period" whereas O'Brien's colonialism is voluntarily embraced and pro-active, at least that is how his critics read the situation.

In his refusal to condemn Camus, O'Brien seems to admit obliquely that if placed in the same situation he himself cannot be sure whose side he would have taken. The humility manifest in the conclusion forms a sharp contrast with the more principled and politically correct tone running right through and may hold the key to O'Brien's later conversion. Gripped by the fear that his beloved country will slip into a civil war, O'Brien is tempted to do away with a vindictive and blazing history and adopts the same humanistic and rationalistic language he had found so repugnant and hypocritical in Camus. Seamus Deane would pick on him precisely for this reason.[40] This impatience for the uses of a serviceable or corruptible history does not prove though that O'Brien has become a defender of colonialism. Frantz Fanon who was the personification of anti-colonialist activism always refused to cross the line that Sartre and later post-structuralist philosophers did when they equated humanism with colonialism. Despite all the horrors being perpetrated under his eyes of combatant, in his sober writing, he continued to resist all demonological and Manichaeist thinking and wished to save the ideal of a universal fellowship. This quest steered him to think that the coloured man had no right to wish the crystallization of culpability in the white man. With words unforgettable in their promise of deliverance and serenity he declared:

> There is no Negro mission; there is no white burden. I am no prisoner of History ... The moral pain in front of the density of the past? I have no right to allow myself being ensnared by the determinations of the past ... The density of History determines none of my actions. And it is by overcoming the historical, instrumental fact that I introduce the cycle of my freedom. As a Negro man, I have no right to confine myself in a world of retroactive reparations.[41]

O'Brien's stance towards Northern Ireland seems to be moulded out of a similar type of sensibility. Like Camus he stops reasoning out of rigid principles and starts reasoning in terms of likely consequences. The argument of a rapprochement between O'Brien and Camus is not pursued in order to impugn the former for contradiction or volte-face like some critics did.[42] After all Frank Wright, Brian Walker and Liam Kennedy have all drawn attention to the reasons why the situation in Northern Ireland is different from Algeria. And in fairness to O'Brien, he was one of the first on the ground, warning as early as September 1971 that the Algerian analogy was seriously flawed and dangerously misleading and that whoever propounded a similar denouement in Northern Ireland "could inadvertently lead the Catholics of Belfast to their doom".[43]

Rather the intention is to show the paradigmatic shift in an Irish context, felt on the pulses as it were, as O'Brien is observing very closely the deteriorating situation in Ulster and trying to fathom out and assimilate unforeseen events. Sectarian violence at its least decorous and most unashamed has thrust forth in his mind, causing his old theories to crumble to dust and proposing hitherto unarticulated and frightening questions. A radically new experience, irreducible to available categories, elicits a typical postmodern brooding from him:

> Northern Ireland is unique: a long, grim history has made it so. The measures to be taken for it and in it should be specific to its problems, not just the application of routines applied elsewhere ... Ulster Protestants have been in Ulster as long as white men have been in what is now the United States. And Irish Catholics have been there, coping with the English Question, much longer still.[44]

In 1988 he stressed again:

> The peculiar slipperiness – the protean character ... of theory, of the concepts involved. Things slide and merge into other things, which would appear to be quite different, and even opposed; this is a field in which the dialectic gets particularly frisky. Category limits that may appear quite distinct and stable conceptually ... become blurred and permeable as they manifest themselves in history.[45]

When he repeatedly delivered this electric shock to the Irish psyche O'Brien was of one mind with the most prescient intellects of the continent. One of them was Hanna Arendt, the German philosopher who had fled Nazi persecution to find asylum in America and whom Conor may have met when between 1965 and 1968 he moved with success around the land of New York intellectuals. In 1953 Arendt reached the frightening conclusion that "the crisis of our century was no mere threat from the outside, no mere result of some aggressive foreign policy of either Germany or Russia, and that it will no more disappear with the death of Stalin than it disappeared with the fall of Nazi Germany".[46] The threat lurked inside, it could leap from any direction and a century which dared to remain smugly entrenched in its rigid and narrow mental grooves played with fire.

Moreover, in assuming the mantle of political relativism, O'Brien also brought to Ireland the endogenous hypothesis. Until then all intellectual and political thought in Ireland pivoted on the central notion that Ireland's skidding off was provoked by external pressures, mainly the divide and conquer tactics of England which pushed the native bourgeoisies to betray the socialist ideals of the Irish revolution and reduce the dreamt Republic into two puppet regimes, one in the North and another in the South, submissively doing the colonizer's bidding. That is why in Marxism and Post-colonialism the religious divide was always disregarded or played down as an artificial foment arising from conquest and imperial tactics. Thus, if over eighty years after the Ulster Volunteers took up arms to resist the break up of the Union and their integration in an independent Ireland partition still existed, it was because the British continuously plotted to keep it intact.

This proposition ran directly contrary to that of O'Brien who chose to define partition not as something imposed from above but as a "secession" occurring because of a severe "breakdown in human relations" and which "no minority is likely to have recourse to it, with all its dangers, unless the pressures on the minority are felt to be intolerable".[47] Thus came a time when the old explanation began to sound increasingly quaint, unconvincing and out of touch with the change in mood and policy in Westminster. As the impasse deepened in the province, marked by sensational legal miscarriages, accusations of shoot to kill tactics and collusions of the army and local police in sectarian killings, some sections of the British Establishment felt that its protracted involvement there had become an onerous drain on the Exchequer and threatened to smear irretrievably its international reputation as a human rights abiding country.

In 1974, after the collapse of the Sunningdale Agreement and the first power-sharing executive, an alarming rumour even began to spread behind the closed doors of ministerial cabinets and in the circles of party meetings to the effect that the English were seriously envisaging the withdrawal of their troops in the near future, regardless of whether the belligerents succeeded in reaching a satisfactory agreement. The other explanation which began to sound also far-fetched and fanciful was the Marxist hypothesis. O'Brien argued that the most formidable rending was vertical with perhaps a few horizontal overlappings. When in the 1960s a radical student avowed that religion was just a red herring, he replied humorously that if it was so it was a red herring of a size of whale.[48] The reasons why Irish Marxism failed are extremely complex and, as we have already seen, some neo-Marxists in the 1970s put forward very sophisticated hypotheses which surpassed the sometimes more anecdotal, impulsive and polemical style of O'Brien. Suffice to say that by showing the inadequacy of all unicausal, monist and structural explanations and the unbridgeable gap between doctrine and reality, O'Brien has been the harbinger of a postmodern consciousness in the political life of Ireland and one of the main architects of the Good Friday Agreement. The Irish were not alone in adhering to the exogenous paradigm. In France, the Marxist orthodoxy in the analysis of the 1789 revolution supposed that the downward spiralling into terror was provoked directly by the class conflict between bourgeois and aristocrats and the military threat posed by the nation's foreign enemies who sought to destroy the Revolution. This situation of double sabotage and the panic it caused, conveniently explained the adoption of exceptionally harsh measures in self-defence. Liberals and Marxists found it difficult to admit that the noble principles of the Rights of Man, popular sovereignty and representative government had caused such a level of state repression.

Their instinct was telling them to protect the sanctity of the Revolution and so they developed a theory of the circumstances to justify the resort by an essentially good revolution to exceptional violence. François Furet exploded this explanation by showing that it was nothing but a repetition of the excuses that had been offered by the architects of the Terror themselves. The Austro-Prussian assault from the East and the reality of several internal revolts in 1793–1794 had certainly put pressure on the Jacobin leadership and pushed it to make fatal mistakes, but when these threats receded, the pace of executions did not slacken in its turn. In fact, it accelerated. The Terror seemed to have a momentum independent of "circumstances".[49] Furet held that the Revolution of 1789 was neither pure nor moderate but that it already contained in embryonic form in its political culture all the dogmatism and intolerance that the Terror unleashed. His argument was for the essential identity of 1789 and 1793–1794.

Revisionism stands in direct opposition to the assumptions of a conventional form of postcolonial theory. For it has argued that the forced regimentation of consciences and the swelling of a political party were caused not by any betrayal on the part of the native bourgeoisie but rather by the very values that triggered the anti-colonial struggle. It is the pivotal idea of organic nation which prevailed in the fight against the old imperialist powers that is henceforth identified as the core of the problem. Even if Ireland's colonial experience has been unique in its *longue durée*, it has also opted for an ethnic definition of the nation at the expense of a contractual and elective one. Partition undoubtedly facilitated and accelerated the pace of cultural contraction with the invasive presence of the Catholic Church in the domain of education and legislation, but the revisionists are inclined to think that this drive towards homogenization and the suppression of dissidence which was rebelling against it, were already latent in the Irish Cultural Revival and have vitiated all benign potential in the movement for independence.

As early as 1965, O'Brien wrote: "We cannot afford, said Parnell, to give up a single Irishman ... Moran and his friends, including many Sinn Féiners and even an increasing number of Gaelic Leaguers, acted as if they could afford to lose a million Irishmen, if those Irishmen did not conform to their idea of what an Irishman ought to be".[50] Roy Foster agreed with O'Brien when he opined that "the emotions focused by cultural revivalism around the turn of the century were fundamentally sectarian and even racialist". He added: "On every front the unpalatable truth was evident as spelt out by D.P. Moran: 'the Irish nation is *de facto* a catholic nation' and the Protestant Ascendancy, no matter how much they learnt, spoke and wrote Irish, or repudiated the ethos of their class and caste, would be considered fundamentally un-Irish".[51]

The problem is that the endogenous hypothesis, also called the self-inflicted wound, conceals also its own temptations. Declan Kiberd foresaw a dangerous drift in revisionist reasoning in that once this theory gained overly credence, it could obscure the damage inflicted to Third World nations by colonialism. He could not help noticing that this thesis conveniently fitted with the assumption shared by all Western Liberals and Conservatives that, when the British or the French departed from their colonies, things only got worse. When native intellectuals endorsed this explanation, their words seemed to echo the old colonialist view that native peoples were incapable of governing their own affairs and that colonialism had been a sort of blessing in disguise because it acted as a buffer between equally sanguinary and obdurate factions, and further assured those Western apologists that they were right to hold these opinions. This was a method by which all remaining British or French guilt about the colonial adventure could be expunged.[52]

Nationalist history is chartered with logocentric assumptions. It assumes the existence of an origin, pure, authentic, unbroken, a Utopian order, egalitarian, proto-socialist, even proto-feminist and envisages the era of conquest as a world uniformly dominated by oppression, taint, corruption and compromising deals. Since that time, the fable goes, a few Promethean, heroic and enlightened minds have sought to heal the wound opened by colonization and reversed its most dire effects. They are saviours who know the path back to the Lost Paradise, or the Golden Age. To identify an ideal and idyllic origin and hasten to treat what follows as accident, complication, deterioration or just evil is the most innate metaphysical gesture in man. The human mind is the site of an irresistible compulsion, which drives him to think within the limits of this conceptual and symbolical order, and often prevents him from seeing beyond. Revisionist writing has turned its back on the narrative of origins and Télos. Ernest Gellner, who contended that nationalism is not the dawning of nations to self-awareness but more the invention of nations where previously they did not exist, influences it.[53] This deconstructionist spirit and method is overtly at work in Roy Foster's defence of a new kind of analysis:

> And when the ostensibly innocent word "tradition" is adopted, it might be worth remembering that historians are increasingly preoccupied by the idea of "the invention of tradition": the artificiality and recentness of many world-views and identifications which are assumed to be venerable and therefore unchangeable ... The search for new words as tools with which to approach the Irish past must be encouraged, if it enables the kaleidoscope to be shaken around a little, and the shapes and colours to be disposed in potentially new patterns.[54]

In typically Derridan fashion, Foster explains that the notion of a Golden Age in the Irish past is unrealistic. The view that past relations were equitably regulated until a brutal invader arrived and spoilt everything is not historical. And yet this is what all parties in the Irish imbroglio, even the Marxist and more pragmatic James Connolly, commonly allege. The Golden Age was variously defined as the period before the arrival of the Normans, the colonial plantation, Daniel O'Connell, the Land War, the 1916 Rebellion, the Civil Rights marches of 1968 and before the coming of the British troops in 1969. This fantasy would not be so costly if those who pandered to it were not doomed to repeat an artificial society, continuously bent on excluding the Other opinion, persuasion or man. This is as true for the Victorian landowner who pines for an exemplary estate without any land agitator as it is for the Gaelic Revivalist who dreams of a blissful and spiritual life in the West of Ireland. Even the Ulster Unionists imagine that the old Stormont regime had created a better society.[55] Desmond Fennell accused revisionists of having given up the battle between good and evil and Michael Laffan replied that they had indeed committed this sin and made no apology for it.[56] In the *Irish Review*, Foster admits that an approach inspired by feelings of guilt or even revenge is not unnatural in itself but he is sceptical as to what heuristic possibilities it holds: "A desire to expiate what are seen as past sins, and a genuine surprise at the appalling record of much of British government in Ireland, is understandable; it is probably good for the English soul; but it must be questioned whether it gets us any nearer understanding".[57] Trying to convey what sort of method revisionism was, he listed among its virtues an ability to appreciate half tones, to separate contemporary intentions from historical effects and to be cautious about imputing praise or blame. The objective was, as he saw it, to explore nineteenth and twentieth century Irish history in all its density, ramifications and complexity.

Revisionist history has indubitably averted its attention from the search for an original sin or a sole culprit, for an overriding criminal act fatalistically shaping all the subsequent march of the nation, and this is why it is not conventionally ethical or should one say, strait-laced? The circumspection that nationalist commentators are more disposed to interpret as moral flabbiness and regard as an absolute abomination is experienced by revisionists as humility and openness of the mind to the otherness of the object of research. Here again in its refusal to yield to the consolations of ontology, the new history displays a profoundly deconstructionist sensibility. In 1967, in *Structure, Sign and Play* Derrida opposed two types of thinking. The first dreams of deciphering a truth, an origin which escapes play and the rule of the sign, and lives as in a state of exile, the necessity of interpretation. The second has broken free from the nostalgic snare of the origin, and affirms play. If man is to establish a more intimate rapport with truth then he will have to relinquish the childish dream of full presence: the reassuring foundation and the end of play.[58]

Part V

Tensions between theoretical intuition and empirical reflex

13 Relativism and its opponents

A captivating facet of the debate on revisionism is that it is criticized on grounds similar to those arraigned against the postmodern school. The danger perceived in them, waved not always in unaffected fashion by Marxists and Nationalists, is something that ought to arrest our attention. On the level of epistemology, they are both accused of overindulging in an enervating relativism, which continually frustrates the formulation of a definite judgement. Relativism can promote more forbearance, optimism and an active dispelling of the ethnocentric habit when it is carved out of an appreciation of the provisional character of situations and the factor of dilapidation inherent in political concepts. However, if used in a calculating manner, relativism can also bury vital questions, blunt the mind's capacity for judgement and tone down responsibilities. The challenge is to succeed in employing relativism without ever letting it run out of one's control. The historian has to strike a delicate balance between opposed imperatives; he needs to display what Wilhelm Dilthey called *verstehen*, which entails entering through empathy into the motives and intentions of past actors without falling into the trap of forgiveness. Daltun O Ceallaigh contends that revisionism has fallen into this very trap. Its tendency to expatiate on the sectarian undercurrents in Irish nationalism hides its hypocrisy because "Presumably the same type of critic, confronted with Nazi crimes in the Germany of the 1930s, would have been quick to opine that the Third Reich was not without its Jewish bigots".[1] O Ceallaigh insinuates that revisionism borders on denial and can turn into a camouflaged defence of all kinds of fascism. Its relativism is blamed for abandoning the harrying of the guilty parties, for spreading a spurious reasoning whose final expression is to pulverize to dust the conventional boundaries between good and evil, empty history of all judgement and shamefully cancel the difference between oppressor and victim.

In the style of postmodern critique, instead of making a value judgement on the manner a past situation was handled, one henceforth raises unusual questions. Ones which pertain to the socio-political conditions that preceded or accompanied the apparition of a certain discourse, the institutional power it serves, its hegemonic propensities and the prohibition on minority rights and claims it imposes in the name of some urgent and yet nebulous unity. For many of its opponents, the apotheosis in this change of the prescribed modes of analysis is the refuge in a servile agnosticism founded on the infamous notion that truth is so multi-faceted that it is ultimately unknowable, thus proclaiming its pursuit vain. To a certain extent, this change is also visible in revisionism although this latter recoils from epistemological nihilism.

Hence, Seamus Deane maintains that revisionism corresponds to a time when the dominant impulse in society is an anxiety to preserve the "status quo" and where relativism is used with a definite purpose in mind: to convince that "historical processes are so complex that any attempt to achieve an overview cannot avoid the distortions and dogmatism of simple-minded orthodoxy".[2] Since they are trained in the tradition of historicism, that is, the notion that truth can be relative to a given moment in history and that truth actually changes as history does, revisionists do welcome a degree of relativism and value neutrality. Their empirical experience has taught them that any judgement hastily entered, soon turns out to be premature and partial as the digging up of fresh evidence contradicts it. Tom Dunne is not blind to the ambivalence in relativism, its manipulability. He concedes the possibility that relativism might promote quietism but argues it can also fashion an inquisitive spirit, lead to a deeper understanding of the past and thus be the basis of a constructive radicalism in the future. With acumen, he adds: "revisionism has produced revolution throughout history, most famously in the contribution of Marxism".[3] So, could it be that the critics of revisionism are uncomfortable with it because it is the nature of Ireland's current revolution they dislike?

Our purpose so far has been to estimate the radicalism of Irish revisionism by comparing it to the postmodern innovations in historical criticism. What is intriguing is that if we cast our glance beyond apparent differences, we soon realize that both schools have a tendency to wrong-foot or ambush themselves. Postmodernism's most original postulation is that truth has its own habitat which varies according to time, space, tribe and experience. This principle is geared to rouse consciences to the need for tolerance toward Otherness. It becomes the bastion for a more authentic democracy. Likewise because it attributes polarization to a mutual refusal to engage emotionally and intellectually with the opposite viewpoint, revisionism has played a central role in the rehabilitation of a controversial and plural history where the espousal of opposed interpretations on the same events is no longer seen as a complete aberration. Roy Foster has drawn attention to the inadequacy of positivism when one tried to fathom "the deep-level trauma" and "uncover the instincts and expectations" which laid at the bottom of the irrational attachment to the Union.[4] But the adoption of relativism at any level, whether cultural or cognitive, raises before long, a sticky problem of logic. If one is to follow closely its logic, relativism has the strange property of not being able to refute any system which contradicts it because by relativism's own principles there are no opposing or false doctrines. Postmodernists challenge the notion of objective analysis, not just as a possibility, but also as an honourable aspiration. The irony is that in destroying the myth of objectivity, postmodernists forget their own critique rests on the same mental logic and is driven by the same impulse. They too, in spite of their denials, believe in this musty ideal and that is why they are loath to reduce their critique of modernity to an ephemeral moment. They too clutch on to the scientific hope. They believe that through their astringent method and the quality of their cogitations, they have come closer to a truth, which one can single out for being superior.

Thus, one catches postmodernism being in blatant violation of its own principles because it does not accept that those principles apply to its own construals too. Its thinkers wish, on the contrary, to retain the privileged status of the author, and do exert jealous control over how their own analyses are interpreted and understood. However, the problem is that once the gateway to relativism is open, one cannot close it again in the interests of one theory without incurring the reproach of bad faith or "self-referential inconsistency", that is the inability to recognize how their doctrine applies to themselves.[5] The same paradox is present in Irish revisionism. The writings of Michel Foucault, Jean-François Lyotard, Roland Barthes and Jacques Derrida were all steeped in the Marxist sensibility. Even if these men gave up the idea of revolution as futile, their unflinching questioning of the authority of all discourses claiming a monopoly on wisdom and advocacy is a pursuit of their Marxism by other means, a sort of sublimation. The evolution of their thought exemplifies the passage from one radicalism to a more ambitious form whereby it is no longer just the deceptions of bourgeois ideology that are exposed but rather the hegemonic drive concealed in any discourse claiming to be truly universal and scientific. Postmodern theory displays a coefficient of radical critique, which carries, embedded in it, the resources for a genuine self-criticism. One which could perhaps enable its representatives to objectify their discourse and countenance with sobriety their own subjectivity. But for a long time it refused to do so. Derrida maintained that "the structuralist invasion" cannot be reduced to a mere topic for the historian of ideas because "what is at stake" is "an adventure of vision, a conversion of the way of putting questions to any object posed before us, to historical objects – his own – in particular". The "anxiety about language" which has infused "universal thought" with "a formidable impulse" is more than just "the sign of an epoch, the fashion of a season, or the symptom of a crisis".[6]

In fact, both Irish revisionism and postmodernism give the impression of being imbued with a similar critical sensibility for neither is prepared to reduce all its musings and harvest to an ideological moment. Thus, the faintheartedness of Irish revisionists when it comes to turning the *radicalité* of their method unto themselves or to push their historicist intuitions to their logical conclusion renders them vulnerable to the charges of inconsistency and bad faith. Vincent Comerford guessed this contradiction when he insisted on the provisional character of all historical interpretations, including and a fortiori, the revisionist ones.[7] Deny any ambition to replace an orthodoxy by another is the only way of keeping one's credibility intact. The philosopher Hans Georg Gadamer insists that the work of reinterpretation is essential to the challenge of dogmas. Yet, while doing so one must beware of the temptation to erect on the basis of this new interpretation a new canon. Yves Boisvert's remarks echo Gadamer's warning since he allows that post-modern *episteme* betrays a tendency of following the same reflex: turning its conclusions into a new dogma.[8] The reason why both revisionism and post-modernism have refused to cross this line is that they both sense that this move is pernicious since it undermines the effort to improve our way of thinking. Not unreasonably, they suspect that in a situation where all statements become interpretations, including this assertion, then the idea of interpretation cancels itself through and leaves everything exactly as it was. In the domain of epistemology, a too radical relativism can lead to a situation when one can no longer defend the scientific validity of one's findings and in the domain of politics it can lead to stasis and paralysis into an unwanted status quo.

Seamus Deane has impugned revisionism for deficiency in self-critique and philosophical innocence. That's why in his opinion it collaborates "unconsciously with the very mentality it wishes to defeat". He concludes: "Revisionists are nationalists despite themselves; by refusing to be Irish nationalists, they simply become defenders of Ulster or British nationalism, thereby switching sides in the dispute while believing themselves to be switching the terms of it".[9] Philosophical innocence is seen as self-defeating and provokes condescension or sometimes as hypocritical and invites cynicism. But if one is prepared to consider seriously that revisionism obeys European patterns of historiographic evolution then it becomes obvious that revisionism is by definition suspicious of all types of nationalism, be they of the Left or of the Right, from the metropolis or from the colony. If it castigates Irish nationalism so implacably, it is because it concurs with Tom Nairn that the most elementary comparative analysis shows nationalism is "at once healthy and morbid. Progress and regression are both inscribed in its genetic code from the beginning".[10] Deane's verdict is final; revisionism has failed because it has fallen into the snares of a timorous method whose real function is to serve as a mouthpiece to the colonialist and unionist mentalities. The implication is that man is so tightly moored to his age he could never unfetter himself from its determinations. Hence, the mind cannot perform the action of stepping outside of itself. If it tries to do so, it will end up re-enacting the most retrograde politics and spreading a scandalous lie. The researcher cannot shed his straitjacket without his efforts catapulting him into another, more damaging of human autonomy of thought and action.

On the contrary, revisionists think that whatever his conditioning, he can intervene against ideology or loosen its stifling embrace. The Traditionalists' strongest objection against revisionism focuses on one daunting anomaly; it cannot claim to have branched off or bypassed tautology. The shift from a *continuiste* to a *discontinuiste* method does not guarantee success because an interpretation is always dependent of the starting point of a researcher. Furthermore, devising a method of opposing a discourse boasting of being superior in its authoritativeness does not promise a disenthralment from the same claim that this discourse makes. Gilbert Larochelle accuses postmodernism of being a discourse, which proceeds from not only a contradictory but also a circular reasoning.[11] Daltun O Ceallaigh attacked revisionism for similar reasons. He questioned its scientific character because its method consisted merely in "recount[ing] orthodoxy", "premis[ing] the opposite" and then "proceed[ing] to see if that can conceivably be validated".[12]

Deane insists that revisionism's claim to offer a more lasting truth rests on an illusion for "it is a retrospective vision – as all history must be", one which has as terminus the Northern problem and "criticises those who did not anticipate or recognize its inevitability and its depth". Curiously, the alternative he puts forward is devoid of any real reflection and is simply an unprepossessing repetition of the usual Manichaeism. Hence, he sees only two possible explanations for the historical underdevelopment of Ireland; it is the result of Irish laziness as the English assume or it is a structural problem caused by colonialism.[13] Still we would not be detracting from our positive judgement of revisionism if we were to concede at least that Deane has identified an unresolved tension, which he exploits skilfully for his own ends.

Indeed, there is a difference between submitting one's method to a theorization and submitting one's discourse to a theorization. In the latter case, one touches on the delicate problem of the epistemological status of history. Herbert Butterfield, who thought of himself as an empirical historian, insisted that the supreme virtue was reflexivity; this homecoming of the mind which can evince the personal stakes or the emotional investment which are often implicit in a principle of selection of evidence, the choice of a paradigm, the choice of a period or the choice of a theme. This tug between the empirical and the theoretical at the heart of revisionism is also elegantly condensed in the *Whig Interpretation of History*. Ostensibly, he shares with other practising historians the "healthy kind of distrust" for "disembodied reasoning". But this can also be a handicap because "they have reflected little upon the nature of their own subject". His first treatise is unapologetically a theoretical reflection, which wishes to find out the precise conditions under which historical knowledge can confidently assert itself and flourish. Bernard Manning claimed it was unfair to saddle one party with the sin of anachronism, as the Whigs were not the only purveyors of a history twisted to their own purposes. Yet, although he did pick profusely on the Whigs, even then Butterfield did hint at the fact that this malpractice was by no means merely their property. Later he openly admitted that the Tories did not escape the Whig interpretation even and especially when "they played tricks with it" as when "they attempted to show that on occasion they themselves, rather then the Whigs, were the real promoters of our present-day liberty".[14]

Nor was he greatly concerned with the temporal logic that caused "mental bias". What he tried to fathom lay rather "in a trick of organization" or "an unexamined habit of mind that any historian may fall into".[15] If anachronism continues to be attractive to historians despite frequent admonitions, it is because it offers simple solutions to the intractable problems raised by historical research. Confronted with the perplexing task of building a coherent story on the basis of primary data which is often conflicting, historians conveniently "cut through complexity". Historians are drawn to "short cuts" because research often yields paradoxes, moments when one realizes a dissonance between the normative requirements of good history and actual practice. In this treatise therefore Butterfield outlines a theory of anachronism by offering a catalogue of errors; errors arousing both out of tensions inherent to the method and "the transference into the past of an enthusiasm for something in the present, an enthusiasm for democracy or freedom of thought or the liberal tradition".[16] This exercise in disclosing the gap between theory and practice is entirely in the service of the historian. It is here to endow him with the quality most prized by postmodern philosophers, self-awareness and teach him that "our assumptions" are venial so long as we remember they are assumptions for "the most fallacious thing ... is to organize our historical knowledge upon an assumption without realizing what we are doing".[17]

The anti-conformist and experimental historian Michel de Certeau voluntarily admits that history is based, like ideology, on the illusion of truth: "History is entirely shaped by the system within which it is developed. Today, as yesterday, the fact of a localized fabrication at such and such a point within this system determines it. Denial of the specificity of place being the very principle of ideology, all theory is excluded".[18] Historians are conjurers or illusionists since their way of recreating the past, its transparency and immediacy, is to naturalize a condition of writing which is everything but natural. If they were to mull openly over the methodological and existential obstacles impending research or how the socio-political climate channels research into certain particular topics at the expense of others and skews its results, then the bubble would burst and the ambiguous constellation collapse. This explains why contrary to sociologists, historians do not always announce their theory before their findings. The kinship between postmodernism and Irish revisionism runs deeper still since both express a similar recalcitrance for the notion of submitting their hypotheses to an overt process of theorization. However, the latter disinclination is harmful because by confining the entire array of their observations to a limp form of discourse, they simply lay themselves open to the criticism that their work is not immune to the pressures of circularity,[19] otherwise they would not hesitate to submit it to such microscopic evaluation. In a nut-shell, by delaying this necessary step, they perpetuate the paralysing question of their political pedigree and feed the rumour that they are upshots of a reactionary type of politics. Hence, Willy Maley claims: "It is precisely because of the Troubles that revisionism is virtually a Theory-free zone, where 'myth' is mocked at rather than mapped out, nation defiled rather than defined and violence decried rather than described".[20] Irish revisionism would be cagey about authentic theoretical engagement because it could lay bare its true political colours. It is as if theory has a precise political sex whereas Irish revisionism is a hermaphrodite creature: an aberration betraying its impotence in the comprehension of historical relations. Like Marxism, Irish nationalism has been dethroned. Both postmodernism and Irish revisionism have been instrumental in unsettling hierarchies of meanings, the idea that some meanings [theories] were superior, more truthful or more fundamental than others. But it is not the opinion of Deane who holds that instead of attacking the notion of a single narrative and supplanting it with a plurality of narratives, revisionism is guilty of underplaying the oppression the 1916 Rising sought to overthrow and upgrading the oppression the Rising itself inaugurated in the name of freedom.[21]

It is perhaps worth noticing that the critique against Irish revisionism is not always rigorous. Deane deploys the French post-structuralist argument to criticize Irish revisionism for its theoretical innocence. However, the irony is that later Terry Eagleton proclaims with the tone of a doomster that the powerful mythologies of liberal humanism and postmodern pluralism entrap Irish historiography and labels Roy Foster a scandalous post-modernist. How it is possible to be at once a scandalous postmodernist and ignorant of its emphasis on the subjectivity of all intellectual effort, he does not tell us. However, Eagleton is interesting to us because although his pairing of postmodernism and Irish revisionism aims at denigrating the latter, it also ostensibly brings grist to our mill.

Superficially, to suggest an identity in rationale between Irish revisionism and postmodernism is close to stating a contradiction in terms. Post-modernism, faithful to its rejection of systems, either political or scholastic, displayed a profound scepticism towards empiricism and the lures of progress. Thus, it did not believe that truth was immanent and could be retrieved through experience. Its most emphatic proposition was that no matter how much meticulous research one brought to bear, one could not attain unimpeachable truths. In contrast, revisionism at least in its early phase was founded on the conviction one could replace popular mythology with a more objective history, purified of its ideological cum mythological sedimentation. Seen from this angle, it seemed the Irish version of the obedience to empiricism. Certainly, *The Whig Interpretation of History*, the alleged Bible for Irish revisionism, never made the claim of having established the conditions for untainted objectivity. It courageously identified the problem of tautology but never purported to have solved it. This is also the opinion of Ciaran Brady according to whom there is no serious evidence attesting to a willingness to create an objective history in the strong sense. He thinks there is an important difference between an aspiration to strive to more objectivity and the staunch confidence perfect objectivity is an attainable goal, and this difference is no less than the product of two completely opposed epistemologies.[22] By hastily collapsing this distinction and declaring it had no analytical significance, Bradshaw neglected the gradations in Irish revisionism's epistemological stance and obviated the truly crucial questions of its originality, precocity and dialectical bend. The distinction is not at all trivial because to devote oneself to objectivity can well be predicated on the supposition that since its realization is logically impossible the only possibility of clarity in argument and equality in dialogue lies on an agreement about the exigency of its pursuit.

To back up his opinion, Brady compares the founders of revisionism with the high priest of value-free social science, Max Weber (1864–1920), a man who greatly influenced twentieth-century historical practice. Brady explains that the adoption of a systematic method in social sciences served not primarily as a guide to objective truth but as weapon against the twin enemies of nihilism and relativism. It is no coincidence if Brady defines Weber's methodology as a rampart against these two temptations given that traditionalists have categorically accused revisionists of succumbing to them. Brady's identification with Weber invites reflection especially when one realizes how conflicted and ambiguous is Weber's method underneath its silences. Surely, he laid down as a principle that the social scientist should purge his analyses of facts from the stain of normative positions. In his words, "all research ... once it has established its methodological principles, will consider the analysis of the data as an end in itself".[23] The safest way of doing so is to clarify for the benefit of oneself and others prior to the work of scientific exposition one's standpoint. This step is crucial because it alerts the scientist to the not at all trifling consideration that the value is neither intrinsic to the subject matter nor specific to its context. The same route awakens one to the futility of proving or disproving with the use of data the validity of "ultimate and final values" which are by essence not amenable, compliant or reducible to empirical operation. It is so not because the realm of immutable metaphysics and the realm of fluctuant reality are incompatible but "on the contrary" because they are "in harmony with each other" since life "with its irrational reality" confirms how "inexhaustible" is "the store of its possible meanings" and so frees the believer to lash himself with even more zeal to his demonic intentions.

But despite such frequent statements, which have often misled into thinking of Weber as a relativist, he was no relativist neither of the ethical nor the cognitive type. As Brady hinted there are effectively signs that he conceived of value-free science as a means to curtail the encroachments of excessive relativism. An intrepidly opinionated man himself, he thought that "what mattered was the trained ability to look at realities of life with an unsparing gaze, to bear these realities and be a match for them inwardly".[24] To train one to look at the realities of life in all their starkness is the irreplaceable role of the teacher. Indeed his first task is to compel his students to accustom themselves to the existence of "inconvenient" facts. The performing of this important task goes beyond mere intellectual feat. It is a "moral achievement" because it teaches one the "abysmal contrast" between a reasoning based on the goodness of intentions and one based on the goodness of consequences. Science's unique contribution consists precisely in making crystal clear the opposition between a form of deontological ethics and a form of consequentialist ethics. The former is represented by the fundamentalist who presumes the purity of intentions justifies the means to achieve them, however dangerous or costly these may be. The latter is represented by the sceptic who finds such absolute or unconditional stance unacceptable, especially in the political domain where the possibility of violence and human suffering always lurk in the background. In so far as science lays bare "the probable evil ramifications" behind the pursuit of a "good" end, equips one with the vital and prerequisite knowledge to choose with care between ends and means its highest function is one of political education. If empirical experience carried over centuries has refuted the superficial maxim that "from good comes only good; but from evil only evil follows" but a man perseveres in this belief, the responsibility for doing so however remains entirely his. Science then can declare, "Here I stand; I can do no other".

So, although Weber would have secretly nourished the hope that the teaching of a value-free science would influence the opinions of the students by putting at their disposition always more complex samples of reality, he stopped resolutely short of developing a philosophical "mechanism for validating in and of themselves" the values he himself deemed superior.[25] Can one substantiate the charge of cognitive relativism against Irish revisionism? Irish revisionism stems from a desire to contain and reverse the fragmentation of truth, Irishness and humanity. As A.T.Q. Stewart put it, the fathers of modern Irish historiography firmly believed in putting the study of Irish history on a basis, which would be interchangeable and mean the same thing for Belfast or Dublin or to someone from either of the competing traditions in the North.[26] Margaret MacCurtain, the pioneer of women's history, remembered how sensitized she became to bias in the teaching of history when she attended a seminar on this question in the early 1960s. Equipped with this new awareness, she grew a faith "in a history that can help reconcile societies". She added: "History can only explain the past, it cannot change behaviour. But the larger dimension of history, when history seeks to reconcile and synthesise the past rather than divide people into camps and set antitheses between ethnic groups and religious sects is something very dear to my heart".[27]

The same idealism infuses the Bulletin of the Students Association, which first appeared in 1956 and was jointly edited by David Thornley of TCD and Owen Dudley Edwards of UCD. R.D. Edwards was the architect of the

Association, which was set up in the late 1940s. Every year, each of the member societies acting as host in turn would convene an annual congress and publish an associated Bulletin. In "The Future of the Congress", to mark the third birthday of the Inter-Varsity Congress, W.A. Hurst voiced the belief that when pursued with accuracy and in an attitude of open-mindedness, history could assist tolerance and ecumenism. The association came about thanks to a few people who were enthused, "By a love of history for its own sake, and also by the conviction that much good could be achieved by a body which had as its aim the bringing together of students from all over the country to discuss, in a spirit of impartial and objective inquiry, those aspects of the subject which were of particular interest to them as students, and perhaps also as citizens of a country where the sense of history is both strong and often distorted".[28] Hurst remarked it was "this spirit of disinterested idealism which had given the Congress its momentum and which was, at the same time, its most salient characteristic". He hoped this spirit would persist and prove infectious to other Irishmen. By insisting on the uncovering of a truth not easily disposable, more sceptical, critical, if not distrustful of both nationalism and unionism, Irish revisionism is determined to oppose those who would argue that the only grounds that count for preferring one interpretation of the past over another are aesthetic, moral or political. There is a truth in the written vestiges of the past that ought to be recounted, irrespective of its political incorrectness. History is not simply about the struggle for a "parity of esteem" coming from two ethnic factions presenting equally valid perspectives on truth.

Rather it is about the crimes, violations and shady deals each entered in the course of a turbulent history in the name of an inalienable right to express in an untrammelled and selfish manner their unique identity. Those remarks suggest rather that cognitive relativism, the principle stipulating that reality and truth are solely matters of perception, does not seem really to chime with the sort of moral rectitude which inspired Irish revisionism. The historians who spearheaded it were too obsessed by the tragic cost of falsehood in Irish society to entertain merrily the opinion that there is no separate or superior truth apart from how each tribe happens to see things. Then again nor is there any absolutism or objectivism in the strong sense in their profile. What one finds is more a commitment to reduce the falsehood and the belief, perhaps naïve, that a more stringent form of historical knowledge could assist the interests of tolerance and pluralism. The way to carry out this chipping away at falsehood seemed to have consisted in widening the compass covered by technical history in order to establish a common ground between all doctrines; Protestantism, Catholicism, Nationalism and Unionism. The belief was that a common language would accrue out of the least common denominator of those things established by historical evidence and that this step would also force at some point some mutual understanding, in the higher regions. At any rate, the belief that disunity is not always liability, that variety is more enriching than uniformity, that those are not a form of error or brainwashing to be purged by paternalistic guidance or raw coercion, was a realization that was to transform profoundly the manner in which this theme was treated in the writing of Irish history. It awakened a sincere respect and curiosity for the insights, forebodings, warnings and apprehensions of all the capricious voices inside and outside of the national-ist family. It put a sudden end to impulsive telescoping, curbed posterity's condescension and started a meticulous scanning into various periods when Irish history might have escaped its violent destiny and streamed along towards more benign and peaceful paths.

14 The problematic of ends and means

Brady's recruitment of Weber to shed light on the revisionist method is not just a tactical choice because there are inside this comparison pregnant similarities. The haunting problematic of ends and means is also the existential and methodological crux around which has hinged the entire project of Irish revisionism. Revisionists oppose deontological ethics in the realm of politics because they do not agree with the proposition that by virtue of its good intentions, one should graciously vouchsafe some indefinite moral exemption or political immunity to Irish nationalism. Nor are they satisfied with the unconvincing separation between the insurgent nationalisms, perceived as virtuous and honourable because they arise out of a decolonizing war and the nationalisms fathered by the imperial powers perceived as racist and exploitative. Rather they reason that Irish nationalism forfeited this privileged status every time it failed to live up to its democratic professions.

Hence, on 19 April 1958 as he observed with consternation the world having collapsed into the nihilism of Cold War, Edwards voiced ethical concerns which had also been monopolizing for some time the agenda of intellectual discussions in Continental Europe. He entreated intelligent people not to upset the "hierarchy of values" because without it one "cannot expect to realize even well-meaning hopes". He called for a clearer appreciation of "the proper dependence of ends and means" in the domain of international affairs and at home, and a schooling into the reasons why "ends and means cannot be switched about at will". After all, he was simply articulating, "the nagging fear" hidden in the hearts of many that "something serious had gone wrong with this order of ends and means". Like many who "worried about the non-stop production of nuclear weapons, especially those in the megaton range", he was dumbfounded, and he dreaded that this dismal development betrayed a complete loss of political direction and was a harbinger of the yet most terrible violation of the fundamental rights of mankind. Confusion reigns when ends are conferred a holy and sublime quality they cannot possess since they are "relics typically human". "The early history of our species" showed that men always "fastened on any evidence" of their "capacity" to remember their distance from God. But now regression had become palpable because he could not detect "any overwhelming manifestation of the same faculty". To din into his fellowmen this perversion of ends and means he magnified it by weighing up technical progress with the disturbing lack of moral leadership; hence, "the fact that the first stage began with stone axes and we are now playing with H-Bombs only adds a touch of cosmic irony to the whole business". To those in power who thought the logic of "balance of the nuclear deterrent" justified the nuclear race, Edwards retorted it did not for it did not stem from a "fully rationalized purpose" but rather from an "attempt to rationalize fear". Prescient he concluded: "The painful thing about the present international situation is that fear is increasingly its motive and not anything grounded in reason. Reason is the mark of the human being. Fear is at times a necessary counsellor but it is proverbially a bad one. No matter how right you are you cannot live on fear as a staple diet".[1]

This question had also been preoccupying a minority of unflinching minds like Arthur Koestler (1905–1983), Albert Camus (1913–1960) and Raymond Aron (1905–1983) who refused to close their eyes to the crimes and the lies of Communist Russia and had stubbornly been pushing this unpalatable truth under the nose of Jean-Paul Sartre (1905–1980) or Harold Laski (1893–1950) and other like-minded Western radicals, who would without demur dismiss the ethical Puritanism that the end does not automatically justify the means as mere anti-communist cant. Camus believed that an extreme utilitarianism – a doctrine which postulated that "you could not make omelettes without breaking eggs", to recall the sardonic phrase used by Aleksander Wat in *My Century* – epitomized not audacity but rather surrender of constructive thought in favour of a hugely precarious logic whose human cost was revealing horrifying. As he saw it, any ideology which placed value on the end of history was dangerous as it meant, "Until then, there is no suitable criterion on which to base a judgment of value. One must act and live in terms of the future. All morality becomes provisional".[2] He held Hegel responsible for this adulteration of Western thought and suspected that both Nazism and Communism were suffused with this vice.

Hegel's historicism later adopted by Marx was premised on the idea that every spirit, personified in a nation or a state, was organically driven to attain its highest fulfilment and that violence was inevitable in the process of defeating all the obstacles on the march to perfection. Because of its teleological thrust, the end assumed supreme importance, it became an absolute priority so much so that the intermediate phases, no matter how plagued with suffering and misery, were ignored. In the ruthless competition to impose their hegemonic will, Hegel had made it normal for states to demote human beings to the demeaning position of tools, mere disposable means in pursuit of transcendental purposes. That the minds of Irish people were also infected by the same poison is evident in the remarks of Prof. R.A. Breathnach who argued that if Republican violence held a powerful attraction on youth it was because of the ostensible lack of serious political leadership. In a language reminiscent of that of continental dissentients, he explained:

Close to the heart of doctrines like Nationalism and Communism stands the false assumption that the end not only justifies but also sanctifies the means. Violence, then, becomes virtue, because it is believed to be the means of establishing the heaven on earth, by whatever name it may be known. So deeply has nationalism affected the minds of our youth that recently I read in a Gaelic paper that it is "an integral part of our Catholic religion"! This is an example of the kind of thinking, a synthesis of political and religious elements, which provides the theoretical motive power behind the guns...[3]

In "Embers of Easter", Conor Cruise O'Brien discloses the depth of his pessimism: a pessimism quite unmatched for the times. He is nagged by a doubt he cannot dispel: "If Pearse and Connolly could have had a foresight of the Ireland of 1966 would they have gone with that high courage to certain death?" Not afraid to face the harsh reality, he comments: "The national objective of Connolly and Pearse is now finally and necessarily buried". The angst is quite unforgettable here and one feels that O'Brien does not see much reason for rejoicing in the coming celebrations of the Rising. His intention instead is to take the political establishment down a peg or two; to remind them of their failure to accomplish any of the ideals for which all the men of 1916 died. Professions of patriotism are unavailing when one does not back them up with practical initiatives to embody that patriotism. Indignant yet lucid he declared: "We were bred to be patriotic, only to find that there was nothing to be patriotic about; we were republicans of a Republic that wasn't there. Small wonder that Pearse's vision of an Ireland 'not free merely but Gaelic as well' did not convince us. The nation for which Pearse died never came to life".[4] He speaks in the shades of the irretrievable. His verdict is irrevocable and does not fail to affect one. After all the man who is condemning, is also confessing. Indeed, he is no stranger to the tradition he dissects with such unflinching intransigence. He admits he is guilty too. He implicates himself in the deceitful enterprise of excitation of the collective imagination. He does not try to relieve himself of the burden of his own mistakes. However, he indicates that he has understood and learnt from these: "The present writer blushes to recall that he devoted a considerable part of his professional activity ... to what was known as 'anti-partition'. The only positive result of this anti-partition activity ... was that it led me to discover the cavernous inanities of anti-partition and of Government propaganda generally". He accuses the Dublin Government of double standards because they "continued to propagate" a "national fantasy" while "punishing those who acted on it". The campaign allowed this hypocrisy to thrive since its more sinister function was "[to] enable the State to punish with a good conscience the young in the IRA. Partition must be ended certainly but there was a right and a wrong way to end it".

In later years, O'Brien became even more contemptuous of this deception as he described the strategy of "taking the gun out of Irish politics" coined by the Costello–MacBride Coalition Government in 1948 as a cosmetic gesture, because the anti-partition campaign and the passing of the Republic of Ireland Act (1949) were, in his opinion, above all designed to appease the IRA.[5] He insisted that both initiatives had been harmful. The move away from the Commonwealth gave "the new Republic's claim to Northern Ireland – already present in Articles two and three of the Constitution – greater salience than it had before". Feeling attacked and wanting to express her gratitude for the way Unionism had helped her through the Second World War, England felt summoned to respond by reassuring Northern Ireland of its membership to the United Kingdom. In retaliation, it introduced the Ireland Act. This Irish move was therefore not exactly congenial to the opening of future discussion between the old antagonists. "A lot of stuff from the past had been stirred up by the Irish move" stuff "which would have been better left unstirred". This led all the parties in Ireland lending their names to a long outpouring of vociferous propaganda which ultimately convinced neither the Americans nor Europe of the propriety of Ireland's refusal to join NATO as long as Britain would "occupy" Northern Ireland.[6] O'Brien's denunciation of the pretence of the Irish government does not bring him much comfort though, for his incredulity at the derisive results of post-revolutionary society is mingled with the niggling suspicion that the Republican dream of territorial unity was never viable. Culturally Ireland remained a region, or rather two regions, of the English-speaking world. Religion became a dangerous substitute for cultural fulfilment. As for partition, one could never mend it by "semantic exercises" as it was "the slightly distorted expression of a long-standing spiritual division which men like Tone and Pearse lived and died to close". Furthermore, this impasse was aggravated by two sets of pressures, "the pressures of reality itself and those resulting from the inability of idealists to accept that reality". He concluded: "Functionally the pseudo-activity of anti-partition helped to deaden the pain of the dawning of reality. That grey and humdrum dawn has now arrived".

There is no doubt in this essay where the heaviest responsibility lies. The decision of the government to persist in the mendacious is inexcusable because it misled a whole youth into destruction, murder and death. This irresponsibility is even harder to forgive when one knows, as O'Brien does, that no serious thinking was encouraged to create an auspicious climate for the realization of the dream. Instead of displaying vision and courage to heal this wound of the heart and the soul, the Establishment was just happy with thrashing about pathetically in a propagandist quagmire that was futile, unconvincing and hostile to peace. Partition is here conceptualized as being only the "tip of the iceberg" and he is truly aghast at the lack of foresight of the Southern leadership. One senses dismay at the extent of the failure as well as regret for not guessing sooner the disastrous effects of this rhetoric. If one compares this essay with others that followed, it is still moderate. Yet, it is no exaggeration to say that in a sense it foreshadows them. His feeling of alienation is profound and transpires in his forthrightness. He does not use kid-glove methods to say what he really thinks, does not spare the suscepti-bilities of those in power and finally does not tolerate the squeamishness of his community. Reality in all its dismal state is here for all to look at. Whoever turns his eyes away from it is a treacherous fool. One draws the impression that already in 1966 O'Brien is psychologically ready to break the umbilical cord. By refusing to act as a protective shield or a moral alibi to his tradition, by putting an end to the justifying reflex, he sets in motion a disenthralling of his society. Because truth has no political sex and is not the monopoly of a single group of people, he turns it against his own family and reveals thereby the depth of his disenchantment.

The disastrous inadequacy of ends and means is also at the heart of F.S.L. Lyons' reflection. During one of his three broadcasted lectures in December 1971 intended for the commemoration of the 50th anniversary of the 1921 Anglo-Irish Treaty, Lyons (1923–1983) declared:

> In the present situation, with the dire past still overhanging the dire present, the need to go back to fundamentals and consider once more the meaning of independence, asserts itself with almost intolerable urgency. The theories of revolution, the theories of nationality, the theo-ries of history, which have brought Ireland to its present pass, cry out for re-examination and the time is ripe to try to break the great enchantment which for too long has made myth so much more conge-nial than reality.[7]

It is patent that this statement was prompted by the debilitating effects of the conflict in Northern Ireland and it is not untrue that the decades of the 1970s and 1980s had seen a pronounced tendency among some revision-ists to blame chiefly nationalist mythology rather than fifty years of Unionist single party rule and discrimination. Still the salient aspect of this passage is its undeniable postmodern accents. The apocalyptic re-evaluation of all the master narratives dramatically prophesized here is infected by an anxiety, and a sense of urgency which are strikingly reminiscent of the tone and style of the most political figure of the Postmodern school, Jean-François Lyotard. The repetition of the word "theory" betrays a typical obsession and strongly appears to be a faithful echo of the assault conducted against it by the icono-clastic project of the new philosophers. Here for the first time one experi-ences the failures of Irish history in a terribly personal way. Lyons is done with the comforting reflex of blaming the old enemy for whatever went awfully wrong in the construction of the Irish nation. Instead, he implies that most of the wounds suffered by Ireland were self-inflicted.

The gaze of the historian has turned away from the most conspicuous explanations and the usual allocations of guilt, such as the tactical decision of the British to play the Orange card and support the unionist veto, the quasi-institutionalization of discrimination against the Catholic minority in the North, the tacit condoning of unjust practices by the British Government, and coiled inwards, at the heart of the most deeply treasured beliefs and dreams of the Irish people; those that had inspired the Irish revolution and the desire for freedom. Lyons does not say these were not laudable values to fight for, but that the theories employed to embody them proved thoroughly inadequate on Irish soil. The theories of nationality, history and revolution are held responsible for the impasse in the North and this view is congruent with the postmodern intuition, of which the most convincing illustration is found in the writings of Lyotard, especially those tackling the Algerian question, that theory, instead of being an enlightening guide to political action, has become an intimate part of the problem. The critic Edna Longley pondered enigmatically: "Whether malign historians have indeed caused subsidence under the Nationalist grand narrative, or whether its foundations have always quaked";[8] thereby suggesting that the theory might have secreted some noxious core from its inception or that the manifest failings of the Nationalist school of history reflected a geological fault in the system itself. At Easter 1916, when he heard about the Rising, W.B. Yeats cast a cold and Delphic eye on it, and his reaction had almost a tone of postmodern scepticism in it as he described the rebels as "innocent and patriotic theorists, carried away by their belief that they must put their theories into practice. They would fail and pay the penalty for rashness".[9] Estimating a number of Marxist analyses, both traditional and more revisionist, on the Northern Irish conflict, Frank Burton accused them all of sacrificing "the complexity of the problem to maintain the plausibility of a theoretical position".[10]

In fact, a consciousness of the limits of theory stamps the epistemologies of both the Revisionist and postmodern schools. As Gilbert Larochelle wrote: "The intellectual program of the interpreters of post-modernity appears, in sum, centred on a theorization of the limits of theory".[11] The disquiet arises out of the presentiment that the theories conceived by Karl Marx, G.W.F. Hegel, Johann Herder, Wilhelm Riehl and Johann Fichte, whose precepts were imposed on Irish soil by James Connolly, Patrick Pearse or D.P. Moran, were dangerous either because the principle that "the end justifies the means" and the principle of the superiority of the Celtic race governed them or because one could never graft them conclusively on the Irish "body". Nationalism and communism were bedfellows which displayed both a natural proclivity to engender and justify violence. There was something rotten in the core of these theories, and reality under the nightmarish transmutation of the Shoa, the Stalinist gulags and one could include the supremacist appetites in Northern Ireland the ethnic cleansing mentality of some more recent European nationalisms, like the War in ex-Yugoslavia, confirmed this. In his conclusion to *Culture and Anarchy*, Lyons wrote:

> The true anarchy during the period from the fall of Parnell to the death of Yeats ... was not primarily an anarchy of violence in the streets, of

contempt for law and order such as to make the island, or any part of it, permanently ungovernable. It was rather an anarchy in the mind and in the heart, an anarchy which forbade not just unity of territories, but also "unity of being", an anarchy that sprang from the collision within a small and intimate island of seemingly irreconcilable cultures, unable to live together or to live apart, caught inextricably in the web of their tragic history.[12]

These remarks are symptomatic of the paradigmatic shift registered in both Irish revisionism and postmodern theory. The vision of the thorough indoctrination of man haunts these two schools. This introjection of power turns into something monstrous and chronically unleashes its violence on society. Resting his analysis of disintegration on the same theme, Lyons queried the appositeness of conventional political history because, "The most important consequence of the 1921 settlement was that by concentrating attention on physical boundaries and questions of political sovereignty, it postponed almost till our own day any serious consideration of the cultural difference that underlay the partition of the country".[13] As an alternative to a type of history that attended only to the superficial causes of conflict, he lobbied for a cultural history which could make one realize that "this malaise is both more deep-seated and harder to cure than the political instability with which we are all familiar, and of which it is a prime cause".[14] Lyons' emphasis on the harm done by theories and his intimation of an anarchy of the heart and mind forbidding unity of territories is curiously evocative of the literature produced by the French post-structuralist school. In *Libidinal Economy*, Jean-François Lyotard speaks of a desire, an energy that resists all settlement, political or other. Conventional means cannot pin down, bolt or contain this force. Faced with these mysterious and irrational forces working unbidden through man, the only thing remaining to do, is to "bear witness" to their inexplicable nature. This chaos, consubstantial with the mind precedes political economy and this is why Marxist theory is doomed to fail when any effort is made to turn it into practice. Angry and remorseless in his criticism of the Left, Lyotard decides that there is no point in engaging in a dialogue with socialism, because it will "always confuse power and force" and choose Fascistic methods as a bugbear to ensure the suppression of these libidinal forces that his socio-political theory cannot check.[15]

F.S.L. Lyons' conclusion, with its undertones of intense distress at the sight of two enemies locked inexorably into an agonistic view of each other, carries something of the post-lapsarian quality (fall from a state of innocence or grace) of the postmodern outlook on the human condition. Ideology has won the battle over man. It holds so much sway over his mind that he can no longer feel the rescuing emotion of empathy let alone remember that in Northern Ireland the two warring factions belong to the same Christian family. Ideology has erased from his mind the memory of brotherhood. Lyons' despondency cuts so deep that he even comes to question his rationalizations. The Olympian *Clercs* to which he belonged had always striven with unerring optimism to smooth the path for reconciliation between the old enemies and displayed a tendency to play down the gravity of religious and cultural fault-lines. They found solace and inspiration in the idea of some deeper unity which they needed to retrieve for the benefit of all. Political, literary or historical minds all descending from an Anglo-Irish lineage had imagined themselves invested with the mission to temper the acrimony and hatred exhaling from the monoliths.[16]

Lyons' loss of faith in his role of mediator, in his ability to perfect a rapprochement is implicit and stems from the realization that culture, instead of being a unifying force in a divided society, a barrier against anarchy as was expounded by Matthew Arnold, can be complicit with it. The co-existence of several cultures, related yet distinct, made it impossible for Irishmen to gain a coherent view of themselves in relation to each other and the outside world. His demolition of the rationalizations of his tradition calls to mind Lyotard's refutation of the notion of false consciousness on which had rested the entire logic of Marxism. Psychologically and politically, both writers are here flirting with nihilism. The fear is that one has to resign oneself to the unthinkable; that is to say, that there is no solution available inside the conventional limits of the theory. It is so because the theory suffers from an inherent weakness as it does not recognise that the will for domination is iron-branded in the human constitution and therefore cannot be expunged at will; all this can be guessed in the interstices of Lyons' solemn conclusion.

His words were not lost on Revisionists, who deeply unsettled by the finality of his scepticism chose paradoxically to interpret them as a rallying cry for the cause of a cultural history especially geared up to dissect the workings of ideology and to salvage once more what Roy Foster called, "liberal, synthesizing historiography".[17] In a way, Lyons' near defeatism was also an oblique challenge to the revisionist school. For although it knew the magnitude of the obstacles given that during forty years it had devoted all its energy to bringing them down, it had also in a typical posture of headstrong confidence thought that its work of correction would suffice to bring about tangible change in the mentalities and the mournful reality of Northern Ireland. Already in 1958, in one of his Algerian journalistic pieces, Lyotard declared: "We need to get rid of a certain kind of patronizing Marxism. An ideology has no less reality (even and above all if it is false) than the objective relations to which this Marxism wants to reduce it".[18] This admonition against blind positivism is also present in Lyons' *Culture and Anarchy*. He too was warning the revisionist school against the same patronizing sin, pointing out to it the limits of its scientism and insisting that a history inspired by logical principles was no magical wand to conjure away either religious fanaticism, sectarianism theocratic states or racist nationalisms. Rationalism was not strong enough to dislodge those phenomena. Lyons' emphasis is on their strange resilience his new wisdom echoes that of Lyotard as both men realize that incredulity alone towards these master narratives or even a fervent effort to sap their intellectual foundations will not necessarily free the minds from their firm clench.

In his overview of the social-science literature on the Northern conflict, John Whyte wrote that "the internal-conflict approach [was] close to becoming a dominant paradigm",[19] indicating that Lyons' endogenous hypothesis had also become fashionable among other writers. Since Lyons' morose verdict, the Olympians have again taken up the torch that Lyons had given up at the end of his book. In *Varieties of Irishness*, Roy Foster recollected the "mingled admiration and reservations", the "exhilaration and doubts" he felt while listening to the lectures on *Culture and Anarchy* Lyons delivered at Oxford in the Hilary Term of 1978. The most disturbing thing was his "bleak pessimism" because it "ran counter to the school of liberal, synthesizing historiography which Lyons had come to embody". However Foster thought that the premise on which Lyons' book was written, "the battle of two civilizations" was too "crude" and "retrospective" to be an accurate picture of the cultural reality of the early 1900s. The ferment of new ideas unleashed around that time was conducive less to confrontation and more to conciliation. Lyons conceded, "Superficially, it seemed, as the 19th century ended, that a new era was opening, an era of constructive thinking and doing in which men and women of different cultures might join in friendly collaboration". But beneath this superficial harmony, he believed that "The old fissures remained and the battle of the two civilizations was drawing up its lines, to culminate in the real battle of 1916".[20]

Foster put flesh on his doubts when he argued that Lyons' reading had been skewed by the Yeatsan interpretation of the period since Parnell's death in which, in the words of Yeats, "a disillusioned and embittered Ireland turned from parliamentary politics; an event was conceived; and the race began ... to be troubled by that event's long gestation".[21] According to Foster, Lyons failed to see that when Yeats and others popularized this lifescoped view they had at the time a bigger intention at the back of their minds; "the idea that cultural revivalism, in the Irish context, deterministically produced extremist politics, and set up a zero-sum game which eliminated all middle ground".[22] Foster rejected this conclusion and uncovered why both the winners and the losers in the post-revolutionary era rushed to espouse the idea of cultural diversity as inevitably confrontational.

Persuasively, he showed that the drift in fatalism was a self-serving ploy that both sides used to justify to others and to themselves their respective miscalculations and failures. Yeats who was a cultural prophet in the pre-revolutionary period was disposed to believe that his predictions had been accurate all along and so the notion of a deeper logic to 1916, one which could be traced back to the influence of his play *Cathleen ni Houlihan*, appealed to him. Predictably, this overshadowed the perhaps more direct reasons for the Easter Rising, such as the dithering of the British Liberal Government over the Ulster Volunteer Force or the "Pavlovian" Fenian reaction to England's involvement in an external war. On the losing side, the Irish Parliamentary Party also preferred to subscribe to the ambient determinism rather than probe too deeply into the way they lost control of the nationalist vote after 1914. Convinced that around 1900, Irish culture was not yet yoked with separatism, Foster advised research to go in the direction of an excavation of this harmonious experience of cultural difference. His recommendation to unearth a time when Ireland was still at the crossroads, when Yeats had "this moment of supernatural insight" in the form of "a sudden certainty that the nation was like soft wax"[23] in his hands, is based on the hope that it will be possible once again to reclaim the lost pacifying energies of the past. It is a humanistic outlook to the core, one founded on the principles that difference and unity do not have to be antinomic and that history's role is to continue pointing at the soundness of pluralism however implausible it may sound sometimes.

Loyal to the spirit of the first revisionist generation, Foster still believes that an open-minded exploration of Irish history can yield meaningful lessons and be a major healing influence. That's why he cannot reconcile himself to Lyons' "sombre concept of colliding cultures, rather like colliding planets, in a universe where interpenetration, fusion or commingling is simply not a physical possibility".[24] On the contrary, Lyons' disillusionment is such that his historical imagination is impaired so that he sees a past, which is terrifyingly a mere dismal prelude to the present deadlock. Here culture no longer holds the promise of a spiritual bridging of differences, instead it is what immures man and condemns him to a state of neurosis and autistic solitude. On 20 June 1983, during a conversation with Ronan Fanning, Lyons confessed:

> My book ends in pessimism and yes, I was pessimistic when I wrote it and am still more so now ... Does pessimism paralyse the historical imagination? Sometimes I think yes ... but on balance, I don't feel paralysed and only feel that I might be paralysed if I believed in progress. Since I don't, I find ample scope in trying to come as close as possible to "how it actually was", of course, not very close. I would really find it hard to be both a conscientious historian and an optimist – there I diverge from Yeats who was ultimately, I think, an optimist.[25]

Two themes stand out from this statement; the loss of faith in modernity in the guise of progress and a feeling that pessimism, far from causing despair and nihilism may contain the dawn of a new wisdom. Paradoxically, the intellectual assumes here a role which is totally at variance with the old prototype from which it originated: the eighteenth-century enlightened philosopher who believed that reason, harmony and progress would triumph and superstition be defeated thanks to knowledge and education. From now on, it is no longer enough to be the critical conscience of the political, the intellectual has to find the courage to admit and bear witness to its limits.

One should not forget that when Lyons confessed his disenchantment, terror reigned in Northern Ireland. The sectarianism which poisoned society did not appear to be susceptible to a political solution, as the failures of the constitutional initiatives, direct rule, the power-sharing executive and the intergovernmental conference set up by the Hillsborough Agreement of November 1985 all evinced. For at least thirty years, the province was a sinister symbol of the systematic demise of politics in the face of incompatible claims. That's why the threat looming over society compelled Lyons in 1979 to think no more in terms of a future ideal project, in an approach designed to praise the qualities of this or that, but rather in terms of how to limit the damage and find a temporary remedy so as to relieve human agony. The emphasis is on the unflagging resistance to evil as opposed to the belief in an immanent good and the accomplishment of a Utopia. The most credible antidote to any totalitarian drift confines itself, henceforth, to a function of strict watchfulness of the state of the world in order to protect mankind from insanity, that is, from itself.

15 Grappling with the problem of objectivity

Brady is definite about one thing; Bradshaw simplifies to the point of distortion the theoretical foundations of the revisionism. Evidently, there is still a risk that the detachment for which historians strive may conceal pitfalls, especially when distance is elevated into an absolute method in the unveiling of the past. But if some historians exhibit a too swift tendency of hiding uncertainties behind the system of distance, some of their opponents exhibit a too swift tendency of hiding other uncertainties behind the opposite system of proximity. The danger that by following too closely their respective systems both may miss something and impede their free judgement is here equally. The paradox is that historians are pressed to persevere where they know there is no final resolution.

François Furet recognized the paradox and yet he saw it as a necessary thing to cling to though, one which in the interests of history should never be renounced. If Existentialism and Marxism with their stress on the pressures of structures had helped combat "the positivist illusion that objectivity is possible", there was now a danger that "the continuing harping of this truism" would "perpetuate professions of faith and polemics that have had their day". True the day would come when the battle over who was the true heir of the French Revolution would seem incredible but "this cooling off of this object" should not be expected only from the passing of time. The task of the historian was to "define the conditions needed to bring it about". These new conditions had already "deeply modified the relation between the historian and his subject" making "less spontaneous and less compelling the historian's identification with the actors, his commemoration of the founders, or his execration of the deviants".[1] Admit the impossibility of full objectivity does not lessen the value of the effort of dissociation, if only because it awakens the scientific mind to the need for improvement of the methods. When Jacques Derrida's project of destabilization of metaphysical oppositions was dismissed as unfeasible, he retorted: "I would say that deconstruction loses nothing in the admission of its impossibility; and also that those who will rejoice in such admission are in for a surprise. The interest of deconstruction, of such a force and desire of which it seems to be animated, is precisely a certain experience of the impossible".[2] The contamination of history by literature, favoured by deconstruction is useful because it highlights the limits of empirical inference and can awake the researcher to ways of utilizing fictional evidence. But Derrida did not mean hereby he wished to dispense altogether with history as a discipline. The prestige traditionally attached to history should remain. His intention when he defended the notion of contamination was not simply to reverse the hierarchy and bestow authority to the non-scientific instead of the scientific discourse.

For out of this exercise, the notion of absolute authority comes out unscathed. It is only transferred from one discipline to another. On the contrary what he wished to obtain by shifting the boundaries and rendering the categories more pervious between one another was above all to loosen the grip of hierarchy in the mind and question the idea of superiority in the social sciences. Still there is a world of difference between recognizing the limitations of a heuristic system and conceding no merit whatsoever to its output. The difference is one of degree or quality in critical rigour. The historian may be surrendering to some elements of literature, like the rhetorical and the allegorical, or even some elements of politics, like the partisan and the propagandist, at the very moment when he detects and denounces them. Even if no one can totally escape this, and if no one is thus responsible for giving in to it, however little one may do so, Derrida insisted that all the ways of giving in to it are not of equal importance.[3] Certain irreducible characteristics of the historical practice, and certain qualities of its unique expertise, will subsist after the work of deconstruction. Only history will no longer be perceived as an infallible Bible for what happened in the past and how it is interpreted in the present. In a nutshell, it will no longer hold a monopoly on truth. To sum up his vision, Derrida added: "What interests me is not strictly speaking, either philosophy or literature. I dream of a writing which would be neither one nor the other, while keeping, I have no desire to relinquish this, the memory of literature and of philosophy".[4]

Even Lévi-Strauss who had done so much to knock history from its pedestal insisted he wished to deny neither its reality nor its scientific status but what he called its mystique; the belief that "the temporal dimension enjoys a special prestige, as if diachrony founded a type of intelligibility, not only superior to the one brought by synchrony, but above all, of a more specifically human order".[5] As a method of enquiry, history could not be contested because like ethnology it was a helpful example of a science of relativity. It was only as a special kind of myth, which "our society had internalised", and whose function was to make mankind believe in an ineluctable march towards freedom that history was dangerously misleading. Jean-François Lyotard, Jacques Derrida and Hayden White have all advocated a levelling between literature and history and not a blunt reversal of this binary opposition with literature and literary criticism assuming henceforth a superior position supposedly because these do not hide their political colours behind the pretence of objectivity. Sometimes one suspects that the thrust of Seamus Deane's attack conspires to do precisely this; to overturn simply the hierarchy not to dissolve it as the theorists of the postmodern sought to do. Willey Maley argues that revisionism is a homogenizing force, which tolerates no opposition to its orthodoxy. He uses Derrida's reflection on violence to clinch his argument that revisionism's placatory veil hides a bellicose character, which is the exact copy of the nationalism it rejects. He adds "Revisionism appears intent upon blaming the victims of colonialism, where nationalist discourse was wont to balm or embalm them, but demonology and sanctification are two sides of the same coin".[6]

Derrida explains indeed that it requires more than simple opposition to escape the magnetic power of a discourse and Maley is convinced that Irish revisionism is caught in this vicious circle. This is an interesting argument, expressed with shrewdness, were it not for the fact that it betrays a complete ignorance of revisionism as a critical practice and a total overshadowing of the context that prompted it. In fact, the coherence of his argument depends on an eclipse of its origins. The critical strategy on which revisionism relies to objectify nationalism is not one of external opposition but one of internal opposition. And this latter, as deconstruction has shown, has more power of destabilization of the authoritarian discourse than the former.

In their majority, revisionists do not just reject Irish nationalism; instead, they explore its tremendous and everlasting appeal on the Irish psyche, its ambivalent role in Ireland's historical processes, that is, at once as instrument of emancipation and instrument of oppression, or tool of dissent and tool of silencing of dissent. Indeed, the new school was the first to have turned into a problem the discourse, of both nationalism and unionism, to have targeted their mendacity and cracked their all-enveloping mirage. Maley then criticizes Steven Ellis' conclusions. Because physical proximity between Ireland and England cancels the possibility of colonization in the strong sense of the word, he retaliates that Ellis merely domesticates the terrifying experience of conquest. Furthermore, because revisionists discount anti-Irish racism because of a lack of "objective criteria such as skin colour", while imputing racism to Irish nationalism, their reading reveals a racism of empiricism, if not a racism of the empire. Despite a witty and theoretical exposition, Maley's tone seems to be as judgemental as the one he gleefully attributes to Irish revisionism, especially when he concludes that by opposing Irish nationalism revisionists intend to do nothing more than defend the British Empire. He patches up his preconceived opinion with a superficial and selective reading of both deconstruction and revisionism; a pre-emptive move which stops him from appreciating how mutually influenced they are. The apex of this pseudo-exegesis is to reduce revisionism to a product of violence, and he agrees with Gerry Smyth who contends that "post-nationalism and post-colonialism are troubled discourses, in the sense that their force and coherence depends to a large extent on the reality of sustained sectarian violence in Northern Ireland".[7]

The truth is that despite its erudition, Maley's critique does not convey the impression of having overcome or short-circuited the condemnatory logic it deplores. He is right to underline the limits of a method based solely on distance. Historicism may not always intercept with circular reasoning. And it is undeniable that the Northern troubles have exerted a negative influence on revisionism, the daily horror of sectarian violence driving it to become more polemical and caricatural in its positions. Besides Ronan Fanning, F.S.L. Lyons and Roy Foster have readily admitted this. Foster wrote: "Partly the result of questioning the monolithic received view of a purely Gaelic nation, it is also, obviously, a result of forced reconsiderations since the detonation of the Ulster crisis".[8] But Maley's intentions are suspect. Does he really want to encourage a close dialogue between historians and other scholars or is his intention to refuse them all credibility by decreeing as he does that their history is simply a reaction to the violence in the North? Paranoia is never far from the surface inside Irish intellectual circles and no one is immune to it no matter how equitable one may try to be. To campaign for interdisciplinarity is a laudable objective but Maley underestimates the extent to which the condescending attitude mocking the professionalism and integrity of these historians and presenting their entire output as expendable forces them to wind back the drawbridge.

Brendan Bradshaw opined that Irish revisionists wrote in a very militant style. Irish revisionism is not so much an aggressive as a passionate discourse. To understand the tension in which it is caught, one could turn to the literary critic Edna Longley, a self-professed revisionist. Her writing is organized around a crucial rhetorical trope; the sense of inhabiting a fallen world, stained by original sin. A society in which for reasons of historical malformation, poetry is forced to step into the realm of the political. The contradiction in her critical approach derives from the abnormal configuration of Northern Ireland. Her work has continuously forced the poem into the bear-pit of the social arena while denying time after time that it should have to do so.[9] The aesthetic object cannot be confined to meditation but needs to turn into an act of dissidence. Its function is to erode the ideologies that re-float or repackage antagonistic images of Irish society.[10] Its prescience can refine and unify sensibilities, that's why one must protect the autonomy of the creative act from any temporal ideologies. Here transcendence and historicity are not mutually exclusive so long as the intervention aims at transcendence. If materialism sees in literature a means to an end, idealism sees in it the promise of an escape from this logic.[11] In *Poetry in the Wars*, she brings back those Irish poets who between the two World Wars and during the sectarian conflict stubbornly refused to manacle their art in the service of the cause. If as a citizen, the poet has a right to defend a cause, his responsibility as a writer is never to forsake the quest for human truth at its most fundamental and universal. The realm of literature reveals the irreducibility of conscience. It is within it that the power of severance of the mind can assert itself. It is what holds the promise of his emancipation from the shackles of his ineluctable social identity. Thanks to it man can escape the parochial blindfolding that is imposed on him. Disunion is not without appeal, it is not final: the Northern Irish people can get the better of their estrangement. She opposes post-structuralism because it has "turned our quaking sod into a quaking text", thereby inhibiting the emergence of genuine criticism in Irish society.

She considers the structuralist word "discourse" a bully and is suspicious of the Field Day intellectuals who celebrate its supposed egalitarian qualities. Discourse is not attractive; on the contrary, it is repulsive because it "abolishes any boundary between poetry and prose, poetry and politics, in the same spirit as 'comrade' abolishes class distinctions. The only casualty is imagination".[12] She attacks Deane's "polarised vista of endlessly competing discourses – rival propagandas?" which "frighteningly rules out any objective language of fact or value".[13] What cancels the differences and demotes the unique contribution of each discipline only leads to an impoverishment of thought. She tries to reconcile opposites in that "her work is an ongoing negotiation between the idealism of truth as it is located in the poetic and the rationality which (in the Irish context) seeks to disrupt the monolith or the definitional".[14] The aesthetic object possesses a transfiguring quality, one stemming from the diversity of wills and consciences, can assist the "witnessing [of] the last spasms of the Green and Orange state-ideologies which literature long ago found unworkable".[15] The structure of Longley's polemics and its tensions are an illustration of the pitfalls that have beset the politicization of revisionism. Once thrown into the political arena, it ran the risk of becoming not so much in its content as in its form a replica of what it opposed. The Ulster crisis forced historians to speak more loudly and Roy Foster advised they pumped up the volume.[16] The imperative of stopping the war, its carnage and the spread of hatred jolted them into stopping meditation and beginning dissuasion, almost by hype and plugging tactics. It was there that the danger lay and it was difficult to steer clear of it in the Ireland of the 1980s and 1990s. For the task of convincing fast and the highest number compelled Irish revisionists to resort almost to a form of proselytism, where as in the case of the separatist intellectuals of the 1900s, it ended unfortunately not only in a grotesque caricature of the enemy but also of the values, intuitions and motives that had inspired their project.

Once turned into activists the "new historians" had to silence their own doubts and hide the aporias detectable in all thought behind a system, in this case empiricism. Hence, the desire to heal the social breach turned into a mechanism of exhortation and hindered the opening of the mind to its own regions of darkness. Naturally, these areas of doubt offered an excellent opportunity of attack for their opponents who applied themselves to magnify them. If there is disequilibrium in tone and feeling in revisionism it does not betray hypocrisy or intolerance, as their critics on both sides of the political spectrum assume, but it is an aspect of the psychology of the historian who writes in an environment saturated with violence, physical and verbal. Those accusations show conspicuously however this self-feeding hermeneutics of suspicion,[17] which some theorists deploy ad nauseam and with delectation while they themselves are simply content with perfunctorily mending the edifice of their convictions and accusing historians of the very sin in which they are yet the first to wallow in; the pursuit of their political agendas through the medium of their discipline. Seamus Deane granted one thing to revisionism; it put the question of the epistemological status of history back on the agenda.[18] However, his verdict was pitiless as he accused it of nursing dogmatic tendencies. Revisionism was not "a conspiracy theory" but rather "a consensus theory".[19] It had succumbed to the illusion of having found superior and indisputable truths. A defender of empiricism herself, Edna Longley reminds us that in his seminal book *The Poverty of Theory*, E.P. Thompson had exposed the "original heresy of metaphysics against knowledge".[20] In his dispute with the Marxist historian, Louis Althusser argued that the past was unfathomable, it was devoid of all meaning and the theoretical impulse, whether one cared to admit or not, preceded and rigidly dictated the parameters of historical investigation. In his invective against the empiricism of revisionism, Seamus Deane squarely repeated Althusser's attack; confirming what we already know, that Field Day had found in radical poststructuralism a strong offensive. Paraphrasing Roland Barthes, Deane wrote: "history is a discourse; events and conditions are not. They are outside discourse, but can only be reached through it. It is a slippery discipline that has the additional merit or demerit of itself being an integral part of the object it addresses".[21]

However Deane's assertion that the revisionists claimed such unblemished objectivity was always wildly exaggerated. In 1954, J.C. Beckett underlined his distance from any doctrinaire scientism. He emphasized his conviction that "No historian is infallible. I would go further, and say that no historian is completely impartial – no matter how scrupulous he is, there are presuppositions that he cannot get rid of".[22] F.S.L. Lyons wrote: "I am not arguing that uncommitted historians are themselves immaculately objective. No historian, I would maintain, can be completely and thoroughly objective. In this sense, we are not only prisoners of our history, but also of our individual biographies".[23] In fact, Lyons acknowledged the conflicting pulls implicit in the art of writing history, but declared himself in favour of their retention. The decision to use the empirical method was founded precisely on the need to contain one's subjectivity. Furthermore Lyons saw a qualitative difference between rootedness in a time and place and partisanship. He was convinced indeed that these two sets of determinations did not exert the same constraint:

> I have always felt uneasy in the company of what are called "committed historians", be they devout Marxists, dedicated Freudians or passionate Nationalists. I am uneasy in, I hope, no pharisaical sense ... But there is a world of difference between the historian who, though enchained by

the very nature of his being, realises the fact and uses his awareness of the human condition as a means towards greater perception, and the historian who voluntarily assumes additional bonds, so shackling himself that he can look only in one direction.[24]

Theorists do not seem to take on board this qualitative difference. They do not see it as an element worthy of being included in the theoretical equation. If anything, they hold the exact opposite opinion. Relative objectivity is, they claim, more likely to be found in those historians, i.e. the Marxists or the Nationalists who openly display their political colours. Post-structuralism argues that history, rooted in an empirical tradition, is of all the ideologies the most insidious and stealthy, precisely because it hides behind a Rankean method which is regarded as superior. Yet in fairness to Lyons, his position was not devoid of theoretical refinement since he pinpointed the twin dangers present in what Butterfield called the Whig fallacy. He ungrudgingly admitted that retrospective history was not solely the cardinal sin of nationalist history but could become that of revisionist history too. This is an important moment in Lyons's thinking because in marked contrast to other fellow revisionists then, he came the closest at recognizing that his method was not such a safe and inviolable redoubt against distortion and infiltration of circularity of thought. Lyons wrote, "Professional historians had been affected by the upsurge of violence" in "a way that was at once highly creditable and potentially dangerous". They had tipped the scales in favour of the parliamentary tradition out of "over-compensation" because they were afraid they had been guilty of "giving undue prominence to the concept of revolutionary militancy" in the past. Justly horrified by the sudden recrudescence of violence, intellectually affronted by the crudity of the assumption that Ireland's modern history began in 1916, Irish historians began to examine their consciences. They wanted to redress the imbalance, correct the excess. Yet Lyons recognized that the profession had not cast its glance far enough to foresee that its desire for compensation concealed the same pitfall it was trying to avoid, simply under a reversed guise. This is why his integrity and foresight obliged him to warn his colleagues that:

> To reactivate the study of constitutional history in revulsion from present violence would merely be to commit in a different form the sin of interpreting the past in the light of the present and would result, as the sin always does result, in a wrong principle of selection and therefore in a distorted interpretation of events.[25]

There was no sure path to the achievement of a balanced approach. Still he reckoned that remembering the emotional truth that violence and non-violence co-existed in each one of us could perhaps help historians to realize that the theory of history which was most likely to mislead would be the one which exalted either to the detriment of the other.[26] These philosophical remarks are very apposite. They show Lyons anticipating criticisms which were aired mostly after his death and prove compellingly that his stance had nothing to do with the dull empiricism arbitrarily attached to the category of Revisionist. Despite all the constraints on the writing of contemporary history, the fact that "it is a mine-field", Lyons came down in favour of persevering in it because it would be a betrayal if people who were trying to assimilate recent horrendous events were abandoned by professional historians and left only with pseudo-history to satisfy their legitimate curiosity. In giving priority to the social function of the historian, Lyons is not without sounding a little like Brendan Bradshaw, except that the latter would tend to abet people's emotions whereas the former would patiently try to reason them out of them, however quixotic and chimerical this may sound. Roy Foster declared that historians were aware of ideology's forays into historical narrative. They spent an increasing amount of time teaching and researching this very problem. Denying absence of self-critique, he argued that they were not so single-minded as to believe they were invulnerable to it or so Machiavellian as to conceal a deliberate agenda. Generally, they knew their limitations and the provisional nature of most verdicts. He then offered his opinion on post-structuralism:

> It is significant that some of these denunciations come from literary critics, because the effect of critical theory on historical discourse is worth noting – in Ireland as in America, in the age of Hayden White and Paul Ricoeur. Some accompanying concepts have added much enlightenment to Irish history, notably the analysis of colonial collusions elsewhere in the Empire. But the recently fashionable idea that the historian/writer is in corrupt and unconscious collusion with the text, and that reference to an ascertainable body of fact is a delusion of the late bourgeois world, leads quickly to the useful position that all history is suspect and all readings questionable. By an easy elision, this sanctions a turning back to the old verities and the old, atavistic antipathies.[27]

Foster recognizes that theory does make a difference to the way Irish history is analysed. Even so, he voices apprehensions about the final principle of post-structuralism, the one that reduces history to a mere discourse, intentionally or unintentionally colluding with the ideologies it tries to defeat. Foster's disquiet is justified. But his conventional manner of defending his craft does not do justice to his own theoretical flair. Ciaran Brady expresses a similar unease. He thinks historians must challenge the relativists and the sceptics who deny the historians' claims to have established a progressive and socially useful branch of knowledge. Perceptive, he rightly identifies deconstruction as the most consummate form of relativism, although his judgement would be more appropriate to a bolshie, vulgar type of deconstruction that has tended in the past to close off all interdisciplinary dialogue and for this reason stymied all realization of common methodo-logical assumptions between theory and history:

> Relativism has reached its most extreme position in the deconstruction-ists' claim that historians' pretensions to recount the past in any more than a wholly fictive manner is both impossible and ideologically repressive. Arguments of this kind have proved quite naturally unac-ceptable to working historians, who continue to believe that, whatever their epistemological muddles, something "real" has intruded upon their imaginations, that events actually occurred in the past for which there is palpable, if all too fragmentary, evidence.[28]

When theorists question the *raison d'être* of the historical discipline, the historians' reflex is to fall back automatically on an essentialist type of argu-ment. In fact, the more one becomes acquainted with the depth of insight behind each discipline, the more one draws the impression that some of the dialogue of the deaf and misunderstanding occurred and still does because philosophy and history have different linguistic habits. In a famous defence of history, the English historian Geoffrey Elton writes: "Ideological theories create preconditioned convictions about the past; philosophical theories deny that the past can ever be reconstituted. The first undermine the histo-rian's honesty, the second his claims to existence".[29] Elton grants that the questions the historian puts to the past may be the ones which suit him and probably he will "include himself in the equation when he explains, inter-prets, even perhaps distorts". Notwithstanding these qualifying clauses he believes that the historian cannot invent the experiment; the subject under investigation is outside of the historian's control. Elton is positive. The his-torian cannot escape the first condition of his job, which is that the matter subjected to his analytical mind has a dead reality independent of the enquiry: "At some time, these things actually once happened, and it is now impossible to arrange them for the purposes of experiment".[30]

He concedes this is not the same thing as to claim that we can know exactly what, when, how or why everything happened. The historian "should not suppose that his knowledge can be either total or finite" but it is because the past has gone, is irrecoverable and unrepeatable, that "its objective reality", its ontological existence, "is guaranteed". He continues: "What is in question here is the subject matter of history, the events of the past, not the evidence they have left behind or the product of the historian's labours. However biased, prejudiced, incomplete and inadequate that product may be, it embodies an account of events that happened quite independent of the existence of him who now looks at them ... the past ... is commandingly there".[31] But Elton has just identified a problem, which cannot be resolved by a simple appeal to common sense. He admits that the historian is concerned with a truth which is more absolute than "mere truth-fulness", that is more truthful than a verified experiment. Thus whilst the historian will rarely be able to say: "This is the truth and no other answer is possible [he] ... will always be able to say; this once existed or took place, and there is therefore a truth to be discovered if only we can find it".[32] The last part of this statement indicates that even Elton, the devotee of empiricism par excellence, is also prone to epistemological doubt. Furthermore, there is misunderstanding here because no earnest theorist has ever denied the inert presence of the past. What they question is the possibility of devising a method capable of making the representation of the past true and objective. Objectivity and truth do not derive from the existence of an object of inquiry but from the internal mechanisms chosen to impart coherence and persuasion to the explanation. Thus if Elton wants to convey an objective knowledge of the past beyond the chronicle, then he will need to discover a method and not content himself with naïvely asserting that a singular explanation carries truth and objectivity just because it has a single object as the focus of its enquiry.

The mere ontological assertion is not enough to give an accurate and comprehensive representation of what happened and it leads nowhere in the explanation of the whys and wherefores of the ontological. Roy Foster invokes the "ascertainable body of facts". He suggests that the presence of a verifiable past is sufficient onto itself, as if this past could speak for itself, as if without any mediation, one could retrieve truth and objectivity by simply dipping into it. However, when we dissolve the logocentric mirage, we realize that these values are not in the past waiting to be discovered. Instead, they are extrinsic evaluations waiting to be applied. Truth and objectivity do not innately belong to the past; they are just terms we use when we evaluate the accounts of the past which historians make. It takes more than simple access to the ontological fact to arrive at true explanations of the states and the conditions of its existence. From the ontological fact, we cannot draw normative values. If we admit the past is impotent and agnostic on the question of the truth then we are also a step closer to the recognition that if the historian does not dissect with a critical eye the written traces of the past, then the subjective intentions of these documents can elude him. Revisionists know this well but their refuge behind empiricism has done them a disservice by burying their precious theoretical intuition born of their personal experience underneath a borrowed system. An essay by Desmond T. Williams reveals that the first generation was conscious of the epistemological hurdles, which afflicted its craft. At the fifth inaugural meeting of the History Students' Society held at UCD on 14 December 1948, he declared:

> Historians as well as other scholars have often been asked what is the purpose and aim of their science. The obvious answer is of course the discovery of the true story of mankind – to find as Ranke put it, *wie es weiklich gewesen*. It may well be remarked however that there is an infinite host of facts from which we select according to our standards and

that it is not the whole truth we seek but only that part which appears relevant. The dangers implicit in this necessary selection are naturally apparent, and we often find our history cut according to the cloth of the historian. Prejudice and passion take on frequently very subtle forms. There is the reverse danger that in the search for as many facts as possible one may lose the wood from the trees. Acton complained once that history was descending into the kitchen in a hunt for irrelevant and unimportant facts, and the great German classicist, Wilamowitz–Moellenderf deplored the decline of historical judgement and imagination caused by research in no way concerned with reality. History in spreading its scope often tends to become dull and as has aptly been said, the historian begins to know more and more about less and less.[33]

Here clearly Williams pronounces himself against the fetishism of facts. He appreciates why this fetishism by no means guarantees access to a noteworthy truth or how it can drive knowledge into a cul-de-sac; a cold erudition, congenitally powerless to confer meaning where its discovery is most urgently needed. Ciaran Brady, who this time shows he is well equipped and willing to quit the essentialist argument, echoes Williams' theoretical acuity:

Historical writing is always conducted by means of synecdoche, in the sense that one set of details is selected from the mass of evidence to represent the whole of the phenomenon described. But because such a selection can never be replicated, and because one synecdoche cannot refute another, historical argument can never be "falsified" in scientific terms.[34]

This study postulates the idea of an intellectual kinship between revisionism in Ireland and postmodernism on the Continent. The connections binding these two schools are profound and natural because in both cases they arise out of a will to think seriously about the general state of knowledge and a prolonged experiment on the methods to apply in order to accomplish a separation between history and politics. When one explores these links and the spontaneous manner in which they burst upon the intelligence of the researcher, one no longer watches with the same credulity the flirt of Irish theorists with post-structuralism. Their appropriation of the body of continental theory is first of all a lot more narrowly selective and capricious and for this reason gives the impression that it has a polemical edge and thrust only. The interpenetration between postmodernism and Irish revisionism has its roots in a common existential experience. In both schools, one notes a very real and consistent effort to think about difference or Otherness, be it Ulster Unionism, Southern Anglo-Irish dissent, the debilitating gap between theory and reality, or the mistakes, shortcomings and tragedies of their respective political tradition, in the case of postmodernism, Marxism and in the case of Irish revisionism, Republican nationalism. Conversely, it is bewildering to note that despite engagement with a very radical and far-seeing theoretical apparatus, the political choices embraced by the Irish critics of revisionism remain strangely traditional. The notion of nationalism as a still viable and desirable prospect for the future emerges intact from this theoretical jaunt. Seamus Deane describes nationalism as an intellectual umbrella which can contain and accommodate all the micro-narratives forming the totality of Ireland's cultural tradition. Nationalism under the reforming spirit of Field Day represents a "story"; a "meta-narrative" which is in essence "hospitable" and can welcome "all the micro-narratives that, from time to time, have achieved prominence as the official version of the true history, political and literary, of the island's past and present".[35]

Autarkical and padlocked, the political certitudes of the intellectuals of Field Day[36] live on in spite of the shattering implications outlined by the theory. One cannot help thinking that this appropriation boils down to an artificial patching: an attempt to boost Irish nationalism by giving it a gloss of theoretical and politive elegance. Irish revisionists, however, more sceptically inclined, do not understand this obstinacy for they think that the past belies this generous portrayal of Irish Nationalism. This latter has, in their view, lamentably failed in its democratic dimension. Very early, the state assumed a conservative and conformist character and imposed the ethos of the majority without so much as a serious thought about the impact of this decision on the other traditions present on the island. Edna Longley suspects this "reconstructed" nationalism of being instrumentalist or expedient in its harnessing of postcolonial and post-structuralist theories and voices her reticence vis-à-vis a domestication which consists in, as it was said by J.J. Lee, "throwing theory at Ireland, hoping that bits of it will stick".[37] She decries the "one-size-fits-all" zeal of these theorists and argues that the phenomenon of territorial expansion internal to European borders represents a more apposite model to explain the historical trajectory of the country than those elaborated by Frantz Fanon and Edward Said.[38] The historian J.J. Lee expresses a similar reservation regarding the chances of success of the foreign socio-economic theories on Irish soil. With a touch of irony, he asks whether the government "conceived of imported ideas as raw materials, as intermediate goods, or as finished products".[39] The notion that the crude importation of a foreign theory is a hazardous exercise is not new and E.P. Thompson in his famous dispute with Louis Althusser had explained its intrinsic defects:

> Internationalism ought not to consist in lying prostrate before the ("Western Marxist") theorists of our choice, or in seeking to imitate their modes of discourse. The reason why this kind of imitation can never produce more than a sickly native growth is complex. The "adoption" of other traditions, that is, adoption which has not been fully

worked through, interrogated and translated into the terms of our own traditions, can very often mean no more than the evacuation of the real places of conflict within our own intellectual culture.[40]

Certainly, it is no extrapolation to say that Irish revisionism was born out of similar presentiments. It rightly feared that a rough or crude importation of postcolonial or post-structuralist theory evacuated the real places of conflict in the Irish historiographic debate. Irish history presented a number of challenging questions, which was in the very nature of good history to try to answer. Why and how did the ethnic theory of the nation prevail in the South during the first decades of independence at the expense of the elective theory? Why the Stormont regime didn't grasp the opportunity to cement the foundations of the Northern State by giving a fair deal to the Catholics inside its borders? Why did the Irishmen of the North and the South eventually opt for cultural isolation and homogenization instead of trying what Ernest Renan called "the daily plebiscite" or the "secular association"? Or more to the point, why a political tradition demanding reverence to its forbears did not itself heed more their advices, as when Thomas Davis warned that: "To mingle politics and religion in such a country is to blind men to their common secular interests, to render political union impossible and national independence hopeless".[41]

But a too literal reading of postcolonial theory had the effect of shelving all these puzzling issues since it posited that the nationalism of the colony was doomed to imitate the paternalistic oppression of the colonizing power in its treatment of its own minorities. Indeed, one could even venture as far as to say that in its ultimate thrust, postcolonial theory made the investigation of the Irish past superfluous. Post-structuralism in its extreme form also presented a tendency to abort inter-cultural dialogue in the Irish situation and abandon the key idea of a single Irishness. That is why if revisionism is influenced by it, it has nonetheless stopped short from endorsing its final two principles. Revisionists do not concede that the authority of their discipline rests on a mere rhetorical game. Nor do they adhere to the opinion that humanism is always hegemonic and duplicitous. It is at this phase of the desertion of revisionists that theorists assume the take-over of theoretical anti-humanism. Luke Gibbons declared:

> The revisionist enterprise in Ireland, based as it is on a liberal-humanistic ethic, was faced with an intractable dilemma as it gradually became apparent that a belief in a human condition, transcending all historical and political divisions, belonged to the kind of cultural fantasy that Sean O'Faolain associated with Nationalism, except that it was now a Humanist rather than a Gaelic mystique.[42]

Some of the principles governing the revisionist school, such as the faith in Reason, the search for truth and the ideal of reconciliation of all Irishmen were also the momentum behind a certain kind of liberal nationalism in Ireland. Gibbons retorts that the refusal to countenance any validity for Irish nationalism places revisionists in a situation of internal contradiction because it amounts to prematurely emptying their own project of an important part of its *raison d'être*. If one censures Irish nationalism's poor record on grounds of the aprioristic impracticality of its objectives then one is also querying the ability of Irish revisionism to accomplish those same goals. Put another way, Gibbons argues that if one accepts that these ideals were never viable in the Irish setting, then nothing can guarantee that Irish revisionism will succeed where Irish nationalism has failed. Peremptorily, he announces that humanism and its entire aggregation of idealistic assumptions have collapsed on the Continent and for this reason the same fate awaits them in Ireland. He demotes humanism to a "cultural fantasy" because it rests on the illusion of a common human condition. Clearly here, Gibbons is also alluding to the derogatory semantic shift, which has affected the term humanism on the Continent, where it is dismissed as a window-dressing disguising hegemonic leanings. But Tom Dunne does not concur with Gibbons' defeatism. Historically liberal humanism emanated precisely out of the acute knowledge of such divisions and was always aware of its own specific history of complicity rooted, as it was, in some of the dominant social, economic and political processes in Europe over the past half-millennium. Dunne does not agree either with the proposition that if liberal humanism has failed in France, it necessarily follows it will also fail in Ireland. If the social ideal of the Enlightenment has not materialized in France and the French intelligentsia jettisoned it because imperialism justified its atrocities by evoking its name, the failure of this experiment should not be erected to the status of general principle. To dismiss its potential in contemporary Ireland is an especially premature gesture since no one has tried it there yet. Ciaran Brady explains again the defiance of Irish historians for the final principle of poststructuralism:

> But least helpful of all is the radical deconstructionist view, most commonly associated with Roland Barthes and on occasion with Hayden White and sometimes threatened by history's critics in Ireland, which denies all of history's claims to be a distinct and defensible form of discourse, and defines it simply as another, rather disingenuous, form of fiction, whose pretension to exercise a special privilege over others should be entirely disregarded. Thus, where the public histories advocated by Bradshaw would seem to threaten Babel, the harsh judgment of the deconstructionists would appear merely to enjoin silence. In heuristic terms, neither has anything constructive to offer the historians in their routine travails.[43]

It is hard not to share his misgivings because a churlish and jejune interpretation of this complex philosophy can lead to the specious conclusion that there is nothing outside the political and that all attempts to escape from its crushing influence are destined to fail. What is denied is the improvement of heuristic tools and it seems that researchers are admonished above all not to budge because the least scientific initiative could but sink them deeper into the quicksand of their ineluctable identities. Once this idea gains credence in the Irish situation, then the path is open again for "British Colonialism and Irish Nationalism to resume the integrity of their old quarrel", as Stephen Howe said.[44] Revisionism was labelled a crude empirical school. Yet, the more interesting question of what sort of concerns underlay this respectful scrutiny of facts was never given the attention it deserves. The critics of history in their sniper attack against empiricism invent and reinforce false dichotomies: the idea that empiricism and philosophy are separated by the most impenetrable partition, that they are opposed categories whose paths never meet.

The pity is that in the Irish historiographic situation this compartmentalization has evacuated the deep layers of theoretical interrogation that had originally triggered off the will to rethink the status of the discipline and rebuild it along more objective lines. Hence the often repeated charge is of putting way too much store on accredited facts instead of looking at the subjective climate of the period under scrutiny and what has not been recorded. For instance, Brendan Bradshaw depicts himself as crying in the wilderness against "a sceptical empiricism [which] resulted in sterile reductionism". Meanwhile, he too is guilty of reductionism for he sees revisionism as a monolithic conspiracy whose designs are to extract the heroism, tragedy and "play of national consciousness" from Irish history.[45] Yet again, this religious obedience to facts is not based on some gullible faith in the ability of facts to speak for themselves. More than anyone else, Irish historians know that facts are not tenacious, that they are precarious, docile, pliable and at every one's beck and call. They know they can be mercilessly distorted to fit the contours of a theory or complacently absorbed in the sluggishness of public opinion. So, facts are not stubborn as Lenin[46] used to believe, but subdued by theory, myth and propaganda, they are reduced to at best empty signifiers, colourless abstractions that are doomed to await the ascription of meaning, a meaning that can vary infinitely. The insistence on the need to free history of these contaminations is not founded on the naïve belief that one can achieve a final separation between fact and myth. Rather it is premised on a knowledge of their seductive power and of the ferocious competition that facts must endure to protect the past and create the conditions for the flowering of a truth at once more comprehensive, critical and compassionate.

There seems to be at the heart of revisionism, a crisis in cognitive faith, a crisis in the strength of conventional forms of epistemology. It is not so much that there is no truth, rather that truth always gets lost and that a traditional form of knowledge that is not willing to take into account the reasons why and how facts are abused, and to examine how the inroads of ideology impede on the production of a reliable knowledge, is unlikely to attain any critical truth worthy of the name. If Irish revisionists unremittingly try to reintroduce these facts it is not because they believe in their immanence, but rather because they cling to the faint yet necessary hope that these latter will eventually rehabilitate themselves, reclaim their authority by dislodging the phantasmagorias of mythology.

Therefore, their quest for facts is inseparable from the veiled fear that these may not suffice when rivalled by morale boosting stories. It is no coincidence if the retrospective anxiety of W.B. Yeats when he wondered in old age about his early nationalist play, *Cathleen ni Houlihan*, "Did that play of mine send out certain men the English shot" became also that of F.S.L. Lyons. Both men feared that their writings might have locked Irishmen into "a hall of distorting mirrors so grotesque that [they] could no longer distinguish the realities of what had happened in this island from the myths [they] had chosen to weave about certain symbolic events".[47] Lyons feared lest the preoccupation with violence had made historians accomplices to a pernicious climate; a climate that had incited to murder and sacrifice in the name of abstractions. What oppressed his conscience was the thought that they had themselves fallen prey to the disembodying call of Manichean heresy and forgotten how much more nuanced and intricate reality truly was. And that maybe their writings had compounded the problem by exorcizing the fear of political murder by glamorizing or ennobling it with beautiful metaphors and semantic artifices. Would such deep-seated anxiety be the characteristic of an empiricist? It is more than doubtful. Of course, the empiricism varies according to the temperament of these historians so it would be wrong to generalize. Still the fact remains that Irish revisionism originated too much in the looming shadow of what Jacques Derrida called the *pharmakon*, the "poison", or the "allurement" or even what Stanley Fish called the insidious appeal of "fine language", by which he meant language that had transgressed the limits of representation and substituted its own forms for the forms of reality to have a positive faith in empiricism.

Irish revisionism is best described as a historical practice, which, although it uses the discourse of empiricism to define itself, fails to be swayed by the dream of "pure experience", or "pure difference". Its disposition is one of scepticism in the possibility of recovering unadulterated truth because it knows all too well how slippery the borders between reality and myth are, how vulnerable it remains itself to the infection of this sophistic disease, and how much dogged persistence it takes to filter it out continuously with no hope of a final elimination. Interestingly, Conor Cruise O'Brien wrote: "I do not claim that anything is proved in the scientific sense at all. The only requirement of the scientific spirit to which I have tried to conform is that of respect for the facts".[48] In his review of Edwards' *Ireland in the Age of the Tudors*, Aidan Clarke remarked it was authorially self-effacing to the point of idiosyncrasy:

Though Edwards did not actually say so, the book was in essence an affirmation of the primacy of the sources, an exemplification of Galbraith's wry contention that while historians may come and go their dispensable ways, the sources endure. The sources became less the evidence that the historian must use than the subject with which he must deal, and the historian became the custodian of the past rather than its interpreter.[49]

The desire to efface the intervention of the historian rings like an admission that the authorial stamp once allowed in, is always going to be disruptive and is uncannily reminiscent of what Leopold von Ranke said in the preface to his *World History*, "I wish I could as it were extinguish myself".[50] Disciplinary hostility has slowly receded in Ireland. One of the personalities who contributed the most to this is Tom Dunne. For many years, he was an exception amongst Irish historians because he encouraged a rapprochement and cross-fertilization between theory and empirical practice. In "A Polemical Introduction", he explained how the adoption of a narrow empiricism, modelled on the English type, was a major factor in the tendency of Irish historians to ignore lingering theoretical quandaries. A number of obstacles were at the bottom of this misunderstanding. The impenetrable jargon, the unreality and affectation of literary theory deterred historians. Likewise, literary specialists were put off by history because they saw it as a useless empirical depository too cluttered to master, instead of identifying in it a literary form, which they were admirably equipped to interpret. Yet Dunne thought there was irony in all this because while historians were stiffly wrestling with the obscure concepts of structuralism and deconstruction, they failed to see how conditioned by and pertinent to historical practice these were. In the eighteenth century, an intimate connection was apparent between history and literature. It was however eroded by the pressures of Romanticism of which the objective was not just to reflect but also to transform reality. The emphasis on the autonomy of the imagination led to the positing of fiction as an absolute alternative to history.

The long influence of Romanticism prolonged the ingrained distrust of the historian, especially as it coincided with the improvement of the historical method along ever more rigid empirical lines. Dunne derived consolation from the fact that most of the theoretical bases had now been laid to knock down this unnatural polarization. Proving his depth of theoretical expertise, Dunne differentiated between a theory that favoured dialogue and a theory that left no room for it. Roland Barthes welcomed the discarding of narrative history because he assumed that the fictive element in it undermined its claims of portraying reality. He could not conceive a middle way and therefore campaigned for a historical genre that concerned itself solely with structures. Partly as a reaction against this overbearing doctrinarism, a strong vindication of the role of the narrative form, its germane quality and relevance for historical research came from American analytical philosophy.

Hence for Hayden White the notion of historical text as literary invention is no longer a weakness but a re-affirmation of the inimitable value of history.[51] White offers a way out of the impasse because his glance is far-reaching enough to turn the post-structuralist argument back on itself. He contends that history's roots in fiction can become its greatest asset:

> It may be observed that if historians were to recognise the fictive element in their narratives, this would not mean the degradation of historiography to the status of ideology or propaganda. In fact, this recognition would serve as a potent antidote to the tendency of historians to become captive of ideological preconceptions that they do not recognise as such but honour as the "correct" perception of "the way things really are". By drawing historiography nearer to its origins in literary sensibility, we should be able to identify the ideological, because it is the fictive element in our own discourse.[52]

In *The Irish Story*, Roy Foster grants the limitations of scientific history and is open to the idea of interdisciplinary collaboration. He welcomes the breaking down of the barriers that separate "historical narrative, personal history and national fictions" and thinks of this new development as "exciting and intellectually stimulating".[53] But he continues to be defiant of an "Irish historical interpretation [that] has too often been cramped into a strict literary mode", because this has resulted in "the narrative drive" ruthlessly eroding "awkward elisions". The function of history is to "ascertain facts and progressions, often unexpected and prove that there is a history beyond received narrative conditioning, though postmodernists may not admit it".[54] Foster is wary of how the difference between the personal and the national can collapse and history become "a kind of scaled-up biography, and biography a microcosmic history".[55] The history he defends is one that "illustrates ambiguities" and as the biographer of W.B. Yeats, he knows that ambiguity is the natural element of the poets and novelists. He admits that the writing of Irish history has been the abode of a compelling fictive impulse, going so far as to state "in Ireland history – or historiography – is our true novel".[56] However, he is also alert to the dangers involved in the breakdown of the barrier between fact and fiction.

It is hard not to concur with him. Post-structuralist theory, once derailed from its scientific track can sanction a cavalier attitude to historical evidence and confer authority to the practice of selective memory, ideological pleading or even sheer mendacity. When the difference between fact and fiction is erased, it becomes well-high impossible to adjudicate on the basis of extra-linguistic criteria. With this tactic, one is free to opt for the one narrative which he finds most appealing without having to care about the degree of truth, if any, behind it. The appropriation of postmodern principles by Field Day fails to convince for yet another reason because in the hands of a devil's advocate, it could be used to confirm the underlying pedigree of Field Day.

One could retort that a certain literary criticism has been hiding its Conservative temperament behind the cloak of postmodern radicalism. Furthermore, the choice of cloak was not a judicious one, because postmodernism has revealed to be in its final expression a flippant or unreliable tool of political analysis that has been accused of colluding with the conclusions of the Right. In fact, Field Day uses the same argument to discredit revisionism. Thus if Irish revisionism is wrong because of its links with postmodernism then the same can be said of Irish traditionalism since it relies on it to launch its attack on Irish revisionism.

Conclusion

In Ireland the subjection of history to politics, the vestige of a colonial past, proved a fertile ground for the incubation of a suspecting and deconstructive spirit. This incestuous closeness entailed that when Moody, Edwards and other gifted allies undertook the work of correction they did not just challenge a venerable historiographic tradition, they also automatically landed a severe blow to the cherished myths of unionism and nationalism.[1] Almost inevitable but worth running was the risk that one would belittle this scientific initiative to the vulgar status of the eternal political battle conducted by other means.

Objectivity, the cornerstone of rationalism, is an ideal difficult to live up to in a divided society. However, the paradox is that the need for it may be all the greater and its advocacy is sometimes assumed with a passion that is regarded as an admission of ulterior motives. Nowhere is this paradox more obvious than in Ireland. The false choice paraded by critics between a stark truth without embellishment and its vanishing behind a multitude of dispensable facts tries to convey the impression that revisionists are somewhat muddled empiricists. They certainly use empirical methods. But it is not the same thing as being an inveterate empiricist who believes one can retrieve objective truth simply by dipping into archival repositories.

At the conclusion of our historiographic journey, it becomes clearer how different methods yield different interpretations and this should be enough for us to realize that discoveries are destined to remain relative, incomplete and provisional. Still history is not reducible to some postmodern puzzle entirely eclectic and permissive of the wildest suppositions. In it, there is an excess, a remainder, the traces of a cognitive effort, which detaches it from the utilitarian knowledge of liberation, or the proselytizing efforts of propaganda. To paraphrase Derrida, there subsists a memory of history which is crucial to preserve if one day we are not to declare defunct the quest for knowledge. Revisionism in Ireland was driven by the desire to assert once and for all the fundamental rights of history to desert the cooped up impressions of the ideologues, reject their raucous, tumultuous and fickle verdicts on the presumed culprits and innocents and unravel a past rich in surprises and unpredictable alliances. Once submitted to this meticulous observation, the notion of Irishness broadened and emptied itself of its violent ontologies. This effort of emancipation of the discipline was therefore an act of dissidence and a political gesture in the strong sense. Historians declared aloud that their professional duty was to give the polysemous truth of the people in all its categories and not to regurgitate the opinions of the Unionist and Nationalist elites.

The time had come, claimed Seamus Deane in 1998, to depress or even flatten the old dichotomy between science and ideology because supposedly the Enlightenment imposed its own rigid regime of rationality and dogmatically brushed aside as mystification any other system which drew its legitimation out of an enquiry into forces and actions irreducible to rational analysis. Rationalism is a more dangerous soporific because unlike nationalism it has refused down to this day to acknowledge its indebtedness to myth. But this assertion is credible only if one exaggerates the break with modernity that postmodernism and its derivatives represent. One must ignore Derrida's confession after the novelty effect had passed and some of the anger and fear subsided that he too operated largely from within a basic humanistic position, anxious to rehabilitate it by understanding why along the way it skidded off and committed grave mistakes. Would we be engaging in hare-brained hypotheses if we say that he wished to put humanism on a better scholarly footing and make it safer and more competent for the future? This is also implicit in his admission that deconstruction was a continuation of the critical spirit of Marxism[2] and the ultimate purpose of any radical philosophical critique was not to stop at iconoclastic negation and lurch in endless denigration but to use this phase in order to arrive at a moment of creative affirmation. Thus in 1984, during an interview with Richard Kearney he stated: "Deconstruction certainly entails a moment of affirmation ... acknowledged or not ... Deconstruction is, by definition, a positive response to an Otherness which necessarily calls, summons or motivates it. Deconstruction is therefore a vocation – a response to a call".[3] Likewise, it would be no aberration to say that Irish revisionism, especially before the outbreak of the Troubles, represented the collective work of historians who retained a faith in the feasibility of political unity but were concerned to show that the means hitherto employed had been counterproductive. They were also deeply convinced that political and religious differences should not be allowed to stand in the way of an appreciation of the cultural unity of Ireland. That the reappearance of sectarian violence punctured this faith, precipitating the younger generations into a more interrogative and subversive mood, is almost a certainty. But what does Seamus Deane imply by his statement? That Irish nationalism is superior because it confesses borrowing from myth whereas the Enlightenment and by extension Irish revisionism are inferior or more precisely less honest because they are chary of doing so?

Deane hastens to impute disingenuous political motives to Irish revisionists and misses an important factor that has been weighing on their minds. If they flinch from such ideas it is not out of dormant colonialist or unionist sympathies, but because in a universe where everything is inescapably political, even and especially knowledge, all efforts of elucidation are before long declared redundant and abortive. All that remains for them to do is fold their arms and wait uncomplainingly for the two great ideological monsters to initiate a dialogue, a move that may prove insufficient because the people would still be indoctrinated. The post-structuralist assault on the cognitive claims of rationalism appeals to the detractors of revisionism because it restores the old polarities and closes the democratic and critical space where dissident and marginalized opinions can once again recover their voice and defend the value of their experience. It is no coincidence if traditionalists swimming against the tide of etymology, stigmatize pluralism as a tyrannical dogma instead of seeing in it a demanding political and intellectual objective.[4] Deane contends that revisionists have assimilated rhetorical and discursive strategies that are strongly redolent of Edmund Burke's style in his *Reflections on the French Revolution*. Revisionism allegedly swings between its ambition to be the voice of a complexity that defies conceptualization and the proverbial and universalizing impulse that gives away the passage of theory in its estimations. Ideology like an indomitable monster crouches in the unconscious of the historian and waits patiently for its ravening jump. Its safest den is precisely this tremendous almost Promethean illusion of deliverance of the mind from what pinches upon, tortures and pigeonholes it. But if this affinity contains anything real then the notion also adopted by Deane and others that scholastic revision can be equated with the pitilessly bowdlerizing force of modernization which tolerates no challenge to its dictates and its vision of the future logically collapses since Burke was the arch opponent of modernity as articulated by the radicalism of the French philosophers.

All throughout the gestation of this study an impression ever more irrepressible and disquieting came to lodge itself in a corner of my mind. What I could no longer repulse was the disconcerting intuition of the infinite manipulability of theory. In short, theory is versatile to one's liking: one can make it say anything one wishes. Some literary critics are capable of exploiting a very sophisticated theoretical apparatus in order to revitalize or boost a nationalism of which the legacy and record remain ambiguous. This prodigious paradox and its occultation cannot fail one day to turn around, like a boomerang, to strike the very essence of theory and cast serious doubts on its ultimate speculative and heuristic value. One is entitled to ask how a theory of such enormous or overwhelming implications like postmodernism can serve to patch up the edifice of convictions of a few nationalist intellectuals instead of propelling them into a more pensive or confessing mood. What is disturbing is the opportunistic hijacking of a post-structuralism which rejects the totalizing impulse, by a nationalism which is its very quintessence.

What is annoying and mystifying is the selective use of postcolonial theory not only for the irreproachable purpose of throwing light on the mechanisms of return of oppression in the new order but also for the more objectionable intention of surreptitiously letting Irish nationalism off the hook for its less than satisfactory record since independence. By the same token, what conceals a tendentious character is the utilization of Albert Memmi's sociological and psychological models by Unionist intellectuals who invest so much zeal in trying to convince one that the settlers were as much victims of the colonial fact as the natives and suggest that all consecutive mistakes are ascribable to the abnormality, imbalance and uncertainty which formed the core of Unionism's relationship with the metropolis. For instance the critic John Wilson Foster writes: "The Ulster Protestant, feeling the perpetual threat of being taken over, already experiences in some sense, and exhibits the symptoms of, the condition of being colonized. His legendary intransigence is the anticipation of a calamity".[5]

The suffocation and schizophrenia caused by the colonial machine as much on the colonizer as on the colonized is no extrapolation. The ravages on the soul, especially on the soul of the colonizer who is a man of the Left, are indeed an important theme in Memmi's demonstration. Colonization could only disfigure the colonizer because it placed him in a dilemma with equally disastrous outcomes: between the daily injustices condoned for his own benefit or the necessary self-sacrifice never consummated. If he consented to this organization of injustice, he corrupted himself, if he refused it, he denied himself.[6] If Wilson Foster's appropriation is problematic, it is because he is within an inch of crowning the colonizer with the aura of victim. However, the colonizer having been the first beneficiary of this high scale organization of injustice, a moral imperative seems to dictate to us that he has no right to claim the status of victim, not even in a metaphorical way. In addition, the single party regime, the discrimination rampant for forty years in Northern Ireland and the reality of state collusion in sectarian attempts to suppress the 1968 Civil Rights movement prompts one to think rather that Unionists are the vanquished; candidates for domination who have failed. The abdication of moral responsibility and reflection under the cover of a theory is a reproach, which can be pointed against all the parties in the Ireland of 1990s; including some historians. That is why, sooner or later, I arrived at a point where I started to spy on myself, wondering whether I was not also engaged in a similarly unsavoury academic exercise.

Was I going to defend a prestigious affiliation between revisionism and postmodernism in a glittering and dazzling fashion and just dodge the question of the impasses of the revisionist method? Was I going to look away when revisionism hides its uncertainties behind the system of empiricism? Too often, a system helps to evacuate or shelve questions for which unfortunately we do not have definitive answers. During the Troubles, the successful broadcasting of the colonial identity of the Northern Ireland problem by the IRA not only stunted research in the ways in which Ireland did present colonial remnants in its mental geography, as Tom Dunne recently said, but it also pushed some historians into the hopeless tangle of a too rigid empirical method.

Hence, those who declare that the proximity between Ireland and England indubitably rules out the possibility of a colonialist relationship, or because of a lack of objective criteria such as skin colour there could not be a racism of the empire, do not prove much except perhaps that the adoption of empiricism in a too literal manner in a singular case like Ireland can lead to odd aberrations. Hence for instance the statement made by the English historian Steven G. Ellis who during an exchange with Brendan Bradshaw opined that "the geographical proximity between Ireland and Great Britain and their long-term economic interdependence favoured a continuous migration between the two islands and therefore close cultural links which cannot be described as colonial"[7] remains problematic. A rationalism of this sort suggests that violence against what is close to us is not violence. Yet the sense of threat that this "same other" posed to British identity was perhaps more frightening, its memory more difficult to erase from the minds. Perhaps the shiver, the squirmy revulsion towards what is close and yet stamped by a coefficient of strangeness, provokes greater intolerance, a more pitiless, crueller violence. The desire to annihilate this so eerily familiar Other may be more imperious. Often, the difference of others challenges us to the core, it questions our being. But the compulsion to strike off the rolls of human society those who apparently are totally alien, even exotic, is easily satisfied. He who can neither read nor write, he who is black like the devil and utters impenetrable sounds, he who practises cannibalism, human sacrifice, infanticide or female circumcision is just a barbarian. No further comment.

The evidence of several tangible differences becomes an incontrovertible testimony to his bestiality. Whereas the being whose most remarkable quality is precisely this deficit in objective criteria of differentiation, the being who defiantly straddles the border between sameness and otherness, worries us, haunts us, no doubt because our bad conscience naggingly reminds us that the accusation of barbarism is here no longer credible and what's more unfair. European history is scattered with examples which clearly show that wars against geographical neighbours for hegemonic expansion, persecution campaigns against schismatics and dissidents of a political doctrine reveal an unimaginable violence. Indeed the more intimate is the difference the more terrifying and threatening it also becomes as its power of insinuation in our psyche and of destabilization of our identity has seemingly no foreseeable limits. Exposed too long to this "undecidable", a gnawing or corrosive doubt creeps in, imperceptibly destroying the foundation of our values, fraying the belief in our intrinsic superiority, and forcing us to realize we do not have all the truth. The proximity argument leaves therefore a lot to be desired because it can be demolished with the use of psychoanalytic and deconstructionist theories but above all because it can be questioned on its own ground by observing the history of European internal colonialism. Traces of an empiricism that is dangerously out of keel seem to invalidate the entire argument of this book. But I prefer to think that a more permanent damage would have been caused by a deliberate glossing over of the weaknesses, aporias and temptations of revisionism, especially as it developed in the 1980s and 1990s.

The disequilibrium caused by colonization and a nationalism determined to defy it, the hypertrophy of imaginations revolution created in its turn, the civil war which brought to a traumatic climax the conflict between loyalties and realities, the putschist resurgences and the unexpected outbreak of violence in Northern Ireland, all those factors plunged Irish historians into a profound crisis. The fear of having perhaps been unwitting accomplices to a tyrannical ideology whose ultimate logic was to bring to power the purest expression of its discourse or threaten chronically the democratic foundations of society, compelled them to become more alert to the insidious intrusions of ideology in the texts they were sifting and conceive a method capable of cushioning the most harmful effects of this nibbling, this usurpation.

They have then adopted discontinuity and synchronicity as heuristic tools; an approach bearing strong resemblance to Michel Foucault's archaeology of knowledge. They have also reflected on the nature of Irish nationalism, how to liberate themselves from the mesmeric mystique of this discourse, and although many, especially among the first and second generations, had a sort of sentimental leaning towards it, they all positively declined to come to its aid particularly when they deemed that the means it had chosen to achieve its ends were unwise and self-defeating. A small minority went so far as to reject it wholesale conferring on it the monopoly of blame. But the majority refused to cross this line. Instead of a frontal opposition, they astutely opted for subversion, a subtler tactic consisting in recovering subtilized incarnations of the Irish Revolution and thus implanting an invincible doubt inside the very intimacy of this ideology. Because its primary objective seemed to have been rather to effect a destabilizing passage through nationalist discourse instead of launching into some final condemnation, revisionism became even more formidable and intuitively followed the path of deconstruction. The consistent effort to separate fact and myth, even if it appears archaic or naïve in the light of postmodern knowledge, is not premised on the notion that these two spheres operate in seclusion, but rather on the notion that they are communicating vessels. For instance, in his 1975 manifesto to rouse consciences to the need to see through the haze spread by romantic politics, Conor Cruise O'Brien did admit that the positivist separation between Yeats' nationalist play *Cathleen Ni Houlihan* and the Easter Rising of 1916 was weak because, "The essential difference between the two transactions remains in the legal and technical orders; in point of reality, they are on the same footing, both real and both symbolic".[8]

However, instead of coming to the conclusion that all such arduous academic exercise of separation was for this reason futile, it only strengthened his resolve in it. Hence it was precisely because "participants in the real life action had taken the fiction as a gospel or sacrament" thus binding Irishmen to it and inviting them to re-enact the same sacrifice that this work of demystification remained vital and could not be flippantly relinquished. There is no sign here of easy denigration of "rhetoric" or "naïve" and "condescending" assertion of the autonomy of the "scientific" as Deane once charged, but the identification of a real problem with ongoing tragic consequences on society which in the opinion of O'Brien cannot be solved by pompously pronouncing all efforts at clarification artificial and misleading.

So there is evidence to counterblast Brendan Bradshaw's accusation that revisionism rests on "a confusing and impoverished notion of myth".[9] By levelling this unfounded accusation, Bradshaw imposes his own impoverishment on the minds of the revisionist school. I hope to have shown that the revisionist school is obsessed by the effects of ideology on the dissolution of brotherhood and the destruction of the social fabric, and the presumption of the thorough indoctrination of man pushes some of them to abandon their rationalizations and conclude in a Nietzschean or Foucaultan fashion that the world of ideas is equal to the world of hard facts when its power on the mind is not actually more inhibiting. One thing is certain. The revisionist tendency to shy away from a more overt and systematic theoretical engagement has been a disservice. It prevented the profession from realizing the degree to which their intuitions and insights, after being judged correct and valuable, have been vindicated and consecrated by postmodern theory. In the long term the invisibility of their thought or the paucity of tangible traces of the movement of their mind, if we except a few isolated cases, could only damage their heuristic project. It played right into the hands of those who wanted to relegate them to the category of proponents of an obscurantist or pedantic knowledge who with the spread of a malign method had vitiated the chances of historical understanding and served a specious morality.

The anti-theoretical stance revealed a dead end for they could have convincingly cut the ground from under their critics' feet if they had shown they were the first to identify major epistemological problems such as the danger of falling captive to ideological intentions in the use of evidence, the challenge of understanding and representing the nature of remote events and phenomena when mental categories are anachronistic and empirical traces finite, the historian's entrapment within the perceptual and conceptual categories of the present when it leads to a telescoped or retrospective vision, the requirement to lay down the right underpinnings for a contemporary history divorced from the official policy, the desirability to balance out official records with the voice of the people and finally the difficulty of overcoming circular reasoning.

The new historians were precursors in addressing all these confounding issues and yet an outsider when surveying the general tenor of the debate in the 1990s, the defensiveness of revisionists, the assertiveness of traditionalists, could be excused for thinking that only the latter were truly acquainted with the higher stakes and challenges of history. Another disastrous effect of this reluctance to avail themselves of the qualities, which grow with the couching of a theoretical reflection, is that it hindered them from taking stock and assimilating all the wisdom they had accumulated individually and collectively over long years of empirical experience. As a result, it also impeded the birth and development of a reasoning competent in the important task of juggling with various levels of truth. Usually conducive to a more obvious dialectical outlook, the theoretical gesture might have offered the promise to resolve those enigmas which they preferred to conceal beneath the inadequate and borrowed system of empiricism. By making this mistake, they became in their turn guilty of the sin they had so proficiently spotted in those who insisted at all costs on enclosing the historical experience of the country in the reductive limits of the colonial paradigm. This behaviour amounted to a form of self-alienation and such separations are rarely propitious to the construction of a well-calibrated attack against shrewd intellectual opponents.

The erasure of the Other from the pages of history haunts the revisionist imagination. The Other is of course the Protestants of Ulster. A people who were not heard enough because the majority was too occupied resorbing their difference by assuming the only obstacle to independence was the covetousness and the machinations of a colonialist power. Its social idealism wants to correct this error of appreciation. Like the ethical project of structuralism, revisionism wants to rein in its own ethnocentrism and arrogance. It wants to dissuade nationalism from applying its own criteria of truth and standards of rationality on Ulster. To triumph over ignorance and misunderstanding requires no longer to extend over Ulster the nationalist culture but to leave one's illusive promontory and through a lucid return on oneself recognize one's limitations.

Both schools are animated by a genuine desire to expiate the sin of condescension of their tradition. Revisionists contest the moral superiority of Irish nationalism. Structuralists contest the moral superiority of Western Enlightenment. Both pin down and denounce the hegemonic tendencies hidden behind their pacifying and inclusive discourse. Both invent a hermeneutic style which insinuates doubt on the legitimacy of this domination. Their generosity targets prejudice, but to defuse its power it is no longer enough to open other minds to reason, one must also and above all open one's mind to the reasons of other beings and draw out of oneself the spiritual resources to empathize with their predicament. As Cruise O'Brien once remarked, if nationalism is not irreproachable then unionism may not be a total vice and aberration. There is perhaps one aspect on which they seem to part company. According to Finkielkraut, the proliferation of cultures and their erection in unbridgeable and insurmountable absolutes that are allowed to escape objective judgement and between which there could never be a rapprochement is a buried drift of the philosophy of decolonization. This tendency is also called cultural or moral relativism and is awfully more dangerous. However, if we except Lyons' pessimistic broodings which seem to echo the structuralist argument gone awry, revisionism in its more analytical form does not obey this spirit. Nor does it propound the levelling that one usually finds in multiculturalism.

Its so-called relativism, which is actually an uncomplicated commitment to pluralism but is so often denounced as an abhorrent travesty of historical truth, does not derive from the principle that all political cultures are good and deserve an equal respect but rather from the presentiment that none of them is worthy of the emotional investment, sacrifice and suffering that men undergo in their name. Instead of insisting on parity of esteem and equal legitimacy for both traditions to use the multiculturalist phraseology of the New Ireland Forum of 1984, revisionism is more disposed to underline their equal illegitimacy; their impudent and scandalous illegitimacy. When Cardinal Cahal Daly declared in "a wild fit of ecumenism" that "unionism and nationalism were both noble aspirations" Edna Longley replied it would be preferable "to demote nationalism to the rank of ignoble status habitually reserved to unionism instead of clutching at the idea of an authentic or good nationalism existing in a zone uncontaminated by the Provisional IRA".[10]

It was predictable though that in the Irish situation such noble philosophical principles would be felt as an especially offensive provocation. Because Irish nationalism is historically an emancipating and democratizing force, it does not have a reputation for harbouring redoubtable colonial tendencies. Because it has courageously fought British imperialism, one thinks that its genetic code ill-fits it to acts of tyranny towards the protestant minority. Logocentric logic is founded on the notion that moral categories are fixed and impervious. There is good and evil, aggressor and victim. No slipping, infiltration or contamination between those is usually conceivable. And yet ever since it has been conscious of itself, mankind knows even dimly that it is locked into what D.H. Akenson calls, "a self-replicating cycle of abuser-abused-abuser-abused".[11] R.F. Foster agrees with Akenson that it is a cycle which if it is to be broken in Ireland will require Irish historians to keep chipping away at the myth of "a Platonic solidarity ... between Irish servants and black slaves throughout the empire".[12]

Hence, revisionism is declared morally dubious because instead of confirming this intransience it lingers on historical cases which contradict it. The barbarian according to Lévi-Strauss is first and foremost the man who believes there is such a thing as barbarism and the colonialist adventure under the pretext of assuring the intellectual and moral awakening of all the peoples on this earth had only succeeded in putting the white man face to face with his own savagery. The exclusive guardians of rationality discover this latter is not a dam against the torrent of violence and that it sometimes secretes it and carries it to even crueller forms.

Sooner or later, Irish nationalism had also to deal with its own disquieting shadows; the skeletons it was hiding in its closets. Indeed the Civil War had already inflicted a grave trauma on an entire generation of Irishmen whose more tormented minds could not help voicing some doubts about the coherence of an ideology which could so inexorably descend into such intimate and vindictive violence. While it is true that this event did blemish the reputation of Irish nationalism, it is the emergence of the hard-line Provisional IRA at the end of 1969 and their attempt to brush aside protests at their lack of mandate with their claim to be a modern manifestation of the blood-sacrifice ideals of 1916 that gave it the finishing stroke. This claim was all the more difficult to repudiate as public opinion in the Republic, the state, the educational system but also the intellectual community all shared the rhetoric and the assumptions that this paramilitary culture represented. This phenomenon of acquiescent or silent complicity seemed to reach its most conspicuous and staggering result when in 1970, Neil Blaney and Charles Haughey, important members of Jack Lynch's Cabinet, were charged with importing arms for supply to the IRA. At this moment the distance between rhetoric and action alarmingly narrowed and the moral difference between the two became less defensible, jolting some intellectuals into the realization that Irish nationalism had most tragically failed to address the question of ends and means and that this had to be remedied before democracy was subverted.

Revisionist interpretations are no less fallacious or partial than the nationalist ones which propose a resemblance between various historical landscapes since the Revisionist just like the Nationalist cannot release themselves from the current events which surround them and influence their academic and methodological choices. The superior objectivity the Revisionist boasts about, and his intoxicating feeling of thinking against himself because he resists the natural compulsion to identify with his parochial ethos, are decoys. His disinterestedness that putatively gives him special access to the truth is but the ultimate fantasy of the brain. Originally used by revisionists to perfect their scientific equipment and contain ideological contamination in their deductions, the structuralist argument is eventually diverted from its heuristic objective and transmuted into an arsenal of total demolition of the historical discipline in Ireland. We are back to square one. The problem with this line of argument as Dunne, Brady, O'Day and Boyce all perceptively remarked is that it does not attend to "the internal demands of historical scholarship".[13] Indeed, in this obsessive problematization with the linguistic, psychic and temporal limits congesting pure experience, the theory came to appear, in the words of the American historian Peter Novick, less as a key than as a lock which sealed the door of the "prison-house of language", a prison to which author, text, context and reader were sentenced for all eternity.[14] E.P. Thompson voiced a similar concern. Instead of acknowledging that empirical experience is valid and effective within determined limits which need to be ascertained in order to be better overcome, post-structuralism, especially of the Althusseran type, proceeded immediately to the unreasonable conclusion that experience or evidence cannot be the sources of knowledge of real historical objects.

Whoever collapsed the difference between empiricism and the empirical mode of investigation was on a Trojan horse because this error could lead him to reject both and introduce a procedure for knowledge production, which instead of allowing for "a dialogue between concept and evidence", would provide for a "theoretical practice" to both "elaborate and verify its own facts".[15] For Thompson, and we have good reasons to assume that Irish revisionists would concur with him, this amounted to epistemological nihilism since it induced a degree of circular reasoning which was much higher than the one which sometimes resulted out of the pressure of identified constraints.

Revisionism has demoted the hitherto central theme of Irish history, the fact of oppression and exploitation for the benefit of a colonial power and prioritized a more troubling and embarrassing theme; the repetition of oppressive patterns this time in the name of the republican revolution. By privileging this theme, revisionism has tried to elucidate the tensions which arise between community and individual in the aftermaths of revolutions. It has widely documented the disenchantment which followed the setting up of the Free State in 1921, the swerve into revolutionary dogmatism and most mysteriously this tyranny of the collective which in the words of Finkielkraut "locks the beneficiaries of independence into the pressure of unanimity".[16] If there was no room for the collective subject in the colonial logic, henceforth everything happens as if there is no room for the individual in the *Volkgeist* logic. Because it is interested in all those minorities whose needs were indefinitely put on ice in order to accomplish the glorious dream of the Irish revolution, and discloses how the elite continued to neglect those legitimate demands after independence, revisionism presents remarkable Marxian accents. Having to contend with two ideologies which have always tried to neutralize the ordeal of exteriority in all its forms and exorcize the threat which dissidence and event represent as these often reveal hazardous, precarious and problematic for the coherence of all system, revisionism responds by applying a reverse logic. Where armouring seems perfect and breach impossible, it finds a means to reintroduce the perverse, the original and the irreducible, all that which refuses to be squeezed into a crude formula. To the culturalist logic where the name of man disappears into the name of his community and where he is no longer but a sample, revisionism opposes the individualist logic through the retrieval of all those lives and opinions which have resisted compartmentalization and its dismal and mediocre solutions. Paradoxically enough, its *discontinuiste* and deconstructionist method tries to reintroduce the freedom between individual and tribe, or knowledge and ideology which Enlightenment anthropology strove to assert and consolidate.

Notes

Preface

1 Richard J. Evans, *Rituals of Retribution. Capital Punishment in Germany. 1600–1987*, (Oxford: OUP, 1996), Introduction.
2 R.D. Edwards, UCDA. File LA 22/1173: "Historical Research and Modern Irish History".

1 The intellectual mood in the 1990s

1 F.S.L Lyons, R.A.J. Hawkins (eds), *Ireland Under the Union: Varieties of Tension. Essays in Honour of T.W. Moody*, (Oxford: Clarendon, 1980), p. 1.
2 "Conor Cruise O'Brien", *Phoenix*, 9/6, 22 March 1991.
3 D.G. Boyce, Alan O'Day (eds), *The Making of Modern Irish History. Revisionism and the Revisionist Controversy*, (London: Routledge, 1996), pp. 120–40.
4 Robert O. Paxton, *Vichy France: Old Guard and New Order. 1940–1944*, (New York: Knopf, Random House, 1972).
5 Stathis N. Kalyvas, "Red Terror: Leftist Violence During the Occupation", in Mark Mazower (ed.), *After the War Was Over. Reconstructing the Family. Nation and State in Greece. 1943–1960*, (Princeton, NJ: Princeton University Press, 2000).
6 Luisa Passerini, *Fascism in Popular Memory. The Cultural Experience of the Turin Working Class*, (Cambridge: Cambridge University Press, 1987).
7 Stanley G. Payne, *The Spanish Civil War, the Soviet Union and Communism*, (New Haven: Yale University Press, 2004).
8 Avi Shlaim, *The Iron Wall: Israel and the Arab World*, (London: Penguin, 2001).
9 Benny Morris, *The Birth of the Palestinian Refugee Problem. 1948 and after: Israel and the Palestinians*, (Cambridge: Cambridge University Press, 1989) *Righteous Victims: A History of the Zionist–Arab Conflict. 1881–1999*, (London: John Murray, Revised Edn, 2000).
10 Hayden White, "Response to Arthur Marwick", *Journal of Contemporary History*, Vol. 30, No. 2, April 1995, p. 244.
11 Michael Bentley (ed.), *Companion to Historiography*, (London: Routledge, 1997), p. 389.
12 Michael Laffan, "The Sacred Memory: Religion, Revisionists and the Easter Rising", in Judith Devlin, Ronan Fanning (eds), *Religion and Rebellion*, Historical Studies No. XX, (Dublin: University College Dublin Press, 1997), p. 181.
13 Gearoid O Tuathaigh, "'Revisionism': State of the Art or Ideological Project?", in Ciaran Brady (ed.), *Interpreting Irish History. The Debate on Historical Revisionism*, (Dublin: Irish Academic Press, 1994), p. 306.

14 R.D. Edwards, UCDA. LA 22/715: "The Scotch-Irish and the Irish in America, considered historically", 27 April 1962.
15 Michael Laffan, "Insular Attitudes: The Revisionists and their Critics", in Mairin Ni Dhonnchadha, Theo Dorgan (eds), *Revising the Rising*, (Derry: Field Day, 1991), p. 114.
16 Ciaran Brady, "'Constructive and Instrumental': The Dilemma of Ireland's First 'New Historians'", in *Interpreting Irish History*, p. 12.

2 The revisionist: a new type of intellectual

1 Jacques Julliard, "Les intellectuels ne veulent plus être des 'politiques'", *Nouvel Observateur*, 30 September to 6 October 1993.
2 Raymond Aron, *Introduction à la philosophie de l'histoire. Essai sur les limites de l'objectivité historique*, (Paris: first edition 1938, re-edition Gallimard 1986), p. 70.
3 R.D. Edwards, UCDA. File LA 22/715: Friday 27 April 1962.
4 J.J. Lee, *Ireland 1912–1985. Politics and Society*, (Cambridge: Cambridge University Press, 1989), pp. 605–6.
5 Maurice Goldring, *Pleasant the Scholar's Life: Irish Intellectuals and the Construction of the Nation State*, (London: Serif, 1993), p. 149.
6 Fintan O'Toole, "Why North has No Time for Doubters", *Irish Times*, 4 April 1991, p. 10.
7 Garret FitzGerald, *All in a Life. An Autobiography*, (Dublin: Gill & Macmillan, 1991), p. 66.
8 Donald Harman Akenson, *Conor. A Biography of Conor Cruise O'Brien*, (Montreal: McGill-Queen's University Press, 1994), p. 347.
9 M.A.G. O Tuathaigh, "'Revisionism': State of the Art or Ideological Project?", in *Interpreting Irish History*, p. 311.
10 Conor Cruise O'Brien, *Power and Consciousness*, (London: University of London Press, 1969), pp. 12–13.
11 Charles C. Ludington, "Visions and Revisions", *History Ireland*, Vol. 4, No. 1, Spring 1996, p. 5.
12 Jacques Julliard, "Les intellectuels ne veulent plus être des 'politiques'", *Nouvel Observateur*, 30 September to 6 October 1993.

3 Internal critique: vicissitudes and potentials

1 Desmond Fennell, "Against Revisionism", in *Interpreting Irish History*, pp. 183, 187.
2 Seamus Deane, *Celtic Revivals: Essays in Modern Irish Literature. 1880–1980*, (London: Faber & Faber, 1985), p. 122.
3 Michael Laffan, "Insular Attitudes: The Revisionists and their Critics", in Theo Dorgan, Mairin Ni Dhonnchadha (eds), *Revising the Rising*, (Derry: Field Day, 1991), p. 113.
4 R.F. Foster, *Modern Ireland. 1600–1972*, (London: Allen Lane, Penguin, 1988), p. 459.
5 Brian Murphy, "The Canon of Irish Cultural History. Some Questions concerning Roy Foster's *Modern Ireland*", in *Interpreting Irish History*, p. 232.
6 Ciaran Brady, "'Constructive and Instrumental': The Dilemma of Ireland's First 'New Historians'", in *Interpreting Irish History*, p. 7.
7 T.W. Moody, "A New History of Ireland", *Irish Historical Studies*, Vol. XVI, No. 63, March 1969, p. 244.
8 Ciaran Brady, "'Constructive and Instrumental': The Dilemma of Ireland's First 'New Historians'", in *Interpreting Irish History*, p. 20.

9 Michel Foucault, *Power/Knowledge. Selected Interviews and Other Writings. 1972–1977*, (Brighton: The Harvester Press, 1980), p. 132.

10 Evi Gkotzaridis "Irish Revisionism and Continental Theory. An Insight into an Intellectual Kinship", *Irish Review*, No. 27, Summer 2001, pp. 121–39.

11 François Furet, *Penser la Révolution française*, (Paris: Gallimard, 1978).

12 Anastasia N. Karakasidou, *Fields of Wheat, Hills of Blood. Passages To Nationhood in Greek Macedonia, 1870–1990*, (Chicago: University of Chicago Press, 1998).

13 Roger Scruton, *A Dictionary of Political Thought*, (London: Pan Books in association with Macmillan, 1982) p. 405.

14 John Bowman, *De Valera and the Ulster Question. 1917–1973*, (Oxford: OUP, 1989), p. 3.

15 Michael Laffan, *The Resurrection of Ireland: The Sinn Féin Party. 1916–1923*, (Cambridge: CUP, 1999), p. 13.

16 F.S.L. Lyons, *John Dillon: A Biography*, (London: Routledge and Kegan Paul, 1968), p. 483.

17 Willy Maley, "Nationalism and Revisionism: Ambiviolences and Dissensus", in Scott Brewster, Virginia Crossman (eds), *Ireland in Proximity. History, Gender, Space*, (London: Routledge, 1999), p. 22.

18 R.D. Edwards, UCDA. File LA 22/1202: *The Leader*, 12 March 1955, Vol. 55, No. 5, p. 3.

19 Ibid.

20 Ibid.

21 Edmund Curtis, "Irish History and its Popular Versions", *Irish Rosary*, No. 39, 1925, pp. 327–8.

22 Ibid. p. 328.

23 Ibid. pp. 328–9.

24 Henri Pirenne, *La tâche de l'historien*, in Le Flambeau, XIV, 1931, p. 20–2.

25 March Bloch, "Pour une histoire comparée des sociétés européennes", *Mélanges Historiques*, (Paris: S.E.V.P.E.N, 1963), pp. 16–40.

26 Tom Garvin, *Nationalist Revolutionaries in Ireland. 1858–1928*, (Oxford: Clarendon Press, 1987).

27 Brian Walker, "Ireland's Historical Position – 'Colonial' or 'European'?", *Irish Review*, No. 9, Autumn 1990, pp. 36–40.

28 Sean Connolly, *Religion, Law, and Power: The Making of Protestant Ireland, 1660–1760*, (Oxford: Clarendon Press, 1992).

29 Liam Kennedy, *Colonialism, Religion, and Nationalism in Ireland*, (Belfast: Institute of Irish Studies, 1996).

30 Alvin Jackson, "Unionist History", in *Interpreting Irish History*, p. 253.

31 David Dickson, "Interview of R.B. McDowell", *History Ireland*, Vol. 1, No. 4, Winter 1993.

32 Richard English, Joseph Morrison Skelly (ed.), *Ideas Matter. Essays in Honour of Conor Cruise O'Brien*, (Dublin: Poolbeg, 1998), p. 138.

33 R.D. Edwards, UCDA. File LA 22/Diary: Sunday 11 November 1956.

34 Garret FitzGerald, *All in a Life: An Autobiography*, pp. 29–30.

35 R.D. Edwards, UCDA. File LA 22/843 (6,7): 24 May 1951.

36 Herbert Butterfield, CUA. File 531/M 142: 12 October 1963.

37 F.X. Martin, "T.W. Moody", *Hermathena*, No. CXXXVI, Summer 1984, pp. 5–7.

38 Michael Tierney, UCDA. File LA 30/117(1–2): 1 March 1930.

39 Edmund Curtis, TCDA. Ms. 2452: 6 February 1936.

40 T.W. Moody, "A New History of Ireland", *Irish Historical Studies*, Vol. XVI, No. 63, March 1969, pp. 245–6.

41 R.D. Edwards, UCDA. File LA 22/Diaries: Tuesday 19 July 1960.

42 Richard Kearney, *Dialogues with Contemporary Continental Thinkers*, (Manchester: MUP, 1987), p. 106.

43 Julia Kristeva, *Nations Without Nationalism*, (New York: Columbia University Press, 1993), p. 165.

44 Aidan Clarke, "Robert Dudley Edwards 1909–88", *Irish Historical Studies*, Vol. XXVI, No. 102, November 1988, p. 124.

45 Tom Dunne, "Maureen Wall (née McGeehin) 1918–1972: a memoir", in Gerard O'Brien (ed.), *Catholic Ireland in the 18th Century. Collected Essays of Maureen Wall*, (Dublin: Geography Publications, 1989).

46 R.D. Edwards, UCDA. File LA 22/381 (44).

47 Patrick O'Farrell, "Fair Exchange. Some Exotic Experiences at Trinity in 1972–73", *Eureka Street* 2, July 1992, pp. 27, 29.

48 Conor Cruise O'Brien, *Memoir. My Life and Themes*, (Dublin: Poolbeg, 1998), p. 123.

49 Herbert Butterfield, *The Whig Interpretation of History*, (London: The Norton Library, 1965) p. V.

50 Owen Dudley Edwards, Fergus Pyle (eds.), *1916: The Easter Rising*, (London: MacGibbon & Kee, 1968).

51 F.X. Martin, "1916 – Myth, Fact, and Mystery", *Studia Hibernica*, No. 7, 1967, pp. 7–125.

52 Francis Shaw, "The Canon of Irish History: A Challenge", *Studies*, LXI, 1972, pp. 117–49.

53 J.A. Murphy, "Further Reflections on Irish Nationalism", *Crane Bag*, Vol. II, No. 1 & 2, 1978, p. 157.

54 Terence Brown, *Ireland: A Social and Cultural History. 1922–85*, (London: Fontana, 1985), p. 18.

55 R.F. Foster (ed.), *The Oxford History of Ireland*, (Oxford: OUP, 1989), p. 534.

56 Tom Garvin, *1922: The Birth of Irish Democracy*, (Dublin: Gill & Macmillan, 1996), pp. 180–1.

57 Clare O'Halloran, *Partition and the Limits of Irish Nationalism. An Ideology under Stress*, (Dublin: Gill & Macmillan, 1987), pp. 3–4.

58 Ibid. pp. 105–6.

59 Michael Laffan, "'Labour must wait': Ireland's Conservative Revolution", in Patrick J. Corish (ed.), *Radicals, Rebels and Establishments*, Historical Studies No. XV, (Belfast: Appletree Press, 1985), p. 217.

60 Ibid. p. 218.

61 Liam O'Dowd, Bill Rolston, Mike Tomlinson, *Northern Ireland: Between Civil Rights and Civil War*, (London: CSE Books, 1980), pp. 73–5.

62 Simon Catterson, "Interview with Declan Kiberd", *Fortnight*, No. 346, January 1996, pp. 31–2.

63 *Catholic Bulletin*, June 1925, p. 540. Cited in Margaret O'Callaghan, "Language, Nationality and Cultural Identity in the Irish Free State, 1922–7. The *Irish Statesman* and the *Catholic Bulletin* reappraised", *Irish Historical Studies*, Vol. XXIV, No. 94, November 1984, p. 242.

64 Seosamh O Neill, "A Response to the Opening of the Dykes", *Irish Statesman*, 2 February 1924, Vol. 1, No. 21.

65 R.F. Foster, *The Irish Story. Telling Tales and Making it up in Ireland*, (London: Penguin, 2001), p. 43.

66 R.D. Edwards, UCDA. File LA 22/793 (43): 20 January 1954.

67 F.S.L. Lyons, *Culture and Anarchy in Ireland 1890–1939*, (Oxford: Clarendon, 1979), p. 112.

68 Michael Tierney, UCDA. File LA 30/353 (2,3): "Partition and a Policy of National Unity", *Studies*, 5–6 February 1935.

69 Daniel A. Binchy, "MacNeill's Study of the Ancient Irish Laws", in F.X. Martin

and F.J. Byrne (eds), *The Scholar Revolutionary: Eoin MacNeill and the Making of the New Ireland*, (Shannon: Irish University Press, 1973), p. 39.

70 Eoin MacNeill, UCDA. File LA1/Q/654. Not dated.
71 Eoin MacNeill, UCDA. File LA1/Q/342: 21 April 1928, *The Freeman*, p. 3.
72 Helen Mulvey, "Thirty Years' Work in Irish History", *Irish Historical Studies*, Vol. XVII, No. 66, September 1970, p. 183.
73 Eoin MacNeill, UCDA. File LA1/F/364: Sean O Luing, "The Dilemma of Eoin MacNeill", *Irish Times*, 24–25 April 1961.
74 F.X. Martin, "Select Documents. Eoin MacNeill on the 1916 Rising", *Irish Historical Studies*, Vol. 12, No. 47, March 1961, p. 229.
75 Ibid. p. 236.
76 W.I. Thompson, *The Imagination of an Insurrection. Dublin, Easter 1916. A Study of an Ideological Movement*, (New York: Harper Colophon Books, 1972), p. 95.
77 F.X. Martin, "Select Documents", *Irish Historical Studies*, Vol.XII, No. 47, March 1961, p. 266.
78 Ibid. p. 240.
79 Ibid. p. 235.
80 Ibid. p. 235.
81 Francis Sheehy-Skeffington, "An Open Letter to Thomas MacDonagh", in *1916: The Easter Rising*, pp. 149–51.
82 Ibid. p. 149.
83 Ibid. pp. 150–1.
84 Ibid. p. 150.
85 Alain Finkielkraut, *L'humanité perdue. Essai sur le XXème siècle*, (Paris: Editions du Seuil, 1996), pp. 95–6.
86 E.M. Henning, "Archeology, deconstruction, and intellectual history", in Dominick La Capra, Steven L. Kaplan (eds), *Modern European Intellectual History. Reappraisals and New Perspectives*, (Ithaca: Cornell University Press, 1982), p. 192.
87 Michael Laffan, "Insular Attitudes. The Revisionists and their Critics", in *Revising the Rising*, pp. 112–13.

4 The loss of history and the new historians' fight against propaganda on the Irish and continental "front"

1 Ciaran Brady, "'Constructive and Instrumental': The Dilemma of Ireland's First 'New Historians'", in *Interpreting Irish History*, p. 18.
2 R.D. Edwards, UCDA. File LA 22/1204: *The Leader*, Vol. 55, No. 2, 29 January 1955, pp. 6–7.
3 R.D. Edwards, UCDA. File LA 22/1219 (2): *The Leader*, 26 January 1957.
4 R.D. Edwards, UCDA. File LA 22/1219 (18): *The Leader*, 26 January 1957, pp. 13–14.
5 Ibid.
6 Tom Dunne, "Maureen Wall (née McGeehin) 1918–1972: A Memoir", in Gerard O'Brein (ed.) *Catholic Ireland in the 18th Century. Collected Essays of Maureen Wall*.
7, Gabriel Doherty, Dermot Keogh (eds), *Michael Collins and the Making of the Irish State*, (Dublin: Mercier, 1998), p. 25.
8 Maureen Wall, "Partition: The Ulster Question (1916–1926)", in Desmond T. Williams (ed.), *The Irish Struggle*, (London: Routledge, 1966), p. 84.
9 Ibid. p. 88.
10 Ibid. p. 88.
11 R.D. Edwards, UCDA. File LA 22/1276: 1950s.
12 Florence O'Donoghue, NLA. Ms. 31, 289: 14 June 1958.

13 Florence O'Donoghue, *No Other Law. The Story of Liam Lynch and the Irish Republican Army. 1916–1923*, (Dublin: Irish Press, 1954).

14 Florence O'Donoghue, NLA. File Ms. 31, 289: 17 June 1958.

15 R.D. Edwards, UCDA. File LA 22/1149: *Irish Historical Studies*, Vol. 8, No. 31, March 1953, pp. 280–4.

16 Brendan Bradshaw, "Nationalism and Historical Scholarship in Modern Ireland", in *Interpreting Irish History*, pp. 191–216.

17 Response to an Anonymous Review of Richard Bennett's, *The Black and Tans*, (Boston: Houghton Mifflin, 1959, 1960), by R.D. Edwards in *Times Literary Supplement*, 31 July 1959, p. 447.

18 R.D. Edwards, UCDA. File LA 22/Diary: 2 March 1957.

19 R.D. Edwards, UCDA. File LA 22/1022: *Irish Press*, 1954.

20 R.D. Edwards, UCDA. File LA 22/1084 (247): 18 April 1966.

21 Ruth Dudley Edwards, "Following Conor", in *Ideas Matter. Essays in Honour of Conor Cruise O'Brien*, p. 140.

22 Herbert Butterfield, "Tendencies in Historical Study in England", *Irish Historical Studies*, Vol. IV, 1944–5, pp. 222–3.

23 R.D. Edwards, UCDA. File LA 22/1207: "Man on his Past", *The Leader*, Vol. 56, No. 1, 14 January 1956.

24 Leonard Krieger, "Elements of Early Historicism: Experience, Theory, and History in Ranke", *History and Theory*, Vol. 14, December 1975.

25 Leonard Krieger, *Ranke: The Meaning of History*, (Chicago: University of Chicago Press, 1977), p. 4.

26 Pietro Rossi, "The Ideological Valences of Twentieth-Century Historicism", *History and Theory*, Vol. 14, December 1975, pp. 15–29.

27 Aidan Clarke, "Robert Dudley Edwards 1909–88", *Irish Historical Studies*, Vol. XXVI, No. 102, November 1988, p. 126.

28 T.W. Moody, TCDA. File 8555/59/79–155, 144, 5 March 1942.

29 Conor McCarthy, *Irish Modernisation: Crisis and Culture in Ireland. 1969–1992*, (Dublin: Four Courts Press, 2000), p. 92.

30 Michel Foucault, *Dits et écrits*, Vol. III, p. 163, in Alain Finkielkraut, *L'Humanité perdue. Essai sur le XXème siècle*, (Paris: Editions du Seuil, 1996), p. 63.

31 R.D. Edwards, UCDA. File LA 22/117. No date.

32 R.D. Edwards, UCDA. File LA 22/467 (75): 29 January 1938.

33 R.D. Edwards, UCDA. File LA 22/419 (12): 13 March 1938, *Irish Times*.

34 R.D. Edwards, UCDA. File LA 22/419 (8): 8 March 1938, *Irish Press*.

35 R.D. Edwards, UCDA. File LA 22/419 (11): 29 March 1938, *Manchester Guardian*.

36 F.S.L. Lyons, "T.W. Moody", in *Ireland Under the Union. Varieties of tension*, pp. 30–1.

37 Peter Novick, *That Noble Dream. The "Objectivity Question" and the American Historical Profession*, (Cambridge: CUP, 1988), pp. 116–32, 206–24.

38 Sidney Bradshaw Fay was an American diplomatic historian who made a first revisionist contribution to the study of the *Origins of the World War*. His book was published in 1928. He asserted that the responsibility for the war was shared by all the powers involved even though Austria, Serbia and Russia were primarily to blame. He was Professor of History at Harvard between 1929 and 1946.

39 Luigi Albertini was a famous Italian journalist and historian. He created and edited the *Corriere della Serra* (Milan), one of the most respected and widely read daily newspapers in Europe. An early and outspoken opponent of fascism, he was also one of the few newspaper editors to resist fascist threats and cajolery. In November 1925, after he was dismissed by the owners of the *Corriere*, Albertini decided to devote the rest of his life to historical studies. He was also an early

revisionist voice. His *Origins of the War of 1914* was published posthumously in 1942.

40 R.D. Edwards, UCDA. File LA 22/1276. No date.

41 James McGuire, "Thomas Desmond Williams (1921–1987)", *Irish Historical Studies*, Vol. XXVI, No. 101, May 1988. pp. 3–7.

42 R.D. Edwards, UCDA. File LA 22/829 (9): 23 February 1949.

43 Herbert Butterfield, CUA. File 531/W207: 4 May 1949.

44 R.D. Edwards, UCDA. File LA 22/1276.

45 Herbert Butterfield, CUA. File 130: 1 April 1949.

46 A.J.P. Taylor, *The Origins of the Second World War*, (New York: Fawcett Premier, 1969), p. 18.

47 R.D. Edwards, UCDA. File LA 22/1276. Article by T.D. Williams entitled "Some Aspects of Contemporary History".

48 Desmond T. Williams, "The Historiography of World War II", Historical Studies No. I, (London: Bowes and Bowes, 1958), pp. 33–49.

49 R.D. Edwards, UCDA. File LA 22/1276.

50 Herbert Butterfield, CUA. File 531/W209: 26 June 1950.

51 Herbert Butterfield, CUA. File 130/4: "Official History: Its Pitfalls and Its Criteria" Paper contributed to a discussion on "Contemporary History" at a meeting of the Historical Society at UCD, 14 December 1948. Appeared in *Studies*, June 1949.

52 Quoted in Arthur Goddard (ed.), *Harry Elmer Barnes, Learned Crusader*, (Colorado: Ralph Myles, 1968), p. 241.

53 At the conclusion of his *The Origins of the World War* (1930), Fay wrote: "One must abandon the dictum of the Versailles Treaty that Germany and her allies were solely responsible. It was a dictum exacted by victors from vanquished, under the influence of the blindness, ignorance, hatred, and the propagandist misconceptions to which war had given rise. It was based on evidence which was incomplete and not always sound".

54 Harry Elmer Barnes has written two important books. The first is a three-volume *Intellectual and Cultural History of the Western World*, in which he strongly comes down in favour of intellectual and cultural freedom. The second is *Genesis of the World War* in which he argued that Serbia, Russia and France were primarily responsible.

55 Anonymous Review of A.J.P. Taylor's *The Origins of the Second World War*, in *The Times Literary Supplement*, Friday 21 April 1961, p. 244.

56 Herbert Butterfield, CUA. File 130/4: "Official History: Its Pitfalls and Its Criteria".

57 Friedrich Meinecke, *German Catastrophe: Reflections and Recollections*, (Cambridge: CUP, 1950), p. 53.

58 Herbert Butterfield, CUA. File 531/W249: 8 November 1955.

59 Linda Colley, *Lewis Namier: A Biography*, (London: Weidenfeld and Nicolson, 1989), pp. 38, 43.

60 Review of Lewis Namier's *Side Lines of History. Vanished Supremacies. Essays on European History. 1812–1918*, (New York: Harper Torchbooks, 1963) by Desmond Williams in *Spectator*, 14 February 1958.

61 A.J.P. Taylor, *The Course of German History*, (London: Hamish Hamilton, 1945).

62 Herbert Butterfield, CUA. File Butt 57/3: 20 December 1957, Letter from Butterfield to Ritter.

63 A.J.P. Taylor, *The Course of German History*, p. 7.

64 A.J.P. Taylor, *The Origins of the Second World War*, p. 293.

65 Desmond Williams, "The Historiography of World War II", Historical Studies No. I, (London: Bowes and Bowes, 1958), pp. 33–49.

66 R.D. Edwards, UCDA. File LA 22/1225: *The Leader*, Vol. 58, No. 24, 1958.

67 Desmond Williams, "The Historiography of World War II", Historical Studies No. I, p. 46.
68 Desmond Williams, "The Anatomy of Appeasement", a Review of *The Eve of War 1939*. Survey of International Affairs 1939–46", *Spectator*, 21 March 1958.
69 Desmond Williams, "Negotiations leading to the Anglo-Polish Treaty of 31 March 1939", in *Irish Historical Studies*, Vol. X, No. 37, March 1956, pp. 59–93. See also I and II in Vol. X, No. 38, September 1956, pp. 156–92, 187–9.
70 Herbert Butterfield, CUA. File 531/W246: 16 May 1955.
71 R.D. Edwards, UCDA. File LA 22/1276.
72 A.J.P. Taylor, *The Origins of the Second World War*, p. 19.
73 Desmond Williams, "Adolph Hitler and the Historians", *University Review*, Vol. I, No. 9, Summer 1956, pp. 37–51, (p. 41).
74 Ibid. p. 41.
75 Geoffrey Barraclough, "German Unification. An Essay in Revision", *Historical Studies*, No. IV, G.A. Hayes-McCoy (ed.), (London: Bowes and Bowes, 1963), pp. 62–81.
76 J.C. Beckett, Review of *Historical Studies No. IV*. G.A. Hayes-McCoy (ed.), (London: Bowes and Bowes, 1962), in *Studia Hibernica*, No. 4, 1964, pp. 233–4.
77 Sean O'Faolain, *King of the Beggars. A Life of Daniel O'Connell*, (Dublin: Poolbeg, 1938).
78 Michael Tierney (ed.), *Daniel O'Connell. Nine Centenary Essays*, (Dublin: Brown and Nolan, 1949).
79 Geoffrey Barraclough, "The 'Historische Zeitschrift'", *Times Literary Supplement*, 14 April 1950, p. 229.
80 Gerhard Ritter, "The 'Historische Zeitschrift'", *Times Literary Supplement*, 12 May 1950.
81 Herbert Butterfield, CUA. File 531/03: 15 June 1950.
82 Herbert Butterfield. CUA. File 531/05: 20 July 1950.
83 Francis Shaw, "The Canon of Irish History – A Challenge", *Studies*, Vol. LXI, 1972, p. 149.
84 Sean Cronin, *Irish Nationalism. A History of its Roots and Ideology*, (Dublin: The Academy Press, 1980) or J.R. Archer, "Necessary Ambiguity: Nationalism and Myth in Ireland", *Eire/Ireland*, Summer 1984, p. 36.
85 Kevin Myers, "Irishman's Diary", *Irish Times*, 16 May 1995, 14 March 1996.
86 Conor Cruise O'Brien, "Nationalism and the Reconquest of Ireland", *Crane Bag*, Vol. I, No. 2, 1977, pp. 8–13.

5 The clash between the new historians and the Bureau of Military History

1 Ronan Fanning, "'The Great Enchantment': Uses and Abuses of Modern Irish History", in *Interpreting Irish History*, p. 154.
2 F.S.L. Lyons, *Ireland since the Famine*, (London: Weidenfeld and Nicolson, 1971), p. 460.
3 Department of an Taoiseach, NAI. File: S. 13081: 5 January 1943.
4 R.D. Edwards, UCDA. File LA 22/462 (18): 10 October 1945.
5 R.D. Edwards, UCDA. File LA 22/465 (3): 3 April 1946.
6 Herbert Butterfield, CUA. File 131: Correspondence 1913–1921, 1948–1958.
7 Herbert Butterfield, CUA. File 130: 9 May 1952.
8 R.D. Edwards, UCDA. File LA 22/333 (111): Sunday 30 October 1955.
9 R.D. Edwards, UCDA. File LA 22/333 (41). No date.
10 R.D. Edwards, UCDA. File LA 22/464 (198). No date.
11 R.D. Edwards, UCDA. File LA 22/335 (167): 14 March 1951.

12 R.D. Edwards, UCDA. File LA 22/335 (167): 14 March 1951.

13 T.W. Moody, TCDA. File 10048/BMH/90/2: 31 March 1951.

14 Florence O'Donoghue, NLA. File Ms. 31, 352 (8): 12 January 1960.

15 Florence O'Donoghue, NLA. File Ms. 31, 355 (1–2): 2 March 1949.

16 Florence O'Donoghue, NLA. File Ms. 31, 355 (1–2): 9 April 1948.

17 Florence O'Donoghue, NLA. File Ms. 31, 355 (1–2): 19 April 1948.

18 Florence O'Donoghue, NLA. File Ms. 31, 355 (1–2): 6 May 1948.

19 Florence O'Donoghue, NLA. File Ms. 31, 355 (1–2): 6 May 1948.

20 R.D. Edwards, UCDA. File LA 22/333 (196). No date.

21 R.D. Edwards, UCDA. File LA 22/333 (147): 14 February 1958.

22 Florence O' Donoghue, NLA. File Ms. 31, 352 (8): 29 April 1960.

23 R.D. Edwards, UCDA. File LA 22/339 (4): 5 September 1959 to 14 March 1960.

24 R.D. Edwards, UCDA. File LA 22/339 (4): 5 September 1959 to 14 March 1960.

25 R.D. Edwards, UCDA. File LA 22/333 (168–169): 31 August 1959.

26 R.D. Edwards, UCDA. File LA 22/339 (8): 18 January 1960.

27 R.D. Edwards, UCDA. File LA 22/451 (55, 56, 57): 8 November 1945.

28 R.D. Edwards, UCDA. File LA 22/809 (20): 12 January 1960.

29 R.D. Edwards, UCDA. File LA 22/464 (127). No date.

30 R.D. Edwards, UCDA. File LA 22/333 (144): 10 February 1958.

31 R.D. Edwards, UCDA. File LA 22/333 (145): 14 February 1958.

32 MAD, File S. 1779: 25 September 1951.

33 Donnchadh O Corráin (ed.), *James Hogan. Revolutionary. Historian and Political Scientist*, (Dublin: Four Courts, 2001).

34 R.D. Edwards, UCDA. File LA 22/793 (3): 14 December 1951.

35 R.D. Edwards, UCDA. File LA 22/793 (71): 28 April 1958.

36 Florence O'Donoghue, NLA. File Ms. 31, 352 (4): 16 January 1947.

37 Florence O'Donoghue, NLA. File Ms. 31, 352 (4): 21 January 1947.

38 Department of an Taoiseach, NAI. File S. 13081: 28 April 1946.

39 MAD. File S. 1860: 23 November 1947.

40 R.D. Edwards, UCDA. File LA 22/1201: *The Leader*, Vol. 52, No. 20, 25 October 1952, p. 19.

41 Ibid.

42 Ibid.

43 R.D. Edwards, UCDA. File LA 22/1202: *The Leader*, Vol. 54. No. 21, 23 October 1954.

44 R.D. Edwards, UCDA. File LA 22/451 (55, 56, 57): 8 November 1945.

45 Herbert Butterfield, CUA. File 531/W385: 3 May 1978.

46 R.D. Edwards, UCDA. File LA 22/451 (121): 8 March 1946.

47 R.D. Edwards, "Rescue the Records", *Irish Archives Bulletin*, Vol. 1, No. 1, May 1971, pp. 7–10.

48 Eoin MacNeill, UCDA. File LA 1/J/228: 1940s.

49 Donal McCartney, "MacNeill and Irish-Ireland", in *The Scholar Revolutionary: Eoin MacNeill and the Making of the New Ireland*, pp. 84–5.

50 Eoin MacNeill, UCDA. LA1/Q/340: "Education – The Idea of the State", *Irish Review*, 25 November 1922.

51 J.J. Lee, *Ireland 1912–1985. Politics and Society*, (Cambridge: CUP, 1989), p. 593.

52 Frank Gallagher, *The Anglo-Irish Treaty*, (London: Hutchinson, 1965), p. 144.

53 Michael Laffan, "Insular Attitudes: The Revisionists and their Critics", in *Revising the Rising*, pp. 108–9.

54 Diarmaid Ferreter, "In Such Deadly Earnest", *Dublin Review*, No. 12, Autumn 2003, p. 41.

55 Department of an Taoiseach, NAI. File S. 13081. Written by Dan Bryan, 24 July 1945.
56 R.D. Edwards, UCDA. File LA 22/465 (30): April 1946 to June 1946, Friday.
57 Willy Maley, "Nationalism and Revisionism: Ambiviolences and Dissensus", in Scott Brewster, Virginia Crossman (eds), *Ireland in Proximity. History, Gender, Space*, (London: Routledge, 1999), p. 21.
58 Patrick Murray, "Obsessive Historian: Eamon de Valera and the Policing of his Reputation", *Proceedings of the Royal Irish Academy*, Vol. 101C, 37–65, December 2001, pp. 48–9.
59 Florence O'Donoghue, NLA. File Ms. 31, 355 (1): "Bureau Journal", 13 June 1946.
60 Ann Dolan, *Commemorating the Irish Civil War. History and Memory 1923–2000*, (Cambridge: CUP, 2003), p. 201.
61 Eunan O'Halpin, "Historical revisit: Dorothy Macardle, *The Irish Republic* (1937)", *Irish Historical Studies*, Vol. XXXI, No. 123, May 1999, pp. 389–94.
62 John M. Regan, *The Irish Counter-Revolution 1921–1936*, (Dublin: Gill & Macmillan, 1999), Preface XV.

6 Weaknesses in ethnographic method

 1 Joel Mokyr, *Why Ireland Starved: A Quantitative and Analytical History of the Irish Economy. 1800–1850*, (London: George Allen & Unwin, 1983), p. 38.
 2 Christopher Morash, "Famine/Holocaust: Fragmented Bodies", *Eire/Ireland*, Vol. 32, No. 1, Spring 1997, p. 141.
 3 Luke Gibbons, *Transformations in Irish Culture*, (Cork: Cork University Press, 1996), p. 176.
 4 Joel Mokyr, *Why Ireland Starved: A Quantitative and Analytical History of the Irish Economy*, p. 43.
 5 Cormac O Grada, *Ireland Before and After the Famine. Explorations in Economic History. 1800–1925*, (Manchester: MUP, 1993), p. 127.
 6 Ibid. p. 132.
 7 R.F. Foster, *Modern Ireland. 1600–1972*, p. 325.
 8 Ibid.
 9 R.F. Foster, *Paddy and Mr Punch. Connections in Irish and English History*, (London: Penguin, 1995), p. 82.
10 Graham Davis, "The Historiography of the Irish Famine", in Patrick O'Sullivan (ed.), *The Meaning of the Famine*, (London: Leicester University Press, 1997), pp. 36–7.
11 George Boyce, *Nineteenth-Century Ireland. The Search for Stability*, (Dublin: Gill & Macmillan, 1990), p. 109.
12 Patrick O'Sullivan, *The Meaning of the Famine*, p. 9.
13 Ibid.
14 Terry Eagleton, "Emily Bronte and The Great Hunger", *Irish Review*, No. 12, Spring 1992, pp. 108–9.
15 S.J. Donnelly, "The Construction of the Memory of the Famine in Ireland and the Irish Diaspora. 1850–1900", *Eire/Ireland*, Vol. 31, No. 1–2, Spring 1997, p. 49.
16 Patrick O'Farrell, "Whose Reality? The Irish Famine in History and Literature", *Historical Studies*, Vol. 20, No. 78, April 1982, p. 3.
17 Graham Davis, "The historiography of the Irish Famine", in *The Meaning of the Famine*, p. 17.
18 Patrick O'Farrell, "Whose Reality? The Irish Famine in History and Literature", Ibid. p. 3.

19 Christopher Morash, "Making Memories: The Literature of the Irish Famine", in *The Meaning of the Famine*, p. 42.

20 Q.S.J. Connolly, "The Great Famine and Irish Politics", in Cathal Pórtéir (ed.), *The Great Irish Famine*, (Dublin: Mercier Press, 1995), p. 49.

21 Terry Eagleton, *Heathcliff and the Great Hunger. Studies in Irish Culture*, (London: Verso, 1995), p. 22.

22 R.D. Edwards, T.D. Williams (eds), *The Great Famine: Studies in Irish History. 1845–1852*, (Dublin: The Lilliput Press, New Introduction by Cormac O Gráda, 1994, 1st edn 1956), p. viii.

23 Edmund Curtis, TCDA. Ms. 2452: 2 October 1916.

24 Ibid.

25 Terry Eagleton, *Heathcliff and the Great Hunger*, p. 22.

26 Cormac O Gráda, *Ireland Before and After the Famine*, p. 101.

27 Ibid. p. 99.

28 Cormac O Gráda, "The Saga of *The Great Famine*", in *Interpreting Irish History*, p. 280.

29 Cecil Woodham-Smith, *The Great Hunger. 1845–1849*, (New York: Old Town Books, 1989), p. 20.

30 Terry Eagleton, "Emily Brontë and The Great Hunger", *Irish Review*, No. 12, Spring 1992, p. 110.

31 R.D. Edwards, UCDA. File LA 22/Diary: 31 October 1955, 3 January 1954.

32 Review of Cecil Woodham-Smith's *The Great Hunger* by F.S.L. Lyons in *Irish Historical Studies*, Vol. XIV, 1964–5, pp. 76–8.

33 Review of R.D. Edwards' and T.D. Williams' *The Great Famine* by F.S.L. Lyons in *Irish Times*, 21 January 1957.

7 Theoretical underpinnings and their impact

1 R.D. Edwards, "An Agenda for Irish History, 1978–2018", in *Interpreting Irish History*, p. 65.

2 Michael Oakeshott, *Experience and its Modes*, (Cambridge: CUP, 1933), p. 129.

3 Michael Oakeshott, "The Activity of Being an Historian", *Historical Studies*, No. I, Desmond T. Williams (ed.), (London: Bowes and Bowes, 1958), p. 15.

4 Cecil Woodham-Smith, *The Great Hunger*, pp. 15–16.

5 Cormac O Gráda, "The Saga of *The Great Famine*", in *Interpreting Irish History*, p. 137.

6 Theodore K. Hoppen, *Ireland since 1800: Conflict and Conformity*, (London: Longman, 1989), p. 53.

7 Peter Gray, "Ideology and the Famine", in *The Great Irish Famine*, pp. 86–103.

8 Christine Kinealy, *This Great Calamity. The Irish Famine. 1845–1852*, (Dublin: Gill & Macmillan, 1994).

9 R.D. Edwards, UCDA. LA 22/File 1225: *The Leader*, Vol. 58, No. 24, 1958.

10 R.D. Edwards, UCDA. LA 22/File 1219 (2): 1957.

11 Ibid.

12 R.D. Edwards, UCDA. LA 22/Diaries: Sunday 24 May 1959.

13 R.D. Edwards, UCDA. LA 22/Diaries: 9 September 1952.

14 R.D. Edwards, UCDA. LA 22/Diaries: 11 September 1952.

15 Willy Maley, "Ambiviolences and Dissensus", in *Ireland in Proximity. History, Gender, Space*, p. 22.

16 R.D. Edwards, UCDA. LA 22/Diaries: 18 February 1963.

17 R.D. Edwards, T.D. Williams (eds), *The Great Famine*, New Introduction by Cormac O Gráda, (Dublin: The Lilliput Press, 1994).

18 Cormac O Gráda, "The Saga of *The Great Famine*", in *Interpreting Irish History*, pp. 282–3.

19 R.D. Edwards, UCDA. LA 22/Diaries: 20 January 1952.

20 R.D. Edwards, UCDA. LA 22/File: 505 (2). Review of *The Great Famine* by Kitson Clark in *University Review*, 8 January 1957.

21 Brendan Bradshaw, "Nationalism and Historical Scholarship", in *Interpreting Irish History*, p. 191.

22 T.D. Williams (ed.), *The Great Famine*, (Dublin, 1994).

23 Mary E. Daly, *The Famine in Ireland*, (Dublin: Dundalgan Press, 1986).

24 Brendan Bradshaw, "Nationalism and Historical Scholarship", *Irish Historical Studies*, Vol. XXVI, No. 104, November 1989, p. 341.

25 Herbert Butterfield, *Christianity and History*, (London: G. Bell & Sons, 1949).

26 Herbert Butterfield, *The Englishman and his History*, (Cambridge: CUP, 1944), p. 6.

27 Brendan Bradshaw, "Nationalism and Historical Scholarship", in *Interpreting Irish History*, p. 207.

28 Ibid. p. 212.

29 Paul Franco, *The Political Philosophy of Michael Oakeshott*, (New Haven: Yale University Press, 1990) pp. 14, 43.

30 E.J. Hobsbawm, *Nations and Nationalism Since 1780. Programme, Myth, Reality*, (Cambridge: CUP, 1990) pp. 12–13.

31 Thomas Babington Macaulay, *History of England from the Accession of James II*, (London: Harper & Brothers, 1862, 1906, 1966), p. 2.

32 Brendan Bradshaw, "Nationalism and Historical Scholarship", in *Interpreting Irish History*, p. 212.

33 Maurice Cowling, "Herbert Butterfield 1900–1979", *Proceedings of the British Academy*, (London: OUP, 1979) Vol. LXV, p. 608.

34 Herbert Butterfield, *The Whig Interpretation of History*, p. 90.

35 Ibid. pp. 92–3.

36 Herbert Butterfield, *George III and the Historians*, (London: Collins Clear-Type Press, 1957), p. 7.

37 Ibid. p. 34.

38 Linda Colley, *Lewis Namier. A Biography*, (London: Weidenfeld and Nicolson, 1989), p. 63.

39 Richard J. Evans, *In Defence of History*, 2nd edn (London: Granta Books, 2000), p. 34.

40 Herbert Butterfield, *George III and the Historians*, p. 8.

41 Ibid. p. 8.

42 Ibid. p. 219.

43 Ibid. p. 214.

44 R.D. Edwards, UCDA. File LA 22/1274: 9 January 1958.

45 R.D. Edwards, UCDA. File LA 22/1274: 24 January 1958.

46 R.D. Edwards, UCDA. File LA 22/1274: 9 January 1958.

47 Herbert Butterfield, *George III and the Historians*, pp. 297–8.

48 Ibid. pp. 297–8.

49 Herbert Butterfield, CUA. File 531/W226: 24 January 1958.

50 Conor McCarthy, *Irish Modernisation, Crisis and Culture in Ireland. 1969–1992*, p. 94.

51 R.F. Foster, *Modern Ireland. 1600–1972*, p. 318.

52 Luke Dodd, "Famine Echoes", *The South Atlantic Quarterly*, Vol. 95, No. 1, Winter 1996, p. 101.

53 J.J. Lee, "Irish Economic History Since 1900", *Irish Historiography, 1970–1979*, (Cork: CUP, 1981), p. 182.

54 Colm Toibin, *The Irish Famine*, (London: Profile Books, 1999), p. 42.

55 Ibid. p. 43.

56 Ibid. p. 44.
57 Cormac O Gráda, *Ireland Before and After the Famine*, p. 100.
58 R.D. Edwards, UCDA. File LA 22/Diaries: Sunday 30 June 1957.
59 Terry Eagleton, *The Illusions of Postmodernism*, (Oxford: Blackwell Publishers, 1996), p. 11.
60 Terry Eagleton (ed.), *Ideology*, (London: Longman, 1994), p. 17.
61 Cormac O Gráda, "Making Irish Famine History in 1995", *History Workshop Journal*, No. 42, Autumn 1996, p. 88.
62 Cormac O Gráda, *Ireland Before and After the Famine*, p. 128.
63 Christopher Morash, "Entering the Abyss", *Irish Review*, No. 17/18, Winter 1995, p. 175.
64 Terry Eagleton, *Heathcliff and the Great Hunger*, p. 13.
65 Alain Finkielkraut, *L'Humanité perdue. Essai sur le XXème siècle*, p. 10.
66 Terry Eagleton, *Heathcliff and the Great Hunger*, p. 13.
67 Michael Longley, "Memory and Acknowledgement", *Irish Review*, No. 17/18, Winter 1995, p. 157.

8 The claims of memory and critique

1 R.D. Edwards, T.D. Williams, *The Great Famine*, p. XIV.
2 Christopher Morash, "Entering the Abyss", *Irish Review*, No. 17/18, Winter 1995, pp. 175–9.
3 Colm Toibin, *The Irish Famine*, p. 47.
4 Roger J. McHugh, "The Famine in Irish Oral Tradition", in *The Great Famine*, p. 436.
5 Graham Davis, "The historiography of the Irish Famine", in *The Meaning of the Famine*, p. 25.
6 "The Irish Century in perspective", Review of George Boyce's, *19th century Ireland: The Search for Stability*, by A.T.Q. Stewart, in *Irish Times*, 16 March 1991.
7 Christine Kinealy, *This Great Calamity: The Irish Famine. 1845–1852*, p. 359.
8 Jacques Derrida, *Spectres of Marx The State of the Debt, the Work of Mourning, and the New International*, (London: Routlege, 1994), p. xix.
9 Ibid. p. 6.
10 Ibid. p. 7.
11 Christopher Morash, "Spectres of the Famine", *Irish Review*, No. 17/18, Winter 1995, pp. 77–8.
12 Ibid. p. 76.
13 Bryan Palmer, *Descent into Discourse: The Reification of Language and the Writing of Social History*, (Philadelphia: Temple University Press, 1990), p. IV.
14 E.P. Thompson, *The Making of the English Working Class*, (New York: Vintage Books, 1963), pp. 12–13.
15 Joyce Appleby, Lynn Hunt, Margaret Jacob, *Telling the Truth About History*, (New York: Norton, 1994), p. 225.
16 Richard Kearney, *Dialogues with Contemporary Continental Thinkers*, (Manchester: MUP, 1984), pp. 123–4.
17 Christopher Morash, *The Hungry Voice: The Poetry of the Irish Famine*, (Dublin: Irish Academic Press, 1989), p. 37.
18 Stuart Sim, *Modern Cultural Theorists. Jean-François Lyotard*, (London: Prentice Hall, Harvester Wheatsheaf, 1996), p. 124.
19 Jean-François Lyotard, *The Postmodern Condition: A Report on Knowledge*, (Manchester: MUP, 1984), p. 24.
20 Christopher Morash, "Making Memories", in *The Meaning of the Famine*, p. 42.
21 Ibid.
22 Canon J. O'Rourke, *The Great Irish Famine*, (Dublin: Veritas, 1874).

23 Charles Gavan Duffy, *Four Years of Irish History*, (London: Cassell, Getter, Galpin, 1883).
24 P.S. O'Hegarty, *A History of Ireland under the Union. 1801–1922*, (London: Methuen, 1952).
25 Cecil Woodham-Smith, *The Great Hunger. 1845–1849*, (London: Old Town Books, 1962).
26 Robert Kee, *The Green Flag*, (London: Weidenfeld & Nicholson, 1972).
27 Thomas Gallagher, *Paddy's Lament. 1846–1847. Prelude To Hatred*, (Dublin: Word River Press, 1985).
28 Christine Kinealy, *This Great Calamity. The Irish Famine. 1845–1852*.
29 Christopher Morash, "Making Memories", in *The Meaning of the Famine*, p. 53.
30 Jean-François Lyotard, *Just Gaming*, (Manchester: MUP, 1985), p. 43.

9 The epistemological and philosophical position of Irish revisionism)

1 A.T.Q. Stewart, *The Narrow Ground: The Roots of Conflict in Ulster. 1609–1969*, (Belfast: Institute of Irish Studies, 1977), p. 16.
2 Ibid.
3 Alain Finkielkraut, *La Défaite de la pensée. Essai sur le XXème siècle*, p. 41.
4 Joe Ruane, Jennifer Todd, *The Dynamics of Conflict in Northern Ireland. Power, Conflict, and Emancipation*, (Cork: Cork University Press, 1996), p. 6.
5 Raymond Williams, *Marxism and Literature*, (Oxford: OUP, 1977), p. 83.
6 Terry Eagleton, *Heathcliff and the Great Hunger*, pp. 250–1, 254.
7 Frantz Fanon, *The Wretched of the Earth*, (New York: Grove Press, 1963), and Frantz Fanon, *Black Skin, White Masks*, (New York: Grove Press, 1967).
8 R.F. Foster, "History and the Irish Question", in *Interpreting Irish History*, p. 131.
9 James Anthony Froude, *The English in Ireland in the Eighteenth Century*, III volumes (London: Longmans, Green and Co., 1872–1874).
10 W.E.H. Lecky, *History of Ireland in the Eighteenth Century*, IV volumes (London: Longmans, Green and Co., 1892, 1913).
11 Homi Bhabha, *The Location of Culture*, (London: Routledge, 1994).
12 Donal McCartney, *W.E.H. Lecky. Historian and Politician. 1838–1903*, (Dublin: The Lilliput Press, 1994) p. 193.
13 F.S.L. Lyons, *Culture and Anarchy in Ireland. 1890–1939*, p. 22.
14 Balachandra Rajan, *The Form of the Unfinished: English Poetics From Spenser to Pound*, (Princeton, NJ: 1985). See also Review of *The Location of Culture*, in *Modern Philology*, Vol. 95, No. 4, May 1998, pp. 490–500.
15 Homi Bhabha, "Remembering Fanon: Self, Psyche and The Colonial Condition", in P. Williams, L. Chrisman (eds), *Colonial Discourse and Postcolonial Theory: A Reader*, (New York: Columbia University Press, 1994), p. 117.
16 Ania Loomba, *Colonialism and Postcolonialism*, (London: Routledge, 1998), p. 91.
17 Terry Eagleton, *Heathcliff and the Great Hunger*, p. 265.
18 George Boyce, "Revisionism and the Revisionist Controversy", in George Boyce, Alan O'Day (eds), *The Making of Modern Irish History*, (London: Routledge, 1996), p. 8.
19 Albert Memmi, *Portrait du colonisateur et du colonisé*, Préface Sartre, Jean-Paul (Paris: Gallimard, 1985), pp. 64–5.
20 Ibid. p. 66.
21 Walter D. Love, "Charles O'Conor of Belanagare and Thomas Leland's 'Philosophical' History of Ireland", in *Irish Historical Studies*, Vol. 13, No. 49, March 1962, pp. 1–25. Or Walter D. Love, "Edmund Burke and an Irish Historiographical Controversy", *History and Theory* 2, 1962–1963, pp. 180–98.

22 Conor Cruise O'Brien, *The Great Melody. A Thematic Biography and Commented Anthology of Edmund Burke*, (London: Sinclair-Stevenson, 1992).

23 S.J. Connolly, *Political Ideas in Eighteenth-Century Ireland*, (Dublin: Four Courts, 2000).

24 Both quotations are drawn from Zeev Sternhell, *La droite révolutionnaire. 1885–1914. Les origins françaises du fascisme*, (Paris: Editions du Seuil, 1978), pp. 152, 162.

25 *Catholic Bulletin*, June 1925.

26 *Catholic Bulletin*, Editorial, June 1926.

27 Maurice Blanchot, *Les intellectuels en question. Ebauche d'une réflexion*, (Paris: Fourbis, 1996), p. 21.

28 Margaret O'Callaghan, "The *Irish Statesman* and the *Catholic Bulletin* reappraised", *Irish Historical Studies*, Vol. XXIV, No. 94, November 1984, pp. 227–44.

29 Conor Cruise O'Brien, *States of Ireland*, (London: Hutchinson, 1972), p. 71.

30 R.F. Foster, *Modern Ireland. 1600–1972*, p. 173.

31 George Boyce, *Nationalism in Ireland*, (London: Routledge, 1995), p. 103.

32 Ibid. p. 105.

33 Benedict Anderson, *Imagined Communities: Reflections on the Origin and Spread of Nationalism*, (London: Verso, 1991), p. 81.

34 George Boyce, *Nationalism in Ireland*, p. 117.

35 R.F. Foster, *Paddy and Mr Punch*, p. 4.

36 George Boyce, *Nationalism in Ireland*, p. 117.

37 Benedict Anderson, *Imagined Communities*, p. 81.

38 Ibid. p. 48.

39 Conor Cruise O'Brien, *The Great Melody*, p. 247.

40 Conor Cruise O'Brien, *The Great Melody*, p. 251.

41 Michel Foucault, *L'archéologie du savoir*, (Paris: Gallimard, 1969), pp. 16–17.

42 Luke Gibbons, "Challenging the Canon: Revisionism and Cultural Criticism", in Seamus Deane (ed.), *The Field Day Anthology of Irish Writing*, Vol. III, (Derry: Field Day, 1991), p. 562.

43 Sean O'Faolain, *King of the Beggars. A Life of Daniel O'Connell*, p. 27.

44 Daniel Corkery, *The Hidden Ireland: A Story of Gaelic Munster in the 18th Century*, (Dublin: Gill & Macmillan, 1967).

45 Louis Cullen, *The Hidden Ireland: Reassessment of a Concept*, (Westmeath: The Lilliput Press, 1988), pp. 1, 5, 16, 19, 25, 36.

46 Steven G. Ellis, "Nationalist Historiography and the English and Gaelic Worlds in the late Middle Ages", *Irish Historical Studies*, Vol. XXV, No. 97, May 1986, pp. 1–18.

47 L.P. Curtis, "The Greening of Irish History", *Eire/Ireland*, Vol. XXIX, No. 2, Summer 1994, pp. 7–28.

48 Brendan Bradshaw, "Nationalism and Historical Scholarship", *Irish Historical Studies*, Vol. XXVI, No. 104, November 1989, p. 332.

49 Steven G. Ellis, "Representations of the Past in Ireland: Whose Past and Whose Present?", *Irish Historical Studies*, Vol. 27, No. 108, 1991, pp. 294–303.

50 Catherine Backs-Clément, *Lévi-Strauss ou la structure et le malheur*, (Paris: Seghers, 1970), p. 182.

51 Herbert Butterfield, *The Whig Interpretation of History*, p. 10.

52 Roy Foster, *The Irish Story. Telling Tales and Making it up in Ireland*, p. 2.

53 Paul Bew, "The Easter Rising: Lost Leaders and Lost Opportunities", *Irish Review*, No. 11, Winter 1991/1992, pp. 9–13.

54 Roy Foster, "We are all Revisionists Now", *Irish Review*, No. 1, 1986, pp. 1–5.

55 Conor Cruise O'Brien, "The Embers of Easter. 1916–1966", in *1916: The Easter Rising*, pp. 227–8.

56 Tom Dunne, "New Histories: Beyond 'Revisionism'", *The Irish Review*, No. 12, 1992, p. 10.
57 R.F. Foster, *The Irish Story. Telling Tales and Making it up in Ireland*, p. xviii.
58 Liam Kennedy, *Colonialism, Religion, and Nationalism in Ireland*, (Belfast: Institute of Irish Studies, 1996), p. 177.
59 Ibid. pp. 221–2.
60 T. Eagleton, F. Jameson, E. Said, *Nationalism, Colonialism, and Literature*, (Mineapolis: University of Minnesota Press, 1990), pp. 7–8.
61 Bill Rolston, "What's Wrong with Multiculturalism?" in David Miller (ed.), *Rethinking Northern Ireland: Culture, Ideology and Colonialism*, (London: Longman, 1998), p. 263.
62 Stephen Howe, *Ireland and Empire. Colonial legacies in Irish History and Culture*, (Oxford: OUP, 2000), p. 130.
63 Maurice Goldring, *Pleasant the Scholar's Life*, pp. 95–125.
64 Oliver MacDonagh, *Ireland: The Union and Its Aftermath*, (London: George Allen & Unwin, 1977), p. 160.
65 Ian R. McBride, *Scripture Politics – Ulster Presbyterians and Irish Radicalism in Late Eighteenth-Century Ireland*, (Oxford: Clarendon, 1998).
66 Thomas Bartlett, *The Fall and Rise of the Irish Nation: The Catholic Question. 1690–1830*, (Dublin: Gill & Macmillan, 1992), pp. 67–9.
67 Ronan Fanning, *Independent Ireland*, (Dublin: Helicon, 1983), p. VII.
68 Ronan Fanning, *"The Four-Leaved Shamrock": Electoral Politics and the National Imagination in Independent Ireland*, (Dublin: National University of Ireland, 1983).
69 Jacob Rogozinski, "Déconstruire-la Révolution", in Jacob Rogozinski, Philippe Lacoue-Labarthe, Jean-Luc Nancy, *Les fins de l'Homme*, (Paris: Edition Galilée, 1980), p. 517.
70 Jacques Derrida, *Marges de la philosophie*, (Paris: Minuit, 1972), p. 162.
71 Roland Barthes, *Mythologies*, (Paris: Editions du Seuil, 1957), p. 246.
72 Colin Graham, "'Liminal Spaces': Post-Colonial Theories and Irish Culture", *Irish Review*, No. 16, Winter 1994, p. 37.
73 Ibid. p. 39.
74 Francis Mulhern, "Postcolonial Melancholy: A Reply to Luke Gibbons", in *The Present Lasts a Long Time: Essays in Cultural Politics*, (Cork: Cork University Press, 1998), pp. 158–63.
75 Peter Gray, "Our man at Oxford. Interview of R.F. Foster", in *History Ireland*, Vol. 1, No. 3, Autumn 1993.
76 Alain Finkielkraut, *La sagesse de l'amour*, (Paris: Gallimard, 1984), p. 117.
77 Michel Foucault, "Nietzsche, la genéalogie, l'histoire", *Hommage à Jean Hyppolite*, (Paris: Presses Universitaires FranÁaises, 1971), p. 160.
78 Alvin Jackson, "Unionist Myths. 1912–1985", *Past and Present*, No. 136, August 1992, pp. 164–85.
79 Dick Walsh, "The end of government from beyond the grave", *Irish Times*, 6 April 1991, p. 8.
80 George Boyce, *Nationalism in Ireland*, (London: Routledge, 2nd edn 1991), p. 408.

10 The revolution comes under revisionist scrutiny

1 Kevin Whelan, "The Region and the Intellectuals", in Liam O'Dowd (ed.), *On Intellectuals and Intellectual Life in Ireland. International, Comparative and Historical Contexts*, (Belfast: Institute of Irish Studies, 1996), p. 126.
2 Sophia Rosenfeld, *A Revolution in Language: The Problem of Signs in Late Eighteenth-Century France*, (Stanford: Stanford University Press, 2001).
3 Sunil Khilnany, *Arguing Revolution. The Intellectual Left in Postwar France*, (New Haven: Yale University Press, 1993), pp. 156–8.

4 David Fitzpatrick, "Commemoration in the Irish Free State: a chronicle of embarrassment", in Ian McBride (ed.), *History and Memory in Modern Ireland*, (Cambridge: CUP, 2001), pp. 184–203.

5 Frank Gallagher, *The Anglo-Irish Treaty*, pp. 193–4.

6 Patrick Pearse, *Collected Works of Padraic H. Pearse: Political Writings and Speeches*, (Dublin: Phoenix, 1922), p. 238.

7 Ibid. pp. 237, 370.

8 George Boyce, "Revisionism and the Northern Ireland Troubles", in *The Making of Modern Irish History*, p. 228.

9 Tom Dunne, *Theobald Wolfe Tone. Colonial Outsider. An Analysis of his Political Philosophy*, (Cork: Tower Books, 1982), p. 17.

10 L.M. Cullen, "The 1798 Rebellion in Wexford: United Irish Organisation, Membership, Leadership", in Kevin Whelan (ed.), *Wexford: History and Society*, (Dublin: Geography Publications, 1987), pp. 248–95.

11 Marianne Elliott, *Wolfe Tone: Prophet of Irish Independence* (New Haven: Yale University Press, 1989).

12 François Furet, *Penser la Révolution française*, p. 37.

13 Ibid. p. 170.

14 Ibid. p. 24.

15 Ibid. p. 91.

16 Vincent Comerford, "Political Myths in Modern Ireland", in The Princess Grace Irish Library (ed.), *Irishness in a Changing Society*, (Gerrards Cross, Colin Smythe, 1988), 2, pp. 6–7.

17 J.C. Beckett, *Confrontations: Studies in Irish History*, (London: Faber & Faber, 1972) p. 150.

18 Ibid. p. 16.

19 R.F. Foster, *Modern Ireland. 1600–1972*, p. 461.

20 F.X. Martin, "1916. Revolution or Evolution?", in F.X. Martin (ed.), *Leaders and Men of the Easter Rising: Dublin 1916*, (London: Methuen, 1967), p. 249.

21 Tom Garvin, *Nationalist Revolutionaries in Ireland. 1858–1928*, (Oxford: Clarendon, 1987), p. 6.

22 Ibid. pp. 3–4.

23 Ibid. p. 4.

24 F.X. Martin, "1916. Revolution or Evolution?", in *Leaders and Men of the Easter Rising*, p. 248.

25 Nicholas Mansergh, "The Unionist Party and The Union. 1886–1916", in *Leaders and Men of the Easter Rising*, p. 83.

26 Ibid. p. 88.

27 François Furet, *Penser la Révolution française*, p. 49.

28 Oliver MacDonagh, *Ireland: The Union and its Aftermath*, p. 15.

29 P.S. O'Hegarty, *A History of Ireland under the Union*, p. 4.

30 George Boyce, *Nationalism in Ireland*, p. 313.

31 Oliver MacDonagh, *Ireland: The Union and its Aftermath*, p. 18.

32 R.F. Foster, *Paddy and Mr Punch. Connections in Irish and English History*, p. 91.

33 François Furet, *Penser la Révolution française*, pp. 33, 45.

34 Kate Soper, *Humanism and Anti-Humanism. Problems of Modern European Thought*, (London: Hutchinson & Co, 1986), p. 140.

35 Seamus Deane, *Strange Country. Modernity and Nationhood in Irish Writing since 1790*, (Oxford: Clarendon, 1997), p. 193.

11 The concept of totalitarianism: comparison and its pitfalls

1 François Furet, *Le passé d'une illusion. Essai sur l'idée communiste au XXème siècle*, (Paris: Robert Laffont/Calmann-Lévy, 1995), p. 192.

2 Hannah Arendt, *The Origins of Totalitarianism*, (New York: Harcourt Brace & Co., 1951).
3 R.F. Foster, "Anglo-Irish Relations and Northern Ireland: Historical Perspectives", in Dermot Keogh (ed.), *Northern Ireland and the Politics of Reconciliation*, (Cambridge: CUP, 1993), p. 14.
4 R.F. Foster, "We are all Revisionists Now", *Irish Review*, 1, 1986, p. 2.
5 Ronan Fanning, "The Meaning of Revisionism", *Irish Review*, 24 September 1987, p. 16.
6 François Furet, Ernst Nolte, *Fascisme et Communisme*, (Paris: Hachette, 1998), p. 17.
7 Ernst Nolte, *Marxismus und Insdustrielle Revolution*, (Stuttgart: Klett-Cotta, 1983), cited in Charles S. Maier, *The Unmasterable Past. History, Holocaust, and German National Identity*, (Harvard: Harvard University Press, 1997), p. 27.
8 Ernst Nolte, "The past that will not pass away", cited in Charles S. Maier, *The Unmasterable Past*, p. 30.
9 François Furet, Ernst Nolte, *Fascisme et Communisme*, p. 37.
10 Ibid.
11 Charles S. Maier, *The Unmasterable Past*, p. 69.
12 David Irving is the author of numerous books about the Second World War, and especially the Third Reich. In 1977, in his book *Hitler's War*, he argued that Hitler knew nothing about the extermination of the Jews, and he gradually became convinced that no such exterminations at all occurred in the concentration camps.
13 Robert Faurisson was professor of French literature at the University of Lyons-2 from 1974 until 1990. He wrote various articles for *The Journal of Historical Review* in which he denied the existence of homicidal gas chambers in Nazi concentration camps and questioned whether there was a systematic killing of European Jews using gas during the Second World War.
14 Michael Oakeshott, *Experience and Its Modes*, (Cambridge: CUP, 1933, 1966, 1978), pp. 167–8.
15 Anthony Coughlan, "Ireland's Marxist Historians", in *Interpreting Irish History*, pp. 300–1.
16 Paul Bew, Henry Patterson, Peter Gibbon, *The State in Northern Ireland. 1921–1972. Political Forces and Social Classes*, (Manchester: MUP, 1979), p. 1.
17 James Connolly, "A Plea for Socialist Unity in Ireland", in *The Connolly–Walker Controversy*, (Cork: Cork Workers' Club, 1974), p. 1.
18 James Connolly, "Sweat Shops Behind the Orange Flag", in *The Workers' Republic. A Selection from the Writings of James Connolly*, edited by Desmond Ryan, (Dublin: At the Sign of the Three Candles, 1951), p. 96.
19 Roger Simon, *Gramsci's Political Thought*, (London: Lawrence & Wishart, 1982), p. 12.
20 Ibid. pp. 13–15.
21 Ibid. p. 22.
22 James Connolly, "A Forgotten Chapter of Irish History", in *Ireland upon the Dissecting Table. James Connolly on Ulster and Partition*, (Cork: Cork Workers' Club, 1975), p. 45.
23 Karl Marx, Frederick Engels, *Collected Works*, (London: Lawrence & Wishart, 1976), Vol. 5, p. 37.
24 Karl Marx, *Idéologie allemande*, Vol. I, p. 153. Cited in Roland Barthes, *Mythologies*, (Paris: Seuil, 1957), p. 229.
25 Bew, Patterson, Gibbon, *The State in Northern Ireland. 1921–1972*, p. 9.
26 Bew, Patterson, Gibbon, *Northern Ireland. 1921–1996. Political Forces and Social Classes*, (London: Serif, 1996), p. 25.

27 James Connolly, "July the 12th", in *Ireland upon the Dissecting Table*, p. 37.
28 Bew, Patterson, Gibbon, *Northern Ireland. 1921–1996*, p. 47.
29 Ibid. p. 18.
30 Ibid. p. 55.
31 Eamonn McCann, *War and an Irish Town*, (London: Pluto Press, New Edition, 1993), p. 293.
32 Austen Morgan, Bob Purdie (eds), *Ireland: Divided Nation/Divided Class*, (London: Ink Links, 1980), pp. 8–9.
33 Bew, Gibbon, Patterson, *Northern Ireland: 1921–1996*, p. 46.
34 Ibid. p. 47.
35 Ibid. p. 46.
36 Ted Benton, *The Rise and Fall of Structural Marxism. Althusser and his Influence*, (London: Macmillan, 1984), p. 15.
37 Bew, Patterson, Gibbon, *Northern Ireland: 1921–1996*, p. 38.

12 Revision, deconstruction, semiology: similar methods?

1 Jean-François Lyotard, *The Postmodern Explained to Children*, (London: Turn-around, 1992), pp. 91–2.
2 F.R. Ankersmit, "Historiography and Postmodernism", *History and Theory*, Vol. XXVIII, No. 2, 1989, p. 146.
3 Julia Kristeva, *Théorie d'ensemble. Foucault, Barthes, Derrida*, (Paris: Edition du Seuil, 1968), pp. 84–5.
4 François Furet, *Penser la Révolution française*, p. 28.
5 Alan Finlayson, "Re-conceptualising the political in Northern Ireland: A Response to Arthur Aughey", *Irish Political Studies*, No. 13, 1998, p. 121.
6 Conor Cruise O'Brien, *Writers and Politics*, (London: Chatto & Windus, 1965), pp. xx–xxii.
7 Donal Harman Akenson, *Conor: A Biography*, (Canada: McGill-Queen's University Press, 1994), p. 471.
8 Roland Barthes, *Mythologies*, (Paris: Editions du Seuil, 1957), pp. 193–246.
9 T.W. Moody, "Irish History and Irish Mythology", in *Interpreting Irish History*, pp. 85–6.
10 Robert Ballagh, *Irish Times*, 21 May 2001.
11 Brian Walker, *Dancing to History's Tune History. Myth and Politics in Ireland*, (Belfast: Institute of Irish Studies, 1996), pp. 5–6.
12 J.C. Beckett, *The Making of Modern Ireland. 1603–1923*, (London: Faber & Faber, 1966).
13 R.F. Foster, *Modern Ireland. 1600–1972*, p. 446.
14 Tom Garvin, *Nationalist Revolutionaries in Ireland. 1858–1928*, p. 124.
15 Roland Barthes, *Mythologies*, p. 225.
16 David Fitzpatrick, *Politics and Irish Life 1913–1921*.
17 Michael Laffan, "Labour must Wait", in *Radicals, Rebels and Establishments*, Historical Studies No. XV, pp. 203–22.
18 Charles Townshend, "Modernization and Nationalism: Perspectives in Recent Irish History", *History: The Journal of the Historical Association*, Vol. 66, No. 217, June 1981, p. 241.
19 David Fitzpatrick, *Politics and Irish Life 1913–1921*, p. 104.
20 Michael Laffan, "Labour must Wait" in *Radicals, Rebels and Establishments*, Historical Studies No. XV, p. 205.
21 Ibid. p. 228.
22 Julia Kristeva, *L'avenir d'une révolte*, (Paris: Calmann-Lévy, 1998), pp. 19–20.
23 Roland Barthes, "Historical Discourse", in Michael Lane (ed.), *Structuralism: A Reader*, (London: Cape, 1970), pp. 145–55.

24 T.W. Moody, Leon O Broin, "The I.R.B. Supreme Council, 1868–78", *Irish Historical Studies*, Vol. 19, No. 75, 1975, p. 314.
25 Maureen Wall, "Plans and Countermand", in Kevin B. Nowlan (ed.), *The Making of 1916: Studies in the History of the Rising*, (Dublin: Stationery Office, 1969), pp. 169–71.
26 F.X. Martin, "Select Documents", *Irish Historical Studies*, Vol. 12, No. 47, March 1961, p. 228.
27 Paul Bew, "The Easter Rising: Lost Leaders and Lost Opportunities", *Irish Review*, No. 11, Winter 1991/1992, pp. 9, 13.
28 R.F. Foster, "Historical Perspectives", in *Northern Ireland and The Politics of Reconciliation*, pp. 28–9.
29 Conor Cruise O'Brien, *Herod: Reflections on Political Violence*, (London: Hutchinson & Co, 1978), p. 12.
30 Claude Lévesque, Christie V. McDonald, *L'oreille de l'autre. Otobiographies, transferts, traductions. Textes et débats avec Jacques Derrida*, (Québec: VLB éditeur, 1988), p. 118.
31 Richard Kearney, "Postmodernity, Nationalism and Ireland", Paper to the Second International Conference of History of European Ideas, (Leuven: Leuven University Press, September 1991).
32 Conor Cruise O'Brien, *The Great Melody*, pp. 603–4.
33 Donald Harman Akenson, *Conor. A Biography*, p. 290.
34 John A. Murphy, "Further Reflections on Irish Nationalism", *Crane Bag*, Vol. 2, No. 1 & 2, 1978, pp. 156–63.
35 John A Murphy, "Easter 1916 – the View from 1984", *Sunday Independent*, 22 April 1984.
36 Conor Cruise O'Brien, *Memoir. My Life and Themes*, (Dublin: Poolbeg, 1998), pp. 446–7.
37 Conor Cruise O'Brien, "Holy War", *New York Review of Books*, Vol. 13, No. 8, 6 November 1969, pp. 9–16.
38 John A. Murphy, "Further Reflections on Irish Nationalism", p. 159.
39 Conor Cruise O'Brien, *Camus*, (Glasgow: Fontana Modern Masters, 1970), p. 85. Originally published under the title "Camus, Algeria, and The Fall", in *The New York Review of Books*, Vol. 13, No. 6, 9 October 1969.
40 Donald Harman Akenson, *Conor: A Biography*, p. 360.
41 Frantz Fanon, *Peau noire, masques blancs*, (Paris: Editions du Seuil, 1952), pp. 185–8.
42 Declan Kiberd, *Inventing Ireland*, (London: Jonathan Cape, 1995), p. 559.
43 Conor Cruise O'Brien, "Violence in Ireland: Another Algeria?", *The New York Review of Books*, Vol. 17, No. 4, 23 September 1971. The differences between Algeria and Northern Ireland were listed as follows in O'Brien's article: Even if all Ireland is taken as the Unit, the Protestants constitute a much larger minority, more than twice as large as did the Europeans of Algeria. They are also more compact. They constitute a clear majority in the Eastern part of Northern Ireland, whereas Europeans did not form a majority in any city of Algeria. O'Brien advanced also the interesting argument that there was not the same emotional solidarity among Irish Catholics generally (embracing North and South) as there was among Algerian Moslems generally, preceding the independence of Algeria and the capitulation of the *colons*. It is an argument that O'Brien seems to have dropped because later he comes to describe the Irish Catholics increasingly in monolithic terms. Finally the Protestants as a community are very much older. The colonization of Ulster began at the beginning of the seventeenth century, that of Algeria only toward the middle of the nineteenth century.
44 Ibid.

45 Conor Cruise O'Brien, *God Land. Reflections on Religion and Nationalism*, (Cambridge, MA: Harvard University Press, 1988), p. 9.

46 Hannah Arendt, "Ideology and Terror: A Novel Form of Government", in Lee A. Jacobus (ed.), *A World of Ideas*, (New York: Bedford/Saint Martin's Press, LLC, 1953).

47 Donald Harman Akenson, *Conor: A Biography*, p. 360.

48 Conor Cruise O'Brien, *States of Ireland*, (London: Hutchinson, 1972), p. 149.

49 David D. Brien, "François Furet, the Terror, and 1789", *French Historical Studies*, Vol. 16, No. 4, Autumn 1990, pp. 777–83.

50 Conor Cruise O'Brien, *Writers and Politics*, (London: Chatto & Windus, 1965), p. 92.

51 R.F. Foster, *Modern Ireland: 1600–1972*, p. 454.

52 Declan Kiberd, "The Elephant of Revolutionary Forgetfulness", in *Revising the Rising*, (Derry: Field Day, 1991) p. 8, or in *Inventing Ireland*, p. 559.

53 Ernest Gellner, *Nations et Nationalisme*, (Paris: Payot, 1989), p. 86.

54 R.F. Foster, *Paddy & Mr Punch*, p. 81.

55 Roy Foster, "Historical Perspectives", in *Northern Ireland and the Politics of Reconciliation*, pp. 31–2.

56 Michael Laffan, "The Sacred Memory", in Judith Devlin, Ronan Fanning (eds), *Religion and Rebellion*, Historical Studies No. XX, (Dublin: University College Dublin Press, 1997), p. 185.

57 R.F. Foster, "We are all Revisionists Now!", *Irish Review*, No. 1, 1986, p. 3.

58 Jacques Derrida, *L'écriture et la différence*, (Paris: Editions du Seuil, 1967), p. 427.

13 Relativism and its opponents

1 Daltun O Ceallaigh (ed.), *Reconsiderations of Irish history and Culture*, (Dublin: Léirmheas, 1994), p. 15.

2 Tom Dunne, "New Histories: Beyond Revisionism", *Irish Review*, No. 12, 1992, p. 8.

3 Ibid.

4 R.F. Foster, *Paddy and Mr Punch*, p. 85.

5 Richard J. Evans, *In Defence of History*, (London: Granta Books, 2nd edn, 2000), p. 232.

6 Jacques Derrida, *Writing and Difference*, (London: Routledge, 2001), pp. 1–2.

7 Vincent Comerford, "Political Myths in Modern Ireland", in *Irishness in a Changing Society*, p. 2.

8 Yves Boisvert, *L'analyse postmoderniste: Une nouvelle grille d'analyse socio-politique*, (Paris: L'harmattan, 1997), p. 45.

9 Seamus Deane, "Wherever Green is Read", in *Interpreting Irish History*, p. 242.

10 Richard Kearney, "The Transitional Crisis of Modern Irish Culture", in *Irishness in a Changing Society*, p. 90.

11 Ibid. p. 60.

12 Daltun O Ceallaigh, *Reconsiderations of Irish history and culture*, p. 25.

13 Seamus Deane, *Strange Country. Modernity and Nationhood in Irish Writing since 1790*, (Oxford: Clarendon, 1997), p. 18.

14 Herbert Butterfield, *The Englishman and his History*, p. 2.

15 Herbert Butterfield, *The Whig Interpretation of History*, p. 30.

16 Ibid. p. 96.

17 Ibid. p. 25.

18 Michel de Certeau, *The Writing of History*, (New York: Columbia University Press, 1988), p. 69.

19 Yves Boisvert, *L'analyse postmoderniste*, p. 60.

20 Willy Maley, "Nationalism and Revisionism: Ambiviolences and Dissensus", in *Ireland in Proximity*, p. 17.
21 Seamus Deane, "Wherever Green is Read", in *Interpreting Irish History*, p. 241.
22 Ciaran Brady, "'Constructive and Instrumental': The Dilemma of Ireland's First 'New Historians'", in *Interpreting Irish History*, p. 16.
23 Edward Shils, Henry Finch, *The Methodology of the Social Sciences*, (New York: Free Press, 1949), p. 66.
24 Max Weber, "The Profession and Vocation of Politics", in Peter Lassman, Ronald Speirs (eds), *Weber: Political Writings*, (Cambridge: CUP, 1994), p. 367.
25 Anthony Giddens, "Weber and Durkheim: Coincidence and Divergence", in Wolfgang J. Mommsen, Jürgen Osterhammel (eds), *Max Weber and his Contemporaries*, (London: The German Historical Institute/Allen & Unwin, 1987), p. 188.
26 Hiram Morgan, "'A Scholar and a Gentleman', Interview of A.T.Q. Stewart", *History Ireland*, Vol. 1, No. 2, Summer 1993.
27 Thomas O'Loughlin, "Interview of Margaret MacCurtain", *History Ireland*, Vol. 2, No. 1, Spring 1994, p. 54.
28 R.D. Edwards, UCDA. File LA 22/117 (176): Published in 1956. Vol. 1, No. 1, May 1971.

14 The problematic of ends and means

1 R.D. Edwards, "A Frightened World", *The Leader*, Vol. 58, No. 8, 19 April 1958.
2 Albert Camus, *The Rebel*, (London: Penguin, 1971), p. 112.
3 R.A. Breathnach, Letters to the Editor, *Irish Times*, 19 January 1957.
4 Conor Cruise O'Brien, "The Embers of Easter", in *1916: The Easter Rising*, pp. 231–4.
5 Conor Cruise O'Brien, *Memoir. My Life and Themes*, pp. 140–8.
6 Ibid. p. 146.
7 Ronan Fanning, "'The Great Enchantment': Uses and Abuses of Modern Irish History", in *Interpreting Irish History*, p. 146.
8 Edna Longley, *The Living Stream: Literature and Revisionism in Ireland*, (Newcastle upon Tyne: Bloodaxe Books, 1994), p. 10.
9 F.X. Martin, "1916 – Myth, Fact and Mystery", *Studia Hibernica*, No. 7, 1967, p. 19.
10 Frank Burton, *The Politics of Legitimacy: Struggles in a Belfast Community*, (London: Routledge & Kegan Paul, 1978), p. 157.
11 Cited in Yves Boisvert, *L'analyse Postmoderniste*, p. 68.
12 F.S.L. Lyons, *Culture and Anarchy in Ireland. 1890–1939*, p. 177.
13 R.F. Foster, "Varieties of Irishness", in Maurna Crozier (ed.), *Cultural Traditions in Northern Ireland*, (Belfast: Institute of Irish Studies, 1989), p. 19.
14 F.S.L. Lyons, *Culture and Anarchy. 1890–1939*, p. 2.
15 Jean-François Lyotard, *Libidinal Economy*, (London: Athlone Press, 1993), pp. 20, 31, 32.
16 John Wilson Foster, "Strains in Irish Intellectual Life", in Liam O'Dowd (ed.), *On Intellectuals and Intellectual Life in Ireland*, p. 78.
17 R.F. Foster, "Varieties of Irishness" in *Cultural Traditions in Northern Ireland*, p. 6, 17.
18 Jean-François Lyotard, *Political Writings*, (London: University College London Press, 1993), p. 199.
19 John Whyte, *Interpreting Northern Ireland*, (Oxford: Clarendon, 1990), p. 203.
20 F.S.L. Lyons, *Culture and Anarchy. 1890–1939*, p. 54.

21 W.B. Yeats, *Autobiographies*, (London: Macmillan & Co., 1955), p. 559.
22 R.F. Foster, "Varieties of Irishness", in *Cultural Traditions in Northern Ireland*, p. 7.
23 W.B. Yeats, *Autobiographies*, p. 199.
24 R.F. Foster, *The Irish Story. Telling Tales and Making it up in Ireland*, p. 39.
25 Ronan Fanning, "'The Great Enchantment': Uses and Abuses of Modern Irish History", in *Interpreting Irish History*, p. 155.

15 Grappling with the problem of objectivity

1 François Furet, *Penser la Révolution française*, pp. 26–7.
2 Jeff Collins, Bill Mayblin, *Introducing Derrida*, (New York: Totem Books, 1997), p. 96.
3 Jacques Derrida, *Writing and Difference*, p. 356.
4 Jeff Collins, Bill Mayblin, *Introducing Derrida*, p. 100.
5 Claude Lévi-Strauss, *La pensée sauvage*, (Paris: Librairie Plon, 1962), p. 339.
6 Willy Maley, "Nationalism and Revisionism: Ambiviolences and Dissensus", in *Ireland in Proximity*, p. 21.
7 Ibid. p. 17.
8 R.F. Foster, *Paddy and Mr Punch*, p. 21.
9 Richard Kirkland, *Literature and Culture in Northern Ireland since 1965: Moments of Danger*, (London: Longman, 1996), p. 90.
10 Edna Longley, "Belfast Diary", *London Review of Books*, No. 14/1, 9 January 1992, p. 21.
11 Edna Longley, *Poetry in the Wars*, (Newcastle upon Tyne: Bloodaxe Books, 1986), p. 10.
12 Ibid. p. 197.
13 Ibid. p. 193.
14 Richard Kirkland, *Literature and Culture in Northern Ireland since 1965*, p. 97.
15 Edna Longley, "Opening Up: A New Pluralism", *Fortnight*, No. 256, November 1987, p. 25.
16 R.F. Foster, "We Are All Revisionists Now", *Irish Review*, No. 1, 1986, p. 5.
17 This expression is borrowed from Paul Ricoeur, *Freud and Philosophy: An Essay on Interpretation*, (New Haven: Yale University Press, 1970). See, for example, the section entitled "Interpretation as Exercise of Suspicion" in Book I, section 2, *Freud and Philosophy*, pp. 32–6. Defining Freud's "reality principle" and "its equivalents in Nietzsche and Marx", Ricoeur concludes: "Over against illusion and the fable-making function, demystifying hermeneutics sets up the rude discipline of necessity", (p. 35).
18 Seamus Deane, "Wherever Green is Read", in *Revising the Rising*, p. 101.
19 Tommy Graham, "A Man with a Mission: Interview with Brendan Bradshaw", *History Ireland*, Vol. 1, No. 1, 1993, p. 53.
20 E.P. Thompson, *The Poverty of Theory and Other Essays*, (London: Merlin Press, 1978), p. 303.
21 Seamus Deane, "Wherever Green is Read", in *Revising the Rising*, p. 101.
22 Alvin Jackson, "J.C. Beckett: Politics, Faith, Scholarship", *Irish Historical Studies*, Vol. XXXIII, No. 130, November 2002, p. 145.
23 F.S.L. Lyons, "The Dilemma of the Irish Contemporary Historian", *Hermathena*, No. CXV, Summer 1973, p. 49.
24 Ibid. p. 58.
25 Ibid. p. 54.
26 Ibid. p. 54.
27 R.F. Foster, *Paddy and Mr Punch*, p. XV.
28 Ciaran Brady (ed.), *Ideology and the Historians*, Historical Studies No. XVII, (Dublin: The Lilliput Press, 1991), p. 6.

29 Geoffrey Elton, *Return to Essentials*, (Cambridge: CUP, 1991), p. 26.
30 Geoffrey Elton, *The Practice of History*, (London: Fontana, 1969), p. 73.
31 Ibid. p. 73.
32 Ibid. p. 74.
33 R.D. Edwards, UCDA. File LA 22/1276.
34 Ciaran Brady (ed.), *Ideology and the Historians*, p. 7.
35 Seamus Deane, "General Introduction", *Field Day Anthology*, Vol. I, (Derry: Field Day, 1989), p. XIX.
36 Field Day was originally the name given to a Theatre Company founded by Stephen Rea and Brian Friel in 1980 in Derry. The Company's first production, the world premiere of Friel's *Translations*, was presented at the Guildhall in Derry in September 1980. With the addition to the board of directors of poets and critics such as Tom Paulin, Seamus Heaney and Seamus Deane, Field Day adopted a more openly political language and articulated its sensibility in a con-troversial pamphlet series. It was an attempt by a group of distinguished Irish artists to define the Northern Irish conflict in a particular way and contribute to its resolution.
37 Edna Longley, *The Living Stream: Literature and Revisionism in Ireland*, p. 28.
38 Ibid. p. 30.
39 J.J. Lee, *Ireland 1912–1985*, p. 627.
40 E.P. Thompson, *The Poverty of Theory and Other Essays*, p. IV.
41 Andrée Sheehy Skeffington, *Skeff. A Life of Owen Sheehy Skeffington*, (Dublin: The Lilliput Press, 1991), p. 223.
42 Luke Gibbons, "Challenging the Canon: Revisionism and Cultural Criticism", in Seamus Deane (ed.), *The Field Day Anthology of Irish Writing*, Vol. III, p. 567.
43 Ciaran Brady, " 'Constructive and Instrumental': The Dilemma of Ireland's First 'New Historians' ", in *Interpreting Irish History*, p. 28.
44 Stephen Howe, *Ireland and Empire. Colonial Legacies in Irish History and Culture*, p. 128.
45 *Free Thought in Ireland*, Supplement to *Fortnight*, No. 297, July 1991, pp. 17–18.
46 Alain Finkielkraut, *L'avenir d'une négation. Redflexion sur la question du génocide*, (Paris: Editions du Seuil, 1982), p. 14.
47 F.S.L. Lyons, "The Burden of Our History", in *Interpreting Irish History*, p. 88.
48 Conor Cruise O'Brien, *Maria Cross: Imaginative Patterns in a Group of Modern Catholic Writers*, (London: Chatto and Windus, 1953).
49 Aidan Clarke, "Robert Dudley Edwards. 1909–1988", *Irish Historical Studies*, Vol. XXVI, No. 102, November 1988, p. 126.
50 Pieter Geyl (ed.), "Ranke in the Light of the Catastrophe", in *Debates with Historians*, (The Hague: Wolters, 1955), p. 7.
51 Tom Dunne (ed.), *The Writer As Witness: Literature as Historical Evidence*, Histor-ical Studies, No. XVI, (Cork: Cork University Press, 1987), pp. 2–4.
52 Hayden White, *Tropics of Discourse*, (Baltimore: Johns Hopkins University Press, 1978), p. 99.
53 R.F. Foster, *The Irish Story. Telling Tales and Making it up in Ireland*, p. xix.
54 R.F. Foster, *The Story of Ireland*, (Oxford: Clarendon, 1995), pp. 29–30.
55 R.F. Foster, *The Irish Story. Telling Tales and Making it up in Ireland*, p. xi.
56 Ibid. p. 4.

Conclusion

1 Joseph Lee, *Ireland 1912–85*, p. 589.
2 Jacques Derrida, *Specters of Marx*, pp. 88, 92, 91.

3 Richard Kearney, *Dialogues with Contemporary Continental Thinkers*, p. 118.

4 Edna Longley, *The Living Stream: Literature and Revisionism in Ireland*, p. 67.

5 John Wilson Foster, *Colonial Consequences: Essays in Irish Literature and Culture*, (Dublin: The Lilliput Press, 1991), p. 271.

6 Albert Memmi, *Portrait du colonisateur et du colonisé*, pp. 159–60.

7 Steven G. Ellis, "Representations of the Past in Ireland: Whose Past and Whose Present?", *Irish Historical Studies*, Vol. 27, No. 108, 1991, p. 294.

8 Conor Cruise O'Brien, "An Unhealthy Intersection", *Irish Times*, 21 August 1975, p. 10.

9 Brendan Bradshaw, "Nationalism", *Irish Historical Studies*, Vol. 26, No. 104, p. 349.

10 Edna Longley, *The Living Stream: Literature and Revisionism in Ireland*, p. 181.

11 Donald Harman Akenson, *If the Irish Ran the World: Montserrat 1630–1730*, (Liverpool: Liverpool University Press, 1997), pp. 174–5.

12 R.F. Foster, *The Irish Story. Telling Tales and Making it up in Ireland*, p. xiv.

13 George Boyce, Alan O'Day, *The Making of Modern Irish History. Revisionism and the Revisionist Controversy*, p. 4.

14 Peter Novick, *That Noble Dream: The "Objectivity Question" and the American Historical Profession*, p. 543.

15 E.P. Thompson, *The Poverty of Theory and Other Essays*, pp. 32–3.

16 Alain Finkielkraut, *La défaite de la pensée*, p. 97.

Bibliography

Manuscript sources

National Archives of Ireland, Dublin (NAD)
Department of an Taoiseach Files: S. 13081

University College Dublin Archives (UCDA)
Files LA 1: Eoin MacNeill
Files LA 22: Robert Dudley Edwards
Files LA 30: Michael Tierney

Trinity College Dublin Archives (TCDA)
Files 10048/BMH/90/2 Files 8555/59/79–155: Theodore William Moody
Ms. 2452: Edmund Curtis

National Library Archives (NLA)
Ms. 31, 289, Ms. 31, 352, Ms. 31, 355: Florence O' Donoghue

Military Archives Dublin (MAD)
Files S. 1779/Files S. 1860

Cambridge University Archives (CUA)
File 130/File 131/File 531 File Butt 57/3: Herbert Butterfield

Primary and secondary sources

Books

Akenson, Donald Harman, *Conor: A Biography of Conor Cruise O'Brien* (Montreal: McGill-Queen's University Press, 1994)
Akenson, Donald Harman, *If the Irish Ran the World: Montserrat 1630–1730* (Liverpool: Liverpool University Press, 1997)
Anderson, Benedict, *Imagined Communities: Reflections on the Origin and Spread of Nationalism* (London: Verso, 1991)

Appleby, Joyce, Hunt, Lynn, Jacob, Margaret, *Telling the Truth About History* (New York: Norton, 1994)

Arendt, Hannah, *The Origins of Totalitarianism* (New York: Harcourt Brace & Co., 1951)

Arendt, Hannah, "Ideology and Terror: A New Form of Government" in Jacobus, Lee. A., *A World of Ideas* (New York: Bedford/Saint Martin's Press, LLC, 1998)

Aron, Raymond, *Introduction à la philosophie de l'histoire. Essai sur les limites de l'objectivité historique* (Paris: first edition 1938, re-edition Gallimard 1986)

Backès-Clément, Catherine, *Lévi-Strauss ou la structure et le malheur* (Paris: Seghers, 1970)

Barraclough, Geoffrey, *History in a Changing World* (Oxford: Basil Blackwell, 1957)

Barraclough, Geoffrey, "German Unification. An Essay in Revision" in Hayes-McCoy, G.A. (ed.), *Historical Studies* No. IV (London: Bowes and Bowes, 1962)

Barthes, Roland, *Mythologies* (Paris: Editions du Seuil, 1957)

Barthes, Roland, "Historical Discourse" in Lane, Michael (ed.), *Structuralism: A Reader* (London: Cape, 1970)

Bartlett, Thomas, *The Fall and Rise of the Irish Nation: The Catholic Question. 1690–1830* (Dublin: Gill & Macmillan, 1992)

Beckett, J.C., *The Making of Modern Ireland. 1603–1923* (London: Faber & Faber, 1966)

Beckett, J.C., *Confrontations: Studies in Irish History* (London: Faber & Faber, 1972)

Bennett, Richard, *The Black and Tans* (Boston: Houghton Mifflin, 1959, 1960)

Bentley, Michael (ed.), *Companion to Historiography* (London: Routledge, 1997)

Benton, Ted, *The Rise and Fall of Structural Marxism. Althusser and his Influence* (London: Macmillan, 1984)

Bew, Paul, Patterson, Henry, Gibbon, Peter, *The State in Northern Ireland. 1921–1972. Political Forces and Social Classes* (Manchester: Manchester University Press, 1979)

Bew, Paul, Patterson, Henry, Gibbon, Peter, *Northern Ireland 1921–1996. Political Forces and Social Classes* Revised and Updated New Edition (London: Serif, 1996)

Bhabha, Homi, *The Location of Culture* (London: Routledge, 1994)

Bhabha, Homi, "Remembering Fanon: Self, Psyche and The Colonial Condition", in Williams, P., Chrisman L. (eds), *Colonial Discourse and Postcolonial Theory: A Reader* (New York: Columbia University Press, 1994)

Blanchot, Maurice, *Les intellectuels en question. Ebauche d'une réflexion* (Paris: Fourbis, 1996)

Bloch, Marc, "Pour une histoire comparée des sociétés européennes", in *Mélanges Historiques* (Paris: S.E.V.P.E.N., 1963)

Boisvert, Yves, *L'analyse postmoderniste: Une nouvelle grille d'analyse socio-politique* (Paris: L'harmattan, 1997)

Bowman, John, *De Valera and the Ulster Question: 1917–1973* (Oxford: Oxford University Press, 1989)

Boyce, George, *Nineteenth-Century Ireland. The Search for Stability* (Dublin: Gill & Macmillan, 1990)

Boyce, George, *Nationalism in Ireland* (London: Routledge, 1995)

Boyce, George, O'Day, Alan (eds), *The Making of Modern Irish History: Revisionism and the Revisionist Controversy* (London: Routledge, 1996)

Brady, Ciaran (ed.), *Ideology and the Historians*, *Historical Studies* No. XVII (Dublin: The Lilliput Press, 1991)

Brady, Ciaran (ed.), *Interpreting Irish History. The Debate on Historical Revisionism* (Dublin: Irish Academic Press, 1994)

Brewster, Scott, Crossman, Virginia (eds), *Ireland in Proximity. History, Gender, Space* (London: Routledge, 1999)

Brown, Terence, *Ireland: A Social and Cultural History. 1922–85* (London: Fontana, 1985)

Burton, Frank, *The Politics of Legitimacy: Struggles in a Belfast Community* (London: Routledge and Kegan Paul, 1978)

Butterfield, Herbert, *The Englishman and his History* (Cambridge: Cambridge University Press, 1944)

Butterfield, Herbert, *Christianity and History* (London: G. Bell & Sons, 1950)

Butterfield, Herbert, *George III and the Historians* (London: Collins Clear-Type Press, 1957)

Butterfield, Herbert, *The Whig Interpretation of History* (New York: The Norton Library, 1965)

Camus, Albert, *The Rebel* (London: Penguin, 1971)

Colley, Linda, *Lewis Namier: A Biography* (London: Weidenfeld and Nicolson, 1989)

Collins, Jeff, Mayblin, Bill, *Introducing Derrida* (New York: Totem Books, 1997)

Comerford, Vincent, "Political Myths in Modern Ireland" in The Princess Grace Irish Library (ed.), *Irishness in a Changing Society* (Gerrards Cross: Colin Smythe, 1988)

Comerford, R. Vincent, *Inventing the Nation: Ireland* (London: Hodder Arnold, 2003)

Connolly, James, *Socialism and Nationalism. A Selection from the Writings of James Connolly*, Introduction by Ryan, Desmond (Dublin: At the Sign of the Three Candles, 1948)

Connolly, James, *The Workers' Republic. A Selection from the Writings of James Connolly* Edited by Ryan, Desmond (Dublin: At the Sign of the Three Candles, 1951)

Connolly, James, *The Connolly-Walker Controversy* (Cork: Cork Workers' Club, 1974)

Connolly, James, *Ireland upon the Dissecting Table. James Connolly on Ulster and Partition* (Cork: Cork Workers' Club, 1975)

Connolly, Sean, *Religion, Law, and Power: The Making of Protestant Ireland, 1660–1760* (Oxford: Clarendon Press, 1992)

Connolly, S.J., *Political Ideas in Eighteenth-Century Ireland* (Dublin: Four Courts Press, 2000)

Corkery, Daniel, *The Hidden Ireland: A Story of Gaelic Munster in the 18th Century* (Dublin: Gill & Macmillan, 1967)

Cronin, Sean, *Irish Nationalism. A History of its Roots and Ideology* (Dublin: The Academy Press, 1980)

Cullen, L.M., "The 1798 Rebellion in Wexford: United Irish Organization, Membership, Leadership", in Kevin Whelan (ed.), *Wexford: History and Society* (Dublin: Geography Publications, 1987)

Cullen, L.M., *The Hidden Ireland: Reassessment of a Concept. Essays and Texts in Irish Cultural History* (Westmeath: The Lilliput Press, 1988)

Daly, Mary, *The Famine in Ireland* (Dublin: Dundalgan Press, 1986)

Deane, Seamus, *Celtic Revivals: Essays in Modern Irish Literature. 1880–1980* (London: Faber & Faber, 1985)

Deane, Seamus (ed.), *The Field Day Anthology of Irish Writing* Vol. III (Derry: Field Day, 1991)

Deane, Seamus, *Strange Country. Modernity and Nationhood in Irish Writing since 1790* (Oxford: Clarendon Press, 1997)

De Certeau, Michel, *The Writing of History* (New York: Columbia University Press, 1988)

Derrida, Jacques, *L'écriture et la différence* (Paris: Editions du Seuil, 1967)

Derrida, Jacques, *Marges de la philosophie* (Paris: Minuit, 1972)

Derrida, Jacques, *Spectres of Marx. The State of the Debt, the Work of Mourning, and the New International* (London: Routledge, 1994)

Derrida, Jacques, *Writing and Difference* (London: Routledge, 2001)

Devlin, Judith, Fanning, Ronan (eds), *Religion and Rebellion, Historical Studies* No. XX (Dublin: University College Dublin Press, 1997)

Doherty, Gabriel, Keogh, Dermot (eds), *Michael Collins and the Making of the Irish State* (Dublin: Mercier Press, 1998)

Dolan, Ann, *Commemorating the Irish Civil War. History and Memory. 1923–2000* (Cambridge: Cambridge University Press, 2003)

Dorgan, Theo, Ni Dhonnchadha, Mairin (eds), *Revising the Rising* (Derry: Field Day, 1991)

Duffy, Charles Gavan, *Four Years of Irish History* (London: Cassell, Getter, Galpin, 1883)

Dunne, Tom, *Theobald Wolfe Tone; Colonial Outsider. An Analysis of his Political Philosophy* (Cork: Tower Books, 1982)

Dunne, Tom (ed.), *The Writer As Witness: Literature as Historical Evidence, Historical Studies* No. XVI (Cork: Cork University Press, 1987)

Dunne, Tom, "Maureen Wall (née McGeehin) (1918–1972): A Memoir" in O'Brien, Gerard (ed.), *Catholic Ireland in the 18th Century. Collected Essays of Maureen Wall* (Dublin: Geography Publications, 1989)

Eagleton, Terry (ed.), *Ideology* (London: Longman, 1994)

Eagleton, Terry, *Heathcliff and the Great Hunger. Studies in Irish Culture* (London: Verso, 1995)

Eagleton, Terry, *The Illusions of Postmodernism* (Oxford: Blackwell Publishers, 1996)

Eagleton, T., Jameson, F., Said, E., *Nationalism, Colonialism, and Literature* (Mineapolis: University of Minnesota Press, 1990)

Edwards, Owen Dudley, Pyle, Fergus (eds), *1916: The Easter Rising* (London: MacGibbon & Kee, 1968)

Edwards, Robert Dudley, Williams, T. Desmond (eds), *The Great Famine. Studies in Irish History. 1845–1852* (Dublin: The Lilliput Press, New Introduction by Cormac O Gráda, 1994)

Elliott, Marianne, *Wolfe Tone: Prophet of Irish Independence* (New Haven: Yale University Press, 1989)

Elton, Geoffrey, *The Practice of History* (London: Fontana, 1969)

Elton, Geoffrey, *Return to Essentials* (Cambridge: Cambridge University Press, 1991)

English, Richard, Skelly, Joseph Morrison (eds), *Ideas Matter. Essays in Honour of Conor Cruise O'Brien* (Dublin: Poolbeg Press, 1998)

Evans, Richard J., *Rituals of Retribution. Capital Punishment in Germany. 1600–1987* (Oxford: Oxford University Press, 1996)

Evans, Richard J., *In Defence of History* 2nd edn (London: Granta Books, 2000)

Fanning, Ronan, *Independent Ireland* (Dublin: Helicon, 1983)

Fanning, Ronan, *"The Four-Leaved Shamrock": Electoral Politics and the National Imagination in Independent Ireland* (Dublin: National University of Ireland, 1983)

Fanon, Frantz, *The Wretched of the Earth* (New York: Grove Press, 1963)

Fanon, Frantz, *Black Skin, White Masks* (New York: Grove Press, 1967)

Fennell, Desmond, *The Revision of Irish Nationalism* (Dublin: Open Air, 1989)

Finas, Lucette, Laporte, Roger (eds), *Ecarts. Quatre essais à propos de Jacques Derrida* (Paris: Editions Fayard. Digraphe, 1973)

Finkielkraut, Alain, *L'avenir d'une négation. Réflexion sur la question du génocide* (Paris: Editions du Seuil, 1982)

Finkielkraut, Alain, *La sagesse de l'amour,* (Paris: Gallimard, 1984)

Finkielkraut, Alain, *La défaite de la pensée* (Paris: Gallimard, 1987)

Finkielkraut, Alain, *L'humanité perdue. Essai sur le XXème siècle* (Paris: Editions du Seuil, 1996)

FitzGerald, Garret, *All in a Life. An Autobiography* (Dublin: Gill & Macmillan, 1991)

Fitzpatrick, David, *Politics and Irish Life 1913–1921. Provincial Experience of War and Revolution* (Dublin: Gill & Macmillan, 1977)

Foster, John Wilson, *Colonial Consequences: Essays in Irish Literature and Culture* (Dublin: The Lilliput Press, 1991)

Foster, R.F., *Modern Ireland. 1600–1972* (London: Allen Lane, Penguin, 1988)

Foster, R.F. (ed.), *The Oxford History of Ireland* (Oxford: Oxford University Press, 1989)

Foster, R.F., "Varieties of Irishness" in Crozier, Maurna (ed.), *Cultural Traditions in Northern Ireland* (Belfast: The Institute of Irish Studies, 1989)

Foster, R.F., "Anglo-Irish Relations and Northern Ireland: Historical Perspectives" in Keogh, Dermot, Haltzel, Michael (eds), *Northern Ireland and The Politics of Reconciliation* (Cambridge: Cambridge University Press, 1993)

Foster, R.F., *Paddy and Mr Punch. Connections in Irish and English History* (London: Penguin, 1995)

Foster, R.F., *The Irish Story: Telling Tales and Making it up in Ireland* (London: Allen Lane, Penguin, 2001)

Foucault, Michel, *L'archéologie du savoir* (Paris: Gallimard, 1969)

Foucault, Michel, "Nietzsche, la généalogie, l'histoire" in *Hommage à Jean Hyppolite* (Paris: Presses Universitaires Françaises, 1971)

Foucault, Michel, *Power/Knowledge. Selected Interviews and Other Writings. 1972–1977* Edited by Gordon, Colin (Brighton: The Harvester Press, 1980)

Franco, Paul, *The Political Philosophy of Michael Oakeshott* (New Haven: Yale University Press, 1990)

Froude, James Anthony, *The English in Ireland in the Eighteenth Century* III Volumes (London: Longmans, Green, and Co., 1872–74)

Furet, François, *Penser la Révolution française* (Paris: Gallimard, 1978)

Furet, François, *Le passé d'une illusion. Essai sur l'idée communiste au XXème siècle* (Paris: Robert Laffont/Calmann-Lévy, 1995)

Furet, François, Nolte, Ernst, *Fascisme et Communisme* (Paris: Hachette, 1998)

Gallagher, Frank, *The Anglo-Irish Treaty* (London: Hutchinson, 1965)

Gallagher, Thomas, *Paddy's Lament. 1846–1847. Prelude To Hatred* (Dublin: Word River Press, 1985)

Garvin, Tom, *Nationalist Revolutionaries in Ireland. 1858–1928* (Oxford: Clarendon Press, 1987)

Garvin, Tom, *1922: The Birth of Irish Democracy* (Dublin: Gill & Macmillan, 1996)

Gellner, Ernest, *Nations et nationalisme* (Paris: Payot, 1989)

Geyl, Pieter (ed.), "Ranke in the Light of the Catastrophe" in *Debates with Historians* (The Hague: Wolters, 1955)

Gibbons, Luke, "Challenging the Canon: Revisionism and Cultural Criticism" in Deane, Seamus (ed.), *The Field Day Anthology of Irish Writing* Vol. III (Derry: Field Day, 1991)

Gibbons, Luke, *Transformations in Irish Culture* (Cork: Cork University Press, 1996)

Giddens, Anthony, "Weber and Durkheim: Coincidence and Divergence" in Mommsen, Wolfgang J., Osterhammel, Jürgen (eds), *Max Weber and his Contemporaries* (London: The German Historical Institute/Allen & Unwin, 1987)

Goddard, Arthur (ed.), *Harry Elmer Barnes: Learned Crusader* (Colorado: Ralph Myles, 1968)

Goldring, Maurice, *Pleasant the Scholar's Life: Irish Intellectuals and the Construction of the Nation State* (London: Serif, 1993)

Hobsbawm, E.J., *Nations and Nationalism Since 1780. Programme, Myth, Reality* (Cambridge: Cambridge University Press, 1990)

Hoppen, Theodore K., *Ireland Since 1800: Conflict and Conformity* (London: Longman, 1989)

Howe, Stephen, *Ireland and Empire. Colonial legacies in Irish History and Culture* (Oxford: Oxford University Press, 2000)

Karakasidou, Anastasia N., *Fields of Wheat, Hills of Blood. Passages To Nationhood in Greek Macedonia, 1870–1990* (Chicago: University of Chicago Press, 1998)

Kearney, Richard, *Dialogues with Contemporary Continental Thinkers* (Manchester: Manchester University Press, 1987)

Kearney, Richard, "The Transitional Crisis of Modern Irish Culture" in The Princess Grace Irish Library (ed.), *Irishness in a Changing Society* (Gerrards Cross: Colin Smythe, 1988)

Kearney, Richard, "Postmodernity, Nationalism and Ireland", Paper to the *Second International Conference of European Ideas* (Leuven: Leuven University Press, September 1991)

Kee, Robert, *The Green Flag* (London: Weidenfeld & Nicholson, 1972)

Kennedy, Liam, *Colonialism, Religion, and Nationalism in Ireland* (Belfast: Institute of Irish Studies, 1996)

Khilnani, Sunil, *Arguing Revolution. The Intellectual Left in Postwar France* (New Haven: Yale University Press, 1993)

Kiberd, Declan, *Inventing Ireland: The Literature of the Modern Nation* (London: Jonathan Cape, 1995)

Kinealy, Christine, *This Great Calamity: The Irish Famine. 1845–1852* (Dublin: Gill & Macmillan, 1994)

Kirkland, Richard, *Literature and Culture in Northern Ireland Since 1965: Moments of Danger* (London: Longman, 1996)

Krieger, Leonard, *Ranke: The Meaning of History* (Chicago: University of Chicago Press, 1977)

Kristeva, Julia, *Théorie d'ensemble. Foucault, Barthes, Derrida* (Paris: Edition du Seuil, Col. Tel Quel, 1968)

Kristeva, Julia, *Nations Without Nationalism* (New York: Columbia University Press, 1993)

Kristeva, Julia, *L'avenir d'une révolte* (Paris: Calmann-Lévy, 1998)

La Capra, Dominick, Kaplan, Steven L. (eds), *Modern European Intellectual History. Reappraisals and New Perspectives* (London: Cornell University Press, 1982)

Laffan, Michael, "Labour must Wait" in Corish, Patrick J. (ed.), *Radicals, Rebels and Establishments Historical Studies* No. XV (Belfast: Appletree Press, 1985)

Laffan, Michael, "Insular Attitudes: The Revisionists and their Critics", in Dorgan, Theo, Ni Dhonnchadha, Mairin (eds), *Revising the Rising* (Derry: Field Day, 1991)

Laffan, Michael, "The Sacred Memory" in Devlin, Judith, Fanning, Ronan (eds), *Religion and Rebellion Historical Studies* No. XX (Dublin: University College Dublin Press, 1997)

Laffan, Michael, *The Resurrection of Ireland: The Sinn Féin Party. 1916–1923* (Cambridge: Cambridge University Press, 1999)

Lecky, W.E.H., *History of Ireland in the Eighteenth Century* 5 Vols (London: Longmans, Green, and Co., 1892, 1913)

Lee, J.J., "Irish Economic History Since 1900" in *Irish Historiography. 1970–1979* (Cork: Cork University Press, 1981)

Lee, J.J., *Ireland 1912–1985. Politics and Society* (Cambridge: Cambridge University Press, 1989)

Lévesque, Claude, McDonald, Christie V., *L'oreille de l'autre. Otobiographies, transferts, traductions. Textes et débats avec Jacques Derrida* (Québec: VLB éditeur, 1988)

Lévi-Strauss, Claude, *La pensée sauvage* (Paris: Librairie Plon, 1962)

Longley, Edna, *Poetry in the Wars* (Newcastle upon Tyne: Bloodaxe Books, 1986)

Longley, Edna (ed.), *Culture in Ireland: Division or Diversity?* (Belfast: Institute of Irish Studies, 1991)

Longley, Edna, *The Living Stream: Literature and Revisionism in Ireland* (Newcastle upon Tyne: Bloodaxe Books, 1994)

Loomba, Ania, *Colonialism and Postcolonialism* (London: Routledge, 1998)

Lyons, F.S.L., *John Dillon: A Biography* (London: Routledge and Kegan Paul, 1968)

Lyons, F.S.L., *Ireland since the Famine* (London: Weidenfeld and Nicolson, 1971)

Lyons, F.S.L., *Culture and Anarchy in Ireland. 1890–1939* (Oxford: Clarendon Press, 1979)

Lyons, F.S.L., Hawkins, R.A.J. (eds), *Ireland Under the Union. Varieties of Tension. Essays in Honour of T.W. Moody* (Oxford: Clarendon Press, 1980)

Lyotard, Jean-François, *The Postmodern Condition: A Report on Knowledge* Translation by Bennington, Geoffrey, Massumi, Brian (Manchester: Manchester University Press, 1984)

Lyotard, Jean-François, *Just Gaming* Translation by Godzich, Wlad (Manchester: Manchester University Press, 1985)

Lyotard, Jean-François, *The Postmodern Explained to Children. Correspondence 1982–1985* Translation by Barry, Don, Maher, Bernadette (London: Turnaround, 1992)

Lyotard, Jean-François, *Libidinal Economy* Translation by Hamilton Grant, Iain (London: Athlone Press, 1993)

Lyotard, Jean-François, *Political Writings* Translation by Readings, Bill, Geiman, Kevin Paul (London: University College London Press, 1993)

Macaulay, Thomas Babington, *History of England from the Accession of James II* (London: Harper & Brothers, 1862, 1906, 1966)

McBride, Ian (ed.), *History and Memory in Modern Ireland* (Cambridge: Cambridge University Press, 2001)

McBride, Ian R., *Scripture Politics – Ulster Presbyterians and Irish Radicalism in Late Eighteenth-Century Ireland* (Oxford: Clarendon Press, 1998)

McCann, Eamonn, *War and an Irish Town* New edn (London: Pluto Press, 1993)

McCarthy, Conor, *Irish Modernisation, Crisis and Culture in Ireland. 1969.1992* (Dublin: Four Courts Press, 2000)

McCartney Donal, *William Edward Hartpole Lecky: Historian and Politician. 1838–1903* (Dublin: The Lilliput Press, 1994)

MacDonagh, Oliver, *Ireland: The Union and its Aftermath* (London: George Allen & Unwin, 1977)

Maier, Charles S., *The Unmasterable Past. History, Holocaust, and German National Identity* (Harvard: Harvard University Press, 1997)

Martin, F.X. (ed.), *Leaders and Men of the Easter Rising: Dublin 1916* (London: Methuen, 1967)

Martin, F.X., Byrne, F.J. (eds), *The Scholar Revolutionary. Eoin MacNeill and the Making of the New Ireland* (Shannon: Irish University Press, 1973)

Marx, Karl, Engels, Frederick, *Collected Works 1845–1947* Vol. V (London: International, 1976)

Mazower, Mark (ed.), *After the War Was Over. Reconstructing the Family, Nation and State in Greece, 1943–1960* (Princeton, NJ: Princeton University Press, 2000)

Meinecke, Friedrich, *German Catastrophe: Reflections and Recollections* Translation by Fay, Sidney B. (Cambridge : Cambridge University Press, 1950)

Memmi, Albert, *Portrait du colonisateur et du colonisé* Preface Sartre, Jean-Paul (Paris: Gallimard, 1985)

Miller, David (ed.), *Rethinking Northern Ireland: Culture, Ideology and Colonialism* (London: Longman, 1998)

Mokyr, Joel, *Why Ireland Starved: A Quantitative and Analytical History of the Irish Economy. 1800–1850* (London: George Allen & Unwin, 1983)

Morash, Christopher, *The Hungry Voice: The Poetry of the Irish Famine* (Dublin: Irish Academic Press, 1989)

Morgan, Austen, Purdie, Bob (eds), *Ireland: Divided Nation/Divided Class* (London: Ink Links, 1980)

Morris, Benny, *The Birth of the Palestinian Refugee Problem. 1948 and After: Israel and the Palestinians* (Cambridge: Cambridge University Press, 1989)

Morris, Benny, *Righteous Victims: A History of the Zionist–Arab Conflict. 1881–1999* (London: John Murray, Revised Edn, 2000)

Mulhern, Francis (ed.), "Postcolonial Melancholy: A Reply to Luke Gibbons" in *The Present Lasts a Long Time: Essays in Cultural Politics* (Cork: Cork University Press, 1998)

Namier, Lewis, *Side Lines of History. Vanished Supremacies. Essays on European History. 1812–1918* (New York: Harper Torchbooks, 1963)

Novick, Peter, *That Noble Dream. The "Objectivity Question" and the American Historical Profession* (Cambridge: Cambridge University Press, 1988)

Oakeshott, Michael, "The Activity of Being an Historian" *Historical Studies* No. I Edited by Williams, Desmond T. (London: Bowes and Bowes, 1958)

Oakeshott, Michael, *Experience and its Modes* (Cambridge: Cambridge University Press, 1978)

O'Brien, Conor Cruise, *Maria Cross: Imaginative Patterns in a Group of Modern Catholic Writers* (London: Chatto and Windus, 1953)

O'Brien, Conor Cruise, *Writers and Politics* (London: Chatto & Windus, 1965)

O'Brien, Conor Cruise, *Power and Consciousness* (London: University of London Press, 1969)

O'Brien, Conor Cruise, *Camus* (Glasgow: Fontana Modern Masters, 1970)

O'Brien, Conor Cruise, *States of Ireland* (London: Hutchinson, 1972)

O'Brien, Conor Cruise, *The Suspecting Glance* (London: Faber & Faber, 1972)

O'Brien, Conor Cruise, *Herod: Reflections on Political Violence* (London: Hutchinson & Co., 1978)

O'Brien, Conor Cruise, *God Land. Reflections on Religion and Nationalism* (Cambridge, MA: Harvard University Press, 1988)

O'Brien, Conor Cruise, *The Great Melody. A Thematic Biography and Commented Anthology of Edmund Burke* (London: Sinclair-Stevenson, 1992)

O'Brien, Conor Cruise, *Memoir. My Life and Themes* (Dublin: Poolbeg Press, 1998)

O'Brien, Gerard, *Irish Governments and the Guardianship of Historical Records, 1922–72* (Dublin: Four Courts Press, 2004)

O Ceallaigh, Daltun (ed.), *Reconsiderations of Irish History and Culture* (Dublin: Léirmheas, 1994)

O Corràin, Donnchadh (ed.), *James Hogan. Revolutionary, Historian and Political Scientist* (Dublin: Four Courts Press, 2001)

O'Donoghue, Florence, *No Other Law. The Story of Liam Lynch and the Irish Republican Army* (Dublin: Irish Press, 1954)

O'Dowd, Liam (ed.), *On Intellectuals and Intellectual Life in Ireland. International, Comparative and Historical Contexts* (Belfast: Institute of Irish Studies, 1996)

O'Dowd, Liam, Rolston, Bill, Tomlinson Mike, *Northern Ireland: Between Civil Rights and Civil War* (London: CSE Books, 1980)

O'Faolain, Sean, *King of the Beggars. A Life of Daniel O'Connell* (Dublin: Poolbeg Press, 1980)

O Gráda, Cormac, *Ireland Before and After the Famine. Explorations in Economic History. 1800–1925* (Manchester: Manchester University Press, 1993)

O'Halloran, Clare, *Partition and the Limits of Irish Nationalism. An Ideology under Stress* (Dublin: Gill & Macmillan, 1987)

O'Hegarty, Patrick Sarsfield, *A History of Ireland under the Union. 1801–1922* (London: Methuen, 1952)

O'Rourke, Canon J., *The Great Irish Famine* (Dublin: Veritas, 1874)

O'Sullivan, Patrick (ed.), *The Meaning of the Famine* (London: Leicester University Press, 1997)

Palmer, Bryan, *Descent into Discourse: The Reification of Language and the Writing of Social History* (Philadelphia: Temple University Press, 1990)

Passerini, Luisa, *Fascism in Popular Memory. The Cultural Experience of the Turin Working Class* (Cambridge: Cambridge University Press, 1987)

Paxton, Robert O., *Vichy France: Old Guard and New Order. 1940–1944* (New York: Knopf, Random House, 1972)

Payne, Stanley G., *The Spanish Civil War, the Soviet Union and Communism* (New Haven: Yale University Press, 2004)

Pearse, Patrick, *Collected Works of Padraic H. Pearse: Political Writings and Speeches* (Dublin: Phoenix, 1922)

Pirenne, Henri, *La tâche de l'historien* Le Flambeau XIV 1931

Pórtéir, Cathal (ed.), *The Great Irish Famine* (Dublin: Mercier Press, 1995)

Rajan, Balachandra, *The Form of the Unfinished: English Poetics From Spenser to Pound* (Princeton, NJ, 1985)

Regan, John M., *The Irish Counter-Revolution 1921–1936* (Dublin: Gill & Macmillan, 1999)

Ricoeur, Paul, *Freud and Philosophy: An Essay on Interpretation* (New Haven: Yale University Press, 1970)

Rogozinski, Jacob, Lacoue-Labarthe, Philippe, Nancy, Jean-Luc, *Les fins de l'Homme* (Paris: Edition Galilée, 1980)

Rosenfeld, Sophia, *A Revolution in Language: The Problem of Signs in Late Eighteenth-Century France* (Stanford: Stanford University Press, 2001)

Ruane, Joe, Todd, Jennifer, *The Dynamics of Conflict in Northern Ireland. Power, Conflict, and Emancipation* (Cork: Cork University Press, 1996)

Scruton, Roger, *A Dictionary of Political Thought*, (London: Pan Books in association with Macmillan, 1982)

Shils, Edward, Finch, Henry, *The Methodology of the Social Sciences* (New York: Free Press, 1949)

Shlaim, Avi, *The Iron Wall: Israel and the Arab World* (London: Penguin, 2001)

Sim, Stuart, *Modern Cultural Theorists. Jean-François Lyotard* (London: Prentice Hall, Harvester Wheatsheaf, 1996)

Simon, Roger, *Gramsci's Political Thought. An Introduction* (London: Lawrence & Wishart, 1982)

Skeffington, Andrée Sheehy, *Skeff. A Life of Owen Sheehy Skeffington* (Dublin: The Lilliput Press, 1991)

Soper, Kate, *Humanism and Anti-Humanism. Problems of Modern European Thought* (London: Hutchinson & Co, 1986)

Sternhell, Zeev, *La droite révolutionnaire. 1885–1914. Les origins françaises du fascisme* (Paris: Editions du Seuil, 1978)

Stewart, A.T.Q., *The Narrow Ground: The Roots of Conflict in Ulster. 1609–1969* (Belfast: Institute of Irish Studies, 1977)

Taylor, A.J.P., *The Course of German History* (London: Hamish Hamilton, 1945)

Taylor, A.J.P., *The Origins of the Second World War* (New York: Fawcett Premier, 1969)

Thompson, E.P., *The Making of the English Working Class* (New York: Vintage Books, 1963)

Thompson, E.P., *The Poverty of Theory and Other Essays* (London: Merlin Press, 1978)

Thompson, W.I., *The Imagination of an Insurrection. Dublin, Easter 1916. A Study of an Ideological Movement* (New York: Harper Colophon Books, 1972)

Tierney, Michael (ed.), *Daniel O'Connell. Nine Centenary Essays* (Dublin: Browne and Nolan, 1949)

Toibin, Colm, *The Irish Famine* (London: Profile Books, 1999)

Walker, Brian, *Dancing to History's Tune: History, Myth and Politics in Ireland* (Belfast: Institute of Irish Studies, 1996)

Wall, Maureen, "Partition: The Ulster Question (1916–1926)" in Williams, Desmond T. (ed.), *The Irish Struggle* (London: Routledge, 1966)

Wall, Maureen, "Plans and Countermand" in Nowlan, Kevin B. (ed.), *The Making of 1916: Studies in the History of the Rising* (Dublin: Stationery Office, 1969)

Wat, Aleksander, *Mon siècle. Confession d'un intellectuel européen* (Paris: Edition de Fallois/L'Age d'Homme, 1989)

Weber, Max, "The Profession and Vocation of Politics", in Lassman, Peter, Speirs, Ronald (eds), "Introduction", *Weber: Political Writings* (Cambridge: Cambridge University Press, 1994)

White, Hayden, *Tropics of Discourse* (Baltimore: Johns Hopkins University Press, 1978)

Williams, Desmond T., "The Historiography of World War II" *Historical Studies* No. I (London: Bowes and Bowes, 1958)

Williams, Raymond, *Marxism and Literature* (Oxford: Oxford University Press, 1977)

Woodham-Smith, Cecil, *The Great Hunger, Ireland 1845–1849* (New York: Old Town Books, 1962)

Whyte, John, *Interpreting Northern Ireland* (Oxford: Clarendon Press, 1990)

Yeats, W.B., *Autobiographies* (London: Macmillan & Co., 1955)

Articles

Ankersmit, F.R., "Historiography and Postmodernism" *History and Theory* Vol. XXVIII No. 2 1989

Archer, J. R., "Necessary Ambiguity: Nationalism and Myth in Ireland" *Eire/Ireland* Summer 1984

Barraclough, Geoffrey, "The 'Historische Zeitschrift'" *Times Literary Supplement* 14 April 1950

Bew, Paul, "The Easter Rising: Lost Leaders and Lost Opportunities" *Irish Review* No. 11 Winter 1991/1992

Bradshaw, Brendan, "Nationalism and Historical Scholarship" *Irish Historical Studies* Vol. XXVI No. 104 November 1989

Breathnach, R.A., "Letters to the Editor" *Irish Times* 19 January 1957

Brien, David D., "François Furet, the Terror, and 1789" *French Historical Studies* Vol. 16 No. 4 Autumn 1990

Butterfield, Herbert, "Tendencies in Historical Study in England" *Irish Historical Studies* Vol. IV 1944–5

Catterson, Simon, "Interview with Declan Kiberd" *Fortnight* No. 346 January 1996

Clarke, Aidan, "Robert Dudley Edwards 1909–88" *Irish Historical Studies* Vol. XXVI No. 102 November 1988

Cowling, Maurice, "Herbert Butterfield 1900–1979" *Proceedings of the British Academy* Vol. LXV, 1979

Curtis, Edmund, "Irish History and its Popular Versions" *Irish Rosary* No. 39 1925

Curtis, L.P., "The Greening of Irish History" *Eire/Ireland*, Vol. XXIX No. 2 Summer 1994 pp. 7–28

Dickson, David, "Interview of R.B. McDowell" *History Ireland* Vol. 1 No. 4 Winter 1993

Dodd, Luke, "Famine Echoes" *South Atlantic Quarterly* Vol. 95 No. 1 Winter 1996

Donnelly, S.J., "The Construction of the Memory of the Famine in Ireland and the Irish Diaspora. 1850–1900" *Eire/Ireland* Vol. 31 No. 1–2 Spring 1997

Dunne, Tom, "New Histories: Beyond 'Revisionism'" *Irish Review* No. 12 1992

Eagleton, Terry, "Emily Brontë and The Great Hunger" *Irish Review* No. 12 Spring 1992

Edwards, R.D., "A Frightened World" *Leader* Vol. 58 No. 8 19 April 1958

Edwards, R.D., "Rescue the Records" *Irish Archives Bulletin* Vol. 1 No. 1 May 1971

Ellis, Steven G., "Nationalist Historiography and the English and Gaelic Worlds in the late Middle Ages" *Irish Historical Studies* Vol. XXV No. 97 May 1986

Ellis, Steven G., "Representations of the Past in Ireland: Whose Past and Whose Present?" *Irish Historical Studies* Vol. 27 No. 108 1991

Ellis, Steven G., "Writing Irish History: Revisionism, Colonialism, and the British Isles" *Irish Review* No. 19 1996

Ferreter, Diarmaid, "In Such Deadly Earnest" *Dublin Review* No. 12 Autumn 2003

Finlayson, Alan, "Re-conceptualising the political in Northern Ireland: A Response to Arthur Aughey" *Irish Political Studies* No. 13 1998

Foster, R.F., "We are all Revisionists Now!" *Irish Review* No. 1 1986

Gkotzaridis, Evi, "Irish Revisionism and Continental Theory. An Insight into an Intellectual Kinship" *Irish Review* No. 27 Summer 2001

Graham, Colin, "'Liminal Spaces': Post-Colonial Theories and Irish Culture" *Irish Review* No. 16 Winter 1994

Graham, Tommy, "A Man with a Mission: Interview with Brendan Bradshaw" *History Ireland* Vol. 1 No. 1 1993

Gray, Peter, "Our Man at Oxford. Interview of R.F. Foster" *History Ireland* Vol. 1 No. 3 Autumn 1993

Jackson, Alvin, "Unionist Myths. 1912–1985" *Past and Present* No. 136 August 1992

Jackson, Alvin, "J.C. Beckett: Politics, Faith, Scholarship" *Irish Historical Studies* Vol. XXXIII No. 130 November 2002

Julliard, Jacques, "Les intellectuels ne veulent plus être des 'politiques'" *Nouvel Observateur* 30 September to 6 October 1993

Krieger, Leonard, "Elements of Early Historicism: Experience, Theory, and History in Ranke" *History and Theory* Vol. 14 December 1975

Longley, Edna, "Belfast Diary" *London Review of Books* No. 14/1 9 January 1992

Longley, Michael, "Memory and Acknowledgement" *Irish Review* No. 17/18 Winter 1995

Love, Walter D., "Charles O'Conor of Belanagare and Thomas Leland's 'Philosophical' History of Ireland" *Irish Historical Studies* Vol. 13 No. 49 March 1962

Love, Walter D., "Edmund Burke and an Irish historiographical controversy" *History and Theory* 2 1962–1963

Ludington, Charles C., "Visions and Revisions" *History Ireland* Vol. 4 No. 1 Spring 1996

Lyons, F.S.L., "The Dilemma of the Irish Contemporary Historian" *Hermathena* No. CXV Summer 1973

McGuire, James, "Thomas Desmond Williams (1921–1987)" *Irish Historical Studies* Vol. XXVI No. 101 May 1988

Martin, F.X., "Select documents. Eoin MacNeill on the 1916 Rising" *Irish Historical Studies* Vol. 12 No. 47 March 1961

Martin, F.X., "1916 – Myth, Fact, and Mystery" *Studia Hibernica*, No. 7 1967

Martin, F.X., "T.W. Moody" *Hermathena* No. CXXXVI Summer 1984

Moody, T.W., "A New History of Ireland" *Irish Historical Studies* Vol. XVI No. 63 March 1969

Moody, T.W., O Broin, Leon, "The I.R.B. Supreme Council, 1868–78" *Irish Historical Studies* Vol. 19 No. 75 1975

Morash, Christopher, "Entering the Abyss" *Irish Review* No. 17/18 Winter 1995

Morash, Christopher, "Spectres of the Famine" *Irish Review* No. 17/18 Winter 1995

Morash, Christopher, "Famine/Holocaust: Fragmented Bodies" *Eire/Ireland* Vol. 32 No. 1 Spring 1997

Morgan, Hiram, "'A Scholar and a Gentleman'. Interview of A.T.Q. Stewart" *History Ireland* Vol. 1 No. 2 Summer 1993

Mulvey, Helen, "Thirty years' work in Irish history" *Irish Historical Studies* Vol. XVII No. 66 September 1970

Murphy, John A., "Further Reflections on Irish Nationalism" *Crane Bag* Vol. 2 No. 1 & 2 1978

Murphy, Joh. A., "Easter 1916 – the View from 1984" *Sunday Independent* 22 April 1984

Murray, Patrick, "Obsessive Historian: Eamon de Valera and the Policing of his Reputation" *Proceedings of the Royal Irish Academy* Vol. 101C 37–65 December 2001

Myers, Kevin, "Irishman's Diary" *Irish Times* 16 May 1995 14 March 1996

O'Brien, Conor Cruise, "Camus, Algeria, and The Fall" *New York Review of Books* Vol. 13 No. 6 9 October 1969

O'Brien, Conor Cruise, "Holy War" *New York Review of Books* Vol. 13 No. 8 6 November 1969

O'Brien, Conor Cruise, "Violence in Ireland: Another Algeria?" *New York Review of Books* Vol. 17 No. 4 23 September 1971

O'Brien, Conor Cruise, "An Unhealthy Intersection" *Irish Times* 21 August 1975

O'Brien, Conor Cruise, "Nationalism and the Reconquest of Ireland" *Crane Bag* Vol. I No. 2 1977

O'Callaghan, Margaret, "Language, Nationality and Cultural Identity in the Irish Free State, 1922–7. The *Irish Statesman* and the *Catholic Bulletin* reappraised" *Irish Historical Studies* Vol. XXIV No. 94 November 1984

O'Farrell, Patrick, "Whose Reality? The Irish Famine in History and Literature", *Historical Studies* Vol. 20 No. 78 April 1982

O'Farrell, Patrick, "Fair Exchange. Some Exotic Experiences at Trinity in 1972–73" *Eureka Street* 2 July 1992

O Gráda, Cormac, "Making Irish Famine History in 1995" *History Workshop Journal* No. 42 Autumn 1996

O'Halpin, Eunan, "Historical revisit: Dorothy Macardle, *The Irish Republic* (1937)" *Irish Historical Studies* Vol. XXXI No. 123 May 1999

O'Loughlin, Thomas, "Interview of Margaret MacCurtain" *History Ireland* Vol. 2 No. 1 Spring 1994

O Luing, Sean, "The Dilemma of Eoin MacNeill" *Irish Times* 24–25 April 1961

O Neill, Seosamh, "A Response to the Opening of the Dykes" *Irish Statesman* Vol. 1 No. 21 2 February 1924

O'Toole, Fintan, "Why North has No Time for Doubters" *Irish Times* 4 April 1991

Ritter, Gerhard, "The 'Historische Zeitschrift'" *Times Literary Supplement* 12 May 1950

Rossi, Pietro, "The Ideological Valences of Twentieth-Century Historicism' *History and Theory* Vol. 14 December 1975

Shaw, Francis, "The Canon of Irish History – A Challenge" *Studies* Vol. LXI 1972

Townshend, Charles, "Modernization and Nationalism: Perspectives in Recent Irish History" *History: The Journal of the Historical Association* Vol. 66 No. 217 June 1981

Walker, Brian, "Ireland's Historical Position – 'Colonial' or 'European'?" *Irish Review* No. 9 Autumn 1990

Walsh, Dick, "The End of Government from Beyond the Grave" *Irish Times* 6 April 1991

White, Hayden, "Response to Arthur Marwick" *Journal of Contemporary History* Vol. 30 No. 2 April 1995

Williams, Desmond T., "Negotiations Leading to the Anglo-Polish Treaty of 31 March 1939" *Irish Historical Studies* Vol. X No. 37 March 1956 pp. 59–93

Williams, Desmond T., "Adolph Hitler and the Historians" *University Review* Vol. I No. 9 Summer 1956 pp. 37–51

Reviews

Anonymous Review of A.J.P. Taylor's *The Origins of the Second World War, Times Literary Supplement* Friday 21 April 1961

Beckett, J.C., Review of *Historical Studies: IV* Edited by G.A. Hayes-McCoy (London 1962), *Studia Hibernica* No. 4 1964 pp. 233–4

Edwards, R.D., Response to an Anonymous Review of Richard Bennett's, *The Black and Tans* (London 1959), *Times Literary Supplement* 31 July 1959

Lyons, F.S.L., Review of R.D. Edwards' and T.D. Williams' *The Great Famine, Irish Times* 21 January 1957

Lyons, F.S.L., Review of Cecil Woodham-Smith's *The Great Hunger, Irish Historical Studies* Vol. XIV 1964–5

Rajan, Balachandra, Review of Homi Bhabha's *The Location of Culture, Modern Philology* Vol. 95 No. 4 May 1998

Stewart, A.T.Q., "The Irish Century in Perspective" Review of George Boyce's, *19th Century Ireland: The Search for Stability*, *Irish Times* 16 March 1991

Williams, Desmond T., Review of Lewis Namier's *Side Lines of History. Vanished Supremacies*, *Spectator* 14 February 1958

Williams, Desmond T., "The Anatomy of Appeasement" Review of *The Eve of War 1939*. Survey of International Affairs 1939–46, *Spectator* 21 March 1958

Index

Dates are only supplied for those individuals who are deceased.